This publication supplements Senate Document 115–8, The Co[nstitution of the] United States of America: Analysis and Interpretation—it sho[uld be inserted] into the pocket on the inside back cover of that vo[lume]

116th Congress 2nd Session	SENATE	DOCUMENT No. 116–20

THE CONSTITUTION

OF THE

UNITED STATES OF AMERICA

ANALYSIS AND INTERPRETATION

2020 SUPPLEMENT

ANALYSIS OF CASES DECIDED BY THE SUPREME
COURT OF THE UNITED STATES TO JULY 14, 2020

PREPARED BY THE
CONGRESSIONAL RESEARCH SERVICE
LIBRARY OF CONGRESS

VALERIE BRANNON
VICTORIA KILLION
ANDREW NOLAN
ATTORNEY EDITORS

GEORGIA GKOULGKOUNTINA
SUMMER NORWOOD
MEGHAN TOTTEN
LEGAL EDITORS

U.S. GOVERNMENT PUBLISHING OFFICE

42-432

WASHINGTON : 2020

Online Version: www.gpo.gov/constitutionannotated; www.constitution.congress.gov

For sale by the Superintendent of Documents, U.S. Government Publishing Office
Internet: bookstore.gpo.gov Phone: toll free (866) 512-1800; DC area (202) 512-1800
Fax: (202) 512-2104 Mail: Stop IDCC, Washington, DC 20402–0001

TABLE OF CONTENTS

ARTICLE I

TABLE OF CONTENTS

[P. 79, delete paragraph starting "Concerns in the scholarly literature . . . " through " . . . most sweeping nature." and substitute with:]

In more recent years, however, the modern application of the *J. W. Hampton* Court's intelligible principle test and the broad deference it affords congressional delegations of authority to the other branches has met with growing skepticism from some members of the Court.[1] The 2019 case of *Gundy v. United States* highlighted an emerging split on the High Court with respect its nondelegation doctrine jurisprudence.[2] In that case, a criminal defendant challenged a provision of the Sex Offender Registration and Notification Act (SORNA) allowing the Attorney General to (1) "specify the applicability" of SORNA's registration requirements to individuals convicted of a sex offense prior to the statute's enactment and (2) "prescribe rules for [their] registration" in jurisdictions where the offender resides, works, or is a student.[3] Writing for a four-Justice plurality, Justice Kagan interpreted this provision as limiting the Attorney General's authority to "require pre-Act offenders to register as soon as feasible,"[4] concluding that the delegation "easily passe[d] constitutional muster."[5] For the plurality, the Attorney General's

---

[1] *See, e.g.*, Dep't of Transp. v. Ass'n of Am. R.R., 575 U.S. ___, No. 13-1080, slip op. at 12 (2015) (Thomas, J., concurring) (arguing that the Court should "return to the original understanding of the federal legislative power" and reject the "boundless standard the 'intelligible principle' test has become"); Gutierrez-Brizuela v. Lynch, 834 F.3d 1142, 1154 (10th Cir. 2016) (Gorsuch, J., concurring) (noting "thoughtful" commentary questioning whether the current intelligible principle test serves "as much as a protection against the delegation of legislative authority as a license for it, undermining the separation between the legislative and executive powers that the founders thought essential").

[2] *See* 139 S. Ct. 2116 (2019). While criticisms of the intelligible principle doctrine have become more pronounced in recent years, some former members of the Court had argued for striking down legislation on nondelegation grounds. *See, e.g.*, Indus. Union Dep't, AFL-CIO v. Am. Petroleum Inst., 448 U.S. 607, 675 (1980) (Rehn quist, J., concurring); Arizona v. California, 373 U.S. 546, 626-27 (1963) (Harlan, J., dissenting).

[3] 34 U.S.C. § 20913(d); *see also Gundy*, 139 S. Ct. at 2122 (plurality opinion) (discussing SORNA's "basic registration scheme").

[4] *See Gundy*, 139 S. Ct. at 2129 (plurality opinion).

[5] *Id.* at 2121.

authority under SORNA, when compared to other delegations the Court had previously upheld, was "distinctly small-bore."[6] Notably, Justice Kagan's opinion was met by a dissent, authored by Justice Gorsuch and joined by Chief Justice Roberts and Justice Thomas, which argued that the statute unconstitutionally provided the Attorney General "unfettered discretion."[7] Further, the dissenters claimed that the modern intelligible principle test has "no basis in the original meaning of the Constitution" or in historical practice.[8] In response, the plurality, noting that delegations akin to the one in SORNA are "ubiquitous in the U.S. Code," argued that as a matter of pragmatism the Court should afford deference to Congress's judgments that such broad delegations are necessary.[9] Providing the fifth vote to affirm the petitioner's conviction was Justice Alito, who, while agreeing that the plurality correctly applied the modern nondelegation case law, indicated he would "support [the] effort" of the dissenting Justices to reconsider the intelligible principle test once a majority of the Court concurred in rethinking the doctrine.[10] Accordingly, *Gundy* witnessed the Court evenly split on how deferential the Court should be with regard to congressional delegations to the other branches, raising questions as to whether the nondelegation doctrine would remain moribund.

CONGRESSIONAL INVESTIGATIONS

Scope of the Power to Investigate

[P. 97, delete sentence starting "In principle, the Court is . . ." and substitute with:]

In addition, Congress may not issue a subpoena for the purpose of law enforcement—that is, to "try" someone before a committee for any "crime or wrongdoing,"[11] as such an action would intrude on powers "assigned under [the] Constitution to the Executive and the Judiciary."[12] Finally, the Court has recognized that recipients of congressional subpoenas "retain common law and constitutional privileges with respect to certain materials," such as privileges associated with attorney-client and internal governmental communications.[13]

---

[6] *Id.* at 2130.

[7] *Id.* at 2143 (Gorsuch, J., dissenting).

[8] *Id.* at 2139.

[9] *Id.* at 2130 (plurality opinion).

[10] *Id.* at 2121 (Alito, J., concurring). Justice Kavanaugh took no part in the consideration or decision in *Gundy*, as he was appointed to the Supreme Court after oral argument occurred in the case.

[11] McGrain v. Daugherty, 273 U.S. 135, 179 (1927).

[12] Quinn v. United States, 349 U.S. 155, 161 (1955).

[13] Trump v. Mazars, 140 S. Ct. 2019, 2032 (2020).

[P. 97, after sentence ending "... given rise to fewer judicial precedents." add:]

With respect to disputes over congressional demands for presidential documents, these disputes typically have not ended up in court.[14] Instead, as the Court in *Trump v. Mazars* recognized, such disputes are typically "hashed out" in the "hurly-burly, the give-and-take of the political process."[15]

Investigations of Conduct of Executive Department

[P. 99, after sentence ending "... in such administration." add new paragraph:]

Notwithstanding the existence of Congress's powers to inquire into the administration of the executive branch, the Court in *Trump v. Mazars* recognized that when Congress seeks the President's records, this power is further limited by separation-of-powers concerns.[16] Writing on behalf of the Court, Chief Justice Roberts began by rejecting the need for a "demanding" standard that would have required Congress to demonstrate a specific need for particular records that were "critical" to a legislative purpose.[17] At the same time, however, the *Mazars* Court concluded that a congressional subpoena for the President's information raised "significant separation of powers issues," and the typical limitations on such subpoenas, such as the requirement of a valid legislative purpose, inadequately shielded the executive branch from congressional aggrandizement.[18] To avoid interfering with the historic practice of resolving information disputes through the political process, the Chief Justice instructed lower courts to perform a "careful analysis" using "[s]everal special considerations" that take "adequate account" of the separation-of-powers principles at stake during a legislative inquiry into

---

[14] *Id.* at 2029.

[15] *Id.* (quoting *Hearings on S. 2170 Before the Subcomm. on Intergov'tal Relations of the S. Comm. on Gov't Operations*, 94th Cong. 87 (1975) (statement of Antonin Scalia, Assistant Att'y Gen., Office of Legal Counsel)) (internal quotation marks omitted).

[16] *See* Trump v. Mazars, 140 S. Ct. 2019, 2035 (2020).

[17] *Id.* at 2032–33 (concluding that imposing a standard akin to that which governs executive privilege claims would "risk seriously impeding Congress in carrying out" inquiries to obtain information it needs to legislate effectively). Importantly, in *Mazars*, the documents at issue were private presidential financial records and therefore did not raise questions of executive privilege. *Id.* at 2032.

[18] *Id.* at 2033–34 (concluding that, because any personal paper possessed by a President could relate to a conceivable subject of legislation, the typical limits on the subpoena power could deter negotiation between the two branches and encourage Congress to seek compliance through the courts). While the papers at stake in *Mazars* were the President's personal records, the Court concluded that the close connection between the Office of the President and its occupant did not diminish the separation-of-powers concerns at issue and may have even posed a "heightened risk" given the records' "less evident connection to a legislative task." *Id.* at 2035. The *Mazars* Court likewise rejected the argument that separation-of-powers concerns were diminished because the records at issue were in the hands of a third party, as opposed to the President himself. *Id.* For the Court, the central issue was that the President's information was at stake, and ruling otherwise would have encouraged side-stepping constitutional requirements. *Id.*

the President's records.[19] Specifically, in such a dispute, courts should, among other considerations: (1) carefully assess whether the confrontation can be avoided by relying on other sources to provide Congress the information it needs in light of its legislative objective; (2) "insist" on a subpoena that is no broader than is reasonably necessary to support Congress's objective; (3) consider the nature of the evidence of Congress's legislative purpose, preferring more detailed and substantial evidence to vague or loosely worded evidence of Congress's purpose; and (4) assess the burdens, such as time and attention, imposed on the President by a subpoena.[20]

Section 2. House of Representatives

Clause 1. Congressional Districting

CONGRESSIONAL DISTRICTING

[P. 112, delete n.275]

[P. 114, at end of n.297, add:]

See also North Carolina v. Covington, 585 U.S. ___, No. 17-1364, slip op. at 9–10 (2018) (per curiam) ("The District Court's decision to override the legislature's remedial map . . . was clear error. '[S]tate legislatures have primary jurisdiction over legislative reapportionment,' and a legislature's 'freedom of choice to devise substitutes for an apportionment plan found unconstitutional, either as a whole or in part, should not be restricted beyond the clear commands' of federal law. A district court is 'not free . . . to disregard the political program of' a state legislature on other bases." (quoting Weiser, 412 U.S. at 795; Burns v. Richardson, 384 U.S. 73, 85 (1966); Upham v. Seamon, 456 U.S. 37, 43 (1982) (per curiam))).

[PP. 114–15, delete paragraph starting "Attacks on partisan gerrymandering . . ." and substitute with:]

Although the Supreme Court had suggested for a number of years that claims of unconstitutional partisan gerrymandering might be justiciable,[21] it held in *Rucho v. Common Cause* that such claims were nonjusticiable, saying that there was no "constitutional directive" nor any "legal standards to guide" the Court.[22] Quoting an earlier plurality opinion

---

[19] *Id.*

[20] *Id.* at 2035–36. The Court observed that "[o]ther considerations may be pertinent as well." *Id.* at 2036.

[21] The Court held in *Davis v. Bandemer* that partisan or political gerrymandering claims were justiciable, but a majority of Justices failed to agree on a single test for determining whether partisan gerrymanders were unconstitutional. 478 U.S. 109, 125 (1986). *See also, e.g.*, Pope v. Blue, 809 F. Supp. 392 (W.D.N.C. 1992) (adjudicating partisan gerrymandering claim as to congressional districts but deciding against plaintiffs on merits), *aff'd*, 506 U.S. 801 (1992); Badham v. Eu, 694 F. Supp. 664 (N.D. Cal. 1988) (same), *aff'd*, 488 U.S. 1024 (1989). In later cases, a majority of the Court continued to suggest that partisan gerrymandering claims might be justiciable, but five Justices could not agree on a test by which to adjudicate such claims. *See* League of United Latin American Citizens v. Perry, 548 U.S. 399 (2006); Vieth v. Jubelirer, 541 U.S. 267 (2004).

[22] 588 U.S. ___, Nos. 18-422, 18-726, slip op. at 34 (2019). The issue is discussed in more detail *infra*, Amend. XIV, § 1, The New Equal Protection.

on the issue, the Court said that "neither § 2 nor § 4 of Article I 'provides a judicially enforceable limit on the political considerations that the States and Congress may take into account when districting.'"[23]

Clause 3. Apportionment

APPORTIONMENT OF SEATS IN THE HOUSE

The Census Requirement

[P. 123, delete sentence starting "Although the Census Clause, . . ." and substitute with:]

Although the Census Clause expressly provides for an enumeration of persons, Congress has historically collected additional demographic information—in some years asking more detailed questions regarding the personal and economic affairs of a subset of respondents.[24]

[P. 124, after sentence ending ". . . for intelligent legislative action." add new paragraph:]

The Court confirmed this understanding of the Enumeration Clause in *Department of Commerce v. New York*.[25] In an opinion on behalf of the Court, Chief Justice Roberts considered whether the Secretary of Commerce's decision to ask a citizenship question on the census questionnaire violated the Enumeration Clause because the question did not relate to the accomplishment of an actual enumeration.[26] The Chief Justice began his analysis by recognizing that the Clause affords virtually limitless authority to Congress in conducting the census, which Congress has, in turn, largely delegated to the Secretary.[27] The Court observed that demographic questions have been asked in every census since 1790, providing a "long and consistent historical practice" that informed the permissibility of the underlying practice.[28] Because of this understanding of the Clause's meaning, the Court held that Congress, and by extension the Secretary, has the power to use the census for broader information-gathering purposes without running afoul of the Enumeration Clause.[29]

---

[23] *Id.* at 29–30 (quoting Vieth v. Jubelirer, 541 U.S. 267, 305 (2004) (plurality opinion)).

[24] *See* Dep't of Commerce v. New York, 588 U.S. ___, No. 18-966, slip op. at 2 (2019).

[25] See Dep't of Commerce, slip op.

[26] *Id.* at 11. In so doing, the Court distinguished the instant challenge against the Secretary of Commerce's decision to collect certain demographic information during the census from prior case law involving the Secretary's decisions on how to *conduct the population count* for the census. *Id.* That case law required decisions about the population count to be reasonably related to accomplishing an actual enumeration. *Id.*

[27] *Id.*

[28] *Id.* at 12–13 ("That history matters. . . . In light of the early understanding of and long practice under the Enumeration Clause, we conclude that it permits Congress, and by extension the Secretary, to inquire about citizenship on the census questionnaire.").

[29] *Id.* at 13. In a separate part of the opinion, the Court invalidated the inclusion of the question on procedural grounds, concluding that the Secretary violated the Administrative

Section 4. Elections

Clause 1. Times, Places, and Manner

LEGISLATION PROTECTING ELECTORAL PROCESS

[P. 127, delete heading "LEGISLATION PROTECTING ELECTORAL PROCESS" and substitute with:]

REGULATION BY CONGRESS

[P. 130, after n. 382, add new section:]

REGULATION BY THE STATE LEGISLATURE

By its terms, Article I, Section 4, Clause 1, also contemplates the times, places, and manner of holding elections being "prescribed in each State by the Legislature thereof," subject to alteration by Congress (except as to the place of choosing Senators). However, the Court did not have occasion to address what constitutes regulation by a state "Legislature" for purposes of the Elections Clause until its 2015 decision in *Arizona State Legislature v. Arizona Independent Redistricting Commission*.[30] There, the Court rejected the Arizona legislature's challenge to the validity of the Arizona Independent Redistricting Commission (AIRC) and AIRC's 2012 map of congressional districts.[31] The Commission had been established by a 2000 ballot initiative, which removed redistricting authority from the legislature and vested it in the AIRC.[32] The Legislature asserted that this arrangement violated the Elections Clause because the Clause contemplates regulation by a state "Legislature" and "Legislature" means the state's representative assembly.[33] The Court disagreed and held that Arizona's use of an independent commission to establish congressional districts is permissible because the Elections Clause uses the word "Legislature" to describe "the power that makes laws," a term that is broad enough to encompass the power provided by the Arizona constitution for the people to make laws through ballot initiatives.[34] In so finding, the Court noted that the word "Legislature" has been construed in various ways depending upon the constitutional provision in which it is used, and its meaning depends upon the function that the entity denominated as the "Legislature" is called upon to exercise in a specific context.[35] Here, in the context of the Elections Clause, the Court found

---

Procedure Act by failing to disclose the actual reason for adding the citizenship question on the census questionnaire. *Id.* at 28.

[30] 576 U.S. ___, No. 13-1314, slip op. (2015).

[31] *Id.* at 2–3.

[32] *Id.*

[33] *Id.* at 2.

[34] *Id.* at 18. The Court also found that the use of the commission was permissible under 2 U.S.C. § 2a(c), a statutory provision that the Court construed as safeguarding to "each state full authority to employ in the creation of congressional districts its own laws and regulations." *Id.* at 19.

[35] *Id.* at 18.

that the function of the "Legislature" was lawmaking and that this function could be performed by the people of Arizona via an initiative consistent with state law.[36] The Court also pointed to dictionary definitions from the time of the Framers;[37] the Framers' intent in adopting the Elections Clause;[38] the "harmony" between the initiative process and the Constitution's "conception of the people as the font of governmental power;"[39] and the practical consequences of invalidating the Arizona initiative.[40]

[P. 130, delete first sentence of third paragraph, "State authority to regulate the 'times, places, and manner' of holding congressional elections has also been tested . . . necessary in order to enforce the fundamental rights involved." and substitute with:]

State authority to regulate the times, places, and manner of holding congressional elections has been described by the Court as "embrac[ing] authority to provide a complete code for congressional elections . . . ; in short, to enact the numerous requirements as to procedure and safeguards which experience shows are necessary in order to enforce the fundamental rights involved."

Section 5. Powers and Duties of the Houses

Clauses 1–4. Judging Elections

POWERS AND DUTIES OF THE HOUSES

Rules of Proceedings

[P. 134, delete last sentence at end of section and substitute with:]

The constitutionality of the filibuster has been challenged in court several times, but those cases have never reached the merits of the issue.[41] More

---

[36] *Id.*

[37] *Id.* at 24 (noting that "dictionaries, even those in circulation during the founding era, capaciously define the word 'legislature'" to include as "[t]he power that makes laws" and "the Authority of making laws").

[38] *Id.* at 25 ("The dominant purpose of the Elections Clause . . . was to empower Congress to override state election rules, not to restrict the way States enact legislation. . . . [T]he Clause 'was the Framers' insurance against the possibility that a State would refuse to provide for the election of representatives to the Federal Congress.'").

[39] *Id.* at 30 ("The Framers may not have imagined the modern initiative process in which the people of a State exercise legislative power coextensive with the authority of an institutional legislature. But the invention of the initiative was in full harmony with the Constitution's conception of the people as the font of governmental power.").

[40] *Id.* at 31, 33 (noting that it would be "perverse" to interpret the term "Legislature" to exclude the initiative, because the initiative is intended to check legislators' ability to determine the boundaries of the districts in which they run, and that a contrary ruling would invalidate a number of other state provisions regarding initiatives and referendums).

[41] *See, e.g.,* Common Cause v. Biden, 748 F.3d 1280 (D.C. Cir. 2014); Judicial Watch, Inc. v. U.S. Senate, 432 F.3d 359 (D.C. Cir. 2005); Page v. Shelby, 995 F. Supp. 23 (D.D.C. 1998). The constitutionality of the filibuster has been a subject of debate for legal scholars. *See, e.g.,*

recently, the Senate interpreted its rules to require only a simple majority to invoke cloture on most nominations.[42]

Section 8. Powers of Congress

Clause 3. Power to Regulate Commerce

POWER TO REGULATE COMMERCE

The Commerce Clause as a Source of National Police Power

Is There an Intrastate Barrier to Congress's Commerce Power?.—

[P. 221, in n.884, after "*E.g.,*" add:]

> McDonnell v. United States, 579 U.S. ___, No. 15-474, slip op. at 24 (2016) (narrowly interpreting the term "official act" to avoid a construction of the Hobbs Act and federal honest-services fraud statute that would "raise[] significant federalism concerns" by intruding on a state's "prerogative to regulate the permissible scope of interactions between state officials and their constituents");

Requirement That Regulation Be Economic.—

[P. 227, at end of last sentence in first paragraph, add new footnote:]

> *See also* Taylor v. United States, 579 U.S. ___, No. 14-6166, slip op. at 3 (2016) (rejecting the argument that the government, in prosecuting a defendant under the Hobbs Act for robbing drug dealers, must prove the interstate nature of the drug activity). The *Taylor* Court viewed this result as following necessarily from the Court's earlier decision in *Raich*, because the Hobbs Act imposes criminal penalties on robberies that affect "all . . . commerce over which the United States has jurisdiction," 18 U.S.C. § 1951(b)(3) (2012), and *Raich* established the precedent that the market for marijuana, "including its intrastate aspects," is "'commerce over which the United States has jurisdiction.'" *Taylor,* slip op. at 6–7. *Taylor* was, however, expressly "limited to cases in which a defendant targets drug dealers for the purpose of stealing drugs or drug proceeds." *Id.* at 9. The Court did not purport to resolve what federal prosecutors must prove in Hobbs Act robbery cases "where some other type of business or victim is targeted." *Id.*

Criminal Law.—

[P. 230, delete last sentence of last paragraph and substitute with:]

Nonetheless, "Congress cannot punish felonies generally" and may enact only those criminal laws that are connected to one of its constitutionally enumerated powers, such as the commerce power.[43] As a consequence, "most federal offenses include . . . a jurisdictional" element that ties the underlying offense to one of Congress's constitutional powers.[44]

Josh Chafetz & Michael J. Gerhardt, *Debate, Is the Filibuster Constitutional?* 158 U. PA. L. REV. PENNUMBRA 245 (2010).

[42] 159 CONG. REC. S8416–18 (daily ed. Nov. 21, 2013).

[43] *See* Cohens v. Virginia, 19 U.S. (6 Wheat.) 264, 428 (1821).

[44] *See* Luna Torres v. Lynch, 578 U.S. ___, No. 14-1096, slip op. at 4 (2016).

[P. 231, n.946, delete second sentence and substitute with:]

Taylor v. United States, 579 U.S. ___, No. 14-6166, slip op. at 3 (2016); Russell v. United States, 471 U.S. 858, 862 (1985).

THE COMMERCE CLAUSE AS A RESTRAINT ON STATE POWERS

Doctrinal Background

[P. 232, after sentence ending ". . . would thereby be brought to an end.", add new footnote:]

See, e.g., Tenn. Wine and Spirits Retailers Ass'n v. Thomas, 588 U.S. ___, No. 18-96, slip op. at 7 (2019) ("[R]emoving state trade barriers was a principal reason for the adoption of the Constitution.").

[P. 233, after sentence ending ". . . lesser measure.", add new footnote:]

Cf. Tenn. Wine and Spirits Retailers Ass'n v. Thomas, 588 U.S. ___, No. 18-96, slip op. at 8 (2019) ("In light of this [historical] background, it would be strange if the Constitution contained no provision curbing state protectionism, and at this point in the Court's history, no provision other than the Commerce Clause could easily do the job.").

[P. 235, after n. 962, add new sentence:]

In 2019, the Supreme Court said in *Tennessee Wine and Spirits Retailers Association v. Thomas* that pursuant to "history" and "established case law," "the Commerce Clause by its own force restricts state protectionism."[45]

[P. 236, delete ", but they do not explain why the Court is empowered under a grant of power to Congress to police state regulatory and taxing decisions."]

[P. 237, n.970, delete "Cf. Quill Corp., 504 U.S. at 318"]

The State Proprietary Activity (Market Participant) Exception.—

[P. 238, at end of n. 975, delete "." and substitute with:]

; see also McBurney v. Young, 569 U.S. 221, 228–29 (2013) (to the extent that the Virginia Freedom of Information Act created a market for public documents in Virginia, the Commonwealth was the sole manufacturer of the product, and therefore did not offend the Commerce Clause when it limited access to those documents under the Act to citizens of the Commonwealth).

---

[45] 588 U.S. ___, No. 18-96, slip op. at 10 (2019).

Congressional Authorization of Otherwise Impermissible State Action.—

[P. 240, delete n.987 and substitute with:]

> Granholm v. Heald, 544 U.S. 460, 487 (2005). *Accord* Tenn. Wine and Spirits Retailers Ass'n v. Thomas, 588 U.S. ___, No. 18-96, slip op. at 24 (2019); Healy v. The Beer Institute, 491 U.S. 324, 340 (1989); Brown-Forman Distillers Corp. v. N.Y. State Liquor Auth., 476 U.S. 573, 579 (1986); Bacchus Imports Ltd. v. Dias, 468 U.S. 263, 276 (1984). *See also infra* Amend. XXI, § 2, Discrimination Against Interstate Commerce.

State Taxation and Regulation: The Modern Law

Taxation.—

[P. 250, n.1044, delete "For recent reiterations of the principle, *see* Quill v. North Dakota ex rel. Heitkamp, 504 U.S. 298, 310 n.5 (1992) (citing cases)."]

[P. 251, delete n.1049 and substitute with:]

> 430 U.S. at 279.

[P. 251, delete sentence "All subsequent cases have been decided in this framework."]

Nexus.—

[P. 251, delete paragraph starting "'The Commerce Clause and the Due Process Clause impose . . ." and substitute with:]

The first prong of the *Complete Auto* test asks whether the tax applies to an activity with a "substantial nexus" with the taxing state, which requires the taxpayer to "avail[] itself of the substantial privilege of carrying on business in that jurisdiction."[46] This requirement runs parallel to the "minimum contacts" requirement under the Due Process Clause that a state must meet to exercise control over a person, that person's property, or a transaction involving the person.[47] Specifically, under the due process requirement, there must be "some definite link, some minimum connection between a state and the person, property, or transaction it seeks to tax."[48] The "broad inquiry" under "both constitutional requirements"[49] is "whether the taxing power exerted by the state bears fiscal relation to protection, opportunities and benefits given by the state"—i.e., "whether the state has given anything for which it can ask return."[50]

---

[46] *See* Polar Tankers, Inc. v. City of Valdez, 557 U.S. 1, 11 (2009) (internal citations and quotations omitted).

[47] *See* MeadWestvaco Corp. v. Ill. Dep't of Revenue, 553 U.S. 16, 24 (2008).

[48] *See* Miller Brothers Co. v. Maryland, 347 U.S. 340, 344–45 (1954).

[49] *See* *MeadWestvaco Corp.* 553 U.S. at 24.

[50] *See* Wisconsin v. J.C. Penney Co., 311 U.S. 435, 444 (1940).

[P. 252, delete sentences starting "The question of the presence of . . ." through n.1054 and substitute with:]

The Court, however, imposed a relatively narrow interpretation of the minimum contacts test in two cases in the latter half of the Twentieth Century, both involving a state's ability to require an out-of-state seller to collect and remit tax from a sale to a consumer within that state. First, in the 1967 case of *National Bellas Hess, Inc. v. Department of Revenue,* the Court considered an Illinois law that required out-of-state retailers to collect and remit taxes on sales made to consumers who purchased goods for use within Illinois.[51] The *Bellas Hess* Court concluded that a mail-order company "whose only connection with customers in the State is by common carrier or the United States mail" lacked the requisite minimum contacts with the state required under either the Due Process Clause or the Commerce Clause.[52] In so doing, the case established a rule that unless the retailer maintained a physical presence with the state, the state lacked the power to require that retailer to collect a local use tax.[53] A quarter of a century later, the Court reexamined *Bella Hess*'s physical presence rule in *Quill v. North Dakota.*[54] In *Quill,* the Court overruled the *Bellas Hess* due process holding,[55] but reaffirmed the Commerce Clause holding,[56] concluding that the physical presence rule was grounded in the substantial nexus requirement of *Complete Auto.*[57]

Twenty-six years after *Quill* and more than half a century after *Bellas Hess,* the Court, in an opinion by Justice Kennedy, overruled both cases in *South Dakota v. Wayfair,* rejecting the rule that a retailer must have a physical presence within a state before the state may require the retailer to collect a local use tax.[58] Several reasons undergirded the *Wayfair* Court's rejection of the physical presence rule. First, the Court noted that the rule did not comport with modern dormant Commerce Clause jurisprudence, which viewed the substantial nexus test as "closely related" to and having "significant parallels" with the due process minimum contacts analysis.[59] Second, Justice Kennedy viewed the *Quill* rule as unmoored from the underlying purpose of the Commerce Clause: to prevent states from engaging in economic discrimination.[60] Contrary to this purpose, the *Quill* rule created artificial market distortions that placed businesses with a physical presence in a state at a competitive

---

[51] 386 U.S. 753, 754–55 (1967).

[52] *Id.* at 758.

[53] *Id.*

[54] *See* 504 U.S. 298 (1992).

[55] *Id.* at 307–08.

[56] *Id.* at 317–18.

[57] *Id.* at 311.

[58] *See* South Dakota v. Wayfair, 585 U.S. ___, No. 17-494, slip op. at 22 (2018).

[59] *Id.* at 10–12. The Court, citing *Burger King Corp. v. Rudzewicz,* 471 U.S. 462, 476 (1985), concluded that it is "settled law that a business need not have a physical presence in a State to satisfy the demands of due process." *See Wayfair,* slip op. at 11.

[60] *See Wayfair* slip op. at 12 (noting that the purpose of the Commerce Clause was to prevent states from engaging in economic discrimination and not to "permit the Judiciary to create market distortions." *Id.*

disadvantage relative to remote sellers.[61] Third, the *Wayfair* Court viewed the physical presence rule, in contrast with modern Commerce Clause jurisprudence, as overly formalistic.[62] More broadly, the majority opinion criticized the *Quill* rule as ignoring the realities of modern e-commerce wherein a retailer may have "substantial virtual connections" to a state without having a physical presence.[63] The Court also maintained that the physical presence rule undermined public confidence in the tax system and in the "Court's Commerce Clause decisions" by providing online retailers an arbitrary advantage over competitors who collect state sales tax.[64] While acknowledging that caution is needed when reconsidering past precedent, the *Wayfair* Court concluded that the doctrine of *stare decisis* could "no longer support" *Bellas Hess* and *Quill,* as the Court "should be vigilant in correcting" an error that prevents the states from "exercising their lawful sovereign powers in our federal system."[65] In particular, Justice Kennedy noted that the financial impact of the *Quill* rule had increased with the prevalence of the Internet, and in recent years, denied states already facing revenue shortages the ability to collect taxes on more than a half a trillion dollars in sales.[66] Ultimately, the *Wayfair* Court concluded that the physical presence rule of *Quill* was "unsound and incorrect," overruling both *Bellas Hess* and *Quill.*[67]

---

[61] *Id.* at 12–13.

[62] *Id.* at 14–15.

[63] *Id.* at 15.

[64] *Id.* at 16–17.

[65] *Id.* at 17. In so concluding, the *Wayfair* Court responded to several arguments as to why *stare decisis* counseled toward maintaining the *Quill* rule. First, Justice Kennedy, while recognizing that Congress has the authority to change the physical presence rule, noted that "Congress cannot change the constitutional default rule," and that it is improper "to ask Congress to address a false constitutional premise of this Court's own creation." *Id.* at 18. The *Wayfair* Court also rejected the argument that the physical presence rule was either easy to apply or had engendered legitimate reliance interests, noting that "[a]ttempts to apply the physical presence rule to online retail sales are proving unworkable" as states are "already confronting the complexities of defining physical presence in the Cyber Age." *Id.* at 19. As a result, the Court viewed the "arguments for reliance based on [the physical presence rule's] clarity" to be "misplaced." *Id.* at 19–20. Likewise, Justice Kennedy rejected the argument that any reliance interests in the *Quill* rule were legitimate considerations, as the tax distortion created by *Quill* largely resulted from consumers "regularly fail[ing] to comply with lawful use taxes." *Id.* at 20. Finally, the *Wayfair* Court, while noting the potential burdens of invalidating the physical presence rule for small businesses that may need to comply with thousands of state and local tax laws, observed that the development of modern software, coupled with legislative and judicial responses, could alleviate undue burdens on commerce. *Id.* at 21.

[66] *Id.* at 19.

[67] *Id.* at 22. Having overruled those two decisions, the Court concluded that the South Dakota law at issue, which required remote retailers delivering more than $100,000 of goods or services into South Dakota or annually engaging in 200 or more separate transactions in the state to collect and remit sales taxes, satisfied the substantial nexus requirement of *Complete Auto*. *Id.* at 23. The Court remanded the case for further consideration of whether the law otherwise complied with the Commerce Clause. *Id.* at 23–24.

Outside of the anomalies of *Bellas Hess* and *Quill*, as the Court in *Wayfair* noted, the substantial nexus inquiry has tended to reject formal rules in favor of a more flexible inquiry.[68]

Apportionment.—

[P. 254, in first paragraph, delete sentence starting "Generally speaking . . ." and substitute with:]

Generally speaking, this factor has been seen as both a Commerce Clause and a due process requisite,[69] although, as one recent Court decision notes, some tax measures that are permissible under the Due Process Clause nonetheless could run afoul of the Commerce Clause.[70]

[P. 255, , after n.1065, at end of second paragraph, add:]

Similarly, the Court held that Maryland's personal income tax scheme—which taxed Maryland residents on their worldwide income and nonresidents on income earned in the state and did not offer Maryland residents a full credit for income taxes they paid to other states—"fails the internal consistency test."[71] The Court did so because, if every state adopted the same approach, taxpayers who "earn[] income interstate" would be taxed twice on a portion of that income, while those who earned income solely within their state of residence would be taxed only once.[72]

---

[68] *See id.* at 14.

[69] *See* Allied-Signal, Inc. v. Dir., Div. of Tax., 504 U.S. 768 (1992); Tyler Pipe Indus. v. Dep't of Revenue, 483 U.S. 232, 251 (1987); Container Corp. of Am. v. Franchise Tax Bd., 463 U.S. 159 (1983); F. W. Woolworth Co. v. N.M. Tax. & Revenue Dep't, 458 U.S. 354 (1982); ASARCO, Inc. v. Id. State Tax Comm'n, 458 U.S. 307 (1982); Exxon Corp. v. Wis. Dep't of Revenue, 447 U.S. 207 (1980); Mobil Oil Corp. v. Comm'r of Taxes, 445 U.S. 425 (1980); Moorman Mfg. Co. v. Bair, 437 U.S. 267 (1978). *Cf.* Am. Trucking Ass'ns Inc. v. Scheiner, 483 U.S. 266 (1987).

[70] Comptroller of the Treasury of Md. v. Wynne, 575 U.S. ___, No. 13-485, slip op. at 13 (2015) ("The Due Process Clause allows a State to tax '*all* the income of its residents, even income earned outside the taxing jurisdiction.' But 'while a State may, consistent with the Due Process Clause, have the authority to tax a particular taxpayer, imposition of the tax may nonetheless violate the Commerce Clause.") (internal citations omitted). The challenge in *Wynne* was brought by Maryland residents, whose worldwide income three dissenting Justices would have seen as subject to Maryland taxation based on their domicile in the state, even though it resulted in the double taxation of income earned in other states. *Id.* at 2 (Ginsburg, J., dissenting) ("For at least a century, 'domicile' has been recognized as a secure ground for taxation of residents' worldwide income."). However, the majority took a different view, holding that Maryland's taxing scheme was unconstitutional under the dormant Commerce Clause because it did not provide a full credit for taxes paid to other states on income earned from interstate activities. *Id.* at 21–25 (majority opinion).

[71] Comptroller of the Treasury of Md. v. Wynne, 575 U.S. ___, No. 13-485, slip op. at 22 (2015). The Court in *Wynne* expressly declined to distinguish between taxes on gross receipts and taxes on net income or between taxes on individuals and taxes on corporations. *Id.* at 7, 9. The Court also noted that Maryland could "cure the problem with its current system" by granting a full credit for taxes paid to other states, but the Court did "not foreclose the possibility" that Maryland could comply with the Commerce Clause in some other way. *Id.* at 25.

[72] *Id.* at 22–23.

Discrimination.—

[P. 257, after n.1074, add:]

> The Court reached the same conclusion as to Maryland's personal income tax scheme, previously noted, which taxed Maryland residents on their worldwide income and nonresidents on income earned in the state and did not offer Maryland residents a full credit for income taxes they paid to other states, finding the scheme "inherently discriminatory."[73]

[P. 257, before sentence starting "Expanding, although neither unexpectedly nor exceptionally . . ." add new paragraph break.]

Regulation.—

[P. 259, after sentence ending ". . . then no balancing is required." add new footnote:]

> *See, e.g.,* Tenn. Wine and Spirits Retailers Ass'n v. Thomas, 588 U.S. ___, No. 18-96, slip op. at 10 (2019) ("[I]f a state law discriminates against out-of-state goods or nonresident economic actors, the law can be sustained only on a showing that it is narrowly tailored to 'advanc[e] a legitimate local purpose.'" (quoting Dep't of Revenue of Ky. v. Davis, 553 U.S. 328, 338 (2008))).

CONCURRENT FEDERAL AND STATE JURISDICTION

The General Issue: Preemption

Preemption Standards.—

[P. 272, in n.1148, delete sentence starting "Recourse to legislative history as one means of ascertaining . . ." and substitute with:]

> Conversely, a state's intentions with regard to its own law "is relevant only as it may relate to 'the scope of the state law that Congress understood would survive'" the preemptive effect of federal law or "the nature of the effect of state law on" on the subject matter Congress is regulating. Gobeille v. Liberty Mut. Ins. Co., 577 U.S. ___, No. 14-181, slip op. at 11 (2016) (internal quotations omitted).

[P. 273, after ". . . theoretically turn on statutory construction," add new footnote:]

> *See, e.g.,* Va. Uranium, Inc. v. Warren, 587 U.S. ___, No. 16-1275, slip op. at 4 (2019) (plurality opinion) (stating that the Court will approach the question of preemption "much as [it] would any other [question] about statutory meaning, looking to the text and context of the law in question and guided by the traditional tools of statutory interpretation"); *see*

---

[73] Comptroller of the Treasury of Md. v. Wynne, 575 U.S. ___, No. 13-485, slip op. at 23 (2015) ("[T]he internal consistency test reveals what the undisputed economic analysis shows: Maryland's tax scheme is inherently discriminatory and operates as a tariff."). In so doing, the Court noted that Maryland could "cure the problem with its current system" by granting a full credit for taxes paid to other states, but it did "not foreclose the possibility" that Maryland could comply with the Commerce Clause in some other way. *Id.* at 25.

also id. at 8 (Ginsburg, J., concurring) (looking to statutory text, context, and history to determine whether a federal statute preempted a state law).

The Standards Applied.—

[P. 274, after n.1155, in second sentence of paragraph starting *"Express Preemption . . . "* delete period immediately after " . . . relatively interpretation free." and add new sentence:]

and the Court has recognized that certain statutory language can guide the interpretation.[74]

[P. 275, after sentence starting "But, more often than not, express preemptive language may be ambiguous . . . ." add new footnote:]

See, e.g., Kansas v. Garcia, 140 S. Ct. 791, 800, 802 (2020) (referring to an Immigration Reform and Control Act of 1986 provision generally prohibiting use of "'any information contained in'" an I-9 form (used for verifying work authorization) as "far more than a preemption provision" because "unlike a typical preemption provision, it applie[d] not just to the States but also to the Federal Government and all private actors" (quoting 8 U.S.C. § 1324a(b)(5))). *But see id.* at 799, 803–04 (holding that § 1324a(b)(5) did not expressly preempt state prosecutions of non-U.S. citizens under state identify-theft and false-information statutes for using on a tax-withholding form the same false Social Security numbers as used on an I-9 form).

---

[74] For example, in *Coventry Health Care of Missouri, Inc. v. Nevils*, the Court noted that it has "'repeatedly recognized' that the phrase 'relate to' in a preemption clause 'express[es] a broad pre-emptive purpose.' Congress characteristically employs the phrase to reach any subject that has 'a connection with, or reference to,' the topics the statute enumerates." 581 U.S. ___, No. 16-149, slip op. at 7 (2017) (quoting Morales v. Trans World Airlines, Inc., 504 U.S. 374, 383–84 (1992)) (internal citation omitted). *Coventry Health Care* involved an express preemption provision of the Federal Employees Health Benefits Act of 1959 (FEHBA) under which any terms of contracts with private carriers for federal employees' health insurance that "relate to the nature, provision, or extent of coverage or benefits (including *payments with respect to benefits*) . . . supersede and preempt any State or local law . . . which relates to health insurance or plans." *Id.* at 1 (quoting 5 U.S.C. § 8902(m)(1)) (internal quotation marks omitted; emphasis added). A federal employee brought an action alleging violations of a Missouri consumer-protection law against a private carrier that asserted a lien against the employee's personal injury settlement under the subrogation and reimbursement terms of a health insurance contract. While there was no dispute that the Missouri law "relates to health insurance," the Court examined whether the contractual subrogation and reimbursement terms "relate to . . . payments with respect to benefits." *Id.* at 2. Based on the statutory language, including "Congress' use of the expansive phrase 'relate to,'" the Court held that such contractual provisions do "'relate to . . . payments with respect to benefits' because subrogation and reimbursement rights yield just such payments. When a carrier exercises its right to either reimbursement or subrogation, it receives from either the beneficiary or a third party 'payment' respecting the benefits the carrier had previously paid." *Id.* at 6–7. The Court also rejected the respondent's argument that allowing a contract to preempt state law violated the Supremacy Clause, which by its terms provides preemptive effect to the "laws of the United States." *Id.* at 9. The Court held "that the regime Congress enacted is compatible with the Supremacy Clause," *id.* at 1–2, because, like "[m]any other federal statutes," FEHBA provides that certain contract terms have preemptive force only to the extent that the contract "fall[s] within the statute's preemptive scope." *Id.* at 9. In this way, the Court concluded that the "statute, not a contract, strips state law of its force." *Id.* For a discussion of preemption in the context of the Supremacy Clause, *see infra* Article VI: Clause 2.

[P. 275, n.1157, delete "Morales v. TWA, 504 U.S. 374 (1992)" and substitute with:]

Morales, 504 U.S. 374.

[P. 275, at end of n.1157, delete "." and substitute with:]

Nw., Inc. v. Ginsberg, 572 U.S. 273 (2014) (holding that the Airline Deregulation Act's preemption provision applied to state common law claims, including an airline customer's claim for breach of the implied covenant of good faith and fair dealing). *But see* Dan's City Used Cars, Inc. v. Pelkey, 569 U.S. 251, 254 (2013) (provision of Federal Aviation Administration Authorization Act of 1994 preempting state law "related to a price, route, or service of any motor carrier . . . with respect to the transportation of property" held not to preempt state laws on the disposal of towed vehicles by towing companies (alteration in original)).

[P. 275, delete n.1159 and substitute with:]

563 U.S. 582 (2011). The *Whiting* majority notably began its analysis of whether the challenged Arizona statute was preempted by federal law with a statement that "[w]hen a federal law contains an express preemption clause, we 'focus on the plain wording of the clause, which necessarily contains the best evidence of Congress' preemptive intent.'" *Id.* at 594. Subsequently, in writing for the majority in *Commonwealth of Puerto Rico v. Franklin California Tax-Free Trust*, Justice Thomas cited this language from *Whiting* in support of the proposition that no presumption against preemption is to be applied when a congressional enactment includes an express preemption clause. *See* 579 U.S. ___, No. 15-233, slip op. at 9 (2016) (declining to apply a presumption against preemption in finding that the federal Bankruptcy Code preempts a Puerto Rico bankruptcy law).

[P. 275, in last sentence of first full paragraph, delete second period immediately preceding n.1160]

[P. 275, delete n.1160 and substitute with:]

Whiting, 563 U.S. at 612 (Breyer, J., dissenting); *id.* at 631 (Sotomayor, J., dissenting).

[P. 277, delete n.1167 and substitute with:]

Gobeille v. Liberty Mut. Ins. Co., 577 U.S. ___, No. 14-181, slip op. at 9 (2016) (holding that ERISA—with its extensive reporting, disclosure, and recordkeeping requirements that are "central to, and an essential part of," its uniform plan administration system—preempted a Vermont law requiring certain entities, including health insurers, to report health care related information to a state agency); Aetna Health, Inc. v. Davila, 542 U.S. 200 (2004) (suit brought against HMO under state health care liability act for failure to exercise ordinary care when denying benefits is preempted); Boggs v. Boggs, 520 U.S. 833 (1997) (decided not on the basis of the express preemption language but instead by implied preemption analysis); De Buono v. NYSA–ILA Med. & Clinical Servs. Fund, 520 U.S. 806 (1997); Cal. Div. of Labor Standards Enf't v. Dillingham Constr., N.A., 519 U.S. 316 (1997); N.Y. State Conf. of Blue Cross & Blue Shield Plans v. Travelers Ins. Co., 514 U.S. 645 (1995) (no preemption of statute that required hospitals to collect surcharges from patients covered by a commercial insurer but not from patients covered by Blue Cross/Blue Shield plan); John Hancock Mut. Life Ins. Co. v. Harris Trust & Sav. Bank, 510 U.S. 86 (1993) (ERISA's fiduciary standards, not conflicting state insurance laws, apply to insurance company's handling of general account assets derived from participating group annuity contract); District of Columbia v. Greater Wash. Bd. of Trade, 506 U.S. 125 (1992) (law requiring employers to provide health insurance coverage, equivalent to existing coverage, for workers receiving workers' compensation benefits); Ingersoll-Rand Co. v. McClendon, 498 U.S. 133 (1990) (ERISA preempts state common-law claim of wrongful discharge to prevent employee attaining benefits under plan covered by ERISA); FMC Corp. v. Holliday, 498 U.S. 52 (1990) (provision of state motor-vehicle financial-responsibility law barring subrogation and reimbursement from claimant's tort recovery for benefits received from a self-insured healthcare plan preempted by ERISA); Fort Halifax Packing Co. v. Coyne, 482 U.S. 1 (1987) (state law requiring employers to provide a one-time severance payment to employees in the event of a plant closing held not preempted by 5–4 vote); Metro. Life Ins. Co. v. Massachusetts, 471 U.S. 724 (1985) (state law mandating that certain minimum mental-health-care benefits be provided to those insured under general health-insurance policy or employee health-care plan is a law "which regulates insurance" and is not preempted); Shaw v. Delta Air Lines, 463 U.S. 85 (1983) (state law forbidding discrimination in employee benefit plans on the basis of pregnancy not preempted, because of another saving provision in ERISA, and provision requiring employers to pay sick-leave benefits to employees unable to work because of pregnancy not preempted under construction of coverage sections, but both laws "relate to" employee benefit plans); Alessi v. Raybestos-Manhattan, Inc., 451 U.S. 504 (1981) (state law prohibiting plans from reducing benefits by amount of workers' compensation awards "relates to" employee benefit plan and is preempted).

[P. 280, after n.1177, add new paragraph:]

In *Virginia Uranium, Inc., v. Warren*, the Supreme Court considered whether a disputed statutory provision was a preemption clause at all.[75] A clause in the Atomic Energy Act provided that nothing in the relevant section should be construed to affect state authority "to regulate activities for purposes other than protection against radiation hazards."[76] A litigant argued this provision displaced "*any* state law . . . if that law was enacted for the purpose of protecting the public against 'radiation hazards.'"[77] Justice Gorsuch disagreed, writing for three members of the Court, instead describing this provision as "a *non-preemption* clause."[78] He said that this statute meant "only state laws that seek to regulate the activities discussed" in that section should be "be scrutinized to ensure their purposes aim at something other than regulating nuclear safety."[79] Three concurring Justices agreed that the effect of this provision was relatively limited, reading the law to address only those "activities" that were already regulated under the statute.[80]

Field Preemption.

[P. 281, n.1185, after "*See*", add:]

Kansas v. Garcia, 140 S. Ct. 791, 804 (2020) (holding that a federal immigration statute regulating the use of information "contained in" I-9 forms for verifying work authorization did not implicitly preempt state prosecutions for using false information on state tax-withholding forms, reasoning that submitting "taxwithholding forms is *fundamentally unrelated* to the federal employment verification system because . . . those forms serve entirely different functions");

---

[75] 587 U.S. ___, No. 16-1275, slip op. at 6 (2019).

[76] *Id.* at 5 (quoting 42 U.S.C. § 2021(k)) (internal quotation mark omitted).

[77] *Id.* at 6.

[78] *Id.*

[79] *Id.*

[80] *Id.* at 7 (Ginsburg, J., concurring).

[P. 282, n. 1186, after "*See also . . .*", add:]

Va. Uranium, Inc. v. Warren, 587 U.S. ___, No. 16-1275, slip op. at 1 (2019 (plurality opinion) (holding that the Atomic Energy Act does not preempt "a state law banning uranium mining"); *id.* at 1 (Ginsburg, J., concurring) (same);

[P. 282, after paragraph ending "leave no room for state or local regulation." add new paragraph:]

The Court has, however, recognized that when a federal statute preempts a narrow field, leaving states to regulate outside of that field, state laws whose "target" is beyond the field of federal regulation are not necessarily displaced by field preemption principles,[81] and such state laws may "incidentally" affect the preempted field.[82] In *Oneok v. Learjet*, gas pipeline companies and the federal government asserted that state antitrust claims against the pipeline companies for alleged manipulation of certain indices used in setting natural gas prices were field preempted because the Natural Gas Act (NGA) regulates wholesale prices of natural gas.[83] The Court disagreed. In so doing, the Court noted that the alleged manipulation of the price indices also affected retail prices, the regulation of which is left to the states by the NGA.[84] Because the Court viewed Congress as having struck a "careful balance" between federal and state regulation when enacting the NGA, it took the view that,[85] "where (as here) a state law can be applied" both to sales regulated by the federal government and to other sales, "we must proceed cautiously, finding preemption only where detailed examination convinces us that a matter falls within the pre-empted field as defined by our precedents."[86] The Court found no such preemption here, in part because the "*target* at which the state law aims" was practices affecting retail prices, something which the Court viewed as "firmly on the States' side of th[e] dividing line."[87] The Court also noted that the "broad applicability" of state antitrust laws supported a finding of no preemption here,[88] as does the states' historic role in providing common law and statutory remedies against monopolies and unfair business practices.[89] However, while declining to find field preemption, the Court left open the possibility of conflict preemption, which had not been raised by the parties.[90]

---

[81] Oneok, Inc. v. Learjet, Inc., 575 U.S. ___, No. 13-271, slip op. at 10–12 (2015).

[82] *Cf.* Hughes v. Talen Energy Mktg., LLC, 578 U.S. ___, No. 14-614, slip op. at 12–13 (2016) (holding that while "States . . . may regulate within the domain Congress assigned to them even when their laws incidentally affect areas" within the federal regulatory field, "States may not seek to achieve ends, however legitimate, through regulatory means that intrude on" the federal government's authority over the field in question) (citing to *Oneok, Inc.*, slip op. at 11).

[83] *See Oneok, Inc.,* slip op. at 3, 10.

[84] *Id.* at 3.

[85] *Id.* at 13.

[86] *Id.* at 10.

[87] *Id.* at 11.

[88] *Id.* at 13.

[89] *Id.* at 14.

[90] *Id.* at 15–16.

Conflict Preemption.

[P. 283, delete n.1193 and substitute with:]

For similar examples of conflict preemption, see Wos v. EMA, 568 U.S. 627 (2013) (holding that a North Carolina statute allowing the state to collect up to one-third of the amount of a tort settlement as reimbursement for state-paid medical expenses under Medicaid conflicted with anti-lien provisions of the federal Medicaid statute where the settlement designated an amount less than one-third as the medical expenses award). *See also* Doctor's Assocs., Inc. v. Casarotto, 517 U.S. 681 (1996) (federal arbitration law preempts state statute that conditioned enforceability of arbitration clause on compliance with special notice requirement); Allied-Bruce Terminix Cos. v. Dobson, 513 U.S. 265 (1995) (federal arbitration law preempts state law invalidating predispute arbitration agreements that were not entered into in contemplation of substantial interstate activity).

[P. 284, before first full paragraph, add new paragraph:]

The Court reached a similar result in *Mutual Pharmaceutical Co. v. Bartlett.*[91] There, the Court again faced the question of whether FDA labeling requirements preempted state tort law in a case involving sales by a generic drug manufacturer. The lower court had held that it was not impossible for the manufacturer to comply with both the FDA's labeling requirements and state law that required stronger warnings regarding the drug's safety because the manufacturer could simply stop selling the drug. The Supreme Court rejected the "stop-selling rationale" because it "would render impossibility pre-emption a dead letter and work a revolution in . . . pre-emption case law."[92]

[P. 284, in first sentence of first full paragraph, after "Pliva, Inc. v. Mensing" add:]

and *Mutual Pharmaceutical Co. v. Bartlett*

[P. 284, delete n.1199 and substitute with new footnote at end of sentence after period:]

Wyeth v. Levine, 555 U.S. 555, 581 (2009); *see also* Merck Sharp & Dohme Corp. v. Albrecht, 587 U.S. ___, No. 17-290, slip op. at 9 (2019) (explaining that pursuant to the standard announced in *Wyeth*, "state law failure-to-warn claims are pre-empted" by federal law "when there is 'clear evidence' that the FDA would not have approved the warning that state law requires," and holding that impossibility preemption based on clear evidence is a question of law for a judge, not a jury, to decide).

[P. 285, delete n.1202 and substitute with:]

See generally Hines v. Davidowitz, 312 U.S. 52, 67 (1941); *see also* Hillman v. Maretta, 569 U.S. 483, 494–97 (2013) (holding that a federal statute establishing a life insurance program for federal employees and allowing the insured to name a beneficiary, preempted a state law providing a cause of action for persons not designated as the beneficiary under such federal contracts, because the state law "interfere[d] with Congress' scheme"); Arizona v. United States, 567 U.S. 387, 403–07 (2012) (holding that a provision of Arizona law making it a

---

[91] 570 U.S. 472 (2013).
[92] *Id.* at 475.

crime for "'an unauthorized alien to knowingly apply for work'" in Arizona was preempted because it "would interfere with the careful balance struck by Congress with respect to unauthorized employment of aliens" in the Immigration Reform and Control Act of 1986 (IRCA)). *But see* Kansas v. Garcia, 140 S. Ct. 791, 806 (2020) (distinguishing *Arizona* because in "enacting IRCA, Congress did not decide that an unauthorized alien who uses a false identity on tax-withholding forms should not face criminal prosecution," and, in fact, "federal law makes it a crime to use fraudulent information on a W-4" withholding form).

COMMERCE WITH INDIAN TRIBES

[P. 295, after n.1255, add new sentence:]

Further, the Court has clarified that "States have *no* authority to reduce federal reservations lying within their borders."[93]

[P. 298, before n.1277, delete ellipsis and substitute with closing period.]

[P. 299, n.1278, delete period at end of second sentence and substitute with:]

; Nebraska v. Parker, 577 U.S. ___, No. 14-1406, slip op. at 5–6 (2016) (noting that "only Congress can divest a reservation of its land and diminish its boundaries," but finding that the statute in question did not clearly indicate Congress's intent to effect such a diminishment of the Omaha reservation); McGirt v. Oklahoma, 140 S. Ct. 2452, 2463 (2020) (stating that to disestablish a reservation, Congress must "clearly express its intent to do so"). In *McGirt*, the Court held that Congress had not expressed a sufficiently clear intent to disestablish the Creek Reservation, concluding that the reservation survived allotment and other intrusions "on the Creek's promised right to self-governance." *Id.* at 2464.

Clause 4. Naturalization and Bankruptcies

ALIENS

[P. 313, at end of n.1363, add:]

Cf. Trump v. Hawaii, 585 U.S. ___, No. 17-965, slip op. at 25 (2018) (assuming without deciding that statutory claims are reviewable and declining to rule on whether "doctrine of consular nonreviewability" rendered claims nonjusticiable).

POSTAL POWER

Clause 7. Post Office

Power To Prevent Harmful Use of the Postal Facilities

[P. 326, delete sentence starting "Pointing out that it is . . ." and substitute with:]

Noting that supplying postal facilities "is by no means an indispensable adjunct to a civil government," the Court held that the "legislative body in

---

[93] McGirt v. Oklahoma, 140 S. Ct. 2452, 2462 (2020) (emphasis added).

thus establishing a postal service may annex such conditions . . . as it chooses."[94]

Clause 8. Copyrights and Patents

COPYRIGHTS AND PATENTS

Patentable Discoveries

[P. 333, after sentence ending ". . . must fall within the constitutional standard." and before sentence starting "Underlying the constitutional tests . . ." add new paragraph break.]

[P. 333, after sentence ending ". . . in encouraging invention by rewarding creative persons for their innovations." and before sentence starting "By declaring . . ." add new footnote:]

As to the nature of the reward to patentees, longstanding case law had defined a patent as the personal property of its holder, similar to title to land. *See, e.g.*, Horne v. Dep't of Agric., No. 14-275, 576 U.S. ___, slip op. at 6 (2015) ("Nothing in this history [of the Takings Clause] suggests that personal property was any less protected against physical appropriation than real property. . . . '[A patent] confers upon the patentee an exclusive property in the patented invention which cannot be appropriated or used by the government itself, without just compensation, any more than it can appropriate or use without compensation land which has been patented to a private purchaser.'" (quoting James v. Campbell, 104 U.S. 356, 358 (1882))); *see also* McCormick Harvesting Mach. Co. v. C. Aultman & Co., 169 U.S. 606, 609 (1898) (concluding that a granted patent "become[s] the property of the patentee, and as such is entitled to the same legal protection as other property"); United States v. Am. Bell Tel. Co., 128 U.S. 315, 370 (1888) ("The United States, by issuing the patents . . . has taken from the public rights of immense value, and bestowed them upon the patentee. . . . This has been taken from the people, from the public, and made the private property of the patentee . . . ."); Brown v. Duchesne, 60 U.S. 183, 197 (1856) ("[B]y the laws of the United States, the rights of a party under a patent are his private property . . . .").

More recently, however, in *Oil States Energy Services, LLC v. Greene's Energy Group, LLC*, 584 U.S. ___, No. 16-712, (2018), the Court called into question this precedent regarding the nature of a patent as private property, at least with respect to certain constitutional claims. In *Oil States*, the Court addressed whether inter partes review, a type of patent validity proceeding conducted by the U.S. Patent and Trademark Office (PTO), violates Article III or the Seventh Amendment of the Constitution. *Id.* at 1. In ruling that such proceedings do not violate either constitutional provision, the Court held that "[i]nter partes review falls squarely within the public-rights doctrine," reasoning "that the decision to grant a patent is a matter involving public rights—specifically, the grant of a public franchise." *Id.* at 6–7. Further, in addressing the precedent suggesting otherwise, the Court stated that these "cases d[id] not contradict [its] conclusion" because "[p]atents convey only a specific form of property right—a public franchise." *Id.* at 10. The Court, however, was careful to "emphasize the narrowness of [its] holding." *Id.* at 16. First, the Court specified that it ruled only on the constitutionality of inter partes review, and not "whether other patent matters, such as infringement actions, can be heard in a non-Article III forum." *Id.* Second, the Court indicated that its holdings were limited to "the precise constitutional challenges that Oil States raised," and therefore did not foreclose constitutional arguments related to "the retroactive application of inter partes review" or a possible "due process challenge." *Id.* at 16–17. Third, the Court noted that "our decision should not be misconstrued as suggesting

---

[94] *Public Clearing House*, 194 U.S. at 506.

that patents are not property for purposes of the Due Process Clause or the Takings Clause." *Id.* at 17.

[P. 334, delete heading "Procedure in Issuing Patents" and entire paragraph starting "The standard of patentability . . ." and ending ". . . thus marking somewhat amorphous the central responsibility."]

Clause 18. Necessary and Proper Clause

NECESSARY AND PROPER CLAUSE

Definition of Punishment and Crimes

[P. 379, after last complete sentence, add new footnote:]

> In *United States v. Kebodeaux*, 570 U.S. 387 (2013), the Court concluded that a sex offender, convicted by the Air Force in a special court-martial, had, upon his release, been subject to state sex offender registration laws, violation of which was prohibited under the Jacob Wetterling Crimes Against Children and Sexually Violent Offender Registration Act, Pub. L. No. 103-322, 108 Stat. 2038, 2038–42 (1994). Kebodeaux was later convicted of failing to register under the "very similar" provisions of the Sex Offender Registration and Notification Act (SORNA), Pub. L. No. 109-248, Title I, 120 Stat. 587, 590 (2006) (codified in scattered sections of 42 U.S.C.), which had superseded the Jacob Wetterling Act. The Court held Congress was well within its authority under the Necessary and Proper Clause to have modified the Jacob Wetterling Act's registration requirements, and Kebodeaux was properly subject to SORNA requirements, even if they were enacted after his release. *Kebodeaux*, 570 U.S. 398–99.

Courts and Judicial Proceedings

[P. 382, delete n.1848 and substitute with:]

> *See* Jinks v. Richland County, 538 U.S. 456, 464–65 (2003); *see also* Artis v. District of Columbia, 583 U.S. ___, No. 16-460, slip op. at 17–18 (2018) (holding that interpreting a federal law to suspend a state statute of limitations both while a state law claim is pending in federal court and for 30 days postdismissal does not "present[] a serious constitutional problem").

Section 9. Powers Denied to Congress

Clause 2. Habeas Corpus Suspension

IN GENERAL

[P. 385, after sentence ending ". . . have been strongest." delete extra space before n.1877 and add new paragraph:]

Building on its statement concerning the "minimum" reach of the Suspension Clause, the Court, in *Department of Homeland Security v. Thuraissigiam,* explored what the habeas writ protected, as it existed in 1789.[95] *Thuraissigiam* involved a Suspension Clause challenge to a

---

[95] 140 S. Ct. 1959, 1968–69 (2020).

provision in IIRIRA limiting when an asylum seeker could seek habeas review to challenge a removal decision and stay in the United States.[96] Proceeding on the assumption that the Suspension Clause only prohibited limitations on the common-law habeas writ,[97] the Court concluded that the writ at the time of the founding "simply provided a means of contesting the lawfulness of restraint and securing release."[98] The asylum seeker in *Thuraissigiam* did not ask to be released from United States custody, but instead sought vacatur of his removal order and a new opportunity to apply for asylum, which if granted would enable him to remain in the United States.[99] The Court concluded that such relief fell outside the scope of the common-law habeas writ.[100] As a consequence, the Court held that, at least with respect to the relief sought by the respondent, Congress did not violate the Suspension Clause by limiting habeas relief for asylum seekers in IIRIRA.[101]

---

[96] In relevant part, IIRIRA limited the review that an alien in expedited removal proceedings could obtain through a habeas petition by allowing habeas review of three matters: (1) whether the petitioner was an alien; (2) whether the petitioner was "ordered removed"; and (3) whether the petitioner had already been granted entry as a lawful permanent resident, refugee, or asylee. *See* 8 U.S.C. § 1252(e)(2)(A)–(C). The asylum seeker in *Thuraissigiam* challenged these jurisdictional limits, arguing they precluded review of a determination that he lacked a credible fear of persecution in his home country, of which an affirmative finding would enable him to enter the United States. *Thuraissigiam*, 140 S. Ct. at 1966–68.

[97] The respondent in *Thuraissigiam* stated "there is no reason" for the Court to consider anything beyond whether the writ of habeas corpus, as it existed in 1789, encompassed the relief sought. *Thuraissigiam*, 140 S. Ct. at 1969 & n.12.

[98] *Id.* at 1969 (discussing the views of William Blackstone and Justice Joseph Story, among others).

[99] *Id.* at 1969–71.

[100] In so concluding, the Court rejected the argument that three bodies of case law—(1) "British and American cases decided prior to or around the time of the adoption of the Constitution;" (2) decisions from the Court during the so-called "finality era" from the late 19th to the mid-20th Century; and (3) two more recent cases—suggested that the Suspension Clause "guarantees a broader habeas right" than the right to contest the lawfulness of restraint and seek release. *Id.* at 1971–82. With regard to the early British and American cases, the *Thuraissigiam* Court viewed those cases to suggest that the habeas writ could only be used to secure a "simple release" from government custody. *Id.* at 1971–76. With respect to the finality-era case law, the Court viewed those cases, including *Nishimura Ekiu v. United States*, 142 U.S. 651 (1892), as simply interpreting the scope of the then-existing habeas statute and not what limitations the Suspension Clause imposes on Congress. *Thuraissigiam*, 140 S. Ct. at 1976–81. Finally, the Court distinguished two more recent cases, *Boumediene v. Bush*, 553 U.S. 723 (2008) and *INS v. St. Cyr*, 533 U.S. 289 (2001), holding that the former case did not pertain to immigration and that the latter case involved using habeas as a vehicle to seek the release of aliens who were in custody pending deportation proceedings. *Thuraissigiam*, 140 S. Ct. at 1981–82.

[101] *Thuraissigiam*, 140 S. Ct. at 1963–64.

Clause 7. Public Money Appropriations

APPROPRIATIONS

[P. 398, n.1972, delete "Knote v. United States, 95 U.S. 149, 154 (1877)" and substitute with:]

> *see also* Knote v. United States, 95 U.S. 149, 154 (1877) ("Moneys once in the treasury can only be withdrawn by an appropriation by law."); Me. Cmty. Health Options v. United States, 140 S. Ct. 1308, 1321 (2020) (stating that the Appropriations Clause does not "address[] whether Congress itself can create or incur an obligation directly by statute," but rather "constrain[s] how federal employees and officers may make or authorize payments without appropriations").

PAYMENT OF CLAIMS

[P. 399, after n.1978, add new sentence:]

> Where, however, Congress creates an "uncapped" obligation to pay particular entities through a statute that is not subject to the availability of appropriations, failure to later appropriate sufficient sums to meet that obligation may not relieve the government of its liability to those entities for the unfulfilled amounts.[102]

Section 10. Powers Denied to the States

Clause 1. Treaties, Coining Money, Etc.

Ex Post Facto Laws

Changes in Punishment.—

[P. 406, after n.2023, add new sentence:]

> The Court adopted similar reasoning regarding changes in the U.S. Sentencing Guidelines: even though the Guidelines are advisory only, an increase in the applicable sentencing range is ex post facto if applied to a previously committed crime because of a significant risk of a lengthier sentence being imposed.[103]

---

[102] Me. Cmty. Health Options v. United States, 140 S. Ct. 1308, 1323–24, 1331 (2020).
[103] Peugh v. United States, 569 U.S. 530 (2013).

Obligation of Contracts

Evaluation of the Clause Today.—

[P. 439, delete sentence starting "More important, the Court . . ."]

[P. 439, delete paragraph starting "'[T]he Contract Clause remains. . ." and substitute with:]

While the Contracts Clause "remains a part of our written Constitution,"[104] not every state law affecting preexisting contracts violates the Constitution.[105] Instead, the Court has applied a two-part test to determine whether a law unconstitutionally impairs a contractual obligation.[106] First, the state law must operate as a "substantial impairment" of a contractual relationship."[107] To determine whether a substantial impairment has occurred, the Court has considered the extent to which the law undermines the contractual bargain, interferes with a party's reasonable expectations, and prevents the party from safeguarding or reinstating his rights.[108] For instance, in *Sveen v. Melin,* the Court held that a Minnesota law automatically revoking upon a couple's divorce any life insurance policies designating a spouse to be the beneficiary did "not substantially impair pre-existing contractual arrangements."[109] Specifically, the *Sveen* Court held as such because the law in question (1) was designed to reflect a policyholder's presumed intent that an ex-spouse not "benefit from [the policyholder's] insurance;"[110] (2) does not upset the beneficiary's expectations, as a divorce court's resolution of the marital assets could have upset the beneficiary designation anyways;[111] and (3) provides a mere default rule that could be reversed "with the stroke of the pen."[112] In rejecting the Contracts Clause challenge, the *Sveen* Court viewed the Minnesota law to be in line with other state laws that imposed default rules facilitating the orderly disposition of property interests.[113]

---

[104] *See* United States Tr. Co. of N.Y. v. New Jersey, 431 U.S. 1, 16 (1977).

[105] *See* El Paso v. Simmons, 379 U.S. 497, 506–07 (1965).

[106] *See* Sveen v. Melin, 584 U.S. ___, No. 16-1432, slip op. at 7 (2018).

[107] *See* Allied Structural Steel v. Spannaus, 438 U.S. 234, 244 (1978).

[108] *See Sveen*, slip op. at 7.

[109] *Id.*

[110] *Id.* at 9.

[111] *Id.* at 9–10.

[112] *Id.* at 10.

[113] *See id.* at 10–12 (equating Minnesota's revocation-on-divorce statute to other laws mandating notifications or filings in order to enforce a contractual right, like state recording statutes that extinguish contractual interests unless timely recorded at government offices). In so concluding, the Court rejected the argument that, unlike state recording statutes, the Minnesota law actually altered the terms of an agreed upon contract. *Id.* at 13. Specifically, the *Sveen* Court found there was "no meaningful distinction" between recording statutes and the Minnesota law, as "they all make contract benefits contingent on some simple filing," which is what is "dispositive" to determine whether there has been a substantial impairment of a contractual obligation. *Id.* at 13–14.

[P. 439, delete paragraph starting "The approach in any event . . ." and substitute with:]

Second, if substantial impairment has occurred, the Court then turns to the "means" and "ends" of the legislation to determine if it violates the Contracts Clause.[114] Specifically, the Court has asked whether the state law is drawn in an "appropriate" and "reasonable" way to advance "a significant and legitimate public purpose."[115] Applying this standard, in two cases in the late 1970s, the Court struck down state legislation that impaired either the government's own contractual obligations or private contracts.[116]

[P. 440, delete sentence starting "Whether these two cases portend . . ." and substitute with:]

These cases seemed to embody more active judicial review of economic regulatory activities, in contrast to the deference shown such legislation under the due process and equal protection clauses.

Clause 3. Tonnage Duties and Interstate Compacts

INTERSTATE COMPACTS

Background of Clause

[P. 447, after sentence ending ". . . upon the just supremacy of the United States." add new sentence:]

Accordingly, congressional approval of a compact is needed when the agreement "might affect injuriously" the interests of other states or when the compact would infringe on the "rights of the national government."[117]

Legal Effect of Interstate Compacts

[P. 449, delete first sentence starting "Whenever, by the agreement of the states . . ." and substitute with:]

Once Congress gives its consent to an interstate compact, the compact, "like any other federal statute," becomes the law of the land.[118]

[P. 449, delete n.2261 and substitute with:]

Texas v. New Mexico, 482 U.S. 124, 128 (1987). In so doing, the Court has noted that "our role in resolving disputes between sovereign States under our original jurisdiction

---

[114] *Id.* at 7.

[115] *See* Energy Reserves Grp. v. Kan. Power & Light Co., 459 U.S. 400, 411 (1983).

[116] *See* Allied Structural Steel v. Spannaus, 438 U.S. 234, 244 (1978); United States Tr. Co. of N.Y. v. New Jersey, 431 U.S. 1, 16 (1977).

[117] *See* Texas v. New Mexico, 583 U.S. ___, No. 141, Orig., slip op. at 4 (2018).

[118] *See* Texas v. New Mexico, 583 U.S. ___, No. 141, Orig., slip op. at 4 (2018).

'significantly differs from the one the Court undertakes in suits between private parties.' 'In this singular sphere,' we have observed, 'the court may regulate and mould the process it uses in such a manner as in its judgment will best promote the purposes of justice.'" Florida v. Georgia, 585 U.S. ___, No. 142, Orig., slip op. at 10 (2018) (quoting Kansas v. Nebraska, 574 U.S. ___, No. 126, Orig., slip op. at 6 (2015); Kentucky v. Dennison, 65 U.S. (24 How.) 66, 98 (1861)). Thus, the Court clarified that it "must approach interstate disputes 'in the untechnical spirit proper for dealing with a quasi-international controversy, remembering that there is no municipal code governing the matter, and that this court may be called on to adjust differences that cannot be dealt with by Congress or disposed of by the legislature of either State alone.'" *Id.* (quoting Virginia v. West Virginia, 220 U.S. 1, 27 (1911) (Holmes, J.)); *see also* Texas v. New Mexico, 583 U.S. ___, No. 141, Orig., slip op. at 5 (2018) (using the Court's "unique authority to mold original actions" to allow the United States to intervene in a dispute).

ARTICLE II

Section 1. The President

Clause 1. Powers and Term of the President

NATURE AND SCOPE OF PRESIDENTIAL POWER

Executive Power: Theory of the Presidential Office

The Youngstown Case.—

[P. 462, delete first sentence starting "The only modern case that has extensively considered . . ." and substitute with:]

The first case in the post-World War II era to consider extensively the "inherent" powers of the President, or the issue of what executive powers are vested by the first section of Article II, was *Youngstown Sheet & Tube Co. v. Sawyer*,[119] but its multiple opinions did not reflect a uniform understanding of these matters.

[P. 463, after n.40, add new section:]

The *Zivotofsky* Case.—The Supreme Court's decision in *Zivotofsky v. Kerry* appears to be the first instance in which the Court held that an act of Congress unconstitutionally infringed upon a foreign affairs power of the President.[120] The case concerned a legislative enactment requiring the Secretary of State to identity a Jerusalem-born U.S. citizen's place of birth as "Israel" on his passport if requested by the citizen or his legal guardian.[121] The State Department had declined to follow this statutory command, citing longstanding executive policy of declining to recognize any country's sovereignty over the city of Jerusalem.[122] It argued the

---

[119] 343 U.S. 579 (1952).

[120] Zivotofsky v. Kerry, 576 U.S. ___, No. 13-628, slip op. (2015). It appears that in every prior instance where the Supreme Court considered executive action in the field of foreign affairs that conflicted with the requirements of a federal statute, the Court had ruled the executive action invalid. *See id.* at 2 (Roberts, C.J., dissenting) ("For our first 225 years, no President prevailed when contradicting a statute in the field of foreign affairs."); Medellin v. Texas, 552 U.S. 491 (2008) (President could not direct state courts to reconsider cases barred from further review by state and federal procedural rules in order to implement requirements flowing from a ratified U.S. treaty that was not self-executing, as legislative authorization from Congress was required); Hamdan v. Rumsfeld, 548 U.S. 557 (2006) (military tribunals convened by presidential order did not comply with the Uniform Code of Military Justice); Youngstown Sheet & Tube Co. v. Sawyer, 343 U.S. 579 (1952); Little v. Barreme, 6 U.S. (2 Cr.) 170 (1804) (upholding damage award to owners of U.S. merchant ship seized during quasi-war with France, when Congress had not authorized such seizures).

[121] Foreign Relations Authorization Act, Fiscal Year 2003, Pub. L. No. 107-228, § 214(d), 116 Stat. 1350, 1366 (2002).

[122] *Zivotofsky*, slip op. at 4. The State Department's Foreign Affairs Manual generally provides that in issuing passports to U.S. citizens born abroad, the passport shall identify the country presently exercising sovereignty over the citizen's birth location. 7 Foreign Affairs Manual § 1330 Appendix D (2008). The Manual provides that employees should

statute impermissibly intruded upon the President's constitutional authority over the recognition of foreign nations and their territorial bounds, and attempted to compel "the President to contradict his recognition position regarding Jerusalem in official communications with foreign sovereigns."[123] The *Zivotofsky* Court evaluated the permissibility of the State Department's non-adherence to a statutory command using the framework established by Justice Jackson's concurring opinion in *Youngstown*, under which executive action taken in contravention of a legislative enactment will only be sustained if the President's asserted power is both "exclusive" and "conclusive" on the matter.[124] The Constitution does not specifically identify the recognition of foreign governments among either Congress's or the President's enumerated powers. But in an opinion that employed multiple modes of constitutional interpretation, the Court concluded that the Constitution not only conferred recognition power to the President, but also that this power was not shared with Congress.

The Court's analysis of recognition began with an examination of "the text and structure of the Constitution," which it construed as reflecting the Founders' understanding that the recognition power was exercised by the President.[125] Much of the Court's discussion of the textual basis for the recognition power focused on the President's responsibility under the Reception Clause to "receive Ambassadors and other public Ministers."[126] At the time of the founding, the Court reasoned, receiving ambassadors of a foreign government was tantamount to recognizing the foreign entity's sovereign claims, and it was logical to infer "a Clause directing the President alone to receive ambassadors" as "being understood to acknowledge his power to recognize other nations."[127] In addition to the Reception Clause, the *Zivotofsky* Court identified additional Article II provisions as providing support for the inference that the President retains the recognition power,[128] including the President's power to "make Treaties" with the advice and consent of the Senate,[129] and to appoint ambassadors and other ministers and consuls with Senate

---

"write JERUSALEM as the place of birth in the passport. Do not write Israel, Jordan or West Bank for a person born within the current municipal borders of Jerusalem." *Id.* at § 1360 Appendix D.

[123] *Zivotofsky*, slip op. at 7 (quoting Brief from Respondent at 48).

[124] *Id.* (quoting Youngstown Sheet & Tube Co., 343 U.S. at 637–38 (Jackson, J., concurring)).

[125] *Id.* at 8–11.

[126] U.S. CONST., art. II, § 3, cl. 4. *Zivotofsky*, slip op. at 9–10.

[127] *Zivotofsky*, slip op. at 9–10. The Court observed that records of the Constitutional Convention were largely silent on the recognition power, but that contemporary writings by prominent international legal scholars identified the act of receiving ambassadors as the virtual equivalent of recognizing the sovereignty of the sending state. *Id.* at 9.

[128] Justice Thomas, writing separately and concurring in part with the majority's judgment, would have located the primary source of the President's recognition power as the Vesting Clause. *Zivotofsky*, slip op. at 1 (Thomas, J., concurring and dissenting in part with the Court's judgment). The controlling five-Justice opinion declined to reach the issue of whether the Vesting Clause provided such support. *Zivotofsky*, slip op. at 10 (majority opinion).

[129] U.S. CONST., art. II, § 2, cl. 2.

approval.[130] The *Zivotofsky* Court emphasized "functional considerations" supporting the Executive's claims of exclusive authority over recognition,[131] stating that recognition is a matter on which the United States must "speak with . . . one voice,"[132] and the executive branch is better suited than Congress to exercise this power for several reasons, including its "characteristic of unity at all times," as well as its ability to engage in "delicate and often secret diplomatic contacts that may lead to a decision on recognition" and "take the decisive, unequivocal action necessary to recognize other states at international law."[133] The Court also concluded that historical practice and prior jurisprudence gave credence to the President's unilateral exercise of the recognition power. Here, the Court acknowledged that the historical record did not provide unequivocal support for this view, but characterized "the weight" of historical evidence as reflecting an understanding that the President's power over recognition is exclusive.[134] Although the Executive had consistently claimed unilateral recognition authority from the Washington Administration onward, and Congress had generally acquiesced to the President's exercise of such authority, there were instances in which Congress also played a role in matters of recognition. But the *Zivotofsky* Court observed that in all earlier instances, congressional action was consistent with, and deferential to, the President's recognition policy, and the Court characterized prior congressional involvement as indicating "no more than that some Presidents have chosen to cooperate with Congress, not that Congress itself has exercised the recognition power."[135] The Court also stated that a "fair reading" of its prior jurisprudence demonstrated a longstanding understanding of the recognition power as an executive function, notwithstanding "some isolated statements" in those cases that might have suggested a congressional role.[136] Having determined that the Constitution assigns the President with exclusive authority over recognition of foreign sovereigns, the *Zivotofsky* Court ruled that the statutory directive that the State Department honor passport requests of Jerusalem-born U.S. citizens to have their birthplace identified as "Israel"

---

[130] *Id.*

[131] *Zivotofsky*, slip op. at 11.

[132] *Id.* (quoting Am. Ins. Ass'n v. Garamendi, 539 U.S. 396, 424 (2003), and Crosby v. Nat'l Foreign Trade Council, 530 U.S. 363, 381 (2000)).

[133] *Id.*

[134] *Id.* at 20.

[135] *Id.* The Court observed that in no prior instance had Congress enacted a statute "contrary to the President's formal and considered statement concerning recognition." *Id.* at 21 (citing Zivotofsky v. Secretary of State, 725 F.3d 197, 203, 221 (D.C. Cir. 2013) (Tatel, J., concurring)).

[136] *See id.* at 14. The Court observed that earlier rulings touching on the recognition power had dealt with the division of power between the judicial and political branches of the federal government, or between the federal government and the states. *Id.* at 14–16 (citing Banco Nacional De Cuba v. Sabbatino, 376 U.S. 398, 410 (1963) (involving the application of the act of state doctrine to the government of Cuba and stating that "[p]olitical recognition is exclusively a function of the Executive"); United States v. Pink, 315 U.S. 203 (1942) (concerning effect of executive agreement involving the recognition of the Soviet Union and settlement of claims disputes upon state law); United States v. Belmont, 301 U.S. 324 (1937) (similar to *Pink*); Williams v. Suffolk Ins. Co., 38 U.S. (13 Pet.) 415 (1839) (ruling that an executive determination concerning foreign sovereign claims to the Falkland Islands was conclusive upon the judiciary)).

was an impermissible intrusion on the President's recognition authority. According to the Court, Congress's authority to regulate the issuance of passports, though wide in scope, may not be exercised in a manner intended to compel the Executive "to contradict an earlier recognition determination in an official document of the Executive Branch" that is addressed to foreign powers.[137]

While the *Zivotofsky* decision establishes that the recognition power belongs exclusively to the President, its relevance to other foreign affairs issues remains unclear. The opinion applied a functionalist approach in assessing the exclusivity of executive power on the issue of recognition, but did not opine on whether this approach was appropriate for resolving other inter-branch disputes concerning the allocation of constitutional authority in the field of foreign affairs. The *Zivotofsky* Court also declined to endorse the Executive's broader claim of exclusive or preeminent presidential authority over foreign relations, and it appeared to minimize the reach of some of the Court's earlier statements in *Curtiss-Wright*[138] regarding the expansive scope of the President's foreign affairs power.[139] The Court also repeatedly noted Congress's ample power to legislate on foreign affairs, including on matters that precede and follow from the President's act of foreign recognition and in ways that could render recognition a "hollow act."[140] For example, Congress could institute a trade embargo; declare war upon a foreign government that the President had recognized, or decline to appropriate funds for an embassy in that country. While all of these actions could potentially be employed by the legislative branch to express opposition to executive policy, they would not impermissibly interfere with the President's recognition power.[141]

---

[137] *See id.* at 29. The Court approvingly cited its description in *Urtetiqui v. D'Arcy*, 34 U.S. (9 Pet.) 692 (1835), of a passport as being, "from its nature and object . . . addressed to foreign powers." *See Zivotofsky*, slip op. at 27.

[138] *See* United States v. Curtiss-Wright Export Co., 299 U.S. 304 (1936). For further discussion of this case, *see supra* Section 1. The President: Clause 1. Powers and Term of the President: Executive Power: Theory of the Presidential Office: The *Curtiss-Wright* Case.

[139] The majority opinion observed that *Curtiss-Wright* had considered the constitutionality of a congressional delegation of power to the President, and that its description of the Executive as the sole organ of foreign affairs was not essential to its holding in the case. *See Zivotofsky*, slip op. at 18.

[140] *Id.* at 13.

[141] *Id.* at 13, 27.

Clauses 2–4. Election

ELECTORAL COLLEGE

Electors as Free Agents

[P. 475, delete sentence starting "But, in Ray v. Blair . . . " and substitute with:]

But, in *Ray v. Blair*, the Court clarified that although electors "exercise a federal function[,] . . . they are not federal officers or agents."[142] Instead, the Constitution provides that they act under state authority.[143]

[P. 475, after n.92, add new sentence:]

By 1832, almost all states used popular presidential elections, and "[b]y the early 20th century, citizens in most States voted for the presidential candidate himself; ballots increasingly did not even list the electors."[144] Instead, parties chose slates of electors, and states then appointed the electors proposed by the party whose presidential nominee won the popular vote statewide.[145]

[P. 475, delete "Electors constitutionally remain free to cast" and substitute with:]

The Constitution does not prohibit electors from casting

[P. 475, after n.94, add new sentence:]

More recently, the 2016 election saw a historic number of faithless electors, with seven electors recorded voting for someone other than their party's nominee.[146]

[PP. 475–77, delete four paragraphs starting "The power either of Congress . . . " and ending at n.99, and substitute with:]

To prevent so-called "faithless electors" from departing from the preferences expressed by voters, today most states require electors to pledge to support their parties' nominees.[147] In *Ray v. Blair*, the Supreme Court rejected a constitutional challenge to a party rule requiring elector candidates to pledge that they would support the nominees elected in the primary in the general election.[148] The Court first concluded that

---

[142] 343 U.S. 214, 224 (1952).

[143] *Id.* at 224–25.

[144] Chiafalo v. Washington, 140 S. Ct. 2316, 2321 (2020).

[145] *Id.*

[146] *See, e.g.*, Alexander Gouzoules, *The "Faithless Elector" and 2016: Constitutional Uncertainty after the Election of Donald Trump*, 28 U. FLA. J.L. & PUB. POL'Y 215, 217 (2017).

[147] *Chiafalo*, 140 S. Ct. at 2321–22.

[148] 343 U.S. 214, 222, 231 (1952). The party rule was adopted under the authority of an

excluding electors who refuse to pledge their support for the party's nominees was "an exercise of the state's right to appoint electors in such manner, subject to possible constitutional limitations, as it may choose."[149] The Court also concluded that the pledge requirement did not violate the Twelfth Amendment, rejecting the argument that "the Twelfth Amendment demands absolute freedom for the elector to vote his own choice, uninhibited by a pledge."[150] Noting the longstanding practice supporting the expectation that electors will support party nominees, the Court said that "even if such promises of candidates for the electoral college are legally unenforceable because violative of an assumed constitutional freedom of the elector under the Constitution, Article II, Section 1, to vote as he may choose in the electoral college, it would not follow that the requirement of a pledge in the primary is unconstitutional."[151]

Ray left open the question of whether states could *enforce* these pledge requirements through sanctions—a question later considered in *Chiafalo v. Washington.*[152] Washington law provided that electors who failed to comply with a pledge to vote for their party nominees would face a civil fine.[153] Three electors who were fined after breaking their pledge in the 2016 presidential election challenged the law.[154] The Supreme Court confirmed that a state's power to appoint an elector includes the "power to condition his appointment," and further clarified that as long as no other constitutional provision prohibits it,[155] the state's appointment power also "enables the enforcement of a pledge" through a law such as Washington's.[156] The Court emphasized that the "barebones" text of Article II and the Twelfth Amendment provide only for "[a]ppointments and procedures" and do not "expressly prohibit[] States from taking away presidential electors' voting discretion."[157] Finally, the Court recognized that historical practice supported Washington's law, as electors "have only

---

Alabama law authorizing parties to determine the qualifications of primary candidates and voters. *Id.* at 222.

[149] *Id.* at 227.

[150] *Id.* at 228.

[151] *Id.* at 230.

[152] *Chiafalo,* 140 S. Ct. at 2319–20. In a companion case, the Supreme Court summarily reversed a Tenth Circuit decision ruling a Colorado faithless-elector law unconstitutional. Colo. Dep't of State v. Baca, 140 S Ct. 2316 (2020) (per curiam). The penalties in the Colorado case were different from a fine: after failing to honor his pledge, an elector's vote was vacated and he was removed as an elector. Baca v. Colo. Dep't of State, 935 F.3d 887, 904 (10th Cir. 2019).

[153] *Chiafalo,* 140 S. Ct. at 2322.

[154] *Id.* at 2322–24.

[155] *See id.* at 2324 n.4 ("A State, for example, cannot select its electors in a way that violates the Equal Protection Clause. And if a State adopts a condition on its appointments that effectively imposes new requirements on presidential candidates, the condition may conflict with the Presidential Qualifications Clause, see Art. II, §1, cl. 5.").

[156] *Id.* at 2324–25.

[157] *Id.*

rarely exercised discretion in casting their ballots for President" and "[s]tate election laws evolved to reinforce" this practice.[158]

Section 2. Powers, Duties of the President

Clause 2. Treaties and Appointment of Officers

THE TREATY-MAKING POWER

Indian Treaties

[P. 542, at end of n.407, delete period and add:]

; *see also* McGirt v. Oklahoma, 140 S. Ct. 2452, 2462 (2020) ("Under our Constitution, States have no authority to reduce federal reservations lying within their borders.").

[P. 542, at end of n.410, add:]

Cf. McGirt, 140 S. Ct. at 2463 (stating that to disestablish a reservation, Congress must "clearly express its intent to do so").

Present Status of Indian Treaties.—

[P. 542, at end of n.412, delete period and add:]

; *see generally, e.g., McGirt*, 140 S. Ct. at 2462 ("[T]he Legislature wields significant constitutional authority when it comes to tribal relations, possessing even the authority to breach its own promises and treaties.").

THE EXECUTIVE ESTABLISHMENT

Office

[P. 563, before heading "Appointments and Congressional Regulation of Offices", add new section:]

 Federal v. Territorial Officers.—Not every office created by Congress is a federal office subject to the strictures of Article II. In *Financial Oversight and Management Board for Puerto Rico v. Aurelius Investment, LLC*, the Court considered the constitutionality of an oversight board (the Board) that Congress created in 2016 to manage the financial issues of the Commonwealth of Puerto Rico, a U.S. territory.[159] Writing for the Court, Justice Breyer explained that provisions in Articles I and IV of the Constitution "empower Congress to create local offices for the District of Columbia and for Puerto Rico and the Territories."[160] Based on the Constitution's text, structure, and history, the Court reasoned that

---

[158] *Id.* at 2326, 2328.
[159] 140 S. Ct. 1649, 1655–56 (2020). Congress created the Board as part of the Puerto Rico Oversight, Management, and Economic Stability Act (PROMESA), Pub. L. No. 114-187, 130 Stat. 549 (2016) (codified at 48 U.S.C. § 2101 et seq.).
[160] *Aurelius Invest., LLC*, 140 S. Ct. at 1659.

creating a local office "does not automatically make its holder an 'Officer of the United States'" within the meaning of Article II's Appointments Clause.[161] At the same time, an official's location in a territory does not, standing alone, exempt that office from the Appointment Clause's reach.[162] Instead, when Congress exercises its Article I or IV powers to create a local or territorial office, the Court examines whether Congress vested that official with "primarily local powers and duties."[163] If so, the official is not an "Officer of the United States" subject to the Appointments Clause.[164]

Based on the text of the 2016 law, the *Aurelius* Court concluded that when Congress created the Board, it exercised its Article IV powers under the Territories Clause.[165] And the Court concluded that the powers and duties that Congress assigned to the Board were "primarily local in nature."[166] Justice Breyer cited several factors that "taken together" demonstrated the Board's local nature: (1) the government of Puerto Rico paid the Board's expenses; (2) the Board developed fiscal plans with the elected government of Puerto Rico and could initiate bankruptcy proceedings for Puerto Rico; and (3) the Board's "broad investigatory powers"—akin to what federal officers exercise—were "backed by Puerto Rican, not federal, law."[167] Accordingly, the Court held that Board members were territorial officers, not federal "Officers," and thus their selection need not comply with the Appointments Clause.[168]

Appointments and Congressional Regulation of Offices

[P. 563, at end of n.504, add:]

See also Ortiz v. United States, 585 U.S. ___, No. 16-1423, slip op. at 25 (2018) (rejecting the argument that the Appointments Clause prohibits an individual already serving as a principal officer on one military tribunal from also serving as an inferior officer on a separate military tribunal).

[P. 565, delete n.511 and substitute with:]

United States v. Germaine, 99 U.S. 508, 509–10 (1879). *See also Buckley*, 424 U.S. at 125; Morrison v. Olson, 487 U.S. 654, 670–73 (1988); United States v. Eaton, 169 U.S. 331, 343 (1898).

---

[161] *Id.* at 1658–59.
[162] *Id.* at 1657–58.
[163] *Id.* at 1661.
[164] *Id.*
[165] *Id.* at 1656; *see also* U.S. CONST. art. IV, § 3, cl. 2.
[166] *Aurelius Invest., LLC*, 140 S. Ct. at 1662.
[167] *Id.* at 1662.
[168] *Id.* at 1662–63.

[P. 568, delete paragraph starting "The *Freytag* decision . . ." and substitute with:]

As a practical matter, the Appointments Clause not only separates principal officers from inferior ones, but also distinguishes both types of constitutional officers from a third class of government officials: mere employees.[169] The general measure established by *Buckley v. Valeo* is that "any appointee exercising significant authority pursuant to the laws of the United States is an 'Officer of the United States.'"[170] In *Freytag v. Commissioner*, the Court applied this standard to hold that special trial judges (STJs) were inferior officers rather than mere employees.[171] The government had argued in part that the STJs were employees because, with respect to the particular agency actions being challenged, STJs lacked "authority to enter a final decision."[172] The Court rejected this argument, saying that it "ignores the significance of the duties and discretion that special trial judges possess."[173] The Court noted that "the duties, salary, and means of appointment" of STJs were established by statute, and that STJs did not operate on a "temporary, episodic basis."[174] The Court also emphasized that STJs exercised "significant discretion" in carrying out a number of "important functions," including the ability to "take testimony, conduct trials, rule on the admissibility of evidence, and . . . enforce compliance with discovery orders."[175] The Court held in the alternative that STJs were officers because the government had conceded that, with respect to other duties, STJs did "act as inferior officers who exercise independent authority."[176] In the view of the Court, STJs could not be "inferior officers for purposes of some of their duties . . . , but mere employees with respect to other responsibilities."[177]

The Court again considered the proper test to distinguish inferior officers from mere employees in *Lucia v. Securities and Exchange Commission (SEC)*.[178] That case involved a challenge to the status of the administrative law judges (ALJs) of the SEC.[179] The Court acknowledged that "*Buckle's* 'significant authority' test" is phrased in "general terms"

---

[169] *See, e.g.*, Lucia v. SEC, 585 U.S. ___, No. 17-130, slip op. at 5 (2018). *See also* Burnap v. United States, 252 U.S. 512, 516 (1920).

[170] 424 U.S. 1, 126 (1976) (per curiam) (quoting U.S. CONST. art. II, § 2, cl. 2). *See also* Go-Bart Importing Co. v. United States, 282 U.S. 344, 352–53 (1931); United States v. Germaine, 99 U.S. 508, 510 (1878).

[171] 501 U.S. 868, 881 (1991).

[172] *Id.*

[173] *Id.*

[174] *Id. See also* Auffmordt v. Hedden, 137 U.S. 310, 327 (1890) (holding that merchant appraiser is not an officer because the "position is without tenure, duration, continuing emolument, or continuous duties, and he acts only occasionally and temporarily"); United States v. Germaine, 99 U.S. 508, 510 (1878) (holding that civil surgeon is not an officer after noting that "the duties are not continuing and permanent, and they are occasional and intermittent").

[175] 501 U.S. at 881–82.

[176] *Id.* at 882.

[177] *Id.*

[178] 585 U.S. ___, No. 17-130, slip op. at 5 (2018) .

[179] *Id.* at 1.

that might one day need refinement, but ultimately concluded that it did not need to further elaborate on that test to resolve the dispute before it, because the SEC ALJs were "near-carbon copies" of the *Freytag* STJs.[180] Without stating that any one factor was either necessary or sufficient to confer status as a constitutional "officer," the Court held that the SEC ALJs met every factor considered by the Court in *Freytag*. Specifically, the Court noted that ALJs (1) hold "a continuing office established by law";[181] (2) exercise "'significant discretion' when carrying out the same 'important functions,'" including the ability to take testimony, conduct trials, rule on the admissibility of evidence, and enforce compliance with discovery orders;[182] and (3) issue decisions with "independent effect."[183] Accordingly, the Court held that the cases were indistinguishable.[184] Because the ALJs were inferior officers, their hiring by SEC staff members violated the Constitution.[185]

The Removal Power

The Removal Power Rationalized.—

[PP. 581–82, delete two paragraphs starting "It is now thus reaffirmed . . . " and ending ". . . are only beginning."]

Inferior Officers.—

[P. 583, delete three sentences starting "In 1940 . . ." and ending ". . . administrative independence."]

[P. 583, before heading "The Presidential Aegis: Demands for Papers," add new section:]

> ***Seila Law.—***In *Seila Law LLC v. Consumer Financial Protection Bureau* (CFPB), the Supreme Court concluded that Congress could not provide for-cause removal protections for the head of the CFPB, an independent financial regulatory agency led by a single Director.[186] The Court described the President's removal power as "unrestricted,"[187] rejecting the view that *Humphrey's Executor* and *Morrison* "establish a

---

180 *Id.* at 6.

181 *Id.* at 8.

182 *Id.* at 8–9 (quoting Freytag v. Commissioner, 501 U.S. 868, 882 (1991)).

183 *Id.* at 9.

184 *Id.* at 10.

185 *Id.* at 5, 12.

186 Seila Law LLC v. Consumer Fin. Prot. Bureau, 140 S. Ct. 2183, 2192 (2020). This case also involved questions of standing. *Id.* at 2195. Among other arguments, a court-appointed amicus curiae claimed that "a litigant wishing to challenge an executive act on the basis of the President's removal power must show that the challenged act would not have been taken if the responsible official had been subject to the President's control." *Id.* at 2196. The Court rejected the idea that such a challenger has to prove this type of counterfactual, finding it sufficient to demonstrate an injury "from an executive act that allegedly exceeds the official's authority." *Id.*

187 *Id.* at 2192.

general rule that Congress may impose 'modest' restrictions on the President's removal power."[188] Instead, "the President's removal power is the rule, not the exception."[189] The Court said that after *Free Enterprise Fund*, only "two exceptions" to the rule requiring removability remained.[190] First, under *Humphrey's Executor*, Congress may sometimes "create expert agencies led by a *group* of principal officers removable by the President only for good cause" if the agency does not exercise executive power.[191] In interpreting this 1935 case, the *Seila Law* Court essentially limited the decision to its facts, saying that this exception permitted for-cause removal protections for "a multimember body of experts, balanced along partisan lines, that performed legislative and judicial functions *and* was said not to exercise any executive power."[192] The Court said that the second exception to the President's removal power allowed at least some removal protections for inferior officers, as in *Morrison*, if those officers have "limited duties and no policymaking or administrative authority."[193]

The Court concluded in *Seila Law* that the CFPB Director did not fall within either of these two exceptions.[194] The single Director was not a multimember expert body, and, in the view of the Court, could not be considered "a mere legislative or judicial aid."[195] Rather than performing merely reporting and advisory functions, the CFPB Director exercised executive power, possessing the authority "to promulgate binding rules fleshing out 19 federal statutes, ... [to] issue final decisions awarding legal and equitable relief in administrative adjudications," and to seek "daunting monetary penalties" in enforcement actions in federal court.[196] Neither could the CFPB Director be considered an inferior officer with limited duties.[197] And the Court ruled that it would not recognize a new exception to the President's removal authority for "an independent agency led by a single Director and vested with significant executive power."[198] The Court described the CFPB's structure as "unprecedented"[199] and

---

[188] *Id.* at 2205. The court-appointed amicus curiae argued that the Court's precedent established that Congress may generally limit the President's removal power, with two exceptions: (1) "Congress may not reserve a role for *itself* in individual removal decisions"; and (2) Congress may not completely eliminate the President's removal power. *Id.*

[189] *Id.* at 2206.

[190] *Id.* at 2198.

[191] *Id.* at 2192, 2199. The Court said its decision in *Wiener* also fell within this exception. *Id.* at 2199 (discussing Wiener v. United States, 357 U.S. 349 (1958)).

[192] *Id.* at 2199 (emphasis added). The Court stressed that "[r]ightly or wrongly, the Court viewed the [Federal Trade Commission ("FTC")] (as it existed in 1935) as exercising 'no part of the [*Humphrey's Executor*] executive power.'" *Id.* at 2198 (quoting Humphrey's Executor v. United States, 295 U.S. 602, 628 (1935)). However, the Court also said that this conclusion "has not withstood the test of time," and that the powers of the FTC—even as they existed in 1935—are now considered executive. *Id.* at 2198 n.2.

[193] *Id.* at 2200. This principle also extended to *Perkins. Id.* at 2199 (discussing United States v. Perkins, 116 U.S. 483 (1886)).

[194] *Id.* at 2200–01.

[195] *Id.*

[196] *Id.* at 2200.

[197] *Id.*

[198] *Id.* at 2201.

[199] *Id.* The Court acknowledged that there were four other relatively recent historical examples of Congress providing good-cause tenure to principal officers leading an agency,

"incompatible with our constitutional structure,"[200] saying that the agency's structure violated the Constitution "by vesting significant governmental power in the hands of a single individual accountable to no one."[201] Consequently, the Court concluded that the provision insulating the Director from removal was unconstitutional, severing the for-cause removal provision from the governing statute.[202]

The Presidential Aegis: Demands for Papers

Prosecutorial and Grand Jury Access to Presidential Documents.—

[P. 587, delete paragraph starting "Rarely will there be situations . . ." and substitute with:]

Recognizing that the "public has a right to every man's evidence," the Court has held that the President may be required to testify or produce documents in criminal proceedings when called upon by the courts.[203] This principle dates to the earliest days of the Republic, when Chief Justice John Marshall presided as the Circuit Justice for Virginia over the infamous treason trial of Aaron Burr. In that case, Chief Justice Marshall concluded that President Thomas Jefferson could be subject to a subpoena to provide a document relevant to the trial.[204] Specifically, he declared that, in contrast to common law privileges afforded the King of England, the President was not "exempt from the general provisions of the constitution," like the Sixth Amendment, that provide for compulsory process for the defense.[205] Nonetheless, Chief Justice Marshall recognized that while the President could be subject to a criminal subpoena, the President could still withhold specific information from disclosure based on the existence of a privilege.[206] In the two centuries since the Burr trial, historical practice by the executive branch[207] and Supreme Court rulings "unequivocally and emphatically endorsed" Chief Justice Marshall's position that the President was subject to federal criminal process.[208] In

---

but dismissed these examples as also being controversial. *Id.* (discussing the Comptroller of the Currency, Office of the Special Counsel, Social Security Administration, and Federal Housing Finance Agency).

[200] *Id.* at 2202.

[201] *Id.* at 2203. The Court noted that the executive branch is the only branch led by a unitary head, and that the President's power is checked through democratic and political accountability. *Id.* Individual executive officials may "still wield significant authority, but that authority remains subject to the ongoing supervision and control of the elected President." *Id.*

[202] *Id.* at 2208–09 (plurality opinion); *id.* at 2224 (Kagan, J., concurring in the judgment with respect to severability and dissenting in part).

[203] *See* Trump v. Vance, 140 S. Ct. 2412, 2420 (2020).

[204] *See* United States v. Burr, 25 F. Cas. 30, 34 (C.C.D. Va. 1807) (No. 14,692D).

[205] *See id.* (observing that while the King is born to power and can "do no wrong," the President, by contrast is "of the people" and subject to the law).

[206] *See* United States v. Burr, 25 F. Cas. 187, 192 (C.C.D. Va. 1807) (No. 14,694).

[207] *See Vance*, 140 S. Ct. at 2423 (discussing historical practices of Presidents Monroe, Grant, Ford, Carter, and Clinton).

[208] Clinton v. Jones, 520 U.S. 681, 704 (1997) (citing United States v. Nixon, 418 U.S. 683, 706 (1974)). In rejecting separation-of-powers challenges to claims that the President is immune from federal criminal process, the Court rejected the argument that criminal

2020, the Court extended this precedent to the context of a *state* criminal proceeding, concluding that the President was not absolutely immune from state criminal subpoenas.[209]

While the President is subject to criminal process, the question remains as to the limits on that process. The Court has recognized several constraints on the ability of a prosecutor to obtain evidence from the President through the use of a criminal subpoena.[210] First, like any citizen, the President can challenge a particular subpoena on the grounds that it was issued in bad faith or was unduly broad.[211] Second, the timing and scope of criminal discovery must be informed by the nature of the office of the President—for example, granting deference in scheduling proceedings to avoid significant interference with the President's official responsibilities.[212] Third, the President can raise subpoena-specific constitutional challenges, arguing that compliance with a particular subpoena would significantly interfere with his efforts to carry out an official duty.[213] As the Court first recognized in *United States v. Nixon*, one particularly notable constitutionally based challenge that a President can lodge against a criminal subpoena is a claim of executive privilege in certain presidential communications.[214]

[P. 587, in sentence starting "Presidential communications, . . ." in front of "Court", add "*Nixon*".]

Congressional Access to Executive Branch Information.—

[P. 591, delete sentences "Congress has considered . . ." through ". . . not remove the disagreements." and substitute with new paragraphs:]

In *Trump v. Mazars*, the Court recognized several separation-of-powers-based limitations on Congress's ability to access presidential records.[215] Writing on behalf of the Court, Chief Justice Roberts began by

---

subpoenas "rise to the level of constitutionally forbidden impairment of the Executive's ability to perform its constitutionally mandated functions." *Id.* at 702–03.

[209] *See Vance*, 140 S. Ct. at 2425–28 (rejecting the categorical argument that state criminal subpoenas would unduly distract the President, impose a stigma on the presidency, or result in harassment by state prosecutors). The *Vance* Court also rejected the argument that a state prosecutor should have to satisfy a heightened standard of need before seeking a sitting President's records, absent any constitutional privileges. *Id.* at 2428–31. Importantly, in *Vance*, the state prosecutor was seeking *private* presidential records, and no claim of executive privilege was at stake. *Id.* at 2432 (Kavanaugh, J., concurring in the judgment). The Court refused to extend the heightened-need standard established in *Nixon* to private records, discussed *infra*, reasoning that: (1) *Burr* and its progeny foreclosed that argument; (2) the heightened-need standard was unnecessary to allow the President to fulfill his Article II functions; and (3) the public interest in fair and effective law enforcement favors "comprehensive access to evidence." *Id.* at 2429–30 (majority opinion).

[210] *See id.*

[211] *Id.*

[212] *Id.* at 2431.

[213] *Id.* at 2431–32.

[214] 418 U.S. 683, 708 (1974).

[215] *See* 140 S. Ct. 2019, 2036 (2020).

acknowledging three central limits on all congressional inquiries, regardless of the target of the inquiry: (1) there must be a valid legislative purpose related to a subject of legislation; (2) the purpose of the inquiry must not be for law enforcement or to expose for the sake of exposure; and (3) certain constitutional and common law privileges can limit disclosures of information.[216] The Court, however, viewed these limitations, standing alone, as inadequately restricting Congress's powers in a dispute with the executive branch.[217] After all, according to *Mazars*, any paper possessed by a President could relate to a conceivable subject of legislation, possibly allowing Congress significant authority to interfere with the executive branch.[218]

Recognizing that the typical limits on the subpoena power did not prevent Congress from attempting to "aggrandize itself at the President's expense," the Chief Justice feared that judicial resolution of such a dispute using only those limits could deter negotiation between the two branches, historically the hallmark of such inquiries, and encourage Congress to seek compliance through the courts.[219] As a result, the Chief Justice instructed lower courts to perform a "careful analysis" using "[s]everal special considerations" that take "adequate account" of the separation-of-powers principles at stake during a legislative inquiry into the President's records.[220] Specifically, in such a dispute, courts should, among other considerations: (1) carefully assess whether the confrontation can be avoided by relying on other sources to provide Congress the information it needs in light of its legislative objective; (2) "insist" on a subpoena that is no broader than is reasonably necessary to support Congress's objective; (3) consider the nature of the evidence of Congress's legislative purpose, preferring more detailed and substantial evidence to vague or loosely worded evidence of Congress's purpose; and (4) assess the burdens, such as time and attention, the subpoena imposes on the President.[221]

---

[216] *Id.* at 2031–32.

[217] *Id.* at 2033.

[218] *Id.* at 2033–34.

[219] *Id.* While the papers at stake in *Mazars* were the President's personal records, the Court concluded that the close connection between the Office of the President and its occupant did not diminish the separation-of-powers concerns at issue, and may have even posed a "heightened risk" given the records' "less evident connection to a legislative task." *Id.* at 2035. The *Mazars* Court likewise rejected the argument that separation-of-powers concerns were diminished because the records at issue were in the hands of a third party, as opposed to the President himself. *Id.* For the Court, the central issue was that the President's information was at stake, and ruling otherwise would have encouraged side-stepping constitutional requirements. *Id.*

[220] *Id.*

[221] *Id.* at 2035–36. The Court observed that "[o]ther considerations may be pertinent as well." *Id.* at 2036. While adopting this four-factor test, the Court rejected the need for a more "demanding" standard that would have required Congress to demonstrate a specific need for particular records that were "critical" to a legislative purpose. *Id.* at 2032–33 (concluding that imposing a standard akin to the one governing executive privilege claims would "risk seriously impeding Congress in carrying out" inquiries to obtain information it needs to legislate effectively).

Clause 3. Vacancies During Recess of Senate

RECESS APPOINTMENTS

[P. 591, after paragraph ending ". . . securing Senate confirmation.", delete remaining paragraphs in section through P. 594, and substitute with:]

Two fundamental textual issues arise when interpreting the Recess Appointments Clause. The first is the meaning of the phrase "the Recess of the Senate." The Senate may recess both between and during its annual sessions, but the time period during which the President may make a recess appointment is not clearly answered by the text of the Constitution. The second fundamental textual issue is what constitutes a vacancy that "may happen" during the recess of the Senate. If the words "may happen" are interpreted to refer only to vacancies that arise during a recess, then the President would lack authority to make a recess appointment to a vacancy that existed before the recess began. For over two centuries the Supreme Court did not address either of these issues,[222] leaving it to the lower courts and other branches of government to interpret the scope of the Recess Appointments Clause.[223]

The Supreme Court ultimately adopted a relatively broad interpretation of the Clause in *National Labor Relations Board v. Noel Canning.*[224] With respect to the meaning of the phrase "Recess of the Senate," the Court concluded that the phrase applied to both inter-session recesses and intra-session recesses. In so holding, the Court, finding the text of the Constitution ambiguous,[225] relied on (1) a pragmatic

---

[222] *See* NLRB v. Noel Canning, 573 U.S. ___, No. 12-1281, slip op. at 9 (2014).

[223] For lower court decisions on the Recess Appointments Clause, *see, e.g.,* Evans v. Stephens, 387 F.3d 1220, 1226–27 (11th Cir. 2004), *cert. denied,* 544 U.S. 942 (2005); United States v. Woodley, 751 F.2d 1008, 1012 (9th Cir. 1985) *(en banc), cert. denied,* 475 U.S. 1048 (1986); United States v. Allocco, 305 F.2d 704, 712 (2d Cir. 1962), *cert. denied,* 371 U.S. 964 (1963); *In re* Farrow, 3 Fed. 112 (C.C.N.D. Ga. 1880). For prior executive branch interpretations of the Recess Appointments Clause, *see* 25 Op. OLC 182 (2001); 20 Op. OLC 124, 161 (1996); 16 Op. OLC 15 (1992); 13 Op. OLC 271 (1989); 6 Op. OLC 585, 586 (1982); 3 Op. OLC 314, 316 (1979); 41 Op. Att'y Gen.463 (1960); 33 Op. Att'y Gen.20 (1921); 30 Op. Att'y Gen.314 (1914); 26 Op. Att'y Gen.234 (1907); 23 Op. Att'y Gen.599 (1901); 22 Op. Att'y Gen.82 (1898); 19 Op. Att'y Gen.261 (1889); 18 Op. Att'y Gen.28 (1884); 16 Op. Att'y Gen.523 (1880); 15 Op. Att'y Gen.207 (1877); 14 Op. Att'y Gen.563 (1875); 12 Op. Att'y Gen.455 (1868); 12 Op. Att'y Gen.32 (1866); 11 Op. Att'y Gen.179 (1865); 10 Op. Att'y Gen.356 (1862); 4 Op. Att'y Gen.523 (1846); 4 Op. Att'y Gen.361 (1845); 3 Op. Att'y Gen.673 (1841); 2 Op. Att'y Gen.525 (1832); 1 Op. Att'y Gen. 631, 633–34 (1823). For the early practice on recess appointments, *see* G. HAYNES, THE SENATE OF THE UNITED STATES 772–78 (1938).

[224] *Noel Canning,* slip op. at 5–33 (2014).

[225] *Id.* at 9–11. More specifically, the Court found nothing in dictionary definitions or common usage contemporaneous to the Constitution that would suggest that an intra-session recess was not a recess. The Court noted that, while the phrase "the Recess" might suggest limiting recess appointments to the single break between sessions of Congress, the word "the" can also be used "generically or universally," *see, e.g.,* U.S. CONST. art. I, § 3, cl. 5. (directing the Senate to choose a President pro tempore "in the Absence of the Vice-President"), and that there were examples of "the Recess" being used in the broader manner at the time of the founding. *Noel Canning,* slip op. at 9–11.

interpretation of the Clause that would allow the President to ensure the "continued functioning" of the federal government when the Senate is away,[226] and (2) "long settled and established [historical] practice" of the President making intra-session recess appointments.[227] The Court declined, however, to say how long a recess must be to fall within the Clause, instead holding that historical practice counseled that a recess of more than three days but less than ten days is "presumptively too short" to trigger the President's appointment power under the Clause.[228] With respect to the phrase "may happen," the majority, again finding ambiguity in the text of the Clause,[229] held that the Clause applied both to vacancies that first come into existence during a recess and to vacancies that initially occur before a recess but continue to exist during the recess.[230] In so holding, the Court again relied on both pragmatic concerns[231] and historical practice.[232] Even under a broad interpretation of the Recess Appointments Clause, the Senate may limit the ability to make recess appointments by exercising its procedural prerogatives. The Court in *Noel Canning* held that, for the purposes of the Recess Appointments Clause, the Senate is in session when the Senate says it is, provided that, under its own rules, it retains the capacity to transact Senate business.[233] In this vein, *Noel Canning* provides the Senate with the means to prevent recess appointments by a President who attempts to employ the "subsidiary method" for appointing officers of the United States (i.e., recess

---

[226] *Noel Canning*, slip op. at 11. ("The Senate is equally away during both an inter-session and an intra-session recess, and its capacity to participate in the appointments process has nothing to do with the words it uses to signal its departure.").

[227] The Court noted that Presidents have made "thousands" of intra-session recess appointments and that presidential legal advisors had been nearly unanimous in determining that the clause allowed these appointments. *Id.* at 12.

[228] *Id.* at 21. The Court left open the possibility that some very unusual circumstance, such as a national catastrophe that renders the Senate unavailable, could require the exercise of the recess appointment power during a shorter break. *Id.*

[229] The Court noted, for instance, that Thomas Jefferson thought the phrase in question could point to both vacancies that "*may happen to be*" during a recess as well as those that "*may happen to fall*" during a recess. *Id.* at 22 (emphasis added).

[230] *Id.* at 1–2.

[231] *Id.* at 26 ("[W]e believe the narrower interpretation risks undermining constitutionally conferred powers [in that] . . . [i]t would prevent the President from making any recess appointment that arose before a recess, no matter who the official, no matter how dire the need, no matter how uncontroversial the appointment, and no matter how late in the session the office fell vacant.").

[232] *Id.* at 34 ("Historical practice over the past 200 years strongly favors the broader interpretation. The tradition of applying the Clause to pre-recess vacancies dates at least to President James Madison.").

[233] *Id.* In the context of *Noel Canning*, the Court held that the Senate was in session even during a pro forma session, a brief meeting of the Senate, often lasting minutes, in which no legislative business is conducted. *Id.* at 38–39. Because the Journal of the Senate (and the Congressional Record) declared the Senate in session during those periods, and because the Senate could, under its rules, have conducted business under unanimous consent (a quorum being presumed), the Court concluded that the Senate was indeed in session. In so holding, the Court deferred to the authority of Congress to "determine the Rules of its Proceedings," *see* U.S. CONST. art. I, § 5, cl. 2, relying on previous case law in which the Court refused to question the validity of a congressional record. *Noel Canning*, slip op. at 39 (citing United States v. Ballin, 144 U.S. 1, 5 (1892)).

appointments) to avoid the "norm"[234] for appointment (i.e., appointment pursuant to the Article II, § 2, cl.2).[235]

Section 3. Legislative, Diplomatic, and Law Enforcement Duties of the President

THE CONDUCT OF FOREIGN RELATIONS

The Power of Recognition

[P. 600, after n.645, add new sentences:]

An examination of this historical practice, along with other functional considerations, led the Supreme Court to hold in *Zivotofsky v. Kerry* that the Executive retains exclusive authority over the recognition of foreign sovereigns and their territorial bounds.[236] Although Congress, pursuant to its enumerated powers in the field of foreign affairs, may properly legislate on matters which precede and follow a presidential act of recognition, including in ways which may undercut the policies that inform the President's recognition decision, it may not alter the President's recognition decision.[237]

PRESIDENTIAL IMMUNITY FROM JUDICIAL DIRECTION

[P. 636, after sentence ending ". . . ordinary criminal process." add new paragraph:]

Putting to the side the question of whether a sitting President is immune from indictment and criminal prosecution,[238] the Court has

---

[234] *Noel Canning*, slip op. at 40.

[235] It should be noted that, by an act of Congress, if a vacancy existed when the Senate was in session, the ad interim appointee, subject to certain exceptions, may receive no salary until he has been confirmed by the Senate. 5 U.S.C. § 5503 (2012). By targeting the compensation of appointees, as opposed to the President's recess appointment power itself, this limitation acts as an indirect control on recess appointments, but its constitutionality has not been adjudicated. A federal district court noted that "if any and all restrictions on the President's recess appointment power, however limited, are prohibited by the Constitution," restricting payment to recess appointees might be invalid. Staebler v. Carter, 464 F. Supp. 585, 596 n.24 (D.D.C. 1979).

[236] Zivotofsky v. Kerry, 576 U.S. ___, No. 13-628, slip op. (2015). The Court identified the Reception Clause, along with additional provisions in Article II, as providing the basis for the Executive's power over recognition. *Id.* at 9–10. *See supra* Clause 1. Powers and Term of the President: Nature and Scope of Presidential Power: Executive Power: Theory of the Presidential Office: The *Zivotofsky* Case.

[237] *See Zivotofsky*, slip op. at 27. While observing that Congress may not enact a law that "directly contradicts" a presidential recognition decision, the Court stated that Congress could still express its disagreement in multiple ways: "For example, it may enact an embargo, decline to confirm an ambassador, or even declare war. But none of these acts would alter the President's recognition decision." *Id.*

[238] *See* Memorandum from Randolph D. Moss, Assistant Atty. Gen., Office of Legal Counsel to the Atty. Gen.: A Sitting President's Amenability to Indictment and Criminal Prosecution, 24 Op. O.L.C. 222, 257 (Oct. 16, 2000) (recognizing that "[n]o court has addressed" the question directly, but expressing the view that "a sitting President is

squarely resolved that the President may be required to testify or produce documents in criminal proceedings when called upon by the courts.[239] This principle dates to the earliest days of the Republic, when Chief Justice John Marshall presided as the Circuit Justice for Virginia over the infamous treason trial of Aaron Burr. In that case, Chief Justice Marshall concluded that President Thomas Jefferson could be subject to a subpoena to provide a document relevant to the trial.[240] Specifically, he declared that, in contrast to common law privileges afforded the King of England, the President was not "exempt from the general provisions of the constitution," like the Sixth Amendment, that provide for compulsory process for the defense.[241] Nonetheless, Chief Justice Marshall recognized that while the President could be subject to a criminal subpoena, the President could still withhold information from disclosure based on the existence of a privilege.[242] In the two centuries since the Burr trial, historical practice by the executive branch[243] and Supreme Court rulings "unequivocally and emphatically endorsed" Chief Justice Marshall's position that the President was subject to federal criminal process.[244] In 2020, the Court extended this precedent to the context of a *state* criminal proceeding, concluding that the President was not absolutely immune from state criminal subpoenas.[245]

[P. 636, delete sentence starting "Finally, most recently, the Court . . ."]

[P. 636, delete "The" at beginning of sentence starting "The President is absolutely immune in . . ." and substitute with:]

Finally, with respect to civil liability, the Court has held that the

---

constitutionally immune from indictment and criminal prosecution").

[239] *See* Trump v. Vance, 140 S. Ct. 2412, 2420 (2020) (recognizing that the "public has a right to every man's evidence").

[240] *See* United States v. Burr, 25 F. Cas. 30, 34 (C.C.D. Va. 1807) (No. 14,692D).

[241] *See id.* (observing that while the King is born to power and can "do no wrong," the President, by contrast is "of the people" and subject to the law).

[242] *See* United States v. Burr, 25 F. Cas. 187, 192 (C.C.D. Va. 1807) (No. 14,694).

[243] *See Vance,* 140 S. Ct. at 2423 (discussing historical practices of Presidents Monroe, Grant, Ford, Carter, and Clinton).

[244] Clinton v. Jones, 520 U.S. 681, 704 (1997) (citing United States v. Nixon, 418 U.S. 683, 706 (1974)). In rejecting separation-of-powers challenges to claims that the President is immune from federal criminal process, the Court rejected the argument that criminal subpoenas "rise to the level of constitutionally forbidden impairment of the Executive's ability to perform its constitutionally mandated functions." *Id.* at 702–03.

[245] *See Vance,* 140 S. Ct. at 2425–29 (rejecting the categorical argument that state criminal subpoenas would unduly distract the President, impose a stigma on the presidency, or result in harassment by state prosecutors). The *Vance* Court also rejected the argument that a state prosecutor should have to satisfy a heightened standard of need before seeking a sitting President's records, absent any constitutional privileges. *Id.* at 2429–31. Importantly, in *Vance,* the state prosecutor was seeking *private* presidential records, and no claim of executive privilege was at stake. *Id.* at 2431 (Kavanaugh, J., concurring in the judgment). The Court refused to extend the heightened-need standard established in *Nixon* to private records, discussed *infra,* reasoning that: (1) *Burr* and its progeny foreclosed that argument; (2) the heightened-need standard was unnecessary to allow the President to fulfill his Article II functions; and (3) the public interest in fair and effective law enforcement favors "comprehensive access to evidence." *Id.* at 2429–30 (majority opinion).

ARTICLE III

Section 1. Judicial Power, Courts, Judges

ORGANIZATION OF COURTS, TENURE, AND COMPENSATION OF JUDGES

Legislative Courts

[P. 667, at end of n.55, add:]

In *Ortiz v. United States*, 585 U.S. ___, No. 16-1423, slip op. at 12 (2018), the Court confirmed that it could exercise appellate jurisdiction over territorial courts "despite their lack of Article III status." The Court also noted that it could exercise appellate jurisdiction over "the non-Article III District of Columbia Courts," *id.* at 13, and "the non-Article III court-martial system," *id.* at 14, emphasizing the judicial nature of all three of these entities.

Review of Legislative Courts by Supreme Court.—

[P. 669, after n.66, add new paragraph:]

In *Ortiz v. United States*, the Supreme Court considered whether it could hear appeals from the Court of Appeals for the Armed Forces (CAAF), the tribunal "atop the court-martial system."[246] The Court rejected the argument that it was divested of appellate jurisdiction solely because the CAAF was a non-Article III court located in the executive branch.[247] Instead, relying on "the judicial character and constitutional pedigree of the court-martial system," the Court held that it could review the CAAF's decisions.[248] Noting that it has appellate jurisdiction over territorial courts and District of Columbia courts, also non-Article III tribunals, the Court concluded that the court-martial system "stands on much the same footing."[249] But the Court cautioned that it was saying "nothing about whether [it] could exercise appellate jurisdiction over cases from other adjudicative bodies in the Executive Branch, including those in administrative agencies."[250]

The "Public Rights" Distinction.—

[P. 670, at end of n.74, add:]

But cf. Ortiz v. United States, 585 U.S. ___, No. 16-1423, slip op. at 8 (2018) (noting that the "essential character" of the military justice system is "in a word, judicial").

[P. 672, at end of n.82, add:]

---

[246] 585 U.S. ___, No. 16-1423, slip op. at 2 (2018).
[247] *Id.* at 6.
[248] *Id.*
[249] *Id.* at 14.
[250] *Id.* at 19.

See also Oil States Energy Servs., LLC v. Greene's Energy Grp., LLC, 584 U.S. ___, No. 16-712, slip op. at 17 (2018) ("This Court's precedents establish that, when Congress properly assigns a matter to adjudication in a non-Article III tribunal, 'the Seventh Amendment poses no independent bar to the adjudication of that action by a nonjury factfinder.'" (quoting *Granfinanciera*, 492 U.S. at 53–54)).

[P. 672, delete sentence after n.83 and add new paragraphs:]

In *Stern v. Marshall*, [251] the Court shifted away from the functionalism of previous cases and back towards the formalism of *Northern Pipeline*. Specifically, the *Stern* Court held that Article III prohibited a bankruptcy court from exercising jurisdiction over a common law claim concerning fraudulent interference with a gift because it did not fall under the public rights exception. [252] The Court limited the public rights exception to claims deriving from a "federal regulatory scheme" or claims in which "an expert Government agency is deemed essential to a limited regulatory objective." [253] In rejecting the application of the public rights exception to the fraudulent interference claim, the Court observed that the claim was not one that could be "pursued only by grace of the other branches" or could have been "determined exclusively" by the executive or legislative branches. [254] Additionally, the underlying claim did not "flow from a federal regulatory scheme" and was not limited to a "particularized area of law." [255] Because the claim involved the "most prototypical exercise of judicial power," adjudication of a common law cause of action not created by federal law, the Court rejected the bankruptcy courts' exercise of jurisdiction over the claim as violating Article III. [256]

Nonetheless, in *Oil States Energy Services, LLC v. Greene's Energy Group, LLC*, the Court noted that it "has not 'definitively explained' the distinction between public and private rights, and its precedents applying the public-rights doctrine have 'not been entirely consistent.'" [257] The Court observed, however, that these "precedents have given Congress significant latitude to assign adjudication of public rights to entities other than Article III courts." [258] In *Oil States*, the Court addressed whether inter partes review, a type of patent validity proceeding conducted by the U.S. Patent and Trademark Office (PTO), violates Article III. [259] The Court held that such proceedings "fall[ ] squarely within the public-rights doctrine," and therefore could constitutionally be conducted by a non-Article III tribunal. [260] In so holding, the Court noted that the "case d[id] not require

---

[251] *See* 564 U.S. 462 (2011).

[252] *Id.* at 487–88.

[253] *Id.* at 465.

[254] *Id.*

[255] *Id.*

[256] *Id.*

[257] 584 U.S. ___, No. 16-712, slip op. at 6 (2018) (quoting N. Pipeline Constr. Co. v. Marathon Pipe Line Co., 458 U.S. 50, 69 (1982) (plurality opinion); *Stern*, 564 U.S. at 488).

[258] *Id.* at 6.

[259] *Id.* at 1.

[260] *Id.* at 6–7.

us to add to the 'various formulations' of the public-rights doctrine."[261] Instead, the Court described the public-rights doctrine as "cover[ing] matters 'which arise between the Government and persons subject to its authority in connection with the performance of the constitutional functions of the executive or legislative departments.'"[262] The Court then held "that the decision to *grant* a patent is a matter involving public rights—specifically, the grant of a public franchise" that "need not be adjudicated in Article III court."[263] Further, because "[i]nter partes review involves the same basic matter as the grant of a patent," the Court concluded that "it, too, falls on the public-rights side of the line."[264] Accordingly, having held that inter partes review falls within the public-rights doctrine, the Court determined that such review did not involve an exercise of Article III judicial power, so Congress constitutionally assigned these proceedings to the PTO.[265]

[P. 673, delete heading "*Constitutional Status of the Court of Claims and the Courts of Customs and Patents Appeals.*—" and from "Although the Supreme Court long accepted the Court of Claims . . ." through n.90.]

Bankruptcy Courts.—

[P. 678, after n.117, add new sentence:]

Nonetheless, as the Court later held in *Wellness International v. Sharif,*[266] a bankruptcy court may adjudicate with finality a so-called *Stern* claim—that is, a core claim that does not fall within the public rights exception—if the parties have provided knowing and voluntary consent, arguably limiting the ultimate impact of *Stern* for federal bankruptcy law.[267]

Agency Adjudication.—

[P. 680, after sentence ending ". . . all ordinary powers of district courts.'", add new footnote:]

See CFTC v. Schor, 478 U.S. 833, 853 (1986). Notwithstanding *Schor's* efforts to distinguish between the context presented in that case and the bankruptcy context, the Court, in *Wellness International v. Sharif,* extended *Schor's* holding to adjudications of private right claims by bankruptcy courts. See 575 U.S. ___, No. 13-935, slip op. (2015). Specifically, the *Wellness International* Court utilized the balancing approach employed by *Schor* to conclude that allowing bankruptcy courts to decide a fraudulent conveyance claim by consent would not "impermissibly threaten the institutional integrity of the Judicial Branch," *id.* at 12 (quoting *Schor,* 478 U.S. at 851), because (1) the underlying class of claims that was being adjudicated by the non-Article III court was "narrow" in nature, resulting in a "de minimis" intrusion on the federal judiciary; (2) the bankruptcy court was ultimately supervised and overseen by a constitutional court and not Congress; and (3) the Court found "no indication"

---

[261] *Id.* at 6 (quoting *N. Pipeline Constr. Co.,* 458 U.S. at 69).
[262] *Id.* (quoting Crowell v. Benson, 285 U.S. 22, 50 (1932)).
[263] *Id.* at 7, 8.
[264] *Id.* at 8.
[265] *Id.* at 9–10.
[266] 575 U.S. ___, No. 13-935, slip op. (2015).
[267] *See id.* at 20.

that Congress, in allowing bankruptcy courts to decide with finality certain private right claims, was acting in "an effort to aggrandize itself or humble the Judiciary." *Id.* at 13–14.

JUDICIAL POWER

Characteristics and Attributes of Judicial Power

[P. 682, after n.142, change "Once" to "One".]

Finality of Judgment as an Attribute of Judicial Power

[P. 686, delete sentence starting "More recently, . . ."]

ANCILLARY POWERS OF FEDERAL COURTS

Sanctions Other Than Contempt

[P. 702, delete n.246 and add:]

> *Id.* at 46–51.

[P. 702, delete n.247 and add:]

> *Id.* at 49–51.

[P. 702, after n.247, add new sentence:]

> Nonetheless, the Court has clarified that because a court's order directing a sanctioned litigant to reimburse the legal fees and costs incurred by the wronged party as a result of bad faith conduct is *compensatory*, rather than *punitive*, in nature, a fee award may go no further than to redress the wronged party "for losses sustained."[268]

Power to Issue Writs: The Act of 1789

Habeas Corpus: Congressional and Judicial Control.—

[PP. 705–08, delete section "Habeas Corpus: Congressional and Judicial Control" through paragraph ending ". . . in the CSRT process."]

---

[268] *See* Goodyear Tire & Rubber Co. v. Haeger, 581 U.S. ___, No. 15-1406, slip op. at 5–6 (2017) (holding that a court, "when using its inherent sanctioning authority," must "establish a causal link—between the litigant's misbehavior and legal fees paid by the opposing party").

The Rule-Making Power and Powers Over Process

Limitations to the Rule Making Power.—

[P. 715, after n.333, add new sentences:]

While the Court has not "precisely delineated the outer boundaries" of a federal court's inherent powers to manage its own internal affairs, the Court has recognized two limits on the exercise of such authority.[269] First, a court, in exercising its inherent powers over its own processes, must act reasonably in response to a specific problem or issue "confronting the court's fair administration of justice."[270] Second, any exercise of an inherent power cannot conflict with any express grant of or limitation on the district court's power as contained in a statute or rule, such as the Federal Rules of Civil Procedure.[271] In applying these two standards, the Court has recognized that a district court, as an exercise of its inherent powers, can in limited circumstances rescind an order to discharge a jury and recall that jury in a civil case.[272] The Supreme Court has also acknowledged that federal courts possess the inherent power to control other aspects of regulating internal court proceedings, including having the inherent power to (1) hear a motion *in limine*;[273] (2) dismiss a case for the convenience of the parties or witnesses because of the availability of an alternative forum;[274] and (3) stay proceedings pending the resolution of parallel actions in other courts.[275]

[P. 716, after n.334, add new sentence:]

Nonetheless, while the exercise of an inherent power can, at times, allow for departures from even long-established, judicially crafted common law

---

[269] *See* Dietz v. Bouldin, 579 U.S. ___, No. 15-458, slip op. at 4 (2016).

[270] *Id.* at 4–5.

[271] *Id.* at 4.

[272] *Id.* at 5–7 (acknowledging that while it is "reasonable" to allow a jury to reconvene after a formal discharge to correct an error and while such an exercise of authority does not conflict with a rule or statute, the exercise of the inherent power to rescind a discharge order needs to be "carefully circumscribed" to guarantee the existence of an impartial jury); *see also id.* at 9–10 (holding that a court, in exercising an inherent power to rescind a discharge order, must consider, among other factors, (1) the length of delay between discharge and recall; (2) whether jurors have spoken to anyone after discharge; (3) any reaction to the verdict in the courtroom; and (4) any access jurors may have had to outside materials after discharge). The rule provided in *Dietz* extends only to civil cases, as additional constitutional concerns—namely, the attachment of the double jeopardy bar—may arise if a court were to recall a jury after discharge in a criminal case. *See id.* at 10.

[273] *See* Luce v. United States, 469 U.S. 38, 41 n.4 (1984). A motion *in limine* is a preliminary motion resolved by a court prior to trial and generally regards the admissibility of evidence. *See* BLACK'S LAW DICTIONARY 1171 (10th ed. 2014).

[274] *See* Gulf Oil Corp. v. Gilbert, 330 U.S. 501, 507–08 (1947). This doctrine is called *forum non conveniens*. *See* BLACK'S LAW DICTIONARY 770 (10th ed. 2014) (defining *forum non conveniens* as the "doctrine that an appropriate forum — even though competent under the law — may divest itself of jurisdiction if, for the convenience of the litigants and the witnesses, it appears that the action should proceed in another forum in which the action might also have been properly brought in the first place").

[275] *See* Landis v. N. Am. Co., 299 U.S. 248, 254 (1936).

rules,[276] courts are not "generally free to discover new inherent powers that are contrary to civil practice as recognized in the common laws."[277]

Section 2. Judicial Power and Jurisdiction

Clause 1. Cases and Controversies

JUDICIAL POWER AND JURISDICTION—CASES AND CONTROVERSIES

Adverse Litigants

[P. 722, after section ending " . . . doubtful character of the legislation in question.", add new paragraphs:]

Concerns regarding adversity also arise when the executive branch chooses to enforce, but not defend in court, federal statutes that it has concluded are unconstitutional. In *United States v. Windsor*,[278] the Court considered the Defense of Marriage Act (DOMA), which excludes same-sex partners from the definition of "spouse" as used in federal statutes.[279] DOMA was challenged by the surviving member of a same-sex couple (married in Canada), who was seeking to claim a spousal federal estate tax exemption. Although the executive branch continued to deny the exemption, it also declined to defend the statute based on doubts as to whether it would survive scrutiny under the equal protection component of the Fifth Amendment's Due Process Clause. Consequently, the Bipartisan Legal Advisory Group of the House of Representatives (BLAG)[280] intervened to defend the statute. The Court held that, despite the decision not to defend, the failure of the United States to provide a refund to the taxpayer constituted an injury sufficient to establish standing, leaving only "prudential" limitations on judicial review at issue.[281] The Court concluded that the "prudential" concerns were outweighed by the presence of BLAG to offer an adversarial presentation of the issue, the legal uncertainty that would be caused by dismissing the case, and the concern that the executive branch's assessment of the constitutionality of the statute would be immunized from judicial review.[282]

---

[276] *See Dietz*, slip op. at 11 (assuming that, even if courts at common law lacked the inherent power to rescind a jury discharge order, a court's exercise of its inherent powers can depart from the common law). The term "common law" refers to the body of English law that was "adopted as the law of the American colonies and supplemented with local enactments and judgments." *See* BLACK'S LAW DICTIONARY 334 (10th ed. 2014).

[277] *See Dietz*, slip op. at 12.

[278] 570 U.S. 744 (2013).

[279] Pub. L. No. 104-199, § 3, 110 Stat. 2419, 1 U.S.C. § 7.

[280] BLAG is a standing body of the House, created by rule, consisting of members of the House Leadership and authorized to direct the House Office of the General Counsel to file suit on its behalf in state or federal court.

[281] *Windsor*, 756–57.

[282] *Id.* at 759–61.

The Court applied *Windsor* in *Seila Law, LLC v. Consumer Financial Protection Bureau* (CFPB), to conclude that even though the parties agreed "on the merits of the constitutional question," the case did not lack adversity.[283] The CFPB, a federal agency, had issued a civil investigative demand asking the petitioners to produce certain information.[284] In response, the petitioners argued that the agency's structure violated the Constitution's separation of powers.[285] Before the Supreme Court, the federal government agreed that the agency's structure was unconstitutional, but maintained that it could nonetheless enforce the civil investigative demand.[286] Viewing the case as akin to *Windsor*, the *Seila Law* Court concluded that the decision below upholding the demand "present[ed] real-world consequences" that supported the Court's jurisdiction to resolve the constitutional question.[287]

Substantial Interest: Standing

Constitutional Standards: Injury in Fact, Causation, and Redressability.—

[P. 729, delete n.395 and substitute with:]

See Lujan v. Defs. of Wildlife, 504 U.S. 555, 506–61 (1992). Importantly, standing is not "dispensed in gross," and, accordingly, a plaintiff must demonstrate standing for each claim "he seeks to press and for each form of relief that is sought." *See* Davis v. FEC, 554 U.S. 724, 734 (2008). Moreover, when there are multiple parties to a lawsuit brought in federal court, "[f]or all relief sought, there must be a litigant with standing, whether that litigant joins the lawsuit as a plaintiff, a coplaintiff, or an intervenor as of right." *See* Town of Chester v. Laroe Estates, Inc., 581 U.S. ___, No. 16-605, slip op. at 6 (2017). A litigant must also maintain standing to pursue an appeal. *See, e.g.*, Hollingsworth v. Perry, 570 U.S. 693, 705 (2013); *see also, e.g.*, Seila Law LLC v. Consumer Fin. Prot. Bureau, 140 S. Ct. 2183, 219 (2020) (stating that a petitioner had "appellate standing" where the petitioner suffered a "concrete injury" that was "traceable to the decision below" and could be redressed by the Court).

[P. 730, after n.403, add new sentence:]

Moreover, while Congress has the power to define injuries and articulate "chains of causation" that will give rise to a case or controversy, a plaintiff does not "automatically satisf[y] the injury-in-fact requirement whenever a statute grants a person a statutory right and purports to authorize a person to sue to vindicate that right."[288]

---

[283] Seila Law LLC v. Consumer Fin. Prot. Bureau, 140 S. Ct. 2183, 2196–97 (2020).

[284] *Id.* at 2194.

[285] *Id.*

[286] *Id.* at 2196.

[287] *Id.*

[288] *See* Spokeo, Inc. v. Robins, 578 U.S. ___, No. 13-1339, slip op. at 9 (2016); *see also* Thole v. U.S. Bank N.A., 140 S. Ct. 1615, 1620 (2020) (rejecting the argument that the existence of a general cause of action for participants in a defined-benefit plan in the Employee Retirement Income Security Act of 1974 sufficed to provide Article III standing). The phrase "chains of causation" originates from Justice Kennedy's concurrence in *Defenders of Wildlife*, in which he states that in order to properly define an injury that can be vindicated in an Article III court, "Congress must . . . identify the injury it seeks to vindicate and relate the

[P. 732, n.408, italicize "*Id.*"]

[P. 732, n.409, change "Communications" to "Commc'ns" and "Services" to "Servs."]

[P. 732, n.409, italicize "*Id.*"]

[P. 732, delete space before n.410 and after n.410, add new paragraphs:]

Beyond these historical anomalies, the Court has indicated that, for parties lacking an individualized injury to seek judicial relief on behalf of an absent third party, there generally must be some sort of agency relationship between the litigant and the injured party.[289] In *Hollingsworth v. Perry*,[290] the Court considered the question of whether the official proponents of Proposition 8,[291] a state measure that amended the California Constitution to define marriage as a union between a man and a woman, had standing to defend the constitutionality of the provision on appeal. After rejecting the argument that the proponents of Proposition 8 had a particularized injury in their own right,[292] the Court considered the argument that the plaintiffs were formally authorized through some sort of official act to litigate on behalf of the State of California.

Although the proponents were authorized by California law to argue in defense of the proposition,[293] the Court found that this authorization, by itself, was insufficient to create standing. The Court expressed concern that, although California law authorized the proponents to argue in favor of Proposition 8, the proponents were still acting as private individuals, not as state officials[294] or as agents that were

---

injury to the class of persons entitled to bring suit." 504 U.S. at 580 (Kennedy, J., concurring).

[289] *See, e.g.*, Thole v. U.S. Bank N.A., 140 S. Ct. 1615, 1620 (2020) (rejecting the argument that uninjured participants in a defined-benefit plan could sue as the plan's representatives because, unlike "guardians, receivers, and executors," the plaintiffs had not been "legally or contractually appointed to represent the plan"); Gollust v. Mendell, 501 U.S. 115, 124–25 (1991) (requiring plaintiff in shareholder-derivative suit to maintain a financial stake in the litigation's outcome to avoid "serious constitutional doubt whether that plaintiff could demonstrate the standing required by Article III's case-or-controversy limitation").

[290] 570 U.S. 693 (2013).

[291] Under the relevant provisions of the California Elections Code, "'[p]roponents of an initiative or referendum measure' means . . . the elector or electors who submit the text of a proposed initiative or referendum to the Attorney General . . . ; or . . . the person or persons who publish a notice or intention to circulate petitions, or, where publication is not required, who file petitions with the elections official or legislative body." CAL. ELEC. CODE § 342 (West 2003).

[292] *Hollingsworth*, 570 U.S. at 704–07.

[293] California's governor and state and local officials declined to defend Proposition 8 in federal district court, so the proponents were allowed to intervene. After the federal district court held the proposition unconstitutional, the government officials elected not to appeal, so the proponents did. The federal court of appeals certified a question to the California Supreme Court on whether the official proponents of the proposition had the authority to assert the state's interest in defending the constitutionality of Proposition 8, *see* Perry v. Schwarzenegger, 628 F.3d 1191, 1193 (2011), which was answered in the affirmative, *see* Perry v. Brown, 265 P.3d 1002, 1007 (Cal. 2011).

[294] *See Hollingsworth*, 570 U.S. at 709–10 (citing Karcher v. May, 484 U.S. 72 (1987)).

controlled by the state.[295] Because the proponents did not act as agents or official representatives of the State of California in defending the law, the Court held that the proponents only possessed a generalized interest in arguing in defense of Proposition 8 and, therefore, lacked standing to appeal an adverse district court decision.[296]

[P. 732, delete "Nonetheless," and substitute with:]

More broadly,

[P. 732, delete n.411 and substitute with:]

See, e.g., Gill v. Whitford, 585 U.S. ___, No. 16-1161, slip op. at 14 (2018) (holding that, in order to have standing to raise a claim of vote dilution as a result of partisan gerrymandering, plaintiffs must allege that their own particular district has been gerrymandered; claims of gerrymandering by those who do not live in a gerrymandered district amount to a generalized grievance); see also United States v. Hays, 515 U.S. 737, 744–45 (1995) (same rationale for allegations of racial gerrymandering).

[P. 732, delete sentence after n.412 and add new paragraphs:]

In a number of cases, particularly where a plaintiff seeks prospective relief, such as an injunction or declaratory relief, the Supreme Court has strictly construed the nature of the injury-in-fact necessary to obtain such judicial remedy. First, the Court has been hesitant to assume jurisdiction over matters in which the plaintiff seeking relief cannot articulate a concrete harm.[297] For example, in *Laird v. Tatum*, the Court held that plaintiffs challenging a domestic surveillance program lacked standing when their alleged injury stemmed from a "subjective chill", as opposed to a "claim of specific present objective harm or a threat of specific future harm."[298] And in *Spokeo, Inc. v. Robins*, the Court explained that a concrete injury requires that an injury must "actually exist" or there must

---

[295] The Court noted that an essential feature of agency is the principal's right to control the agent's actions. Here, the proponents decided "what arguments to make and how to make them." *Id.* at 725. The Court also noted that the proponents were not elected to their position, took no oath, had no fiduciary duty to the people of California, and were not subject to removal. *Id.*

[296] *Id.* at 709–10. Similarly, in *Virginia House of Delegates v. Bethune-Hill*, the Court concluded that one chamber of the Virginia legislature lacked standing to represent the Commonwealth's interests for two reasons: (1) Virginia law designated the Virginia Attorney General as the Commonwealth's exclusive representative in litigation; and (2) the chamber claimed earlier in the litigation that it was vindicating its own interests, as opposed to those of Virginia. *See* 139 S. Ct. 1945, 1951–52 (2019).

[297] *See generally* Summers v. Earth Island Inst., 555 U.S. 488, 496 (2009) ("[D]eprivation of a . . . right without some concrete interest that is affected by the deprivation . . . is insufficient to create Article III standing."); *see, e.g.,* Thole v. U.S. Bank N.A., 140 S. Ct. 1615, 1618, 1621–22 (2020) (holding that participants in a defined-benefit plan lacked a concrete stake in a lawsuit seeking monetary and injunctive relief to remedy alleged mismanagement of the plan where the plaintiffs' monthly payments were fixed and not tied to plan performance); Cal. Bankers Ass'n v. Shultz, 416 U.S. 21, 73 (1974) (plaintiffs alleged that Treasury regulations would require them to report currency transactions, but made no additional allegation that any of the information required by the Secretary will tend to incriminate them).

[298] 408 U.S. 1, 14–15 (1972).

be a "risk of real harm," such that a plaintiff who alleges nothing more than a bare procedural violation of a federal statute cannot satisfy the injury-in-fact requirement.[299]

Second, the Court has required plaintiffs seeking equitable relief to demonstrate that the risk of a future injury is of a sufficient likelihood; past injury is insufficient to create standing to seek prospective relief.[300] The Court has articulated the threshold of likelihood of future injury necessary for standing in such cases in various ways,[301] generally refusing to find standing where the risk of future injury is speculative.[302] More recently, in *Clapper v. Amnesty International USA*, the Court held that, in order to demonstrate Article III standing, a plaintiff seeking injunctive relief must prove that the future injury, which is the basis for the relief sought, must be "certainly impending"; a showing of a "reasonable likelihood" of future injury is insufficient.[303] Moreover, the Court in *Amnesty International* held that a plaintiff cannot satisfy the imminence requirement by merely "manufacturing" costs incurred in response to speculative, non-imminent injuries.[304] A year after *Amnesty International*,

---

[299] *See* 578 U.S. ___, No. 13-1339, slip op. at 8–10 (2016). Nonetheless, the *Spokeo* Court cautioned that "intangible" injuries, such as violations of constitutional rights like freedom of speech or the free exercise of religion, can amount to "concrete" injuries. *Id.* at 8–9 ("'Concrete' is not, however, necessarily synonymous with 'tangible.'"). In determining whether an intangible harm amounts to a concrete injury, the Court noted that history and the judgment of Congress can inform a court's conclusion about whether a particular plaintiff has standing. *Id.* at 9.

[300] *See* City of Los Angeles v. Lyons, 461 U.S. 95, 110 (1983) (holding that a victim of a police chokehold seeking injunctive relief was unable to show sufficient likelihood of recurrence as to him).

[301] *See* Davis v. FEC, 554 U.S. 724, 734 (2008) ("[T]he injury required for standing need not be actualized. A party facing prospective injury has standing to sue where the threatened injury is real, immediate, and direct.").

[302] *See, e.g.*, Rizzo v. Goode, 423 U.S. 362, 372 (1976) ("[I]ndividual respondents' claim to 'real and immediate' injury rests not upon what the named petitioners might do to them in the future . . . but upon what one of a small, unnamed minority of policemen might do to them in the future because of that unknown policeman's perception of departmental disciplinary procedures."); O'Shea v. Littleton, 414 U.S. 488, 497 (1974) (no "sufficient immediacy and reality" to allegations of future injury that rest on the likelihood that plaintiffs will again be subjected to racially discriminatory enforcement and administration of criminal justice).

[303] 568 U.S. 398, 410–11 (2013). In adopting a "certainly impending" standard, the five-Justice majority observed that earlier cases had not uniformly required literal certainty. *Id.* at 414 n.5. *Amnesty International*'s limitation on standing may be particularly notable in certain contexts, such as national security, where evidence necessary to prove a "certainly impending" injury may be unavailable to a plaintiff.

[304] *Id.* at 410–11. In *Amnesty International*, defense attorneys, human rights organizations, and others challenged prospective, covert surveillance of the communications of certain foreign nationals abroad as authorized by the FISA Amendments Act of 2008. The Court found the plaintiffs lacked standing because they failed to show, inter alia, what the government's targeting practices would be, what legal authority the government would use to monitor any of the plaintiffs' overseas clients or contacts, whether any approved surveillance would be successful, and whether the plaintiffs' own communications from within the United States would incidentally be required. *Id.* at 411–14. Moreover, the Court rejected that the plaintiffs could demonstrate an injury-in-fact as a result of costs that they had incurred to guard against a reasonable fear of future harm (such as, travel expenses to conduct in person conversations abroad in lieu of conducting less costly electronic communications that might be more susceptible to surveillance) because those costs were the

the Court in *Susan B. Anthony List v. Driehaus*[305] reaffirmed that pre-enforcement challenges to a statute can occur "under circumstances that render the threatened enforcement sufficiently imminent."[306] In *Susan B. Anthony List*, an organization planning to disseminate a political advertisement, which was previously the source of an administrative complaint under an Ohio law prohibiting making false statements about a candidate or a candidate's record during a political campaign, challenged the prospective enforcement of that law. The Court, in finding that the plaintiff's future injury was certainly impending, relied on the history of prior enforcement of the law with respect to the advertisement, coupled with the facts that "any person" could file a complaint under the law, and any threat of enforcement of the law could burden political speech.[307]

[P. 733, delete sentence starting "There must be a causal connection . . ." and substitute with:]

A plaintiff must show its injuries are fairly traceable to the conduct complained of.[308]

[P. 733, delete n.414 and substitute with:]

See Duke Power Co. v. Carolina Envtl. Study Grp., 438 U.S. 59, 79 (1978); *see, e.g.,* Food Mktg. Inst. v. Argus Leader Media, 588 U.S. ___, No. 18-481, slip op. at 4–5 (2019) (holding that a ruling allowing, but not requiring, an agency to withhold information under the Freedom of Information Act redresses injuries resulting from disclosure when the

---

result of an injury that was not certainly impending. *Id*. at 415–18.

[305] 573 U.S. ___, No. 13-193, slip op. (2014).

[306] Relying on *Amnesty International*, the Court in *Susan B. Anthony List* held that an allegation of future injury may suffice if the injury is "'certainly impending' or there is a 'substantial risk' that the harm may occur." *Susan B. Anthony List*, slip op. at 8 (quoting *Amnesty Int'l*, slip op. at 10, 15, n.5). *cf.* Thole v. U.S. Bank N.A., 140 S. Ct. 1615, 1621 (2020) (concluding that participants in a defined-benefit plan lacked standing because they failed to adequately plead that the plan managers had "substantially increased the risk that the plan and the employer would fail and be unable to pay the participants' future pension benefits"). The Court framed the imminence requirement similarly in *Department of Commerce v. New York*, a suit brought by the State of New York to enjoin the inclusion of a question on the census about a person's citizenship. *See* 588 U.S. ___, No. 18-966, slip op. at 9 (2019). In holding that the state had standing to sue, the Court deferred to the lower court's findings that New York's alleged injury of being deprived of federal funding as a result of the reinstatement of a citizenship question on the census had a "sufficient likelihood," given evidence in the record of lower response rates by noncitizen households and the likely decrease in federal funding resulting from an undercount. *Id*. at 9–10.

While previous Court decisions have viewed pre-enforcement challenges as a question of "ripeness," *see* Article III: Section 2. Judicial Power and Jurisdiction: Clause 1. Cases and Controversies; Grants of Jurisdiction: Judicial Power and Jurisdiction-Cases and Controversies: The Requirements of a Real Interest: Ripeness, *infra*, *Susan B. Anthony List* held that the doctrine of ripeness ultimately "boil[s] down to the same question" as standing and, therefore, viewed the case through the lens of Article III standing. *Susan B. Anthony List*, slip op. at 7 n.5.

[307] *Id*. at 14–17 (internal quotation marks omitted).

[308] *See* Lujan v. Defenders of Wildlife, 504 U.S. 555, 560–61 (1992). *Cf., e.g.,* Dep't of Commerce v. New York, 588 U.S. ___, No. 18-966, slip op. at 10 (2019) (reasoning that a causal link between including a citizenship question on the census and harms that would flow from lower response rates was not "speculat[ive]" based on the "predictable effect" of some households choosing not to respond, even if failure to respond is unlawful).

government has "unequivocally" stated that it will not disclose the contested information absent a court order); Wittman v. Personhuballah, 578 U.S. ___, No. 14-1504, slip op. at 4–5 (2016) (dismissing a challenge to a redistricting plan by a congressman, who conceded that regardless of the result of the case he would run in his old district, any injury suffered could not be redressed by a favorable ruling). Although "causation" and "redressability" were initially articulated as two facets of a single requirement, the Court now views them as separate inquiries. *See* Sprint Commc'ns Co., LP v. APCC Servs., 554 U.S. 269, 286–87 (2008). The former examines a causal connection between the allegedly unlawful conduct and the alleged injury, whereas the latter examines the likelihood that the judicial relief requested would redress that injury. *Id.* at 273, 286–87.

[P. 734, after n.418, add new sentence:]

And in a case where a creditor challenged a bankruptcy court's structured dismissal of a Chapter 11 case that denied the creditor the opportunity to obtain a settlement or assert a claim with "litigation value," the Court held that a decision in the creditor's favor was likely to redress the loss.[309]

Standing to Assert the Rights of Others.—

[P. 737, after ". . . the interests of his patients.", add new footnote:]

Tileston, 318 U.S. at 46. *But cf.* June Med. Servs. LLC v. Russo, 140 S. Ct. 2103, 2118–19 (2020) (plurality opinion) (observing that the Court has "long permitted abortion providers to invoke the rights of their actual or potential patients in challenges to abortion-related regulations" and has "generally permitted plaintiffs to assert third-party rights in cases where the 'enforcement of the challenged restriction *against the litigant* would result indirectly in the violation of third parties' rights'" (quoting Kowalski v. Tesmer, 543 U.S. 125, 130 (2004))).

[P. 739, delete sentence "However, a 'next friend' whose . . ." and substitute with:]

A "next friend" that is asserting the rights of another must establish that he has a "close relationship" with the real party in interest who is unable to litigate his own cause because of a "hindrance,"[310] such as mental incapacity, lack of access to the courts, or other disability.[311]

---

[309] *See* Czyzewski v. Jevic Holding Corp., 580 U.S. ___, No. 15-649, slip op. at 11 (2017) (holding that the "mere possibility" that a plaintiff's injury will not be remedied by a favorable decision is insufficient to conclude the plaintiff lacks standing because of want of redressability); *see also* Clinton v. City of New York, 524 U.S. 417, 430–31 (1998) (holding that the imposition of a "substantial contingent liability" qualifies as an injury for purposes of Article III standing).

[310] *See* Kowalski v. Tesmer, 543 U.S. 125, 130 (2004); *see also* Powers v. Ohio, 499 U.S. 400, 411 (1991). The Court has held that a parent-child relationship "easily satisfies" the "close relationship" requirement for "next friend" standing. *See* Sessions v. Morales-Santana, 582 U.S. ___, No. 15-1191, slip op. 7 (2017).

[311] *See* Whitmore v. Arkansas, 495 U.S. 149, 163 (1990) (rejecting "next friend" standing for a death row inmate who knowingly, intelligently, and voluntarily chose not to appeal his sentence); *see also* Morales-Santana, 582 U.S. at ___, slip op. at 7 (holding that the death of the real party in interest meets the "hindrance" requirement for "next friend" standing).

Standing of Members of Congress.—

[P. 742, after sentence ending ". . . as a predicate to standing.", add new footnote:]

> *See, e.g.,* Wittman v. Personhuballah, 578 U.S. ___, No. 14-1504, slip op. at 6 (2016) (concluding that two congressmen could not invoke federal jurisdiction to challenge a redistricting plan when they could not provide any evidence that the plan might injure their reelection chances).

[P. 742, at end of first paragraph, delete "What that injury in fact may consist of, however, is the basis of the controversy." and substitute with:]

What such injury in fact may consist of, however, has been the subject of debate.

[P. 743, at end of first paragraph, delete "The status of this issue thus remains in confusion."]

[P. 744, delete third paragraph starting "It may be observed . . ." and ending "deprived of the effectiveness of their votes?" and substitute with:]

In a subsequent case, the Court reaffirmed the continued viability of *Coleman*[312] in concluding that legislators, when authorized by the legislature, could have standing to assert an "institutional injury" to that legislative body.[313] Specifically, the Court held in *Arizona State Legislature v. Arizona Independent Redistricting Commission* that the Arizona legislature had standing to challenge the validity of the Arizona Independent Redistricting Commission and the commission's 2012 map of congressional districts because the legislature had been "stripped" of what the plaintiff considered its "exclusive constitutionally guarded role" in redistricting.[314] Comparing the Arizona legislature's role to the "institutional injury" suffered by the plaintiffs in *Coleman,* the Court viewed the Arizona legislators' injury as akin to that of the *Coleman* legislators. Specifically, the Court likened the instant case to *Coleman* because the Arizona Constitution and the ballot initiative that provided for redistricting by an independent commission would have "completely nullif[ied]" any vote "now or 'in the future'" by the legislature "purporting to adopt a redistricting plan."[315] However, in *Arizona State Legislature,* the Court left open the question of whether Congress, in a lawsuit against the President over an institutional injury to the legislative branch, would

---

[312] *See* Coleman v. Miller, 307 U.S. 433 (1939).

[313] Ariz. State Legislature v. Ariz. Indep. Redistricting Comm'n, 576 U.S. ___, No. 13-1314, slip op. at 14 (2015).

[314] *Id.* at 10.

[315] *Id.*

likewise have standing, as such a lawsuit would "raise separation-of-powers concerns absent" in the case before the Court.[316]

Notwithstanding *Coleman* and *Arizona State Legislature,* the Court continued to express skepticism about standing questions concerning legislative plaintiffs. In *Virginia House of Delegates v. Bethune-Hill,* the Court held that a single chamber of the Virginia legislature—the House of Delegates of its General Assembly—lacked standing to defend state redistricting legislation that the lower court had invalidated.[317] In so holding, the Court, citing *Raines,* reasoned that just as individual members "lack standing to assert the institutional interests of a legislature," "a single House of a bicameral legislature lacks capacity to assert interests belonging to the legislature as a whole."[318] In response to the argument that redistricting altered the composition of the House of Delegates and therefore amounted to an Article III injury, the Court observed that the House had "no cognizable interest in the identity of its members," as the public chose its members.[319] As a consequence, while the Court has recognized the a single chamber of a legislature may be able to assert injuries unique to that chamber,[320] the *Virginia House of Delegates* decision indicates that the invalidation of a law does not necessarily inflict a discrete, cognizable injury on "each organ of government that participated in the law's passage."[321]

The Requirement of a Real Interest

Mootness.—

[P. 756, delete n.540 and substitute with:]

See Preiser v. Newkirk, 422 U.S. 395, 401 (1975). Under *United States v. Munsingwear,* when a case has become moot on its way to the Supreme Court, the Court's "established practice

---

[316] *Id.* at 14 n.12.

[317] *See* 587 U.S. ___, No. 18-281, slip op. at 7 (2019).

[318] *Id.* at 8. The *Virginia House of Delegates* Court distinguished *Arizona State Legislature* on two grounds, observing that in that case (1) both the Arizona House and Senate collectively brought the lawsuit and (2) the underlying law being challenged permanently altered the legislature's role in the redistricting process. *Id.* at 8–9. In contrast, the Court reasoned that the House of Delegates was alone in bringing its appeal, and that its appeal did not alter the Virginia legislature's ongoing role in redistricting. *Id.* at 9. The *Virginia House of Delegates* Court also distinguished *Coleman,* concluding that, unlike the legislators in the earlier case, the Virginia House of Delegates was not contesting the results of a vote in its chamber, but instead was defending the constitutionality of a "concededly enacted redistricting plan." *Id.* at 10.

[319] *Id.* at 10–11. In so concluding, the Court distinguished *Sixty-Seventh Minnesota State Senate v. Beens,* 406 U.S. 187 (1972) (per curiam), in that *Beens* involved a challenge to an order reducing the Minnesota Senate's membership in half, altering—in contrast to the injuries of the Virginia House of Delegates—the *manner* in which the legislative body "goes about its business." *See Va. House of Delegates,* slip op. at 10–11 & n.6.

[320] *See, e.g., Va. House of Delegates,* slip op. at n. 5 (noting that both the House of Representatives and the Senate had standing to defend the one-house veto in *INS v. Chadha,* 462 U.S. 919, 929–31 & nn. 5–6, 939–40 (1983), because the statute at issue granted *each* chamber of Congress an ongoing power to veto certain executive branch decisions).

[321] *Id.* at 7.

. . . is to reverse or vacate the judgment below and remand with a direction to dismiss." *See* 340 U.S. 36, 39 (1950). The logic of this rule is based, in part, out of a concern that plaintiffs, after obtaining a favorable judgment, would thereafter take voluntary action to moot the case in order to retain the benefit of the judgment and shield that judgment from review. *See* Arizonans for Official English v. Arizona, 520 U.S. 43, 67 (1997). The fact that the claim becomes moot before a party seeks review from the Supreme Court does not limit the Court's discretion to apply the *Munsingwear* rule. *See* Azar v. Garza, 584 U.S. ___, No. 17-654, slip op. at 4 (2018) (collecting various cases).

[P. 757, n.541, delete last four sentences "If this foundation exists . . . 508 U.S. 83 (1993)."]

[P. 757, at end of paragraph, add new sentence:]

> So long as concrete, adverse legal interests between the parties continue, a case is not made moot by intervening actions that cast doubt on the practical enforceability of a final judicial order.[322]

[P. 758, n.544, delete initial citation sentence and substitute with:]

> *E.g.*, United States v. Microsoft Corp., 584 U.S. ___, No. 17-2 (2018); Lewis v. Continental Bank Corp., 494 U.S. 481 (1990); Richardson v. Wright, 405 U.S. 208 (1972); Diffenderfer v. Central Baptist Church, 404 U.S. 412 (1972); Sanks v. Georgia, 401 U.S. 144 (1971); Hall v. Beals, 396 U.S. 45 (1969); United States v. Alaska Steamship Co., 253 U.S. 113 (1920); Pennsylvania v. Wheeling & Belmont Bridge Co., 54 U.S. (13 How.) 518 (1852).

[P. 758, n.544, after "Lewis v. Continental Bank Corp., 494 U.S. 481 (1990)", add:]

> ; N.Y. State Rifle & Pistol Ass'n, Inc. v. City of New York, 140 S. Ct. 1525, 1526 (2020) (per curiam)

[P. 758, n.544, after citation sentence referencing *City of Mesquite v. Aladdin's Castle, Inc.*, add:]

> ; *see also* Decker v. Nw. Envtl. Def. Ctr., 568 U.S. 597, 609–10 (2013) (action to enforce penalty under former regulation not mooted by change in regulation where violation occurred before regulation was changed).

[PP. 758–59, delete sentence starting "This exception has its . . ." and substitute with:]

> This exception has its counterpart in civil litigation, as well, where the Court has held that even the remote possibility of recovery can obviate mootness concerns.[323]

---

[322] Chafin v. Chafin, 568 U.S. 165, 175–76 (2013) (appeal of district court order returning custody of a child to her mother in Scotland not made moot by physical return of child to Scotland and subsequent ruling of Scottish court in favor of the mother continuing to have custody).

[323] *See, e.g.*, Mission Prod. Holdings, Inc. v. Tempnology, LLC, 587 U.S. ___, No. 17-1657, slip op. at 2–3, 6–7 (2019) (concluding that the prospect of obtaining monetary damages even if recovery was uncertain or unlikely was a merits question and did not implicate mootness concerns); *cf.* Chafin v. Chafin, 568 U.S 165, 175 (2013) (observing that courts "often

[P. 759, after n.551, add new sentence:]

This amounts to a "formidable burden" of showing with absolute clarity that there is no reasonable prospect of renewed activity.[324]

[P. 759, after n.552, add new sentence:]

In this vein, the Court in *Campbell-Ewald Co. v. Gomez*, informed by principles of contract law, held that an *unaccepted* offer to settle a lawsuit amounts to a "legal nullity" that fails to bind either party and therefore does not moot the litigation.[325]

[PP. 759–60, at end of n.554, add:]

However, in *United States v. Sanchez-Gomez*, 584 U.S. ___, No. 17-312, slip op. at 12 (2018), the Court unanimously held that it would not presume that persons convicted of illegal entry or reentry offenses would be likely to again illegally reenter the United States, notwithstanding evidence suggesting that such behavior was likely. The Court distinguished *Honig*, 484 U.S. at 320–21, as a civil case in which the litigant was unable, "for reasons beyond [his] control, to prevent [himself] from" repeating the challenged conduct. *Sanchez-Gomez*, slip op. at 12.

[PP. 759–60, delete last sentence on P. 759, which continues on top of P. 760, and substitute with:]

This exception is frequently invoked in cases involving situations of comparatively limited duration, such as elections,[326] pregnancies,[327] short sentences in criminal cases,[328] the award of at least some short-term

---

adjudicate disputes where the practical impact of any decision is not assured.").

[324] Already, LLC v. Nike, Inc., 568 U.S. 85, 91–92 (2013) (dismissal of a trademark infringement claim against rival and submittal of an unconditional and irrevocable covenant not to sue satisfied the burden under the voluntary cessation test) (citing Friends of the Earth v. Laidlaw Envtl. Servs., 528 U.S. 167, 190 (2000)). *See also* Trinity Lutheran Church of Columbia, Inc. v. Comer, 582 U.S. ___, No. 15-577, slip op. at 5 n.1 (2017) (holding that a Governor's announcement that religious organizations could compete for state monetary grants did not moot a case challenging a previous policy of issuing grants only to non-religious entities as the state had failed to carry its "heavy burden" of "making absolutely clear" that it could not revert to its policy of excluding religious organizations from the grant program).

[325] 577 U.S. ___, No. 14-857, slip op. at 7–9 (2016) ("[W]ith no settlement offer still operative, the parties remained adverse; both retained the same stake in the litigation that they had at the outset."). The *Campbell-Ewald* decision was limited to the question of whether an *offer* of complete relief moots a case. The Court left open the question of whether the *payment* of complete relief by a defendant to a plaintiff *can* render a case moot. *Id.* at 11.

[326] *See, e.g.*, Storer v. Brown, 415 U.S. 724, 737 n.8 (1974); Rosario v. Rockefeller, 410 U.S. 752, 756 n.5 (1973); Moore v. Ogilvie, 394 U.S. 814, 816 (1969).

[327] *See, e.g.*, Roe v. Wade, 410 U.S. 113, 124–25 (1973).

[328] *See, e.g.*, Sibron v. New York, 392 U.S. 40, 49–58 (1968). *See also* Gerstein v. Pugh, 420 U.S. 103 (1975).

federal government contracts,[329] and the issuance of injunctions that expire in a brief period.[330]

[P. 760, at end of sentence starting "An interesting and potentially significant . . .", add new footnote:]

The Court recently emphasized, however, that its class action precedents do not create "a freestanding exception to mootness outside the class action context." United States v. Sanchez-Gomez, 584 U.S. ___, No. 17-312, slip op. at 5 (2018).

[P. 761, at end of n.561, delete ", although the value of this interest was at best speculative." and add:]

. *Cf.* Genesis Healthcare Corp. v. Symczyk, 569 U.S. 66 (2013) (in the context of a "collective action" under the Fair Labor Standards Act where a plaintiff's individual claim was moot and no other individuals had joined the suit, holding that a plaintiff had no personal stake in the case that provided the court with subject matter jurisdiction). In a slightly different context, the Court, in *Campbell-Ewald Co. v. Gomez*, held that neither an unaccepted settlement offer or an offer of judgment provided *prior* to class certification would moot a potential lead plaintiff's case. 577 U.S. ___, No. 14-857, slip op. at 11 (2016). According to the majority opinion, this holding avoided placing defendants in the "driver's seat" with respect to class litigation wherein a defendant's offer of settlement could eliminate a court's jurisdiction to adjudicate potentially costly class actions. *Id.*

Retroactivity Versus Prospectivity.—

[P. 764, delete n.582 and substitute with:]

For an example of the application of the *Teague* rule in federal collateral review of a federal court conviction, see Chaidez v. United States, 568 U.S. 342 (2013). *See also* Welch v. United States, 578 U.S. ___, No. 15-6418, slip op. at 7 (2016) (assuming, without deciding, that the *Teague* framework "applies in a federal collateral challenge to a federal conviction as it does in a federal collateral challenge to a state conviction").

[P. 764, delete "A" at beginning of first full sentence and substitute with:]

However, "[a]

[P. 764, delete n.583 and substitute with:]

Whorton v. Bockting, 549 U.S. 406, 416 (2007).

[P. 764, after n.583, add new sentences and new paragraph:]

Put another way, a new rule will be applied in a collateral proceeding only if it places certain kinds of conduct "beyond the power of the criminal law-making authority to prescribe" or constitutes a "new procedure[ ] without

---

[329] *See, e.g.,* Kingdomware Techs., Inc. v. United States, 579 U.S. ___, No. 14-916, slip op. at 7 (2016) ("We have previously held that a period of two years is too short to complete judicial review of the lawfulness of [a] procurement.") (citing S. Pac. Terminal Co. v. ICC, 219 U.S. 498, 514–16 (1911)).

[330] *See, e.g.,* Carroll v. President & Commr's of Princess Anne, 393 U.S. 175 (1968). *See* Neb. Press Ass'n v. Stuart, 427 U.S. 539 (1976) (short-term court order restricting press coverage).

which the likelihood of an accurate conviction is seriously diminished."[331] In *Montgomery v. Louisiana,* the Court extended the holding of *Teague* beyond the context of federal habeas review, such that when a new substantive rule of constitutional law controls the outcome of a case, state collateral review courts must give retroactive effect to that rule in the same manner as federal courts engaging in habeas review.[332]

As a result, at least with regard to the first exception, the Court has held that the *Teague* rule is constitutionally based,[333] as substantive rules set forth categorical guarantees that place certain laws and punishments beyond a state's power, making "the resulting conviction or sentence . . . by definition . . . unlawful."[334] In contrast, procedural rules are those that are aimed at enhancing the accuracy of a conviction or sentence by regulating the manner of determining the defendant's guilt.[335] As a consequence, with respect to a defendant who did not receive the benefit of a new *procedural* rule, the possibility exists that the underlying conviction or sentence may "still be accurate" and the "defendant's continued confinement may still be lawful" under the Constitution.[336] In this vein, the Court has described a substantive rule as one that alters the range of conduct that the law punishes, or that prohibits "a certain category of punishment for a class of defendants because of their status or offense."[337] Under the second exception it is "not enough under *Teague* to say that a new rule is aimed at improving the accuracy of a trial. More is required. A rule that qualifies under this exception must not only improve accuracy, but also alter our understanding of the *bedrock procedural elements* essential to the fairness of a proceeding."[338]

---

[331] Teague v. Lane, 489 U.S. 288, 307, 311–13 (1989) (plurality opinion); *see also* Butler v. McKellar, 494 U.S. 407, 415–16 (1990).

[332] *See* Montgomery v. Louisiana, 577 U.S. ___, No. 14-280, slip op. at 12 (2016) ("If a State may not constitutionally insist that a prisoner remain in jail on federal habeas review, it may not constitutionally insist on the same result in its own postconviction proceedings."). The Court reasoned as such because new substantive rules constitute wholesale prohibitions on the state's power to convict or sentence a criminal defendant under certain circumstances, making the underlying conviction or sentence void and providing the state with no authority to leave the underlying judgment in place during collateral review. *Id.* at 10–11; *see also id.* at 12 ("A penalty imposed pursuant to an unconstitutional law is no less void because the prisoner's sentence became final before the law was held unconstitutional. There is no grandfather clause that permits States to enforce punishments the Constitution forbids.").

[333] *See Montgomery,* slip op. at 8 ("[T]he Constitution requires substantive rules to have retroactive effect regardless of when a conviction became final.")

[334] *Id.* at 9.

[335] *Id.*

[336] *Id.*

[337] *See Welch,* slip op. at 11; *see also* Schriro v. Summerlin, 542 U.S. 348, 353 (2004); Penry v. Lynaugh, 492 U.S. 302, 330 (1989). Accordingly, the Court has rejected the argument that the underlying "source" of a constitutional rule—i.e., the fact that a constitutional rule on its face creates substantive or procedural rights—can determine the retroactivity of a ruling. *See Welch,* slip op. at 10 ("[T]his Court has determined whether a new rule is substantive . . . by considering the function of the rule, not its underlying constitutional source.").

[338] Sawyer v. Smith, 497 U.S. 227, 242 (1990) (internal quotations and citations omitted). For application of these principles, see *Montgomery,* slip op. at 14–17 (holding that the Court, in interpreting the Eighth Amendment to prohibit mandatory life without parole for juvenile

Political Questions

The Doctrine Reappears.—

[P. 776, n.655, delete "*See also* Davis v. Bandemer, 478 U.S. 109 (1986) (challenge to political gerrymandering is justiciable). *But see* Vieth v. Jubelirer, 541 U.S. 267 (2004) (no workable standard has been found for measuring burdens on representational rights imposed by political gerrymandering)."]

[P. 777, before paragraph starting "In short, the political question doctrine . . .", add new paragraph:]

In *Rucho v. Common Cause*, the Supreme Court articulated a slightly different statement of the political question doctrine in holding that claims of unconstitutionally partisan gerrymandering—that is, claims that the boundaries of a legislative district were impermissibly based on partisan considerations—were nonjusticiable.[339] Quoting a prior opinion from Justice Kennedy, the Court said that "[a]ny standard for resolving such claims must be grounded in a 'limited and precise rationale' and be 'clear, manageable, and politically neutral.'"[340] After looking to the Constitution and to various tests proposed by the parties, the *Rucho* Court concluded that it could identify no "limited and precise standard that is judicially discernable and manageable"[341] for evaluating "when partisan activity goes too far."[342] Viewing plaintiffs in political gerrymandering cases to be asking "courts to make their own political judgment about how much representation particular political parties *deserve*," the Court held that "federal courts are not equipped to apportion political power as a matter of fairness."[343] Chief Justice Roberts's opinion for the Court emphasized that intervening in disputes over partisan redistricting meant that federal courts would be injecting themselves "into the most heated partisan issues,"[344] and that courts "would risk assuming political, not legal, responsibility for a process that often produces ill will and

---

offenders, "did announce a new substantive rule" because the prohibition necessarily placed beyond the power of a state a particular punishment with respect to the "vast majority of juvenile offenders"). *See also Welch*, slip op. at 9–11 (holding that a conviction under a statute that was later found to be void for vagueness is a substantive rule, as the invalidity of the law under the Due Process Clause altered the "range of conduct or class of persons that the law punishes."); *Schriro*, 542 U.S. at 352 (holding that the requirement that aggravating factors justifying the death penalty be found by the jury was a new procedural rule that did not apply retroactively).

[339] 588 U.S. ___, Nos. 18-422, 18-726, slip op. at 34 (2019).

[340] *Id.* at 15 (quoting Vieth v. Jubelirer, 541 U.S. 267, 306, 308 (2004) (Kennedy, J., concurring)).

[341] *Id.* at 21.

[342] *Id.* at 26; *see also id.* at 28 (concluding that the Court was left with an "unanswerable question": "How much political motivation and effect is too much?" (quoting *Vieth*, 541 U.S. at 296–97 (plurality opinion))).

[343] *Id.* at 17.

[344] *Id.* (quoting Davis v. Bandemer, 478 U.S. 109, 145 (1986) (O'Connor, J., concurring in the judgment) (internal quotation mark omitted)).

distrust."[345] It was against this background that the Court concluded that it was "vital" to "act only in accord with especially clear standards."[346]

[P. 777, delete paragraph starting "In short, the political question doctrine . . ."]

JUDICIAL REVIEW

Limitations on the Exercise of Judicial Review

Disallowance by Statutory Interpretation.—

[P. 790, delete n.724 and substitute with:]

Bond v. United States, 572 U.S. 844 (2014); United States v. X-Citement Video, Inc., 513 U.S. 64, 69 (1994); Rust v. Sullivan, 500 U.S. 173, 190–91 (1991); Pub. Citizen v. DOJ, 491 U.S. 440, 465–67 (1989) (quoting Crowell v. Benson, 285 U.S. 22, 62 (1932)); Edward J. DeBartolo Corp. v. Fla. Gulf Coast Bldg. & Constr. Trades Council, 485 U.S. 568, 575 (1988).

[P. 791, delete n.729 and substitute with:]

See Whole Woman's Health v. Hellerstedt, 579 U.S. ___, No. 15-274, slip op. at 37 (2016) (noting that while as a "general matter" courts will honor a legislature's preference with regard to severability, severability clauses do not impose a requirement on courts that are confronted with *facially* unconstitutional statutory provisions, as such an approach would "inflict enormous costs on both courts and litigants" in parsing out what remains of the statute); *see also* Ayotte v. Planned Parenthood of N. New Eng., 546 U.S. 320, 329 (2006) (discussing how a severability clause is not grounds for a court to "devise a judicial remedy that . . . entail[s] quintessentially legislative work."); Reno v. ACLU, 521 U.S. 844, 884–85 n.49 (1997) (noting the limits on how broadly a court can read a severability clause); *see generally* Dorchy v. Kansas, 264 U.S. 286, 290 (1924) (concluding that a severability clause is an "aid merely; not an inexorable command.")

Stare Decisis in Constitutional Law.—

[P. 791, delete n.730 and substitute with:]

Burnet v. Coronado Oil & Gas Co., 285 U.S. 393, 406–08 (1932) (Brandeis, J., dissenting), *overruled by* Helvering v. Mountain Producers Corp., 303 U.S. 376 (1938). *See also, e.g.,* Ramos v. Louisiana, 140 S. Ct. 1390, 1405 (2020) ("[T]he doctrine [of stare decisis] is 'at its weakest when we interpret the Constitution[.]'" (quoting Agostini v. Felton, 521 U.S. 203, 235 (1997))).

---

[345] *Id.* (quoting *Vieth*, 541 U.S. at 307 (Kennedy, J., concurring) (internal quotation mark omitted)).

[346] *Id.*

JURISDICTION OF SUPREME COURT AND INFERIOR FEDERAL COURTS

Cases Arising Under the Constitution, Laws, and Treaties of the United States

When a Case Arises Under.—

[P. 794, after sentence ending ". . . more restrictive course.", add new footnote:]

> *See* Merrill Lynch, Pierce, Fenner & Smith Inc. v. Manning, 578 U.S. ___, No. 14-1132, slip op. at 9–10 (2016) ("This Court has long read the words 'arising under' in Article III to extend quite broadly, to all cases in which a federal question is an ingredient of the action . . . . In the statutory context, however, we . . . give those same words a narrower scope in the light of § 1331's history, the demands of reason and coherence, and the dictates of sound judicial policy.") (internal brackets, citations, and quotations omitted).

Federal Questions Resulting from Special Jurisdictional Grants.—

[P. 799, delete n.782 and substitute with:]

> For example, when federal statutes create new duties without explicitly creating private federal remedies for their violation, the willingness of the federal courts to infer private causes of action will implicate the federal courts' workload. During the mid-20th century, the Court would imply causes of action that were not explicit in the text of a statute as a routine matter. *See, e.g.,* Allen v. State Bd. of Elections, 393 U.S. 544, 557 (1969) ("We have previously held that a federal statute passed to protect a class of citizens, although not specifically authorizing members of the protected class to institute suit, nevertheless implied a private right of action."); Sullivan v. Little Hunting Park, Inc., 396 U.S. 229, 239 (1969) ("The existence of a statutory right implies the existence of all necessary and appropriate remedies."). In the late 1970s, the Court began to move away from such an approach, *see* Cannon v. *University of Chicago,* 441 U.S. 677, 717 (1979) ("When Congress intends private litigants to have a cause of action to support their statutory rights, the far better course is for it to specify as much when it creates those rights."), and more recently has instead held that for a court to recognize a statutory cause of action, the statute itself must "displa[y] an intent to create" both a private right and a private remedy. *See* Alexander v. Sandoval, 532 U.S. 275, 286 (2001).
>
> In the context of constitutional rights, the Court in 1971 recognized (in the absence of any federal statute) an implied damages remedy to compensate persons injured by federal officers who violated the Fourth Amendment's prohibition against unreasonable searches and seizures. *See* Bivens v. Six Unknown Named Agents, 403 U.S. 388, 397 (1971). Since *Bivens,* the Court has recognized a similar remedy for a violation of the equal protection component of the Fifth Amendment's Due Process Clause, *see Davis v. Passman,* 442 U.S. 228, 248–49 (1979), and an Eighth Amendment Cruel and Unusual Punishment Clause violation, *see Carlson v. Green,* 446 U.S. 14, 19 (1980). However, these three cases are anomalous and represent the "only instances in which the Court has approved of an implied damages remedy under the Constitution itself." *See* Ziglar v. Abbasi, 137 S. Ct. 1843, 1855 (2017). Instead, in a series of cases, the Court has rejected extending the *Bivens* remedy to other constitutional contexts. *See* Minneci v. Pollard, 565 U.S. 118, 120 (2012) (rejecting an Eighth Amendment-based *Bivens* claim against employees of a privately operated federal prison); Wilkie v. Robbins, 551 U.S. 537, 547–48, 562 (2007) (refusing to recognize a *Bivens* claim against officials of the Bureau of Land Management accused of harassment and intimidation aimed at extracting an easement across private property in violation of the Fourth and Fifth Amendments); Correctional Services Corp. v. Malesko, 534 U.S. 61 (2001) (refusing to extend *Bivens* to allow recovery against a private corporation operating a halfway house under contract with the Bureau of Prisons); FDIC v. Meyer, 510 U.S. 471 (1994) (declining to imply

a *Bivens* cause of action directly against an agency of the Federal Government); Schweiker v. Chilicki, 487 U.S. 412 (1988) (refusing to infer a damages action against individual government employees alleged to have violated due process in their handling of Social Security applications); United States v. Stanley, 483 U.S. 669, 671-72, 683–84 (1987) (holding that *Bivens* does not extend to any claim incident to military service); Bush v. Lucas, 462 U.S. 367, 389 (1983) (declining to create a *Bivens* remedy against individual Government officials for a First Amendment violation arising in the context of federal employment); Chappell v. Wallace, 462 U.S. 296, 298 (1983) (declining to extend *Bivens* to claims by military personnel against superior officers). Recognizing that "it is a significant step under separation-of-powers principles for a court to determine that it has the authority . . . to create and enforce a cause of action for damages against federal officials in order to remedy a constitutional violation," the Court in *Ziglar v. Abbasi,* without overturning *Bivens,* held that if a case is different in a meaningful way from the three previous instances in which the Court recognized a damages remedy, *Bivens* should not be extended to a new context if there are "special factors" counseling hesitation. *See Ziglar,* 137 S. Ct. at 1856–60. In particular, if there are reasons to think that Congress might have questioned the need for a damages remedy, courts must refrain from creating such a remedy. *Id.* at 1856. Moreover, the Court supported its conclusion by noting that courts generally are not well-suited, absent congressional action or instruction, to consider and weigh the costs and benefits of allowing a damages action to proceed. *Id.* at 1857. The Court cited *Ziglar* in 2020 when it declined to extend *Bivens* to the "markedly new" context of a claim based on a U.S. border patrol agent's cross-border shooting of a Mexican teenager. Hernández v. Mesa, 140 S. Ct. 735, 739, 742–743 (2020). In the Court's view, such an extension would have "foreign relations and national security implications." *Id.* at 739, 744–47. The Court also reasoned that declining to extend a *Bivens* remedy was warranted because when Congress authorized damages against federal officials in other statutes, Congress precluded claims based on conduct occurring abroad. *Id.* at 749–50.

In addition "federal common law" may exist in a number of areas where federal interests are involved and federal courts may take cognizance of such suits under their "arising under" jurisdiction. *See, e.g.,* Illinois v. City of Milwaukee, 406 U.S. 91, 100 (1972); Int'l Paper Co. v. Ouellette, 479 U.S. 481, 488 (1987). The Court, however, has been somewhat wary of finding "federal common law" in the absence of some congressional authorization to formulate substantive rules, *see Texas Industries v. Radcliff Materials,* 451 U.S. 630, 640 (1981), and Congress may always statutorily displace the judicially created law. *City of Milwaukee,* 451 U.S. at 107.

Supreme Court Review of State Court Decisions.—

[P. 805, at end of n.816, add:]

Whereas declining to review judgments of state courts that rest on an adequate and independent determination of *state* law protects the sovereignty of states, the Court has emphasized that review of state court decisions that invalidate state laws based on interpretations of *federal* law, "far from *undermining* state autonomy, is the only way to *vindicate* it" because a correction of a state court's federal errors necessarily returns power to the state government. *See* Kansas v. Carr, 577 U.S. ___, No. 14-449, slip op. at 9 (2016) (quoting Kansas v. Marsh, 548 U.S. 163, 184 (2006) (Scalia, J., concurring)).

Cases of Admiralty and Maritime Jurisdiction

Power of Congress to Modify Maritime Law.—

[P. 812, after sentence starting "The law administered by federal courts . . .", add new footnote:]

See, e.g., Dutra Group v. Batterton, 588 U.S. ___, No. 18-266, slip op. at 1 (2019).

[P. 812, after sentence starting "The law administered by federal courts . . .", add new sentence:]

The Supreme Court has said that courts exercising common-law authority in this area of the law should be guided by legislative enactments.[347] Courts may only "depart from the policies found in the statutory scheme in discrete instances based on long-established history," and must "do so cautiously."[348]

Admiralty and Maritime Cases.—

[P. 814, after n.868, add:]

products liability suits,[349]

[P. 814, delete sentence starting "The Court has expressed a willingness . . ." and n.870]

Admiralty and Federalism.—

[P. 822, at end of n.918, add:]

See also, e.g., Dutra Group v. Batterton, 588 U.S. ___, No. 18-266, slip op. at 4–8 (2019) (tracing the development of unseaworthiness claims).

Cases to Which the United States is a Party

Suits Against United States Officials.—

[P. 832, n.977, delete sentence starting "An emerging variant is . . ." and ending " . . . 457 U.S. 800 (1982)."]

Suits Against Government Corporations.—

[P. 832, at end of n.979, add:]

Id. at 250. Further, the Court recognized that under some circumstances, constitutional concerns might give rise to "implied exceptions" to "sue and be sued" clauses. *Id.* at 245. However, in *Thacker v. Tennessee Valley Authority*, the Supreme Court declined to read a constitutionally based objection into such a clause. 587 U.S. ___, No. 17-1201, slip op. at 7 (2019). The government had argued that allowing litigants to challenge the performance of "discretionary functions" would violate "separation-of-powers principles" by subjecting the agency to "judicial second-guessing." *Id.* at 6 (internal quotation marks omitted). The Court rejected this argument, explaining that Congress holds the power to determine federal agencies' immunity and that Congress's exercise of that power, even though it may subject the government to the judicial process, "raises no separation of powers problems." *Id.* at 7–8. The Court left open the possibility that in a future case, "suits challenging the [government] entity's *governmental* activity"—as opposed to its *commercial* activity—"may

---

[347] Miles v. Apex Marine Corp., 498 U.S. 19, 27 (1990).

[348] *Dutra Group*, No. 18-266, slip op. at 1–2.

[349] *See, e.g.*, Air & Liquid Sys. Corp. v. DeVries, 139 S. Ct. 986, 993 (2019); E. River S.S. Corp. v. Transamerica Delaval, 476 U.S. 858, 865 (1986).

run into an implied limit on its sue-and-be-sued clause." *Id.* at 9. But the Court emphasized that this immunity would be available "only if it is 'clearly shown' that prohibiting the 'type[] of suit [at issue] is necessary to avoid grave interference' with a governmental function's performance." *Id.* (quoting *Burr*, 309 U.S. at 245).

Suits Between Two or More States

Modern Types of Suits Between States.—

[P. 834, after sentence ending "... but they have not been confined to any one region.", add new footnote:]

See, e.g., Florida v. Georgia, 585 U.S. ___, No. 142, Orig., slip op. at 1 (2018) ("This case concerns the proper apportionment of the water of an interstate river basin. Florida, a downstream State, brought this lawsuit against Georgia, an upstream State, claiming that Georgia has denied it an equitable share of the basin's waters.").

[P. 834, after sentence ending "... between conflicting state interests.", add new footnote:]

See also Florida, 585 U.S. at ___, slip op. at 10 ("Where, as here, the Court is asked to resolve an interstate water dispute raising questions beyond the interpretation of specific language of an interstate compact, the doctrine of equitable apportionment governs our inquiry." (citing Colorado v. New Mexico, 459 U.S. 176, 183 (1982); Virginia v. Maryland, 540 U.S. 56, 74 n.9 (2003) ("Federal common law governs interstate bodies of water, ensuring that the water is equitably apportioned between the States and that neither State harms the other's interest in the river."))).

[P. 834, before sentence starting "In *New Jersey v. New York*, . . .", add new paragraph break.]

[PP. 834–35, remove quotation marks around sentence starting "A river is more . . ." and ending ". . . as best they may be." and block quote the entire quotation.]

[P. 835, after n.997, add new paragraph:]

More recently, in *Florida v. Georgia*, the Supreme Court summarized the "several related but more specific sets of principles" that govern the doctrine of equitable apportionment in interstate disputes between two states.[350] *Florida v. Georgia* involved a dispute brought by Florida, the downstream state, against Georgia over the division of water

---

[350] 585 U.S. ___, No. 142, Orig., slip op. at 10 (2018). Specifically, when asked to resolve such a dispute under the doctrine of equitable apportionment, the Court should consider the following principles: (1) that the two states "possess an equal right to make a *reasonable use* of the waters of the stream"; (2) that "the Court's 'effort always is to secure an equitable apportionment without quibbling over formulas' . . . [and w]here '[b]oth States have real and substantial interests in the River,' those interests 'must be reconciled as best they may be'"; (3) that, "in light of the sovereign status and 'equal dignity' of States, . . . the complaining State must demonstrate that it has suffered a 'threatened invasion of rights' that is 'of serious magnitude'"; and (4) that "where a complaining State meets its 'initial burden of showing 'real or substantial injury,' this Court, recalling that equitable apportionment is 'flexible,' not 'formulaic,' will seek to 'arrive at a just and equitable apportionment of an interstate stream' by 'consider[ing] 'all relevant factors.'" *Id.* at 11–14 (citations omitted).

from an interstate river basin known as the Apalachicola-Chattahoochee-Flint River Basin.[351] At the outset, the Court noted that, "given the complexity of many water-division cases, the need to secure equitable solutions, the need to respect the sovereign status of the States, and the importance of finding flexible solutions to multi-factor problems, we typically appoint a Special Master and benefit from detailed factual findings."[352] The Court remanded the case to the Special Master assigned to the dispute, concluding that the Special Master had not applied the proper standard to evaluate the case.[353] The Court further advised that, "[c]onsistent with the principles that guide our inquiry in this context, answers need not be 'mathematically precise or based on definite present and future conditions.' Approximation and reasonable estimates may prove 'necessary to protect the equitable rights of a State.' . . . Flexibility and approximation are often the keys to success in our efforts to resolve water disputes between sovereign States that neither Congress 'nor the legislature of either State' has been able to resolve."[354]

The Problem of Enforcement: Virginia v. West Virginia.—

[P. 838, after paragraph ending ". . . agreement with Virginia to pay it.", add new section "Enforcement Authority Includes Ordering Disgorgements and Reformation of Certain Agreements":]

Enforcement Authority Includes Ordering Disgorgement and Reformation of Certain Agreements.—More recently, the Court, noting that proceedings under its original jurisdiction are "basically equitable," has taken the view that its enforcement authority encompasses ordering disgorgement of part of one state's gain from its breach of an interstate compact, as well as reforming certain agreements adopted by the states.[355] In so doing, the Court emphasized that its enforcement authority derives both from its "inherent authority" to apportion interstate streams between states equitably and from Congress's approval of interstate compacts. As to its inherent authority, the Court noted that states bargain for water rights "in the shadow of" the Court's broad power to apportion them equitably and it is "difficult to conceive" that a state would agree to enter

---

[351] *Id.* at 1–2.

[352] *Id.* at 14.

[353] *Id.* at 15.

[354] *Id.* at 37 (quoting Idaho *ex rel.* Evans v. Oregon, 462 U.S. 1017, 1026 (1983); Virginia v. West Virginia, 220 U.S. 1, 27 (1911)).

[355] Kansas v. Nebraska, 574 U.S. ___, No. 126, Orig., slip op. at 14–17 (2015). Equity is "the system of law or body of principles originating in the English Court of Chancery." BLACK'S LAW DICTIONARY 656 (10th ed. 2014). Persons who sought equitable relief "sought to do justice in cases for which there was no adequate remedy at common law," A.H. MANCHESTER, MODERN LEGAL HISTORY OF ENGLAND AND WALES, 1750–1950 135–36 (1980), i.e., cases in which the English courts of law could afford no relief to a plaintiff. While eventually courts of law and courts providing equitable relief merged into a single court in most jurisdictions, an equitable remedy refers to a remedy that equity courts would have historically granted. *See* 1 DAN B. DOBBS, DOBBS LAW OF REMEDIES: DAMAGES—EQUITY—RESTITUTION § 2.1(2), at 59–61 (2d ed. 1993). Compensatory damages are a classic "legal" remedy, whereas an injunction is a classic "equitable" remedy. *See* RICHARD L. HASEN, REMEDIES 141 (2d ed. 2010).

an agreement as to water rights if the Court lacked the power to enforce the agreement.[356] The Court similarly reasoned that its remedial authority "gains still greater force" because a compact between the states, "having received Congress's blessing, counts as federal law."[357] The Court stated, however, that an interstate compact's "legal status" as federal law could also limit the Court's enforcement power because the Court cannot order relief that is inconsistent with a compact's express terms.[358]

Controversies Between Citizens of Different States

The Law Applied in Diversity Cases.—

[P. 855, delete sentence starting "Despite, then, Justice Brandeis' assurance . . ." and substitute with:]

> As a result, notwithstanding Justice Brandeis's oft-quoted statement that there is "no federal general common law,"[359] there are areas of law where "federal judges may appropriately craft the rule of decision."[360] Nonetheless, because legislative power is vested in Congress, federal common law plays a "necessarily modest role"[361] under the Constitution, and such common lawmaking must at a minimum be "necessary to protect uniquely federal interests."[362]

Clause 2. Original and Appellate Jurisdiction

THE ORIGINAL JURISDICTION OF THE SUPREME COURT

[P. 861, at end of n.1154, add:]

> *Cf.* Florida v. Georgia, 585 U.S. ___, No. 142, Orig., slip op. at 3 (2018). This Court has recognized for more than a century its inherent authority, as part of the Constitution's grant of original jurisdiction, to equitably apportion interstate streams between States.' But we have long noted our 'preference' that States 'settle their controversies by mutual accommodation and agreement.'" (quoting Kansas v. Nebraska, 574 U.S. ___, No. 126, Orig., slip op. at 7 (2015); Arizona v. California, 373 U.S. 546, 564 (1963))).

---

[356] *See Kansas,* slip op. at 8 (quoting Texas v. New Mexico, 462 U.S. 554, 567 (1983)).

[357] *Id.*

[358] *Id.*

[359] *See* Erie R.R. Co. v. Tompkins, 304 U.S. 64, 78 (1938).

[360] *See* Rodriguez v. FDIC, 140 S. Ct. 713, 717 (2020).

[361] *Id.*

[362] Texas Indus., Inc. v. Radcliff Materials, Inc., 451 U.S. 630, 640 (1981) (quoting Banco Nacional de Cuba, 376 U.S. at 426) (internal quotation marks omitted); *see, e.g., Rodriguez,* 140 S. Ct. at 717–18 (concluding that a federal common law rule inappropriately developed by the lower courts concerning allocation of a refund to an affiliated group of corporations did not implicate any significant federal interests and did not necessitate discarding the application of state law with respect to the tax dispute).

POWER OF CONGRESS TO CONTROL FEDERAL COURTS

The Theory of Plenary Congressional Control

Appellate Jurisdiction.—

[P. 864, after sentence ending ". . . has been applied in later cases.", change period to comma and after n.1166, add:]

including recently in *Patchak v. Zinke*.[363]

Jurisdiction of the Inferior Federal Courts.—

[P. 866, after n.1178, add new paragraph break.]

[P. 867, after n.1182, add new sentences:]

More recently, in *Patchak v. Zinke*, the Court confirmed that "Congress' greater power to create lower federal courts includes its lesser power to 'limit the jurisdiction of those Courts.' So long as Congress does not violate other constitutional provisions, its 'control over the jurisdiction of the federal courts' is 'plenary.'"[364] In *Patchak*, a neighboring landowner challenged the authority of the Secretary of the Interior to invoke the Indian Reorganization Act[365] and take into trust a property on behalf of the Match-E-Be-Nash-She-Wish Band of Pottawatomi Indians, which planned to build a casino on the property.[366] While the suit was on remand in a district court, Congress enacted the Gun Lake Trust Land Reaffirmation Act, which "reaffirmed as trust land" the Tribe's Property and provided that "an action . . . relating to [that] land shall not be filed or maintained in a Federal court and shall be promptly dismissed."[367] In response, the district court dismissed the suit, and the U.S. Court of Appeals for the D.C. Circuit affirmed.[368] On appeal, the Supreme Court affirmed the dismissal, holding that the Gun Lake Act did not violate Article III.[369] In so holding, the Court clarified that "Congress generally does not infringe the judicial power when it strips jurisdiction because, with limited exceptions, a congressional grant of jurisdiction is a

---

[363] 583 U.S. ___, No. 16-498, slip op. at 7–8 (2018) (plurality opinion) ("Congress' greater power to create lower federal courts includes its lesser power to 'limit the jurisdiction of those Courts.' So long as Congress does not violate other constitutional provisions, its 'control over the jurisdiction of the federal courts' is 'plenary.'" (quoting United States v. Hudson, 11 U.S. (7 Cranch) 32, 33 (1812); Brotherhood of R.R. Trainmen Enter. Lodge, No. 27 v. Toledo, P. & W.R. Co., 321 U.S. 50, 63–64 (1944))).

[364] *Id.* at 7–8 (2018) (plurality opinion) (quoting Hudson, 11 U.S. (7 Cranch) at 33; *Trainmen*, 321 U.S. at 63–64).

[365] 25 U.S.C. § 5108.

[366] *Patchak*, slip op. at 1–2.

[367] Gun Lake Trust Land Reaffirmation Act, Pub. L. No. 113-79, § 2, 128 Stat. 1913, 1913–14 (2014).

[368] *Patchak*, slip op. at 4.

[369] *Id.*

prerequisite to the exercise of judicial power."[370] Furthermore, the Court stated, "when Congress strips federal courts of jurisdiction, it exercises a valid legislative power no less than when it lays taxes, coins money, declares war, or invokes any other power that the Constitution grants it."[371]

The Theory Reconsidered

[P. 872, after n.1208, delete sentence starting "*Klein* thus stands for the proposition . . ." and substitute with:]

While the precise import of *Klein*—with its broad language prohibiting Congress prescribing a "rule of decision" that unduly invades core judicial functions—has puzzled legal scholars,[372] it appears that *Klein* broadly stands for the proposition that Congress may not usurp the judiciary's power to interpret and apply the law by directing a court "how pre-existing law applies to particular circumstances" before it.[373] Few laws, however, have been struck down for improperly prescribing a "rule of decision" that a court must follow, and the Court has, in more recent years, declined to interpret *Klein* as inhibiting Congress from "amend[ing] applicable law."[374]

Instead, the Court has recognized that Congress may, without running afoul of *Klein*, direct courts to apply newly enacted legislation to pending civil cases, even when such an application would alter the outcome in the case.[375] Moreover, the general permissibility under Article

---

[370] *Id.* (citing Steel Co. v. Citizens for Better Env't, 523 U.S. 83, 94–95 (1998)).

[371] *Id.* Moreover, not only does Congress have the power to restrict the jurisdiction of lower courts, it also has significant discretion in structuring how appellate courts review lower court judgments. *See* Ayestas v. Davis, 584 U.S. ___, No. 16-6795, slip op. at 14 (2018) (rejecting the argument that appellate review must occur through the traditional Article III hierarchy, as "[n]othing in the Constitution ties Congress to the typical structure of appellate review established by statute.").

[372] *See* Bank Markazi v. Peterson, 578 U.S. ___, No. 14-770, slip op. at 13 & n.18 (2016) (noting various secondary sources describing the *Klein* opinion as being "deeply puzzling," "delphic," and "baffling").

[373] *See id.* at 12–13 & n.17. The Court in *Bank Markazi* noted that the precise constitutional concern in *Klein* was tied to the President's pardon power. *Id.* at 14–15. Specifically, the Court viewed *Klein* as a case in which the Congress, lacking the authority to impair *directly* the effect of a pardon, attempted to alter *indirectly* the legal effect of a pardon by directing a court to a particular outcome, and, in so doing, was compelling a court to a result that required the judiciary to act unconstitutionally. *See id.* at 15 & n.19 (noting the constitutional infirmity identified by *Klein* was that the challenged law "attempted to direct the result without altering the legal standards governing the effect of a pardon—standards Congress was powerless to prescribe.").

[374] *See, e.g., id.* at 15 (holding that *Klein*'s prohibition "cannot" be taken "at face value" because Congress has the power to "make valid statutes retroactively applicable to pending cases") (quoting R. FALLON, J. MANNING, D. MELTZER, & D. SHAPIRO, HART AND WECHSLER'S THE FEDERAL COURTS AND THE FEDERAL SYSTEM 324 (7th ed. 2015)); Plaut v. Spendthrift Farm, Inc., 514 U.S. 211, 218 (1995) (noting that *Klein*'s "prohibition does not take hold when Congress 'amend[s] applicable law'") (quoting Robertson v. Seattle Audubon Soc'y, 503 U.S. 429, 441 (1992)); *Robertson*, 503 U.S. at 437–38, 441.

[375] *See Bank Markazi*, slip op. at 16. While retroactive legislation, standing alone, may not violate *Klein*'s prohibition, other constitutional provisions—including Article I's

III of legislation affecting pending litigation extends to statutes that direct courts to apply a new legal standard even when the underlying facts of a case are undisputed, functionally leaving the court with nothing to decide. For example, in *Bank Markazi v. Peterson*, the Court upheld a provision of the Iran Threat Reduction and Syria Human Rights Act of 2012 that made a designated set of assets available for recovery to satisfy a discrete and finite set of default judgments, notwithstanding the fact that the change in the underlying law made the result of the pending case all but a "forgone conclusion."[376] In addition, the *Bank Markazi* Court, recognizing Congress's authority to legislate on "one or a very small number of specific subjects," rejected the argument that particularized congressional legislation that alters the substantive law governing a specific case—standing alone—impinges on the judicial power in violation of Article III.[377] The Court held as such, even though the legislation in question identified a case by caption and docket number and did not apply to similar enforcement actions involving any other assets.[378] Accordingly, *Klein*'s prohibition on congressionally prescribed "rule[s] of decision" appears to be limited to instances where Congress "fails to supply any new legal standard effectuating the lawmakers' reasonable policy judgment" and instead merely compels a court to make particular findings or results under the old law.[379]

In *Patchak v. Zinke*, the Court reiterated the distinction "between permissible exercises of the legislative power and impermissible infringements of the judicial power."[380] In *Patchak*, a neighboring landowner challenged the authority of the Secretary of the Interior to invoke the Indian Reorganization Act[381] and take into trust a property on behalf of the Match-E-Be-Nash-She-Wish Band of Pottawatomi Indians, which planned to build a casino on the property.[382] While the suit was on

---

prohibitions on ex post facto laws and bills of attainder and the Fifth Amendment's Due Process and Takings Clauses—may otherwise restrict Congress's ability to legislate retroactively. *See id.* (quoting Landgraf v. USI Film Prods., 511 U.S. 244, 266–67 (1994)). *See also* Patchak v. Zinke, 583 U.S. ___, No. 16-498, slip op. at 5 (2018) (plurality opinion) ("[T]he legislative power is the power to make law, and Congress can make laws that apply retroactively to pending lawsuits, even when it effectively ensures that one side wins.").

[376] *Bank Markazi*, slip op. at 16; *see also Robertson*, 503 U.S. at 434–39 (upholding a statute permitting timber harvesting, altering the outcome of pending litigation over the permissibility of such harvesting).

[377] *Bank Markazi*, slip op. at 21.

[378] *Id.* The Court's holding in *Bank Markazi* may have been influenced by the case touching on foreign affairs, "a domain in which the controlling role of the political branches is both necessary and proper." *Id.* at 22. In concluding its opinion in *Bank Markazi*, the Court, citing to long-established historical practices in the realm of foreign affairs, "stress[ed]" that congressional regulation of claims over foreign-state property generally does not "inva[de] upon the Article III judicial power." *Id.* at 22–23.

[379] *See id.* at 18–19. For example, the *Bank Markazi* Court noted that a statute that directs that in a hypothetical case—"Smith v. Jones"—that "Smith wins," would violate the principle of *Klein*. Nonetheless, Congress can alter the underlying *substantive* law affecting such a case, allowing Congress to accomplish *indirectly* what the rule of *Klein directly* prohibits. *See id.* at 12–13 n.17.

[380] *Patchak*, slip op. at 5–6.

[381] 25 U.S.C. § 5108.

[382] *Patchak*, slip op. at 1–2, (plurality opinion).

remand in a district court, Congress enacted the Gun Lake Trust Land Reaffirmation Act, which "reaffirmed as trust land" the Tribe's Property and provided that "an action . . . relating to [that] land shall not be filed or maintained in a Federal court and shall be promptly dismissed."[383] In response, the district court dismissed the suit, and the U.S. Court of Appeals for the D.C. Circuit affirmed.[384] On appeal, the Supreme Court affirmed the dismissal, holding that the Gun Lake Act did not violate Article III.[385]

Citing *Plaut v. Spendthrift Farm, Inc.*, a plurality of the Court restated that Congress may not exercise the judicial power, but its legislative power permits Congress to make laws that apply retroactively to pending lawsuits, even when the law effectively ensures that one side will win.[386] The plurality opinion stated that "[t]o distinguish between permissible exercises of the legislative power and impermissible infringements of the judicial power, this Court's precedents establish the following rule: Congress violates Article III when it 'compel[s] . . . findings or results under old law.' But Congress does not violate Article III when it 'changes the law.'"[387] In sum, when congressional action compels an Article III court to make certain findings under old law, the plurality agreed with the dissenters that Congress cannot usurp the judiciary's power by saying, for example, "'[i]n *Smith v. Jones*, Smith wins.'"[388] Furthermore, while the Court could not agree on a broader principle of when a facially neutral law is permissible, four Justices concluded that a facially neutral law that strips the courts of jurisdiction did not raise an Article III concern, even when the natural result of the law ensured that the government would win the only pending case the law would implicate. Under these principles, the Court concluded that in the Gun Lake Act Congress changed the law, which was "well within Congress' authority and d[id] not violate Article III."[389]

---

[383] Gun Lake Trust Land Reaffirmation Act, Pub. L. No. 113-79, § 2, 128 Stat. 1913, 1913–14 (2014).

[384] *Patchak*, slip op. at 4.

[385] *Id.*

[386] *Id.* at 5 ("The separation of powers, among other things, prevents Congress from exercising the judicial power. One way that Congress can cross the line from legislative power to judicial power is by 'usurp[ing] a court's power to interpret and apply the law to the [circumstances] before it.' . . . At the same time, the legislative power is the power to make law, and Congress can make laws that apply retroactively to pending lawsuits, even when it effectively ensures that one side wins." (citing Plaut v. Spendthrift Farm, Inc., 514 U.S. 211, 218 (1995)) (quoting Bank Markazi v. Peterson, 578 U.S. ___, No. 14-770, slip op. at 12 (2016))).

[387] *Id.* at 5–6 (quoting Robertson v. Seattle Audubon Soc., 503 U.S. 429, 438 (1992); *Plaut*, 514 U.S. at 218).

[388] *Id.* at 5.

[389] *Id.* at 6.

FEDERAL-STATE COURT RELATIONS

Conflicts of Jurisdiction: Rules of Accommodation

Abstention.—

[P. 883, at end of n.1272, delete "." and substitute with:]

; Sprint Commc'ns, Inc. v. Jacobs, 571 U.S. 69 (2013).

Conflicts of Jurisdiction: Federal Court Interference with State Courts

Federal Restraint of State Courts by Injunctions.—

[P. 892, delete last paragraph and substitute with:]

Beyond criminal prosecutions, the Court extended *Younger*'s general directive to bar interference with pending state civil cases that are akin to criminal prosecutions.[390] *Younger* abstention was also found appropriate when a judgment debtor in a state civil case sought to enjoin a state court order to enforce the judgment.[391] The Court further applied *Younger*'s principles to bar federal court interference with state administrative proceedings of a judicial nature, in which important state interests were at stake.[392] Nonetheless, the Court has emphasized that "only exceptional circumstances justify a federal court's refusal to decide a case in deference to the States."[393] In *Sprint Communications, Inc. v. Jacobs*,[394] the Court made clear that federal forbearance under *Younger* was limited to three discrete types of state proceedings: (1) ongoing state criminal prosecutions; (2) particular state civil proceedings that are akin to criminal prosecutions; and (3) civil proceedings involving orders uniquely in furtherance of the state courts' ability to perform their judicial functions.[395] In so doing, the *Sprint Communications* Court clarified that

---

[390] Middlesex Cty. Ethics Comm. v. Garden State Bar Ass'n, 457 U.S. 423 (1982); Moore v. Sims, 442 U.S. 415 (1979); Trainor v. Hernandez, 431 U.S. 434 (1977); Juidice v. Vail, 430 U.S. 327 (1977); Huffman v. Pursue, Ltd., 420 U.S. 592 (1975) (state action to close adult theater under the state's nuisance statute and to seize and sell personal property used in the theater's operations).

[391] Pennzoil Co. v. Texaco, Inc., 481 U.S. 1 (1987) (holding that federal abstention was warranted in a federal court action to block a state court order issued under the state's "lien and bond" authority). It was "the State's [particular] interest in protecting 'the authority of the judicial system, so that its orders and judgments are not rendered nugatory' "that merited abstention, and not merely a general state interest in protecting ongoing civil proceedings from federal interference. *Id.* at 14 n.12 (quoting *Juidice*, 430 U.S. at 336 n.12).

[392] Oh. Civil Rights Comm'n v. Dayton Christian Sch., Inc., 477 U.S. 619 (1986). The "judicial in nature" requirement is more fully explicated in *New Orleans Public Service, Inc. v. Council of City of New Orleans*, 491 U.S. 350 (1989).

[393] *See New Orleans Pub. Serv., Inc*, 491 U.S. at 368.

[394] 571 U.S. 69 (2013).

[395] *Id.* at 72–73.

the types of cases previously held to merit abstention under the *Younger* line defined *Younger*'s scope and did not merely exemplify it.[396]

Habeas Corpus: Scope of the Writ.—

[P. 904, delete paragraph starting "For the future . . . "]

---

[396] *Id.* at 78.

ARTICLE IV

Section 1. Full Faith and Credit

JUDGMENTS: EFFECT TO BE GIVEN IN FORUM STATE

Jurisdiction: A Prerequisite to Enforcement of Judgments

[P. 925, n.28, before "Rogers v. Alabama," add:]

> *See* V.L. v. E.L., 577 U.S. ___, No. 15-648, slip op. at 6 (2016) (per curiam) (holding that where a Georgia judgment appeared on its face to have been issued by a court with jurisdiction and there was no established Georgia law to the contrary, the Alabama Supreme Court erred in refusing to grant the Georgia judgment full faith and credit); *see also*

RECOGNITION OF RIGHTS BASED UPON CONSTITUTIONS, STATUTES, COMMON LAW

Development of the Modern Rule

[P. 943, delete n.109 and substitute with:]

> *E.g.,* Allstate Ins. Co. v. Hague, 449 U.S. 302 (1981); Carroll v. Lanza, 349 U.S. 408 (1955); Pacific Emps. Ins. Co. v. Industrial Accident Comm'n, 306 U.S. 493 (1939); Alaska Packers Ass'n v. Industrial Accident Comm'n, 294 U.S. 532 (1935).

[P. 943, delete remainder of section following n.109 and substitute with:]

As such, a state need not "substitute for its own statute, applicable to persons and events within it, the statute of another state reflecting a conflicting and opposed policy," so long as the state does not adopt a "policy of hostility to the" public acts of that other state in so doing.[397] In recent years, the Court has, in protracted litigation by a Nevada citizen in a Nevada court over alleged abusive practices by a California state agency, twice interpreted the "policy of hostility" standard.[398] In 2003, in *Franchise Tax Board of California v. Hyatt,* the Supreme Court held that the Nevada Supreme Court did not exhibit "hostility" in declining to apply a California law affording *complete* immunity to state agencies, because the state high court had, in considering "comity principles with a healthy regard for California's sovereign status," legitimately relied on "the contours of Nevada's own sovereign immunity from suit as a benchmark for its analysis."[399] Thirteen years later, after the case had been remanded and the Nevada Supreme Court had crafted a "special rule" for damages in the matter wherein the California state agency could not rely on the Nevada sovereign immunity statute limiting liability to $50,000, the

---

[397] *See Carroll,* 349 U.S. at 412–13.

[398] *See* Franchise Tax Bd. of Cal. v. Hyatt *(Franchise Tax Bd. II),* 578 U.S. ___, No. 14-1175, slip op. (2016); Franchise Tax Bd. of Cal. v. Hyatt *(Franchise Tax Bd. I),* 538 U.S. 488 (2003).

399 See Franchise Tax Bd. I, 538 U.S. at 499.

Supreme Court reviewed whether the Nevada court's ruling conflicted with the Full Faith and Credit Clause.[400] In contrast to the 2003 ruling, the 2016 ruling held that the Nevada Supreme Court *had* acted in violation of the Full Faith and Credit Clause. Specifically, the High Court concluded that upholding the Nevada Supreme Court's "special rule"—which was supported by a "conclusory statement" respecting California's lack of oversight of its own agencies and was viewed by the Court as reflecting a "policy of hostility to the public Acts' of a sister State"—would allow for a "system of special and discriminatory rules" that conflicted with the Constitution's "vision of 50 individual and equally dignified States."[401] While the *Franchise Tax Board* litigation demonstrates that the "policy of hostility" standard still exists as a threshold inquiry into whether a state is providing full faith and credit to the public acts of a sister state, ordinarily a state has significant discretion in applying their own choice of law provisions in matters arising in that state's courts, and the Court will not engage in any broad "balancing-of-interests" approach to determine the appropriate application of a given state law.[402]

Workers' Compensation Statutes.—

[P. 950, delete n.134 and substitute with:]

See Crider v. Zurich Ins. Co., 380 U.S. 39 (1965); Carroll v. Lanza, 349 U.S. 408 (1955); Cardillo v. Liberty Mutual Co., 330 U.S. 469 (1947); Pacific Emp'rs Ins. Co. v. Indus. Accident Comm'n, 306 U.S. 493 (1939); Alaska Packers Ass'n v. Indus. Accident Comm'n, 294 U.S. 532 (1935).

Section 2. Interstate Comity

Clause 1. State Citizenship: Privileges and Immunities

STATE CITIZENSHIP: PRIVILEGES AND IMMUNITIES

All Privileges and Immunities of Citizens in the Several States

---

[400] *See* Franchise Tax Bd. II, slip op. at 3–4.

[401] *See id.* at 7. In 2018, the Supreme Court granted certiorari for a third time in the litigation to decide whether the Constitution prohibited altogether the Nevada citizen's suit against the California tax board. Franchise Tax Bd. of Cal. v. Hyatt (Franchise Tax Board III), 587 U.S. ___, No. 17-1299, slip op. at 1, 18 (2019). Overruling prior precedent, the Court held that the California agency was entitled to sovereign immunity in Nevada's courts as a constitutional matter. *Id.* at 1, 18; *see also id.* at 3–4 n.1 (explaining that the board had "raised an immunity-based argument from [the] suit's inception, though it was initially based on the Full Faith and Credit Clause").

[402] *Franchise Tax Bd. II*, slip op. at 7–8 (noting that while the Court, in the instant case, could "safely conclude" that Nevada's special rule violated the Constitution, the Court had "abandoned" any broader balancing test with respect to the Full Faith and Credit Clause and "public acts").

[P. 962, at end of first partial paragraph, add new sentence:]

Contrariwise, accessing public records through a state freedom of information act was held not to be a fundamental activity, and a state may limit such access to its own citizens.[403]

Section 3. New States

Clause 1. Admission of New States to Union

DOCTRINE OF THE EQUALITY OF STATES

[P. 972, delete first sentence in last paragraph and substitute with:]

The equal footing doctrine is generally a limitation upon the terms by which Congress admits a state.[404]

[P. 973, delete n.271 and substitute with:]

See Minnesota v. Mille Lacs Band of Chippewa Indians, 526 U.S. 172, 204–05 (1999); Coyle v. Smith, 221 U.S. 559, 573–74 (1911); Bolln v. Nebraska, 176 U.S. 83, 89 (1900); Escanaba Co. v. City of Chicago, 107 U.S. 678, 688 (1882); Withers v. Buckley, 61 U.S. (20 How.) 84, 92 (1857); Pollard's Lessee v. Hagan, 44 U.S. (3 How.) 212, 224–25, 229–30 (1845).

[P. 974, after sentence starting "Similarly, Indian treaty rights . . .", add new footnote:]

Minnesota v. Mille Lacs Band of Chippewa Indians, 526 U.S. 172, 204 (1999).

[P. 974, delete n.281 and substitute with:]

Id. In *Herrera v. Wyoming*, 587 U.S. ___, No. 17-532, slip op. at 10 (2019), the Supreme Court confirmed that *Mille Lacs* "upended" the reasoning of *Ward v. Race Horse*, 163 U.S. 504 (1896), which had applied the "equal footing" doctrine to overrule a treaty granting hunting rights to certain tribes. In *Herrera*, the Court said that "[s]tatehood is irrelevant" to an analysis of whether Congress abrogated "an Indian treaty right . . . . unless a statehood Act otherwise demonstrates Congress' clear intent to abrogate a treaty, or statehood appears as a termination point in the treaty." Slip op. at 10.

---

[403] McBurney v. Young, 569 U.S. 221, 224, 237 (2013). The Court further found that any incidental burden on a nonresident's ability to earn a living, own property, or exercise another "fundamental" activity could largely be ameliorated by using other available authorities. *Id.* at 227–28. The Court emphasized that the primary purpose of the state freedom of information act was to provide state citizens with a means to obtain an accounting of their public officials. *Id.* at 236–37.

[404] *See* South Carolina v. Katzenbach, 383 U.S. 301, 328–29 (1966). However, in recent years the Court has relied on the general principle of "constitutional equality" among the states to strike down both federal and state laws. *See, e.g.*, Franchise Tax Bd. of Cal. v. Hyatt, 578 U.S. ___, No. 14-1175, slip op. at 7 (2016); Shelby Cty. v. Holder, 570 U.S. 529, 544 (2013) (citing Nw. Austin Mun. Util. Dist. No. One v. Holder, 557 U.S. 193, 203 (2009)).

Clause 2. Property of the United States

PROPERTY AND TERRITORY: POWERS OF CONGRESS

Territories: Powers of Congress Thereover

[P. 980, after n.327, add new sentences:]

Congress may also establish non-judicial territorial offices.[405] If the powers and duties assigned to these offices are "primarily local" in nature, then Congress may prescribe the manner of appointment for officials to these positions without having to comply with the requirements of Article II's Appointments Clause.[406]

---

[405] Fin. Oversight & Mgmt. Bd. for P.R. v. Aurelius Inv., LLC, 140 S. Ct. 1649, 1655 (2020).

[406] *Id.* at 1665. *See supra* "Federal v. Territorial Officers."

ARTICLE VI

Clause 2. Supremacy of the Constitution, Laws, and Treaties

NATIONAL SUPREMACY

Task of the Supreme Court Under the Clause: Preemption

[P. 1006, after ". . . will be necessary.", add new footnote:]

For a discussion of express preemption, see *supra* Article I: Section 3: Clause 3.

The Operation of the Supremacy Clause

[P. 1007, after n.9, add new paragraph:]

At the same time, however, the Supremacy Clause is not the "source of any federal rights,"[407] and the Clause "certainly does not create a cause of action."[408] As such, individual litigants cannot sue to enforce federal law through the Supremacy Clause, as such a reading of the Clause would prevent Congress from limiting enforcement of federal laws to federal actors.[409] Instead, without a statutory cause of action, those wishing to seek injunctive relief against a state actor that refuses to comply with federal law must rely on the inherent equitable power of courts, a judge-made remedy that may be overridden by Congress.[410]

Obligation of State Courts Under the Supremacy Clause

[P. 1009, at end of n.19, delete "." and substitute with:]

; *see also* James v. City of Boise, 577 U.S. ___, No. 15-493, slip op. at 2 (2016) ("The Idaho Supreme Court, like any other state or federal court, is bound by this Court's interpretation of federal law."); DIRECTV, Inc. v. Imburgia, 577 U.S. ___, No. 14-462, slip op. at 5 (2015) (holding that the Supreme Court's interpretation of a federal law is an "authoritative interpretation of that Act," requiring the "judges of every State" to "follow it."). Moreover, the Court has interpreted the Supremacy Clause to require that a state court, when reviewing a prisoner's collateral claims that are controlled by federal law, "has a duty to grant the relief that federal law requires." *See* Montgomery v. Louisiana, 577 U.S. ___, No. 14-280, slip op. at 13 (2016) (quoting Yates v. Aiken, 484 U.S. 211, 218 (1988)). For an extended discussion on *Montgomery* and the obligations of state collateral review courts when reviewing substantive constitutional rules, see *supra* Article III: Section 2. Judicial Power and Jurisdiction: Clause 1. Cases and Controversies; Grants of Jurisdiction: Judicial Power and Jurisdiction-Cases and Controversies: The Requirements of a Real Interest: Retroactivity Versus Prospectivity.

---

[407] *See* Golden State Transit Corp. v. Los Angeles, 493 U.S. 103, 107 (1989).

[408] *See* Armstrong v. Exceptional Child Ctr., Inc., 575 U.S. ___, No. 14-15, slip op. at 3 (2015).

[409] *Id.*

[410] *Id.* at 5–6.

Supremacy Clause Versus the Tenth Amendment

[P. 1018, delete sentence starting "Federal laws of general applicability . . ."]

[P. 1019, delete paragraph starting "The scope of the rule thus expounded . . ."]

[P. 1019, delete paragraph starting "A partial answer was provided . . ." and substitute with:]

Three years later in *Reno v. Condon*, the Court upheld the Driver's Privacy Protection Act of 1994 (DPPA) against a charge that it offended the anti-commandeering doctrine.[411] That law restricted the disclosure and dissemination of personal information provided in applications for driver's licenses.[412] Equating the congressional enactment at issue in *Condon* to the law that was upheld in *South Carolina v. Baker*, the Court concluded that the DPPA did not require states in their sovereign capacity to regulate their own citizens.[413] Instead, the law regulated states as the "owners of databases" of driver's license data, and, therefore, applying the principle of *Garcia*, the Court upheld the law as one that applied equally to state and private actors.[414]

The Court's most recent consideration of the anti-commandeering principle occurred in 2018 in *Murphy v. NCAA*.[415] In *Murphy*, Justice Alito, writing on behalf of the Court, invalidated on anti-commandeering grounds a provision in the Professional and Amateur Sports Protection Act (PASPA) that prohibited states from authorizing sports gambling schemes.[416] Noting the rule from *New York* and *Printz* that Congress lacks "the power to issue orders directly to the States,"[417] the Court concluded that PASPA's prohibition of state authorization of sports gambling violated the anti-commandeering rule by putting state legislatures under the "direct control of Congress."[418] In so concluding, Justice Alito rejected the argument that the anti-commandeering doctrine only applies to "affirmative" congressional commands, as opposed to when Congress prohibits certain state action.[419] Finding the distinction between

---

[411] 528 U.S. 141, 151 (2000).

[412] *Id.* at 146–47.

[413] *Id.* at 150–51.

[414] *Id.* at 151; *see also* Murphy v. NCAA, 584 U.S. ___, No. 16-476, slip op. at 20 (2018) (describing the holding of *Condon*).

[415] *See Murphy*, slip op. at 14–24.

[416] *See* Pub. L. No. 102-559, § 2(a), 106 Stat. 4227, 4228 (1992) (codified at 28 U.S.C. § 3702).

[417] *See Murphy*, slip op. at 14. *Murphy* offered three justifications for the anti-commandeering rule: (1) to protect liberty by ensuring a "healthy balance of power" between the states and the federal government; (2) to promote political accountability by avoiding the blurring of which government is to credit or blame for a particular policy; (3) to prevent Congress from shifting the costs of regulation to the states. *Id.* at 17–18.

[418] *Id.* at 18.

[419] *Id.* at 18–19.

affirmative requirements and prohibitions "empty," the Court held that both types of commands equally intrude on state sovereign interests.[420]

In holding that Congress cannot command a state legislature to refrain from enacting a law, the *Murphy* Court reconciled its holding with two related doctrines.[421] First, the Court noted that while cases like *Garcia* and *Baker* establish that the anti-commandeering doctrine "does not apply when Congress evenhandedly regulates activity in which both States and private actors engage,"[422] PASPA's anti-authorization provision was, in contrast, solely directed at the activities of state legislatures.[423] Second, the Court rejected the argument that PASPA constituted a "valid preemption provision" under the Supremacy Clause.[424] While acknowledging that the "language used by Congress and this Court" with respect to preemption is sometimes imprecise,[425] Justice Alito viewed "every form of preemption" to be based on a federal law that regulates the conduct of private actors—either by directly regulating private entities or by conferring a federal right to be free from state regulation.[426] In contrast, PASPA's anti-authorization provision did not "confer any federal rights on private actors interested in conducting sports gambling operations" or "impose any federal restrictions on private actors."[427] As a result, the *Murphy* Court viewed the challenged provision to be a direct command to the states in violation of the anti-commandeering rule.[428]

---

[420] *Id.* at 19.

[421] *Id.* at 19–24.

[422] *Id.* at 20.

[423] *Id.* at 21. The Court also distinguished two other cases in which the Court rejected anti-commandeering challenges to federal statutes. First, the *Murphy* Court found PASPA to be distinct from the "cooperative federalism" of the law at issue in *Hodel v. Virginia Surface Mining & Reclamation Ass'n, Inc.*, 452 U.S. 264 (1981), in which, unlike PASPA, Congress provided the states with the *choice* of either implementing a federal program or allowing the federal program to preempt contrary state laws. *See Murphy*, slip op. at 20. Likewise, the *Murphy* Court found *FERC v. Mississippi*, 456 U.S. 742 (1982) inapplicable, as the law at issue in *FERC* did not, like PASPA, issue a command to a state legislature. *See Murphy*, slip op. at 20. Instead, the *Murphy* Court viewed the law in *FERC* as imposing the "modest requirement" that states "consider, but not necessarily" adopt federal regulations pertaining to the consumption of oil and natural gas. *Id.*

[424] *See Murphy*, slip op. at 21. *Murphy* identified two requirements for a preemption provision to be deemed valid: (1) the provision must represent an exercise of power conferred on Congress by the Constitution; (2) the provision must regulate private actors and not the states. *Id.* In so concluding, the Court noted that the Supremacy Clause was not an independent grant of legislative power and that "pointing to the Supremacy Clause" as the basis for Congress's authority "will not do." *Id.* (citing Armstrong v. Exceptional Child Ctr., Inc., 575 U.S. ___, No. 14-15, slip op. at 3 (2015)).

[425] *Id.* at 22–23. In particular, the Court noted that while express preemption clauses in federal statutes often appear to operate directly on the states, it would be a "mistake to be confused by the way in which a preemption provision is phrased" because Congress is not required to "employ a particular linguistic formulation when preempting state law." *Id.* at 22 (quoting Coventry Health Care of Missouri, Inc. v. Nevils, 581 U.S. ___, No. 16-149, slip op. at 10–11 (2017)).

[426] *Id.* at 23–24.

[427] *Id.* at 24 (noting that if a private actor started a sports gambling operation, either with or without state authorization, PASPA's anti-authorization provision would not be violated).

[428] *Id.* The Court ultimately invalidated PASPA in its entirety, holding that other

The Doctrine of Federal Exemption From State Taxation

Taxation of Salaries of Federal Employees.—

[P. 1025, delete subheading "Taxation of Salaries of Federal Employees" and substitute with:]

Taxation of Federal Employees' Compensation.—

[P. 1026, delete sentence starting "This principle, the Court has held . . . " and substitute with:]

The Court has since held that the nondiscrimination language in the quoted statute, 4 U.S.C. § 111, is "coextensive with the prohibition against discriminatory taxes embodied in the modern constitutional doctrine of intergovernmental tax immunity."[429]

The Supreme Court has on multiple occasions confronted the question of when a state tax is discriminatory within the meaning of § 111 because it violates constitutional "principles of intergovernmental tax immunity."[430] For example, *Davis v. Michigan Department of the Treasury* involved a Michigan law that exempted state and local government employees' retirement benefits from taxation while subjecting federal employees' retirement benefits to taxation.[431] In evaluating whether the law ran afoul of the nondiscrimination principle, the Court reasoned that "the relevant inquiry is whether the inconsistent tax treatment is directly related to, and justified by, 'significant differences between the two classes.'"[432] The Court found no "significant differences" between federal and state retirees, rejecting the state's argument that the differential tax treatment was justified by the relative amount of benefits afforded to retirees in each class.[433] Accordingly, the Court held that the law violated the intergovernmental tax immunity doctrine.[434] The Court reached a similar conclusion in *Barker v. Kansas*, holding that Kansas could not tax

provisions of the law that *did* regulate private conduct were not severable from the anti-authorization provision and therefore could exist independently from the unconstitutional provision. *See id.* at 24–30.

[429] *Davis*, 489 U.S. at 813; *see also* Dawson v. Steager, 586 U.S. ___, No. 17-419, slip op. at 2 (2019) ("Section 111 codifies a legal doctrine almost as old as the Nation.").

[430] *Davis*, 489 U.S. at 817; *see also id.* at 814 (stating that "the scope of the immunity granted or retained by the nondiscrimination clause [in § 111] is to be determined by reference to the constitutional doctrine").

[431] *Id.* at 806.

[432] *Id.* at 816 (quoting Phillips Chem. Co. v. Dumas Indep. Sch. Dist., 361 U.S. 376, 383–85 (1960)).

[433] The Court reasoned that even accepting the state's argument that federal employees generally received greater retirement benefits than their state counterparts, any difference in amount failed to justify the "blanket exemption" in Michigan's law. *Id.* at 817 (reasoning that a "tax exemption truly intended to account for differences in retirement benefits would not discriminate on the basis of the source of those benefits, as Michigan's statute does; rather, it would discriminate on the basis of the amount of benefits received by individual retirees").

[434] *Id.*

U.S. military retirees' benefits while simultaneously exempting state and local government retirees' benefits from the same tax.[435]

The Court did, however, uphold a local occupational tax as nondiscriminatory in *Jefferson County v. Acker*.[436] In that case, two federal judges who adjudicated cases in Jefferson County, Alabama, challenged a county law requiring persons working within the county who were not already subject to a license fee to pay an occupational tax.[437] The Court held that this requirement did not discriminate against federal judges based on "the federal *source* of their pay."[438] The Court reasoned that even though federal judges could not qualify for the licensing exemption, their "similarly situated" state counterparts—state court judges—also had to pay the tax, so there was no evidence of discrimination between those classes of employees.[439]

The Court's unanimous 2019 decision in *Dawson v. Steager* further clarified the scope of the nondiscrimination principle, holding that a violation of § 111 occurs any time a state "treats retired state employees more favorably than retired federal employees and no 'significant differences between the two classes' justify the differential treatment."[440] In that case, West Virginia had "expressly afford[ed] state law enforcement retirees a tax benefit that federal retirees [could not] receive."[441] The state conceded that there were no "significant differences" between the petitioner's "former job responsibilities [in the U.S. Marshals Service] and those of the tax-exempt state law enforcement retirees," which included state police, firefighters, and deputy sheriffs.[442] However, West Virginia argued that the differential tax treatment was permissible because federal law enforcement officials were on the same footing as most state retirees, the state having extended the challenged tax benefit to only a subset of state employees.[443] The Court disagreed, holding that a tax benefit can discriminate against federal employees even when only *some* state employees qualify for the benefit and *other* state employees who are similarly situated to the federal employees do not qualify for it.[444] What mattered was not "whether federal retirees are similarly situated to state retirees who *don't* receive a tax benefit," but "whether they are similarly situated to those who *do*."[445] And in making the latter determination, the

---

[435] 503 U.S. 594, 598, 605 (1992) (reasoning that although U.S. military retirees remain in the military after retiring from active duty, their retirement benefits are still "deferred pay for past services," not "current compensation for reduced current services," and thus "are not significantly different from the benefits paid to Kansas's state and local government retirees").

[436] 527 U.S. 423, 443 (1999).

[437] *Id.* at 427.

[438] *Id.* at 443.

[439] *Id.*

[440] Dawson v. Steager, 586 U.S. ___, No. 17-419, slip op. at 3 (2019) (quoting Davis v. Mich. Dep't of Treasury, 489 U.S. 803, 814–16 (1989)).

[441] *Id.* at 3.

[442] *Id.* at 3, 6.

[443] *Id.* at 4.

[444] *Id.* at 4–7.

[445] *Id.* at 7.

Court clarified, courts should look to how the state itself has defined the "favored class."[446] In this case, West Virginia "define[d] the favored class" by the retirees' former occupations rather than other criteria, such as age or differences among types of pension benefits, and so the Court believed it was appropriate to focus on the "comparable duties" of these officials.[447]

---

[446] *Id.* at 6.
[447] *Id.* at 6–7.

AMENDMENTS TO THE CONSTITUTION

BILL OF RIGHTS

First Through Tenth Amendments

The Fourteenth Amendment and Incorporation.—

[PP. 1049–50, n.26, delete sentence starting "The language of this process . . ." through end of footnote]

[P. 1052, at end of paragraph ending with n.37, add new sentence:]

> The modern doctrine of incorporation, like some of the earlier cases described above, asks whether a right is "both 'fundamental to our scheme of ordered liberty' and 'deeply rooted in this Nation's history and tradition.'"[448]

[P. 1053, n.37, before "Cruel and unusual punishment—", add:]

> Excessive Bail—McDonald v. City of Chicago, 561 U.S. 742, 764 n.12 (2010); Schilb v. Kuebel, 404 U.S. 357, 365 (1971).

> Excessive Fines—Timbs v. Indiana, 139 S. Ct. 682, 687 (2019).

[P. 1053, n.37, after *"Provisions not applied are,"* delete sentences starting "Eighth Amendment—" through end of footnote]

[P. 1054, delete sentence starting "The latter result . . ." and substitute with:]

> The Supreme Court, however, has since clarified that incorporated rights are generally enforced according to federal standards.[449]

---

[448] Timbs v. Indiana, 139 S. Ct. 682, 689 (2019) (quoting McDonald v. City of Chicago, 561 U.S. 742, 767 (2010).

[449] Timbs v. Indiana, 139 S. Ct. 682, 687 (2019). In *Timbs*, the Court noted that one exception was the Sixth Amendment's guarantee of jury unanimity. *Id.* at 687 n.1; *see also* Apodaca v. Oregon, 406 U.S. 404, 405 (1972) (plurality opinion) (concluding that the Sixth Amendment does not require jury unanimity); Johnson v. Louisiana, 406 U.S. 356, 375 (1972) (Powell, J., concurring) (arguing that "at least in defining the elements of the right to jury trial, there is no sound basis for interpreting the Fourteenth Amendment to require blind adherence by the States to all details of the federal Sixth Amendment standards"). A year later, in *Ramos v. Louisiana*, the Supreme Court overruled this contrary precedent and clarified that "the Sixth Amendment's unanimity requirement applies to state and federal criminal trials equally." 140 S. Ct. 1390, 1397 (2020).

FIRST AMENDMENT

RELIGION

An Overview

Court Tests Applied to Legislation Affecting Religion.—

[P. 1064, n.28, delete first citation sentence and substitute with:]

See Am. Legion v. Am. Humanist Ass'n, 588 U.S. ___, Nos. 17-1717, 18-18, slip op. at 15, 28 (2019) (declining to use *Lemon* to evaluate "the use, for ceremonial, celebratory, or commemorative purposes, of words or symbols with religious associations" and upholding public display of cross after looking to the history of the display); Town of Greece v. Galloway, 572 U.S. 565, 591–92 (2014) (upholding legislative prayers on the basis of historical tradition); Lee v. Weisman, 505 U.S. 577, 587 (1992) (declining to consider case under *Lemon* because the practice of invocations at public high school graduations was invalid under established precedents prohibiting coercive government practices); Marsh v. Chambers, 463 U.S. 783, 790–91 (1983) (upholding legislative prayers on the basis of historical practice).

[P. 1064, delete sentence starting "Nonetheless, the Court employed the *Lemon* tests . . ." and substitute with:]

Notwithstanding steady criticism of the standard,[450] the Court continued to employ the *Lemon* tests in various Establishment Clause decisions,[451] expressly rejecting a litigant's request to "abandon *Lemon*'s purpose test" in 2005.[452]

[P. 1064, at the end of sentence starting "Other tests, however, . . .", add new footnote:]

Under some circumstances, the Court has concluded that the normal tests are wholly inapplicable. *See, e.g.*, Trump v. Hawaii, 585 U.S. ___, No. 17-965, slip op. at 30 (2018) ("[T]his Court has engaged in a circumscribed judicial inquiry when the denial of a visa allegedly burdens the constitutional rights of a U.S. citizen."); *see also id.* at 32 (asking whether "the policy is facially legitimate and bona fide," and whether "it can reasonably be understood to result from a justification independent of unconstitutional grounds").

---

[450] *See, e.g.*, *Am. Legion*, slip op. at 14 (2019) (collecting examples of criticism).

[451] *See, e.g.*, Santa Fe Indep. Sch. Dist. v. Doe, 530 U.S. 290, 395 (2000) (holding unconstitutional under the *Lemon* purpose test a school district policy permitting high school students to decide by majority vote whether to have a student offer a prayer over the public address system prior to home football games); Agostini v. Felton, 521 U.S. 203, 234–35 (1997) (upholding under the *Lemon* test the provision of remedial educational services by public school teachers to elementary and secondary schoolchildren on the premises of religious schools).

[452] McCreary Cty. v. ACLU, 545 U.S. 844, 861 (2005). *See also, e.g.*, Zelman v. Simmons-Harris, 536 U.S. 639, 668 (2002) (O'Connor, J., concurring) (describing *Lemon* as "a central tool" in Establishment Clause analysis).

[P. 1064, after sentence starting "Other tests, however . . .", add new sentence:]

Two decisions from the Roberts Court suggest that the Court may be moving towards a new test, holding that at least in the areas of legislative prayer and longstanding government-sponsored monuments involving religious symbols, the Supreme Court will look to historical practice, evaluating government actions by reference to established traditions rather than the *Lemon* factors.[453]

[P. 1064, at end of n.30, add:]

Justice Kennedy's "coercion" analysis should be distinguished from the views of Justice Thomas, who has argued repeatedly that government actions violate the Establishment Clause only if they "involve actual legal coercion" resembling historical religious establishments. Elk Grove Unified Sch. Dist. v. Newdow, 542 U.S. 1, 52 (2004) (Thomas, J., concurring); *accord, e.g.,* Town of Greece v. Galloway, 572 U.S. 565, 608 (2014) (Thomas, J., concurring).

[P. 1065, delete sentence starting "In two Establishment Clause decisions . . ." through end of n.37.]

[P. 1065, at end of n.42, add:]

But see Masterpiece Cakeshop, Ltd. v. Colo. Civil Rights Comm'n, 584 U.S. ___, No. 16-111, slip op. at 18 (2018) (holding that the presence of government hostility to religion in an administrative adjudication violated the Free Exercise Clause without articulating the appropriate level of scrutiny governing the Court's decision).

Government Neutrality in Religious Disputes.—

[P. 1067, after n.50, delete rest of sentence and substitute with:]

the Supreme Court expanded on this "neutral principles" approach.

---

[453] Am. Legion v. Am. Humanist Ass'n, 588 U.S. ___, Nos. 17-1717, 18-18, slip op. at 21 (2019); Town of Greece v. Galloway, 572 U.S. 565, 577 (2014). In *American Legion*, it appears that a majority of Justices voted to limit *Lemon*'s applicability, but the fractured nature of the opinions make it difficult to determine when *Lemon* might apply in the future. A four-Justice plurality of the Court said that several considerations "counsel against" *Lemon* governing the Court's evaluation of "longstanding monuments, symbols, and practices," and instead said that such actions should be held constitutional so long as they comport with historical traditions. *American Legion*, slip op. at 16, 28 (plurality opinion). At least two concurring Justices, however, would have more broadly overruled the *Lemon* test. *Id.* at 6 (Thomas, J., concurring); *id.* at 7–8 (Gorsuch, J., concurring). The plurality opinion is narrower than the concurring opinions, because it would only have partially overruled *Lemon*, likely making it controlling in the future. Marks v. United States, 430 U.S. 188, 193 (1977) (explaining that when "no single rationale explaining the result [of a case] enjoys the assent of five Justices," the position representing the narrowest grounds is the holding of the Court). Accordingly, courts might still use *Lemon* to evaluate Establishment Clause claims that do not involve "longstanding monuments, symbols, and practices." *American Legion*, slip op. at 16 (plurality opinion).

[P. 1068, delete paragraph starting "Thus, it is unclear . . ." and substitute with:]

Stemming from these general principles of "religious autonomy"[454] or "ecclesiastical abstention"[455] is the "ministerial exception" doctrine.[456] In *Hosanna-Tabor Evangelical Lutheran Church & School v. EEOC*, the Supreme Court extended prior cases prohibiting judicial involvement in matters of church governance to limit the scope of certain employment discrimination laws.[457] A teacher at a Lutheran school claimed that she had been fired in violation of the federal Americans with Disabilities Act of 1990.[458] The school sought to dismiss her claim, arguing that the suit was barred under the "ministerial exception," a doctrine recognized by the lower courts precluding the application of federal antidiscrimination law to certain employment disputes.[459] The Court agreed, recognizing the existence of the ministerial exception and ruling that "[r]equiring a church to accept or retain an unwanted minister, or punishing a church for failing to do so" impermissibly "interferes with the internal governance of the church," violating both the Free Exercise and Establishment Clauses.[460]

The Court further held that this ministerial exception applied to the teacher's claim in *Hosanna-Tabor* even though she was not "the head of a religious congregation."[461] The Court identified four factors leading to the conclusion that the teacher qualified "as a minister."[462] First, the Court observed that the church labeled her "as a minister, with a role distinct from that of most of its members."[463] Second, the Court stressed that the church gave her this title only after "significant . . . religious training" and "a formal process of commissioning."[464] Third, the teacher held herself out as a minister of the church, in part by claiming a federal tax exemption available only to ministers.[465] And fourth, the Court said that her job duties, including her responsibilities in leading religious

---

[454] *See, e.g.,* Roman Catholic Archdiocese of San Juan v. Feliciano, 140 S. Ct. 696, 699 (2020) (per curiam).

[455] *See, e.g.,* Puri v. Khalsa, 844 F.3d 1152, 1162 (9th Cir. 2017); Winkler v. Marist Fathers of Detroit, Inc., 901 N.W.2d 566, 573 (Mich. 2017); St. Joseph Catholic Orphan Soc'y v. Edwards, 449 S.W.3d 727, 738 (Ky. 2014).

[456] Hosanna-Tabor Evangelical Lutheran Church & Sch. v. EEOC, 565 U.S. 171, 188 (2012).

[457] *Id.* at 185; *see also, e.g.,* Serbian E. Orthodox Diocese v. Milivojevich, 426 U.S. 696, 710 (1976) ("This principle [limiting the role of civil courts in resolving religious controversies] applies with equal force to church disputes over church polity and church administration.")

[458] *Hosanna-Tabor*, 565 U.S. at 179.

[459] *Id.* at 180.

[460] *Id.* at 188–89 ("By imposing an unwanted minister, the state infringes the Free Exercise Clause, which protects a religious group's right to shape its own faith and mission through its appointments. According the state the power to determine which individuals will minister to the faithful also violates the Establishment Clause, which prohibits government involvement in such ecclesiastical decisions.").

[461] *Id.* at 190.

[462] *Id.*

[463] *Id.* at 191.

[464] *Id.*

[465] *Id.* at 191–92.

activities, "reflected a role in conveying the [c]hurch's message and carrying out its mission."[466] The Court declined, however, to say whether any of these factors, standing alone, could be sufficient to qualify a teacher as a minister.[467]

In *Our Lady of Guadalupe School v. Morrissey-Berru*, the Court suggested that the last factor from *Hosanna-Tabor*—the individual's job functions—was the most important for determining whether a particular employee falls within the ministerial exception.[468] *Our Lady of Guadalupe* consolidated two cases involving employment discrimination claims brought by teachers fired by religious schools.[469] The Court ruled that the two teachers fell within the doctrine[470] even though, relative to the teacher in *Hosanna-Tabor*, they did not have the title of "minister," had less religious training, and were not practicing members of their employer's religion.[471] Instead, the Court said that "[w]hat matters, at bottom, is what an employee does."[472] Specifically, the Court recognized "that educating young people in their faith, inculcating its teachings, and training them to live their faith are responsibilities that lie at the very core of the mission of a private religious school."[473] The Court further understood that the two teachers in the combined cases "performed vital religious duties," emphasizing that they provided religious instruction, prayed with their students, and were "expected to guide their students, by word and deed, toward the goal of living their lives in accordance with the faith."[474] Consequently, "judicial intervention" in either dispute would, in the Court's view, "threaten[] the school's independence in a way that the First Amendment does not allow."[475]

---

[466] *Id.* at 192.

[467] *See id.*

[468] Our Lady of Guadalupe Sch. v. Morrissey-Berru, 140 S. Ct. 2049, 2059 (2020). However, the Court emphasized that "a variety of factors may be important" in any given case. *Id.* at 2063.

[469] *Id.* at 2055–56.

[470] The majority opinion seemed to move away from using the term "ministerial exception," referring instead to "the *Hosanna-Tabor* exception," *id.* at 2062, or "the exemption we recognized in *Hosanna-Tabor*," *id.* at 2066. This nomenclature choice could be related to the substance of the decision: elsewhere, the Court emphasized that not all religions use the title of "minister," cautioning against "attaching too much significance to titles." *Id.* at 2064.

[471] *Id.* at 2056, 2068.

[472] *Id.* at 2064.

[473] *Id.*

[474] *Id.* at 2066.

[475] *Id.* at 2069.

Establishment of Religion

Governmental Encouragement of Religion in Public Schools: Prayers and Bible Reading.—

[P. 1093, delete n.170 and substitute with:]

> The Court distinguished *Marsh v. Chambers*, 463 U.S. 783, 792 (1983), holding that the opening of a state legislative session with a prayer by a state-paid chaplain does not offend the Establishment Clause. The *Marsh* Court had distinguished *Abington* on the basis that state legislators, as adults, are "presumably not readily susceptible to 'religious indoctrination' or 'peer pressure'" and the *Lee* Court reiterated this distinction. 505 U.S. at 596–97. This distinction was again relied on by a plurality of Justices in *Town of Greece v. Galloway*, 572 U.S. ___, No. 12-696, slip op. (2014), in a decision upholding the use of legislative prayer at a town board meeting. *Id.* at 18–24. Justice Kennedy, on behalf of himself and Chief Justice Roberts and Justice Alito, distinguished the situation in *Lee*, in that with legislative prayer, at least in the context of *Town of Greece*, those claiming offense at the prayer were "mature adults" who are not "susceptible to religious indoctrination or peer pressure" and were free to leave a town meeting during the prayer without any adverse implications. *Id.* at 22–23 (quoting *Marsh*, 463 U.S. at 792).

Religion in Governmental Observances.—

[P. 1102, at end of section, add new paragraph:]

The Court likewise upheld the use of legislative prayers in the context of a challenge to the use of sectarian prayers to open a town meeting. In *Town of Greece v. Galloway*,[476] the Court considered whether such legislative prayers needed to be "ecumenical" and "inclusive." The challenge arose when the upstate New York Town of Greece recruited local clergy, who were almost exclusively Christian, to deliver prayers at monthly town board meetings. Basing its holding largely on the nation's long history of using prayer to open legislative sessions as a means to lend gravity to the occasion and to reflect long-held values, the Court concluded that the prayer practice in the Town of Greece fit within this tradition.[477] The Court also voiced pragmatic concerns with government scrutiny respecting the content of legislative prayers.[478] As a result, after *Town of Greece*, absent a "pattern of prayers that over time denigrate, proselytize, or betray an impermissible government purpose," First Amendment challenges based solely on the content of a legislative prayer appear unlikely to be successful.[479] Moreover, absent situations in which a legislative body discriminates against minority faiths, governmental

---

[476] 572 U.S. ___, No. 12-696, slip op. (2014).

[477] *Id.* at 9–18. The Court suggested that a pattern of prayers that over time "denigrate, proselytize, or betray an impermissible government purpose" could establish a constitutional violation. *Id.* at 17.

[478] *Id.* at 12 ("To hold that invocations must be nonsectarian would force the legislatures that sponsor prayers and the courts that are asked to decide these cases to act as supervisors and censors of religious speech, a rule that would involve government in religious matters to a far greater degree than is the case under the town's current practice . . . .").

[479] *Id.* at 17.

entities that allow for sectarian legislative prayer do not appear to violate the Constitution.[480]

Religious Displays on Governmental Property.—

[P. 1102, delete "was twice before the Court, with varying results." and substitute with:]

has yielded varying results before the Court.

[P. 1105, after n.240, add new sentence:]

A plurality of the Court would have used a different analysis to uphold the monument. Chief Justice Rehnquist argued that the *Lemon* test was "not useful in dealing with the sort of passive monument that Texas has erected on its Capitol grounds."[481] Instead, the plurality's decision was "driven both by the nature of the monument and by our Nation's history."[482]

[P. 1106, after n.243, add new paragraphs:]

The Supreme Court considered the constitutionality of another Latin Cross erected as a World War I memorial in *American Legion v. American Humanist Association*.[483] In upholding the memorial, Justice Alito's opinion for the Court relied on some of the factors highlighted by Justice Breyer's concurring opinion in *Van Orden*—namely, the fact that this particular monument had "stood undisturbed for nearly a century"[484] and had "acquired historical importance" to the community.[485] The majority opinion said that while the cross is a Christian symbol, that symbol "took on an added secular meaning when used in World War I memorials."[486] Under these circumstances, the Court concluded that requiring the state to "destroy[] or defac[e]" the cross "would not be neutral" with respect to religion "and would not further the ideals of respect and tolerance embodied in the First Amendment."[487]

More broadly, however, in *American Legion*, a majority of the Justices limited *Lemon's* scope. Writing for a four-Justice plurality, Justice Alito declared that several considerations "counseled against" applying the *Lemon* test to "longstanding monuments, symbols, and practices,"[488] saying that they should instead be considered constitutional so long as they "follow in" a historical "tradition" of religious

---

[480] *Id.*

[481] *Id.* at 685 (plurality opinion).

[482] *Id.*

[483] 588 U.S. ___, Nos. 17-1717, 18-18 (2019).

[484] *Id.*, slip op. at 31.

[485] *Id.* at 28.

[486] *Id.*

[487] *Id.* at 31.

[488] *Id.* at 16 (plurality opinion).

accommodation.[489] Justices Thomas and Gorsuch wrote separate concurrences disapproving of *Lemon* more generally, expressing their own views on how courts should evaluate Establishment Clause claims.[490] Therefore, a majority of Justices—the plurality, plus Justices Thomas and Gorsuch—voted to limit *Lemon*'s applicability in future cases involving the constitutionality of religious displays on government land.

[P. 1106, after sentence ending ". . . and instead remanded the case for further consideration.", add new section:]

Trump v. Hawaii.—An entirely different standard governs the constitutionality of a President's "national security directive regulating the entry of aliens abroad" that is "facially neutral toward religion," as the Court held in *Trump v. Hawaii.*[491] The plaintiffs in that case sought a preliminary injunction against a presidential proclamation that suspended or restricted the entry of foreign nationals from specified countries, arguing, in relevant part, that the proclamation "was issued for the unconstitutional purpose of excluding Muslims."[492] While the text of the document was facially neutral, restricting entry on the basis of national origin, the plaintiffs highlighted "a series of statements by the President and his advisors" suggesting that the President had intended to target immigration of Muslims.[493] The Court held that the proper standard to evaluate this Establishment Clause claim was the "circumscribed judicial inquiry" prescribed "when the denial of a visa allegedly burdens the constitutional rights of a U.S. citizen."[494] Under this standard, the Court would consider "whether the entry policy [was] plausibly related to the Government's stated objective to protect the country and improve vetting processes," and the plaintiffs' "extrinsic evidence" would not render the policy unconstitutional "so long as [the policy could] reasonably be understood to result from a justification independent of unconstitutional grounds."[495] Under this lenient standard, the Court upheld the proclamation, concluding that the plaintiffs had "not demonstrated a likelihood of success on the merits of their constitutional claim."[496]

---

[489] *Id.* at 28.

[490] *Id.* at 6 (Thomas, J., concurring) ("I would . . . overrule the *Lemon* test in all contexts."); *id.* at 7 (Gorsuch, J., concurring) ("*Lemon* was a misadventure."). Justice Kavanaugh also concurred and suggested that he would no longer apply *Lemon* in any case, although he had joined the plurality opinion. *See id.* at 1 (Kavanaugh, J., concurring) ("[T]his Court no longer applies the old test articulated in *Lemon* . . . .");

[491] 585 U.S. ___, No. 17-965, slip op. at 29 (2018).

[492] *Id.* at 24.

[493] *Id.* at 26.

[494] *Id.* at 30. The Court cited *Kleindienst v. Mandel*, a case in which American citizens who wished to receive the speech of a foreign national challenged the denial of the speaker's visa under the First Amendment. 408 U.S. 753, 756–57 (1972).

[495] *Hawaii*, slip op. at 32.

[496] *Id.* at 38.

Free Exercise of Religion

[P. 1108, at end of n.252, add:]

Cf. Sause v. Bauer, 585 U.S. ___, No. 17-742, slip op. at 2 (2018) (per curiam) ("There can be no doubt that the First Amendment protects the right to pray. Prayer unquestionably constitutes the 'exercise' of religion.").

[P. 1109, after ". . . can work both ways, the Court ruled in", add:]

Locke v. Davey,

[P. 1110, after n.263, add new paragraphs:]

The Court distinguished *Locke,* however, in *Trinity Lutheran Church,* explaining that *Locke'*s holding hinged on that the fact that the State of Washington was prohibiting the dissemination of scholarship money because of what the theology student "proposed *to do*" with the money as opposed to "who he *was.*"[497] In particular, the Court noted that the Washington scholarship program in *Locke* could be used by students to attend pervasively religious schools, but the program could not be used for the training of the clergy.[498] In contrast, the *Trinity Lutheran Church* Court held that the State of Missouri's decision to exclude an otherwise qualified church from a government grant program on the basis of the church's *religious status* violated the Free Exercise Clause.[499] In so holding, the Court concluded that while the First Amendment allows the government to limit the extent government funds can be put to religious use, the government cannot discriminate based on one's religious status and, in so doing, put the recipient of a government benefit to the choice between maintaining that status or receiving a government benefit.[500]

The Court built on *Trinity Lutheran'*s nondiscrimination principle in *Espinoza v. Montana Department of Revenue,* ruling that Montana could not bar religious schools from participating in a tax credit program benefiting private school students.[501] The Montana Supreme Court concluded that the program violated a state constitutional provision, known as the No-Aid Clause, which prohibited the government from providing direct or indirect financial support to religious schools.[502] The State argued that *Trinity Lutheran* should not apply because the No-Aid Clause excluded religious schools based on how they would *use* the funds— for religious education.[503] The Supreme Court disagreed, stating that the

---

[497] *See also* Trinity Lutheran Church of Columbia, Inc. v. Comer, 582 U.S. ___, No. 15-577, slip op. at 12 (2017) (emphases in original).

[498] *Id.* at 13 (citing *Locke,* 540 U.S. at 724).

[499] *Id.* at 14–15.

[500] *Id.* at 13–14 ("In this case, there is no dispute that Trinity Lutheran *is* put to the choice between being a church and receiving a government benefit. The rule is simple: No churches need apply.") (emphasis added).

[501] 140 S. Ct. 2246, 2255–56 (2020).

[502] *Id.* at 2254.

[503] *Id.* at 2255.

text of the state constitutional provision barred religious schools from public benefits solely because of their religious character.[504] Distinguishing *Locke*, the Court emphasized that Montana had not merely excluded any "particular 'essentially religious' course of instruction," but barred all aid to religious schools.[505] Further, unlike the "'historical and substantial' state interest in not funding the training of clergy" at issue in *Locke*, there was no similar historically grounded interest in disqualifying religious schools from public aid more generally.[506] Based on this religious discrimination, the Court evaluated the state's application of the No-Aid Clause under a strict scrutiny analysis and ultimately ruled it unconstitutional.[507] The Court held that, while the state was not required to "subsidize private education," once it decided to do so, it could not "disqualify some private schools solely because they are religious."[508]

The Belief-Conduct Distinction.—

[P. 1110, at end of n.264, add:]

See also Sause v. Bauer, 585 U.S. ___, No. 17-742, slip op. at 2 (2018) (per curiam) (noting that while "the right to pray" would normally be protected under the First Amendment, "there are clearly circumstances in which a police officer may lawfully prevent a person from praying at a particular time and place").

Free Exercise Exemption from General Governmental Requirements.—

[P. 1121, at end of n.333, add:]

See also Masterpiece Cakeshop, Ltd. v. Colo. Civil Rights Comm'n, 584 U.S. ___, No. 16-111, slip op. at 3 (2018) ("[T]he delicate question of when the free exercise of . . . religion must yield to an otherwise valid exercise of state power [must] be determined in an adjudication in which religious hostility on the part of the State itself would not be a factor in the balance the State sought to reach.").

[PP. 1122–23, delete paragraph starting "It does appear that . . ."]

[P. 1124, at beginning of n.350, add new sentence:]

See Burwell v. Hobby Lobby Stores, Inc., 573 U.S. ___, No. 13–354, slip op. (2014) (holding that RFRA applied to for-profit corporations and that a mandate that certain employers provide their employees with "[a]ll Food and Drug Administration approved contraceptive methods, sterilization procedures, and patient education and counseling for women with reproductive capacity" violated RFRA's general provisions); *see also*

---

[504] *Id.*

[505] *Id.* at 2257 (quoting Locke v. Davey, 540 U.S. 712, 721 (2004)).

[506] *Id.* at 2257–58 (quoting *Locke*, 540 U.S. at 722).

[507] *Id.* at 2260–61.

[508] *Id.* at 2261.

Religious Disqualification.—

[P. 1125, delete section "Religious Disqualification" and substitute with:]

The Supreme Court has recognized that the Free Exercise Clause "protect[s] religious observers against unequal treatment" and subjects laws that target the religious for "special disability" based on their "religious status" to strict scrutiny.[509] For example, in *McDaniel v. Paty*, the Court struck down a Tennessee law barring "[ministers] of the Gospel, or [priests] of any denomination whatever" from serving as a delegate to a state constitutional convention.[510] While the Court splintered with respect to its rationale, at least seven Justices agreed that the law violated the Free Exercise Clause by unconstitutionally conditioning the right of free exercise of one's religion on the "surrender" of the right to seek office as a delegate.[511]

Similarly, in *Trinity Lutheran Church v. Comer,* the Court held that a church that ran a preschool and daycare center could not be disqualified from participating in a Missouri program that offered funding for the resurfacing of playgrounds because of the church's religious affiliation.[512] Specifically, Chief Justice Roberts, on behalf of the Court,[513] noted that Missouri's policy of excluding an otherwise eligible recipient from a public benefit solely because of its religious character imposed an unlawful penalty on the free exercise of religion triggering the "most

---

[509] *See* Church of Lukumi Babalu Aye, Inc. v. Hialeah, 506 U.S. 520, 533, 542 (1993).

[510] 435 U.S. 618, 620 (1978).

[511] *See* 435 U.S. at 626 (plurality opinion). A plurality opinion by Chief Justice Burger, joined by Justices Powell, Rehnquist, and Stevens noted that the absolute prohibition on the government regulating religious beliefs (as established by *Torasco v. Watkins*, 367 U.S. 488 (1961)) was inapplicable to the case because the Tennessee disqualification was a prohibition based on religious "status," not belief. *See id.* at 626–27. Nonetheless, the plurality opinion concluded that the (1) Tennessee law was governed by the balancing test established under *Sherbert v. Verner*, 374 U.S. 498, 406 (1963), and (2) the law's regulation of religious status could not be justified based on the state's outmoded views of the dangers of clergy participation in the political process. *Id.* at 627–28.

Justice Brennan, joined by Justice Marshall, relying on *Torasco*, argued that the challenged provision, by establishing as a "condition of office the willingness to eschew certain protected religious practices," violated the Free Exercise Clause. *Id.* at 632 (Brennan, J., concurring). Justice Brennan's concurrence also maintained that the exclusion created by the Tennessee law could violate the Establishment Clause. *Id.* at 636. In a separate opinion, Justice Stewart noted his agreement with Justice Brennan's conclusion that *Torasco* controlled the case. *Id.* at 642 (Stewart, J., concurring). Rather than relying on the Free Exercise Clause to invalidate the Tennessee law, Justice White's concurrence suggested that the law was unconstitutional under the Equal Protection Clause of the Fourteenth Amendment. *Id.* at 643 (White, J., concurring).

[512] *See also* Trinity Lutheran Church of Columbia, Inc. v. Comer, 582 U.S. ___, No. 15-577, slip op. at 5 n.1 (2017).

[513] Three Justices (Kennedy, Alito, and Kagan) joined Chief Justice Roberts' entire opinion, while Justices Thomas and Gorsuch joined in all but a single footnote of the decision. The footnote that Justices Thomas and Gorsuch declined to join was a footnote that disclaimed that the instant case was examining "express discrimination based on religious identity with respect to playground resurfacing" and did not "address religious uses of funding or other forms of discrimination." *Id.* at 18 n.3.

exacting scrutiny."[514] In so holding, the Court rejected the State of Missouri's argument that declining to extend funds to the church did not prohibit it from engaging in any religious conduct or otherwise exercising its religious rights.[515] Relying on *McDaniel*, Chief Justice Roberts concluded that because the Free Exercise Clause protects against "indirect coercion or penalties on the free exercise of religion," as well as "outright" prohibitions on religious exercise, Trinity Lutheran had a right to participate in a government benefit program without having to disavow its religious status.[516] Moreover, the Court held that Missouri's policy of requiring organizations like the plaintiff to renounce its religious character in order to participate in the public benefit program could not be justified by a policy preference to achieve greater separation of church and state than what is already required under the Establishment Clause.[517] As a result, the Court held that Missouri's policy violated the Free Exercise Clause.[518]

A year after *Trinity Lutheran*, the Court suggested that it is equally unconstitutional for hostility to religion to play a role in the government's decisions about how to *apply* its laws.[519] In *Masterpiece Cakeshop, Ltd. v. Colorado Civil Rights Commission*, the Court set aside state administrative proceedings enforcing Colorado's anti-discrimination laws against a baker who had, in the view of the state, violated those laws by refusing to make a cake for a same-sex wedding.[520] The Court held that the state had violated the Free Exercise Clause because the Colorado Civil Rights Commission had not considered the baker's case "with the religious neutrality that the Constitution requires."[521] As a general rule, the Court announced that "the delicate question of when the free exercise of [the baker's] religion must yield to an otherwise valid exercise of state power needed to be determined in an adjudication in which religious hostility on the part of the State itself would not be a factor in the balance the State sought to reach."[522] The Court highlighted two aspects of the state proceedings that had, in its view, demonstrated impermissible religious hostility: first, certain statements by some of the Commissioners during the proceedings before the Commission[523]; and second, "the difference in treatment between [the petitioner's] case and the cases of other bakers

---

[514] *Id.* at 10.

[515] *Id.*

[516] *Id.* at 10–11. As a result, the Court characterized the church's injury not so much as being the "denial of a grant" itself, but rather the "refusal to allow the Church . . . to compete with secular organizations for a grant." *Id.* at 11.

[517] *Id.* at 14. Both parties agreed, and the Court accepted, that the Establishment Clause did not prevent Missouri from including the church in the state's grant program. *Id.* at 6.

[518] *Id.* at 14–15.

[519] Masterpiece Cakeshop, Ltd. v. Colo. Civil Rights Comm'n, 584 U.S. ___, No. 16-111, slip op. at 18 (2018).

[520] *Id.* at 3.

[521] *Id.*

[522] *Id.* at 3.

[523] *Id.* at 13–14.

who objected to a requested cake on the basis of conscience and prevailed before the Commission."[524]

FREEDOM OF EXPRESSION—SPEECH AND PRESS

Adoption and the Common Law Background

[P. 1131, delete first full paragraph and substitute with:]

The First Amendment by its terms applies only to laws enacted by Congress and not to the actions of private persons.[525] As such, the First Amendment is subject to a "state action" (or "governmental action") limitation similar to that applicable to the Fifth and Fourteenth Amendments.[526] The Supreme Court has stated that "a private entity can qualify as a state actor in a few limited circumstances," such as "[1] when the private entity performs a traditional, exclusive public function; [2] when the government compels the private entity to take a particular action; or [3] when the government acts jointly with the private entity."[527] In addition, some private entities established by the government to carry out governmental objectives may qualify as state actors for purposes of the First Amendment. For example, in *Lebron v. National Railroad Passenger Corp.*, the Court held that the national passenger train company Amtrak, "though nominally a private corporation," qualified as "an agency or instrumentality of the United States" for purposes of the First Amendment.[528] It did not matter, in the Court's view, that the federal statute establishing Amtrak expressly stated that Amtrak was not a federal agency because Amtrak was "established and organized under federal law for the very purpose of pursuing federal governmental objectives, under the direction and control of federal governmental appointees."[529]

The question of when broadcast companies are engaged in governmental action subject to the First Amendment has historically divided the Court. In *Columbia Broadcasting System v. Democratic*

---

[524] *Id.* at 14. *See also id.* at 16 ("A principled rationale for the difference in treatment of these two instances cannot be based on the government's own assessment of offensiveness.").

[525] Through interpretation of the Fourteenth Amendment, the prohibition extends to the states as well. *See* Bill of Rights: The Fourteenth Amendment and Incorporation, *infra.* Of course, the First Amendment also applies to the non-legislative branches of government—to every "government agency—local, state, or federal." Herbert v. Lando, 441 U.S. 153, 168 n.16 (1979).

[526] *See* Fourteenth Amendment: Equal Protection of the Laws: Scope and Application: State Action, *infra.*

[527] Manhattan Cmty. Access Corp. v. Halleck, 587 U.S. ___, No. 17-702, slip op. at 6 (2019) (internal citations omitted) (citing Jackson v. Metro. Edison Co., 419 U.S. 345, 352–54 (1974), Blum v. Yaretsky, 457 U.S. 991, 1004–05 (1982), and Lugar v. Edmondson Oil Co., 457 U.S. 922, 941–42 (1982), respectively).

[528] 513 U.S. 374, 383, 394 (1995); *see also* Dep't of Transp. v. Ass'n of Am. R.R., 575 U.S. ___, No. 13-1080, slip op. at 11 (2015) (extending the holding of *Lebron*, such that Amtrak was considered a governmental entity "for purposes of" the Fifth Amendment due process and separation-of-powers claims presented by the case).

[529] *Lebron*, 513 U.S. at 391–93, 398.

National Committee, the Court considered whether a radio station that had a license from the government to broadcast over airwaves in the public domain needed to comply with the First Amendment when it sold air time to third parties.[530] The radio station had a policy of refusing to sell air time to persons seeking to express opinions on controversial issues.[531] Three Justices joined a plurality opinion concluding that the radio station was not engaged in governmental action when it enforced this policy.[532] They reasoned that the federal government had not partnered with or profited from the broadcaster's decisions and that Congress had "affirmatively indicated" that broadcasters subject to federal law retained certain journalistic license.[533] In the view of those Justices, if the Court were "to read the First Amendment to spell out governmental action in the circumstances presented . . . , few licensee decisions on the content of broadcasts or the processes of editorial evaluation would escape constitutional scrutiny."[534] In contrast, three other Members of the Court would have held that the radio station was engaged in governmental action because of the degree of governmental regulation of broadcasters' activities and the station's use of the airwaves, a public resource.[535] And three Justices would not have decided the state action question.[536] Nevertheless, these three Justices joined the Court's opinion concluding that even if the broadcaster was engaged in governmental action, the First Amendment did not require "a private right of access to the broadcast media."[537]

More recently, in *Manhattan Community Access Corp. v. Halleck*, the Supreme Court held that Manhattan Neighborhood Network (MNN), a private, nonprofit corporation designated by New York City to operate public access channels in Manhattan, was not a state actor for purposes of the First Amendment because it did not exercise a "traditional, exclusive public function."[538] Emphasizing the limited number of functions that met this standard under the Court's precedents,[539] the Court reasoned that operating public access channels "has not traditionally and exclusively been performed by government" because "a variety of private and public actors" had performed the function since the 1970s.[540] Moreover, the Court reasoned, "merely hosting speech by others is not a traditional, exclusive

---

[530] 412 U.S. 94 (1973).

[531] *Id.* at 98.

[532] *Id.* at 120 (plurality opinion of Burger, C.J., and Stewart and Rehnquist, JJ.).

[533] *Id.* at 119–20.

[534] *Id.* at 120.

[535] *Id.* at 150 (Douglas, J., concurring in the judgment); *id.* at 172–73 (Brennan and Marshall, JJ., dissenting).

[536] *See id.* at 171 (Brennan, J., dissenting) (noting that Justices White, Blackmun, and Powell would not have reached the state action question).

[537] *Id.* at 129 (majority opinion).

[538] 587 U.S. ___, No. 17-702, slip op. at 2–3, 6 (2019).

[539] *Id.* at 6–7 (stating that while "running elections" and "operating a company town" qualify as traditional, exclusive public functions, "running sports associations and leagues, administering insurance payments, operating nursing homes, providing special education, representing indigent criminal defendants, resolving private disputes, and supplying electricity" do not).

[540] *Id.* at 7.

public function and does not alone transform private entities into state actors subject to First Amendment constraints."[541] In the majority's view, the city's selection of MNN and the state's extensive regulation of MNN did not in and of themselves create state action.[542]

Freedom of Belief

Flag Salutes and Other Compelled Speech.—

[P. 1164, at end of n.556, add:]

> *See also* Janus v. American Federation of State, County, and Municipal Employees, Council 31, 585 U.S. ___, No. 16-1466, slip op. at 9 (2018) (noting that compelled speech imposes a distinct harm by "forcing free and independent individuals to endorse ideas they find objectionable").

[P. 1166, after "anonymous campaign literature," delete "and"]

[P. 1166, after "wish to convey" delete "." and substitute with:]

,

[P. 1166, after n.564, add:]

and a California law that required certain pro-life centers that offer pregnancy-related services to provide certain notices.[543]

[P. 1166, after "By contrast, the Supreme Court has" add:]

at times

---

[541] *Id.* at 10.

[542] *See id.* at 11 (reasoning that absent performance of a traditional and exclusive public function, a private entity is not a state actor merely because the government licenses, contracts with, grants a monopoly to, or subsidizes it); *id.* at 12 (reasoning that state regulations that "restrict MNN's editorial discretion" and effectively require it to "operate almost like a common carrier" do not make MNN a state actor). *Cf.* Pub. Utils. Comm'n v. Pollak, 343 U.S. 451, 462 (1952). The majority also rejected the argument that MNN was simply standing in for New York City in managing government property, reasoning that the record did not show that any government owned, leased, or otherwise had a property interest in the public access channels or the broader cable network in which they operated. *Manhattan Cmty. Access Corp.*, slip op. at 14–15.

[543] *See* Nat'l Inst. of Family and Life Advocates v. Becerra, 585 U.S. ___, No. 16-1140, slip op. at 7 (2018). Specifically, in *National Institute of Family and Life Advocates v. Becerra*, the Court reviewed a California law that, in relevant part, required medically licensed crisis pregnancy centers to notify women that the State of California provided free or low-cost services, including abortion. *Id.* at 2–4 (describing the California law). For the Court, "[b]y requiring [licensed clinics] to inform women how they can obtain state-subsidized abortions—at the same time [those clinics] try to dissuade women from choosing that option," the California law "plainly alters the content" of the clinics' speech, subjecting the law to heightened scrutiny. *Id.* at 7 (internal citations and quotations omitted).

[P. 1166, delete "disclosures in commercial speech . . ." through ". . . political propaganda." and substitute with:]

the disclosure of information in a commercial or professional setting.

[P. 1167, after n.567, add new paragraphs:]

Moreover, the Court has upheld regulations of professional conduct that only incidentally burden speech. For example, in *Planned Parenthood of Southeastern Pennsylvania v. Casey,* the Court considered a law requiring physicians to obtain informed consent before they could perform an abortion.[544] Specifically, the law at issue in *Casey* required doctors to tell their patients prior to an abortion about the nature of the procedure, the health risks involved, the age of the unborn child, and the availability of printed materials from the state about various forms of assistance.[545] In a plurality opinion, the Court rejected a free-speech challenge to the informed consent requirement, viewing the law as "part of the practice of medicine" and an incidental regulation of speech.[546]

However, the Court has cautioned that reduced scrutiny for compelled commercial and professional speech is limited to particular contexts. For example, limited scrutiny of compelled commercial disclosures is restricted to requirements that professionals provide "purely factual" and "uncontroversial information" in their commercial dealings.[547] As a result, in considering the constitutionality of a California law requiring certain medically licensed, pro-life crisis pregnancy centers to disclose information to patients about the availability of state-subsidized procedures, including abortions, the Court in *National Institute of Family and Life Advocates v. Becerra* concluded that the *Zauderer* rule for compelled disclosures of purely factual, uncontroversial information was inapplicable.[548] Specifically, the Court noted that the notice requirements were unrelated to services that the clinics provided and that

---

[544] *See* 505 U.S. 833, 881 (1992) (plurality opinion).

[545] *Id.*

[546] *Id.* at 884.

[547] *See, e.g.,* Nat'l Inst. of Family and Life Advocates v. Becerra, 585 U.S. ___, No. 16-1140, slip op. at 8 (2018).

Moreover, even under *Zauderer,* commercial disclosure requirements cannot be unjustified or unduly burdensome. *See* 471 U.S. at 651. Applying this limit on the *Zauderer* rule, the *National Institute of Family and Life Advocates* Court reviewed a separate provision of the California law discussed above that required *unlicensed* crisis pregnancy centers to notify women that California has not licensed the clinics to provide medical services. *Id.* at 4–5 (describing the requirements for the unlicensed centers). The Court, noting the lack of evidence in the record that pregnant women were unaware that the covered facilities were not staffed by medical professionals and remarking on the breadth of the regulations that required a posting of the notice "no matter what the facilities say on site or in their advertisements," concluded that the regulations of unlicensed crisis pregnancy centers unduly burdened speech. *Id.* at 18–19.

[548] *Id.* at 9.

the notice included information about abortion, "anything but an 'uncontroversial' topic."[549]

In that same ruling, the Court rejected the argument that the California law's disclosure requirements were comparable to the informed consent regulations upheld in *Casey*.[550] In contrast to the law in *Casey,* the *National Institute of Family and Life Advocates* Court concluded that the disclosure requirements were not tied to a particular medical procedure and did not require the disclosure of information about the risks or benefits of any medical procedures the clinics provided.[551] In this sense, the California law, unlike the informed consent law in *Casey*, did not incidentally burden speech, but instead "regulat[ed] speech as speech."[552]

[P. 1167, delete "Regarding compelled labeling of foreign political propaganda," and substitute with:]

The Supreme Court has also found no First Amendment concern with respect to the compelled labeling of foreign political propaganda. Specifically, in *Meese v. Keene,*

Right of Association

Conflict Between Organizations and Members.—

[P. 1180, after n.646, add new paragraph:]

The Supreme Court held in *Janus v. American Federation of State, County, and Municipal Employees, Council 31*, that "public sector agency-shop arrangements violate the First Amendment,"[553] overruling a forty-year old precedent, *Abood v. Detroit Board of Education*, that had generally approved of such arrangements.[554] However, even *Abood* itself had only permitted some aspects of compelled fee regimes,[555] and the Court had, for years prior to *Janus*, signaled its growing discomfort with *Abood*.[556] Understanding the historical course of the jurisprudence

---

[549] *Id.*

[550] *Id.* at 11.

[551] *Id.*

[552] *Id.*

Having concluded that the California disclosure requirements for licensed crisis pregnancy centers should be evaluated under a more rigorous form of scrutiny than what the Court employed in *Zauderer* or *Casey*, the *National Institute of Family and Life Advocates* Court, employing intermediate scrutiny, held that the California law likely violated the First Amendment. *Id.* at 14. Specifically, the Court viewed the law to be both underinclusive—the law excluded several similar clinics without explanation—and overinclusive—the state could have employed other methods, such as a state-sponsored advertising campaign, to achieve its purpose of informing low-income women about its services without "burdening a speaker with unwanted speech." *Id.* at 14–16 (internal citations omitted).

[553] 585 U.S. ___, No. 16-1466, slip op. at 33 (2018).

[554] 431 U.S. 209, 229 (1977).

[555] *Id.* at 235.

[556] *See, e.g.,* Harris v. Quinn, 573 U.S. ___, No. 11-681, slip op. (2014). In *Friedrichs v. California Teachers Association*, the Court was equally divided on the question of whether

governing compelled agency fees is important to understand the ramifications of *Janus*.

[P. 1183, after n.663, add new paragraph:]

Doubts on the constitutionality of mandatory union dues in the public sector intensified in *Harris v. Quinn*.[557] The Court openly expressed reservations on *Abood*'s central holding that the collection of an agency fee from public employees withstood First Amendment scrutiny because of the desirability of "labor peace" and the problem of "free ridership." Specifically, the Court questioned (1) the scope of the precedents (like *Hanson* and *Street*) that the *Abood* Court relied on; (2) *Abood*'s failure to appreciate the distinctly political context of public sector unions; and (3) *Abood*'s dismissal of the administrative difficulties in distinguishing between public union expenditures for collective bargaining and expenditures for political purposes.[558] Notwithstanding these concerns about *Abood*'s core holding, the Court in *Harris* declined to overturn *Abood* outright. Instead, the Court focused on the peculiar status of the employees at issue in the case before it: home health care assistants subsidized by Medicaid. These "partial-public employees" were under the direction and control of their individual clients and not the state, had little direct interaction with state agencies or employees, and derived only limited benefits from the union.[559] As a consequence, the Court concluded that *Abood*'s rationale—the labor peace and free rider concerns—did not justify compelling dissenting home health care assistants to subsidize union speech.[560]

In *Janus v. American Federation of State, County, and Municipal Employees, Council 31*, the Supreme Court formally overruled *Abood* and held "that public sector agency-shop arrangements violate the First Amendment."[561] The Court rejected the governmental interests said to justify the compelled fees in *Abood*, holding that labor peace can be achieved through less restrictive means and that the government does not have a "compelling interest" in avoiding free riders.[562] The majority opinion criticized *Abood*'s extension of *Hanson* and *Street*, saying neither of those cases "gave careful consideration to the First Amendment" and arguing that *Abood*'s reliance on those cases led it to apply an overly deferential standard to analyze public-sector agency fee arrangements.[563] In the Court's view, granting too much deference to legislative judgments about the strength of asserted government interests or about whether the challenged action truly supports those interests "is inappropriate in

---

to overrule *Abood*. 578 U.S. ___, No. 14-915, slip op. at 1 (2016).

[557] 573 U.S. ___, No. 11-681, slip op. (2014).

[558] *Id.* at 8–20.

[559] *Id.* at 24–27.

[560] *Id.* at 27.

[561] 585 U.S. ___, No. 16-1466, slip op. at 33 (2018).

[562] *Id.* at 12–13.

[563] *Id.* at 36.

deciding free speech issues."[564] The Court also disagreed with additional justifications said to justify the agency-shop arrangements, notably holding that they could not be upheld under *Pickering v. Board of Education*,[565] a case in which the Court acknowledged that public employers may sometimes place certain restrictions on employees' speech.[566] Accordingly, after *Janus*, "States and public-sector unions may no longer extract agency fees from nonconsenting employees."[567]

Particular Government Regulations that Restrict Expression

Government as Employer: Free Expression Generally.—

[P. 1208, after first partial paragraph, add new paragraph:]

In distinguishing between wholly unprotected "employee speech" and quasi-protected "citizen speech," sworn testimony outside of the scope of a public employee's ordinary job duties appears to be "citizen speech." In *Lane v. Franks*,[568] the director of a state government program for underprivileged youth was terminated from his job following his testimony regarding the alleged fraudulent activities of a state legislator that occurred during the legislator's employment in the government program. The employee challenged the termination on First Amendment grounds. The Court held generally that testimony by a subpoenaed public employee made outside the scope of his ordinary job duties is to be treated as speech by a citizen, subject to the *Pickering-Connick* balancing test.[569] The Court noted that "[s]worn testimony in judicial proceedings is a quintessential example of speech as a citizen for a simple reason: Anyone who testifies in court bears an obligation to the court and society at large, to tell the truth."[570] In so holding, the Court confirmed that *Garcetti*'s holding is limited to speech made in accordance with an employee's official job duties and does not extend to speech that merely concerns information learned during that employment.

The Court in *Lane* ultimately found that the plaintiff's speech deserved protection under the *Pickering-Connick* balancing test because the speech was both a matter of public concern (the speech was testimony about misuse of public funds) and the testimony did not raise concerns for the government employer.[571] After *Lane*, some question remains about the scope of protection for public employees, such as police officers or official representatives of an agency of government, who testify pursuant to their

---

[564] *Id.* at 37.

[565] 391 U.S. 563 (1968).

[566] *Janus*, slip op. at 26.

[567] *Id.* at 48.

[568] 573 U.S. ___, No. 13-483, slip op. (2014).

[569] *Id.* at 9.

[570] *Id.*

[571] *Id.* at 12–13. The Court, however, held that because no relevant precedent in the lower court or in the Supreme Court clearly established that the government employer could not fire an employee because of testimony the employee gave, the defendant was entitled to qualified immunity. *Id.* at 13–17.

official job duties, and whether such speech falls within the scope of *Garcetti.*

[P. 1209, in n.799, delete last sentence starting "In Waters v. Churchill . . ." and substitute with:]

In *Waters v. Churchill,* 511 U.S. 661 (1994), a plurality of a divided Court concluded that a public employer does not violate the First Amendment if the employer (1) had reasonably believed that the employee's conversation involved personal matters and (2) dismissed the employee because of that reasonable belief, even if the belief was mistaken. *Id.* at 679-80 (plurality opinion) (O'Connor, J., joined by Rehnquist, C.J., Souter & Ginsburg, JJ.). More than two decades later, a six-Justice majority approvingly cited to the plurality opinion from *Waters,* concluding that the employer's motive is dispositive in determining whether a public employee's First Amendment rights had been violated as a result of the employer's conduct. *See* Heffernan v. City of Paterson, 578 U.S. ___, No. 14-1280, slip op. at 5 (2016). In so doing, the Court held that the converse of the situation in *Waters*—a public employer's firing of an employee based on the mistaken belief that the employee *had* engaged in activity *protected* by the First Amendment—was actionable as a violation of the Constitution. *See id.* at 6 ("After all, in the law, what is sauce for the goose is normally sauce for the gander."). Put another way, when an employer demotes an employee to prevent the employee from engaging in protected political activity, the employee is entitled to challenge that unlawful action under the First Amendment, "even if . . . the employer makes a factual mistake about the employee's behavior." *Id.* The Court concluded that the employer's motivation is central with respect to public employee speech issues because of (1) the text of the First Amendment—which "focus[es] upon the activity of the Government"; and (2) the underlying purposes of the public employee speech doctrine, which is to prevent the chilling effect that results when an employee is discharged for having engaged in protected activity. *Id.* at 6–7.

[P. 1209, at end of sentence starting "If the speech does relate . . .", add new footnote:]

The Court stated in *Janus v. American Federation of State, County, and Municipal Employees, Council 31,* 585 U.S. ___, No. 16-1466, slip op. at 23–24 (2018), that this analysis "requires modification" when a court considers "general rules that affect broad categories of employees." In such a case, "the government must shoulder a correspondingly 'heav[ier]' burden and is entitled to considerably less deference in its assessment that a predicted harm justifies a particular impingement on First Amendment rights." *Id.* at 24 (quoting United States v. National Treasury Employees Union, 513 U.S. 454, 466 (1995)) (alteration in original).

Government as Regulator of the Electoral Process: Elections and Referendums.—

[P. 1215, after n.830, add new sentence:]

The Supreme Court also struck down a Minnesota law banning all "political" apparel at polling places as unreasonable, even while recognizing the state's general interest in regulating polling places.[572]

[P. 1215, delete n.830 and substitute with:]

See Republican Party of Minn. v. White, 536 U.S. 765, 776 (2002). In the only case post-*White* concerning speech restrictions on candidates for judicial office, however, the Court in

---

[572] Minnesota Voters Alliance v. Mansky, 585 U.S. ___, No. 16-1435, slip op. at 12–13 (2018).

Williams-Yulee v. Florida Bar, upheld a more narrow restriction on candidate speech. *See* 575 U.S. ___, No. 13-1499, slip op. (2015). The *Williams-Yulee* Court held that a provision within Florida's Code of Judicial Conduct that prohibited judicial candidates from personally soliciting campaign funds served a compelling interest in preserving public confidence in the judiciary through a means that was "narrowly tailored to avoid unnecessarily abridging speech." *Id.* at 8–9.

[P. 1222, after n.870, add new paragraph:]

In *McCutcheon v. FEC,*[573] however, a plurality of the Court[574] appeared to signal an intent to scrutinize limits on contributions more closely to ensure a "fit" between governmental objective and the means utilized.[575] Considering aggregate limits on individual contributions— that is, the limits on the amount an individual can give in one campaign cycle[576]—the plurality opinion distinguished between the government interest in avoiding even the appearance of quid pro quo corruption and the government interest in avoiding potential "'influence over or access to' elected officials of political parties" as the result of large contributions; only the interest in preventing actual or apparent quid pro quo corruption constituted a legitimate objective sufficient to satisfy the First Amendment.[577] Given the more narrow interest of the government, the *McCutcheon* Court struck down the limits on aggregate contributions by an individual donor. The plurality opinion viewed the provision in question as impermissibly restricting an individual's participation in the political process by limiting the number of candidates and organizations to which the individual could contribute (once that individual had reached the aggregate limit).[578] Moreover, the plurality opinion held that the aggregate limits on individual contributions were not narrowly tailored to prevent quid pro quo corruption, as the limits prevent any contributions (regardless of size) to any individual or organization once the limits are reached.[579] The plurality likewise rejected the argument that the restriction prevented circumvention of a separate restriction on base contributions to individual candidates, as such circumvention was either illegal (because of various anti-circumvention rules) or simply improbable.[580] Collectively, the Court concluded that the aggregate limits violate the First Amendment because of the poor "fit" between the

---

[573] 572 U.S. 185 (2014).

[574] Chief Justice Roberts wrote the plurality opinion, joined by Justices Scalia, Kennedy and Alito. Justice Thomas, concurring in the judgment, declined to join the reasoning of the plurality, arguing that, to the extent that *Buckley* afforded a lesser standard of review to restrictions on contributions than to expenditures, it should be overruled.

[575] The Court declined to revisit the differing standards for contributions and expenditures established in *Buckley*, holding that the issue in question, aggregate spending limits, did not meet the demands of either test. *McCutcheon*, 572 U.S. at 199–200.

[576] In 2014, these aggregate limits capped total contributions per election cycle to $48,600 to all federal candidates and $74,600 to all other political committees, of which only $48,600 could be contributed to state or local party committees and PACs. 2 U.S.C. § 441a(a)(3) (2012); 78 Fed. Reg. 8,532 (Feb. 6, 2013).

[577] *McCutcheon*, 572 U.S. at 207–08.

[578] *Id.* at 203–04.

[579] *Id.* at 210–11.

[580] *Id.* at 210–18.

interests proffered by the government and the means by which the limits attempt to serve those interests.[581]

[P. 1230, at end of n.913, add:]

In *Thompson v. Hebdon*, issued in 2019, the Supreme Court vacated and remanded an opinion upholding Alaskan campaign contribution limits after concluding that the U.S. Court of Appeals for the Ninth Circuit had improperly failed to consider and apply *Randall*. 140 S. Ct. 348, 350–51 (2019) (per curiam). The Court noted that Alaska's law contained some of the same "danger signs" identified in *Randall* and remanded the case to the lower court for reconsideration. *Id.* at 351.

Government as Regulator of Labor Relations.—

[P. 1232, n.926, delete "Abood v. Detroit Bd. of Educ., 431 U.S. 209 (1977) (public employees),"]

Government as Administrator of Prisons.—

[P. 1238, at end of n.962, add:]

In a related, but distinct context, however, state laws that restrict the First Amendment rights of former prisoners that are still under the supervision of the state appear to be subject to strict scrutiny. For example, in *Packingham v. North Carolina*, the Court struck down a North Carolina law making it a felony for registered sex offenders to use commercial social networking websites that allow minor children to be members, such as Facebook. 582 U.S. ___, No. 15-1194, slip op. (2017). The Court held that the North Carolina law impermissibly restricted lawful speech because it was not narrowly tailored to serve the significant government interest in protecting minors from registered sex offenders. *Id.* at 8 (holding that it was "unsettling to suggest that only a limited set of websites can be used even by persons who have completed their sentences").

Government and the Power of the Purse.—

[P. 1245, after n.996, add new paragraph:]

In contrast, in *Agency for International Development v. Alliance for Open Society International, Inc.*,[582] the Court found that the federal government could not explicitly require a federal grantee to adopt a public policy position as a condition of receiving federal funds. In *Alliance for Open Society International*, organizations that received federal dollars to combat HIV/AIDS internationally were required: (1) to ensure that such funds were not being used "to promote or advocate the legalization or practice of prostitution or sex trafficking" and (2) to have a policy "explicitly opposing prostitution."[583] While the first condition ensured that the government was not funding speech that conflicted with the grant's purposes, the second requirement, in the Court's view, improperly affected the recipient's protected conduct outside of the federal program.[584]

---

[581] *Id.* at 218–19.

[582] 570 U.S. 205 (2013).

[583] *Id.* at 208 (quoting 22 U.S.C. § 7631(e), (f) (2012).

[584] *See id.* at 217–19.

Further, the Court concluded that the organization could not, as in previous cases, avoid the requirement by establishing an affiliate to engage in opposing advocacy because of the "evident hypocrisy" that would entail.[585] In a follow-on case seven years later, however, the Supreme Court ruled that the First Amendment did not preclude the government from applying this second condition to foreign organizations outside U.S. territory—even with respect to foreign affiliates of U.S. companies.[586] Because these affiliates were "foreign organizations operating abroad" and were legally distinct entities from their U.S. counterparts, the Court concluded they did not possess First Amendment rights.[587]

[P. 1247, after n.1012, add new section:]

The Government Speech Doctrine.—As an outgrowth of the government subsidy cases, such as *Rust v. Sullivan,*[588] the Court has established the "government speech doctrine" that recognizes that a government entity "is entitled to say what it wishes"[589] and to select the views that it wants to express.[590] In this vein, when the government speaks, the government is not barred by the Free Speech Clause of the First Amendment from determining the content of what it says and can engage in viewpoint discrimination.[591] The underlying rationale for the government speech doctrine is that the government could not "function" if the government could not favor or disfavor points of view in enforcing a program.[592] And the Supreme Court has recognized that the government speech doctrine even extends to when the government receives private assistance in helping deliver a government controlled message.[593] As a consequence, the Court, relying on the government speech doctrine, has rejected First Amendment challenges to (1) regulations prohibiting recipients of government funds from advocating, counseling, or referring patients for abortion;[594] (2) disciplinary actions taken as a result of statements made by public employees pursuant to their official duties;[595] (3) mandatory assessments made against cattle merchants when used to fund advertisements whose message was controlled by the government;[596] (4) a city's decision to reject a monument for placement in a public park;[597]

---

[585] *Id.* at 219.

[586] Agency for Int'l Dev. v. All. for Open Soc'y, 140 S. Ct. 2082, 2087 (2020).

[587] *Id.*

[588] 500 U.S. 173 (1991).

[589] Rosenberger v. Rector & Visitors of Univ. of Va., 515 U.S. 819, 829 (1995).

[590] *Id.* at 833.

[591] *See* Pleasant Grove City v. Summum, 555 U.S. 460, 467–68 (2009). Nonetheless, while the First Amendment's Free Speech Clause has no applicability with regard to government speech, it is important to note that other constitutional provisions—such as the Equal Protection principles of the Fifth and Fourteenth Amendments—may constrain what the government can say. *Id.* at 468–69.

[592] *See id.* at 468 ("Indeed, it is not easy to imagine how government could function if it lacked this freedom.").

[593] *See* Johanns v. Livestock Mktg. Ass'n, 544 U.S. 550, 562 (2005).

[594] *See* Rust v. Sullivan, 500 U.S. 173, 194 (1991).

[595] *See* Garcetti v. Ceballos, 547 U.S. 410, 421–22 (2006).

[596] *See Livestock Mktg. Ass'n,* 544 U.S. at 562.

[597] *See Pleasant Grove City,* 555 U.S. at 472.

and (5) a state's decision to reject a design for a specialty license plate for an automobile.[598]

A central issue prompted by the government speech doctrine is determining when speech is that of the government, which can be difficult when the government utilizes or relies on private parties to relay a particular message. In *Johanns v. Livestock Marketing Association,* the Court held that the First Amendment did not prohibit the compelled subsidization of advertisements promoting the sale of beef because the underlying message of the advertisements was "effectively controlled" by the government.[599] Four years later, in *Pleasant Grove City v. Summum,* the Court shifted from an exclusive focus on the "effective control" test in holding that "permanent monuments displayed on public property," even when provided by private parties, generally "represent government speech."[600] In so concluding, the Court relied not only on the fact that a government, in selecting monuments for display in a park, generally exercises "effective control" and has "final approval authority" over the monument, but also on (1) the government's long history of "us[ing] monuments to speak for the public"; and (2) the public's common understanding as to monuments and their role in conveying a message from the government.[601] In *Walker v. Texas Division, Sons of Confederate Veterans,* the Court relied on the same analysis used in *Pleasant Grove City* to conclude that the State of Texas, in approving privately crafted designs for specialty license plates, could reject designs the state found offensive without running afoul of the Free Speech Clause.[602] Specifically, the *Walker* Court held that license plate designs amounted to government speech because (1) states historically used license plates to convey government messages; (2) the public closely identifies license plate designs with the state; and (3) the State of Texas maintained effective control over the messages conveyed on its specialty license plates.[603]

More recently, in *Matal v. Tam,* the Supreme Court held that trademarks do not constitute government speech, concluding that it is "far-fetched to suggest that the content of a registered mark is government speech."[604] The Court distinguished trademarks from the license plates at issue in *Walker,* a case the Court stated "likely marks the outer bounds of the government-speech doctrine."[605] First, the Court noted that, unlike license plates, trademarks do not have a history of use to convey messages by the government. Second, the Court further reasoned that the government does not maintain direct control over the messages conveyed in trademarks—indeed, "[t]he Federal Government does not dream up

---

[598] *See* Walker v. Tex. Div., Sons of Confederate Veterans, Inc., 576 U.S. ___, No. 14-144, slip op. at 1 (2015).

[599] *See Livestock Mktg. Ass'n,* 544 U.S. at 560.

[600] *See Pleasant Grove City,* 555 U.S. at 470.

[601] *Id.* at 470–73.

[602] *See Walker,* slip op. at 1.

[603] *See id.* at 7–12.

[604] 582 U.S. ___, No. 15-1293, slip op. at 14 (2017).

[605] *Id.* at 17–18 ("Trademarks are private, not government, speech.").

these marks, and it does not edit marks submitted for registration." And third, the public, according to the *Tam* Court, does not closely identify trademarks with the government.[606] Thus, while *Tam* demonstrates the Court's continuing reliance on the multi-factor test for determining government speech from *Walker* and *Summum*, that test is not so flexible as to allow for expression like trademarks to be deemed the speech of the government.

Government Regulation of Communications Industries

Commercial Speech.—

[P. 1250, after first paragraph ending ". . . a certified financial planner.", add new paragraph:]

More recently, the Court has distinguished between laws that regulate the conduct of sellers versus those that regulate a seller's speech. In *Expressions Hair Design v. Schneiderman*, the Court held that a New York State statute that prohibits businesses from displaying a cash price alongside a surcharge for credit card purchases burdens speech.[607] Relying on Supreme Court precedent suggesting that "price regulation alone regulates conduct, not speech," the lower court held that the statute was constitutional.[608] The Supreme Court disagreed, stating "[w]hat the law does regulate is how sellers may communicate their prices," and "[i]n regulating the communication of prices rather than prices themselves, [the statute] regulates speech."[609] The Court, however, remanded the case to the lower court to determine in the first instance whether the law survives First Amendment scrutiny.[610]

Government Restraint of Content of Expression

[P. 1268, after n.1123, delete sentences starting "Invalid content regulation includes not only . . . " and ending ". . . accurate description of the purpose and effect of the law.'" and substitute with:]

The constitutionality of content-based regulation is determined by a compelling interest test derived from equal protection analysis: the government "must show that its regulation is necessary to serve a compelling state interest and is narrowly drawn to achieve that end."[611] Narrow tailoring in the case of fully protected speech requires that the government "choose[ ] the least restrictive means to further the

---

[606] *Id.* at 17 (quoting *Walker*, slip op. at 10).
[607] 581 U.S. ___, No. 15-1391, slip op. (2017).
[608] *Id.* at 5.
[609] *Id.* at 9–10.
[610] *Id.* at 1.
[611] Ark. Writers' Project, Inc. v. Ragland, 481 U.S. 221, 231 (1987).

articulated interest."[612] Application of this test ordinarily results in invalidation of the regulation.[613]

The Court has recognized two central ways in which a law can impose content-based restrictions, which include not only restrictions on particular viewpoints, but also prohibitions on public discussions of an entire topic.[614] First, a government regulation of speech is content-based if the regulation on its face draws distinctions based on the message a speaker conveys.[615] For example, in *Boos v. Barry,* the Court held that a Washington D.C. ordinance prohibiting the display of signs near any foreign embassy that brought a foreign government into "public odiom" or "public disrepute" drew a content-based distinction on its face.[616] Second, the Court has recognized that facially content-neutral laws can be considered content-based regulations of speech if a law cannot be "justified without reference to the content of speech" or was adopted "because of disagreement with the message [the speech] conveys."[617] As a result, in an example provided in *Sorrell v. IMS Health,* the Court noted that if a government "bent on frustrating an impending demonstration," passed a law demanding two years' notice before the issuance of parade permits, such a law, while facially content-neutral, would be content-based because its purpose was to suppress speech on a particular topic.[618]

Importantly, for a law that falls within the first category of recognized content-based regulations—those laws that are content-based on their face—the government's justifications or purposes for enacting that law are irrelevant to determine whether the law is subject to strict scrutiny.[619] Put another way, for laws that facially draw distinctions based on the subject-matter of the underlying speech, there is no need for a court to look into the purpose of the underlying law being challenged under the First Amendment; instead, that law is automatically subject to strict scrutiny.[620]

---

[612] Sable Commc'ns of Cal., Inc. v. FCC, 492 U.S. 115, 126 (1989).

[613] *See, e.g.,* Nat'l Inst. of Family and Life Advocates v. Becerra, 585 U.S. ___, No. 16-1140, slip op. at 6–7 (2018) (describing the standard for when courts review content-based regulations of speech as "stringent."). *But see* Williams-Yulee v. Fla. Bar, 575 U.S. ___, No. 13-1499, slip op. (2015) (upholding a provision of the state judicial code prohibiting judicial candidates from personally soliciting campaign funds); Burson v. Freeman, 504 U.S. 191 (1992) (plurality opinion) (upholding state law prohibiting the solicitation of votes and the display or distribution of campaign literature within 100 feet of a polling place).

[614] *See* Ark. Writers' Project, Inc. v. Ragland, 481 U.S. 221, 230 (1987) (citing Consol. Edison Co. v. Pub. Serv. Comm'n, 447 U.S. 530, 537 (1980)).

[615] *See* Ward v. Rock Against Racism, 491 U.S. 781, 791 (1989); *see also* Renton v. Playtime Theatres, Inc., 475 U.S. 41, 48 (1986) (holding that content-neutral "speech regulations are those that are *justified* without reference to the content of the regulated speech.") (internal quotations and citations omitted).

[616] *See* 485 U.S. 312, 315 (1988).

[617] *See Ward,* 491 U.S. at 791.

[618] *See* 564 U.S. 552, 566 (2011).

[619] *See* Turner Broad. Sys., Inc. v. FCC, 512 U.S. 622, 642–43 (1994) ("Nor will the mere assertion of a content-neutral purpose be enough to save a law which, on its face, discriminates, based on content.").

[620] *See* Reed v. Town of Gilbert, 576 U.S. ___, No. 13-502, slip op. at 8 (2015) ("But *Ward*'s .

As such, in *Reed v. Town of Gilbert,* the Court, in invalidating provisions of a municipality's sign code that imposed more stringent restrictions on signs directing the public to an event than on signs conveying political or ideological messages, determined the sign code to be content-based and subject to strict scrutiny, notwithstanding the town's "benign," non-speech related motives for enacting the code.[621] In so holding, the Court reasoned that the First Amendment, by targeting the "abridgement of speech," is centrally concerned with the operations of laws and not the motivations of those who enacted the laws.[622] In this vein, the Court concluded that the "vice" of content-based legislation is not that it will "always" be used for invidious purposes, but rather that content-based restrictions necessarily lend themselves to such purposes.[623]

A law generally regulating speech that *exempts* certain speech on the basis of its content may also raise constitutional concerns. In *Barr v. American Ass'n of Political Consultants,* the Court examined whether an exception in the Telephone Consumer Protection Act of 1991 (TCPA) created invalid, content-based distinctions in the regulatory scheme.[624] Since its enactment in 1991, the TCPA prohibited robocalls to cell phones, with exceptions for emergency calls or automated calls following the prior consent of the receiver.[625] In 2015, Congress amended the TCPA to exempt calls made to collect federal debt, such as student loan debt.[626] In a plurality opinion,[627] Justice Kavanaugh wrote that this "government-debt exception" was content-based on its face, explaining: "A robocall that says, 'Please pay your government debt' is legal. A robocall that says, 'Please donate to our political campaign' is illegal."[628] In the plurality's view, the distinction created by the 2015 amendment was "about as content-based as it gets."[629] The government conceded—and the plurality agreed—that

---

framework applies only if a statute is content-neutral.") (internal citations and quotations omitted).

[621] *Id.* at 8. The *Reed* Court ultimately held that the sign code was not narrowly tailored to further the justifications for the law—aesthetics and traffic safety—because the code did allow many signs that threatened the beauty of the town and because the town could not demonstrate that directional signs posed a greater threat to safety than other types of signs that were treated differently under the code. *Id.* at 14–15.

[622] *Id.* at 10.

[623] *Id.*

[624] 140 S. Ct. 2335 (2020) (plurality opinion).

[625] *Id.* at 2344.

[626] *Id.* at 2344–45.

[627] Justice Kavanaugh's plurality opinion on the First Amendment issue was joined by three other Justices, though, in total, five Members of the Court viewed the government-debt exception as impermissibly content-based, and six Members concluded—one on alternative grounds—that it violated the First Amendment. *Id.* at 2344; *see also id.* at 2356 (Sotomayor, J., concurring in the judgment) (agreeing with "much of the partial dissent's explanation that strict scrutiny should not apply to all content-based distinctions," but concluding that the government-debt exception nevertheless "fails intermediate scrutiny" because it is not "narrowly tailored"); *id.* at 2364 (Gorsuch, J., concurring in the judgment in part and dissenting in part) ("In my view, the TCPA's rule against cellphone robocalls is a content-based restriction that fails strict scrutiny."). Seven Members of the Court concluded that the government-debt exception could be severed without invalidating the TCPA in its entirety. *Id.* at 2342 (plurality opinion).

[628] *Id.* at 2346.

[629] *Id.*

the exception did not satisfy strict scrutiny because the government had not "sufficiently justified the differentiation between government-debt collection speech and other important categories of robocall speech, such as political speech, charitable fundraising, issue advocacy, commercial advertising, and the like."[630]

While content-based restrictions on protected speech are presumptively unconstitutional, the Supreme Court has recognized that the First Amendment permits restrictions upon the content of speech in a "few limited areas," including obscenity, defamation, fraud, incitement, fighting words, and speech integral to criminal conduct.[631] This "two-tier" approach to content-based regulations of speech derives from *Chaplinsky v. New Hampshire*, wherein the Court opined that there exist "certain well-defined and narrowly limited classes of speech [that] are no essential part of any exposition of ideas, and are of such slight social value as a step to truth" such that the government may prevent those utterances and punish those uttering them without raising any constitutional issues.[632] As the Court has generally applied *Chaplinsky* over the past seventy years, if speech fell within one of the "well-defined and narrowly limited" categories, it was unprotected, regardless of its effect. If it did not, it was covered by the First Amendment, and the speech was protected unless the restraint was justified by some test relating to harm, such as the clear and present danger test or the more modern approach of balancing the presumptively protected expression against a compelling governmental interest.

For several decades now, the cases reflect a fairly consistent and sustained movement by the Court toward eliminating or severely narrowing the "two-tier" doctrine. As a result, expression that before would have been held absolutely unprotected (*e.g.*, seditious speech and seditious libel, fighting words, defamation, and obscenity) received protection. While the movement was temporarily deflected by a shift in position with respect to obscenity and by the creation of a new category of non-obscene child pornography,[633] the most recent decisions of the Court reflect a reluctance to add any new categories of excepted speech and to interpret narrowly the excepted categories of speech that have long-established roots in First Amendment law.[634]

---

[630] *Id.* at 2347.

[631] *See* United States v. Stevens, 559 U.S. 460, 468 (2010).

[632] 315 U.S. 568, 571–72 (1942).

[633] *See* New York v. Ferber, 458 U.S. 747, 759 (1982).

[634] *See, e.g.*, Hustler Magazine v. Falwell, 485 U.S. 46, 55 (1988) (refusing to restrict speech based on its level of "outrageousness"); *see also* Nat'l Inst. of Family and Life Advocates v. Becerra, 585 U.S. ___, No. 16-1140, slip op. at 8, 12–14 (2018) (declining to recognize "professional speech" as a separate category of speech, noting the "dangers associated with content-based regulations of speech . . . in the context of professional speech"); United States v. Alvarez, 567 U.S. 709, 718 (2012) (plurality opinion) ("Absent from those few categories where the law allows content-based regulation of speech is any general exception to the First Amendment for false statements."); Brown v. Entm't Merchs. Ass'n, 564 U.S. 786, 794–96 (holding that the obscenity exception to the First Amendment does not

Even if a category of speech is *unprotected* by the First Amendment, regulation of that speech on the basis of viewpoint may be *impermissible*. In *R.A.V. v. City of St. Paul*,[635] the Court struck down a hate crimes ordinance that the state courts had construed to apply only to the use of "fighting words." The difficulty, the Court found, was that the ordinance discriminated further, proscribing only those fighting words that "arouse[ ] anger, alarm or resentment in others . . . on the basis of race, color, creed, religion or gender."[636] This amounted to "special prohibitions on those speakers who express views on disfavored subjects."[637] The fact that the government may proscribe areas of speech such as obscenity, defamation, or fighting words does not mean that these areas "may be made the vehicles for content discrimination unrelated to their distinctively proscribable content. Thus, the government may proscribe libel; but it may not make the further content discrimination of proscribing *only* libel critical of the government."[638]

Group Libel, Hate Speech.—

[P. 1280, after n.1194, add new paragraph:]

Legislation intended to prevent offense of individuals and groups of people has also been struck down as unconstitutional. For example, in *Matal v. Tam*, the Supreme Court considered a federal law prohibiting the registration of trademarks that "may disparage . . . or bring . . . into contempt[ ] or disrepute" any "persons, living or dead."[639] In *Tam*, the Patent and Trademark Office rejected a trademark application for THE SLANTS for an Asian-American dance-rock band because it found the mark may be disparaging to Asian Americans.[640] The Court held that the disparagement provision violates the Free Speech Clause as "[i]t offends a bedrock First Amendment principle: Speech may not be banned on the ground that it expresses ideas that offend."[641] Two years later, the Court invalidated another statutory trademark restriction—one prohibiting the registration of "immoral" or "scandalous" marks—on similar grounds.[642]

---

cover violent speech); *Stevens*, 559 U.S. at 472 (declining to "carve out" an exception to First Amendment protections for depictions of illegal acts of animal cruelty).

[635] 505 U.S. 377 (1992).

[636] *Id.* at 391.

[637] *Id.*

[638] *Id.* at 383–84.

[639] 582 U.S. ___, No. 15-1293, slip op. (2017).

[640] *Id.* at 1.

[641] *Id.* at 1–2.

[642] Iancu v. Brunetti, 588 U.S. ___, No. 18-302, slip op. at 2 (2019) (quoting 15 U.S.C. § 1052(a)). *See also infra* Amend. 1, Non-obscene But Sexually Explicit and Indecent Expression.

Non-obscene But Sexually Explicit and Indecent Expression.—

[P. 1315, after sentence ending ". . . but its reliance on secondary effects suggests that they could not.", add new paragraph:]

Regardless of the government's interests in regulating indecent expression, it may not restrict such expression in a viewpoint discriminatory way, as the Supreme Court reaffirmed in *Iancu v. Brunetti.*[643] *Iancu* involved a provision of the Lanham Act, the federal law governing trademarks, that prohibited the registration of "immoral" or "scandalous" marks.[644] Drawing on dictionary definitions of those terms, the Court concluded that "the statute, on its face, distinguishes between two opposed sets of ideas: those aligned with conventional moral standards and those hostile to them; those inducing societal nods of approval and those provoking offense and condemnation," thus discriminating on the basis of viewpoint.[645] In holding this provision unconstitutional, the Court declined to construe the statute, as the government urged, as prohibiting certain *ways* of expressing ideas such as vulgarity or profanity rather than barring expression of the ideas themselves.[646] The Court reasoned that the law by its own terms reached content beyond sexually explicit and profane speech.[647]

Speech Plus—The Constitutional Law of Leafleting, Picketing, and Demonstrating

The Public Forum.—

[P. 1318, delete n.1396 and substitute with:]

E.g., Minnesota Voters Alliance v. Mansky, 585 U.S. ___, No. 16-1435, slip op. at 13 (2018) (polling places); ISKCON v. Lee, 505 U.S. 672, 679 (1992) (publicly owned airport terminal); Perry Educ. Ass'n v. Perry Local Educators' Ass'n, 460 U.S. 37, 46 (1983) (interschool mail system); United States Postal Service v. Council of Greenburgh Civic Ass'ns, 453 U.S. 114, 128 (1981) (private mail boxes); Greer v. Spock, 424 U.S. 828, 838 (1976) (military bases); Lehman v. City of Shaker Heights, 418 U.S. 298, 304 (1974) (plurality opinion) (advertising space in city rapid transit cars); Adderley v. Florida, 385 U.S. 39, 47–48 (1966) (jails).

[P. 1321, at end of sentence starting "The Court has defined . . .", add new footnote:]

E.g., Minnesota Voters Alliance v. Mansky, 585 U.S. ___, No. 16-1435, slip op. at 7 (2018).

---

[643] 588 U.S. ___, No. 18-302, slip op. (2019).

[644] *Id.* at 2 (quoting 15 U.S.C. § 1052(a)).

[645] *Id.* at 6, 8. The Court illustrated how the statute "favors" and "disfavors" certain viewpoints with the following examples: "'Love rules'? 'Always be good'? Registration follows. 'Hate rules'? 'Always be cruel'? Not according to the Lanham Act's 'immoral or scandalous' bar." *Id.* at 6.

[646] *Id.* at 8–9.

[647] *Id.* Accordingly, the Court declined to reach the question of whether "a statute limited to lewd, sexually explicit, and profane marks" would comport with the First Amendment. *Id.* at 10 n.*.

[P. 1321, delete sentence starting "First, . . ." and substitute with:]

First, there is the traditional public forum—places such as streets and parks that have traditionally been used for public assembly and debate.[648] In such a forum, the government "may impose reasonable time, place, and manner restrictions on private speech, but restrictions based on content must satisfy strict scrutiny, and those based on viewpoint are prohibited."[649]

[P. 1321, after sentence starting "Second, . . .", add new footnote:]

Minnesota Voters Alliance, slip op. at 11. See also *Summum*, 555 U.S. at 469–70.

[P. 1321, delete sentence starting "Third, . . ." and substitute with:]

Third, in a "nonpublic forum," or "a space that 'is not by tradition or designation a forum for public communication,'"[650] the government "may reserve the forum for its intended purposes, communicative or otherwise, as long as the regulation on speech is reasonable and not an effort to suppress expression merely because public officials oppose the speaker's view."[651]

[P. 1322, delete sentence starting "The distinction between . . ."]

[PP. 1322–23, delete paragraph starting "The Court held that . . ." and substitute with:]

Whether a speech restriction will be reviewed under strict scrutiny or only for reasonableness thus may turn in part on whether the government has "intentionally open[ed] a nontraditional forum for public discourse," creating a designated public forum.[652] To determine whether a forum is a designated public forum or a nonpublic forum, the Court will look to the government's intent in opening the forum,[653] the restrictions

---

[648] Pleasant Grove City v. Summum, 555 U.S. 460, 469 (2009).

[649] *Minnesota Voters Alliance*, slip op. at 11. *See also Summum*, 555 U.S. at 469. *Cf.* Clark v. Cmty. for Creative Non-Violence, 468 U.S. 288, 293 (1984) ("[T]ime, place, or manner restrictions . . . . are valid provided that they are justified without reference to the content of the regulated speech, that they are narrowly tailored to serve a significant governmental interest, and that they leave open ample alternative channels for communication of the information.").

[650] *Minnesota Voters Alliance*, slip op. at 7 (quoting *Perry Educ. Ass'n*, 460 U.S. at 46).

[651] *Perry Educ. Ass'n*, 460 U.S. at 46.

[652] *See* Cornelius v. NAACP Legal Def. & Educ. Fund, 473 U.S. 788, 802 (1985). *See also* United States v. Am. Library Ass'n, 539 U.S. 194, 206 (2003) (plurality opinion) ("To create such a [designated public] forum, the government must make an affirmative choice to open up its property for use as a public forum."); United States v. Kokinda, 497 U.S. 720, 727 (1990) (plurality opinion) (holding certain sidewalks were a nonpublic forum because the government owner had not "expressly dedicated" them "to any expressive activity"). *Cf.* Members of City Council of Los Angeles v. Taxpayers for Vincent, 466 U.S. 789, 814 (1984) ("Appellees' reliance on the public forum doctrine is misplaced. They fail to demonstrate the existence of a traditional right of access respecting such items as utility poles for purposes of their communication comparable to that recognized for public streets and parks . . . .").

[653] *Cornelius*, 473 U.S. at 803.

initially placed on speakers' access to the forum,[654] and the nature of the forum.[655] For example, in *Cornelius v. NAACP Legal Defense and Educational Fund*, the Court held that the Combined Federal Campaign (CFC), "an annual charitable fundraising drive conducted in the federal workplace,"[656] was a nonpublic forum.[657] Notwithstanding the fact that the federal government had opened the forum for solicitation by *some* charitable organizations, the Court concluded that "neither [the government's] practice nor its policy [was] consistent with an intent to designate the CFC as a public forum open to *all* tax-exempt organizations."[658] Accordingly, the Court upheld the government's decision to exclude certain charitable organizations as reasonable in light of the purpose of the forum.[659] Similarly, the Court concluded in another case that a school district had not created a public forum with its system for internal school mail because the district had not, "by policy or by practice," "opened its mail system for indiscriminate use by the general public."[660] The Court therefore concluded that the school district could permissibly exclude a teacher's association from using the mail system, while also allowing a different teacher's association—the teachers' exclusive representative—to use the mail system, because the school's policy was reasonable and consistent with the purposes of the forum.[661]

However, although the government has greater discretion to restrict speech in nonpublic forums,[662] the First Amendment still prohibits certain restrictions even in nonpublic forums. For instance, the Court held in *Minnesota Voters Alliance v. Mansky* that "[a] polling place in Minnesota qualifies as a nonpublic forum."[663] After reviewing the long history of state regulation of polling places on election day,[664] the Court concluded that because the polling place was "government-controlled

---

[654] *See Perry Educ. Ass'n*, 460 U.S. at 47–48.

[655] *Cornelius*, 473 U.S. at 803.

[656] *Id.* at 790.

[657] *Id.* at 805.

[658] *Id.* at 804 (emphasis added).

[659] *Id.* at 809.

[660] *See* Perry Educ. Ass'n v. Perry Local Educators' Ass'n, 460 U.S. 37, 47 (1983). The Court also stated, however, that "even if we assume that by granting access to the Cub Scouts, YMCA's, and parochial schools, the School District has created a 'limited' public forum, the constitutional right of access would in any event extend only to other entities of similar character. While the school mail facilities thus might be a forum generally open for use by the Girl Scouts, the local boys' club, and other organizations that engage in activities of interest and educational relevance to students, they would not as a consequence be open to an organization such as [the Perry Local Educators' Association], which is concerned with the terms and conditions of teacher employment." *Id.* at 48. In *United States v. Kokinda*, 497 U.S. 720, 730 (1990) (plurality opinion), the Court interpreted this language to mean that in a limited public forum, "regulation of the reserved nonpublic uses would still require application of the reasonableness test."

[661] *Perry Educ. Ass'n*, 460 U.S. at 50–51. *See also* Hazelwood Sch. Dist. v. Kuhlmeier, 484 U.S. 260, 269–70 (1988) (holding that a student newspaper created as part of "a supervised learning experience" was not a public forum).

[662] *See, e.g.*, United States v. Am. Library Ass'n, Inc., 539 U.S. 194, 204–05 (2003) (plurality opinion).

[663] Minnesota Voters Alliance v. Mansky, 585 U.S. ___, No. 16-1435, slip op. at 8 (2018).

[664] *Id.* at 1–3.

property set aside for the sole purpose of voting,"[665] it qualified as "a special enclave, subject to greater restriction."[666] Although the forum's designation as a nonpublic forum meant that the Court did not apply strict scrutiny, the Court nonetheless struck down a Minnesota law that barred all "political" apparel from polling places as unreasonable.[667] The Court acknowledged that the state could permissibly seek to "prohibit certain apparel" in polling places "because of the message it conveys,"[668] but concluded that the particular scheme followed by Minnesota was not "capable of reasoned application."[669] In the Court's view, the breadth of the term "political" and the state's "haphazard interpretations"[670] of that term failed to provide "objective, workable standards" to guide the discretion of the election judges who implemented the statute.[671]

[PP. 1323–24, delete first full paragraph starting "Application of the doctrine . . ." through first full paragraph starting "Nevertheless, . . ." and substitute with:]

Application of these principles continues to raise often difficult questions. In *United States v. Kokinda*, a majority of Justices that ultimately upheld a ban on soliciting contributions on postal premises under the "reasonableness" review governing nonpublic fora could not agree on the public forum status of a sidewalk located entirely on postal service property.[672] Two years later, in *International Society for Krishna Consciousness, Inc. v. Lee*, the Court similarly divided as to whether non-secured areas of airport terminals, including shops and restaurants, constitute public fora.[673] A five-justice majority held that airport terminals are not public fora and upheld regulations banning the repetitive solicitation of money within the terminals.[674]

A decade later, the Court considered the public forum status of the Internet. In *United States v. American Library Association, Inc.*, a four-justice plurality held that "Internet access in public libraries is neither a 'traditional' nor a 'designated' public forum."[675] The plurality therefore did

---

[665] *Id.* at 8.

[666] *Id.* (quoting Int'l Soc'y for Krishna Consciousness, Inc. v. Lee, 505 U.S. 672, 680 (1992)) (internal quotation marks omitted).

[667] *Id.* at 13.

[668] *Id.* at 12.

[669] *Id.* at 19.

[670] *Id.* at 13.

[671] *Id.* at 18.

[672] 497 U.S. 720, 727 (1990) ("[R]egulation of speech activity where the Government has not dedicated its property to First Amendment activity is examined only for reasonableness.").

[673] 505 U.S. 672 (1992).

[674] *Id.* at 683 ("[N]either by tradition nor purpose can the terminals be described as satisfying the standards we have previously set out for identifying a public forum.").

[675] 539 U.S. 194, 205–06 (2003) ("We have 'rejected the view that traditional public forum status extends beyond its historic confines.' The doctrines surrounding traditional public forums may not be extended to situations where such history is lacking." (quoting Ark. Educ. TV Comm'n v. Forbes, 523 U.S. 666, 679 (1998))). While decided on constitutional vagueness grounds, in *Reno v. American Civil Liberties Union*, the Court struck down a provision of the

not apply strict scrutiny in upholding the Children's Internet Protection Act, which provides that a public school or "library may not receive federal assistance to provide Internet access unless it installs software to block images that constitute obscenity or child pornography, and to prevent minors from obtaining access to material that is harmful to them."[676]

More recently, in *Packingham v. North Carolina*, the Court appeared to equate the Internet to traditional public fora like a street or public park. Specifically, Justice Kennedy, writing for the Court, observed that, "[w]hile in the past there may have been difficulty in identifying the most important places (in a spatial sense) for the exchange of views, today the answer is clear. It is cyberspace—the 'vast democratic forums of the Internet' in general, and social media in particular."[677] Consequently, the Court struck down a North Carolina law making it a felony for registered sex offenders to use commercial social networking websites that allow minor children to be members, such as Facebook. Applying strict scrutiny, the Court held that the North Carolina law impermissibly restricted lawful speech as it was not narrowly tailored to serve the government's interest in protecting minors from registered sex offenders because it "foreclose[d] access to social media altogether," thereby "prevent[ing] the user from engaging in the legitimate exercise of First Amendment rights."[678]

Communications Decency Act of 1996 that prohibited the use of an "interactive computer service" (i.e., the Internet) to display indecent material "in a manner available to a person under 18 years of age." 521 U.S. 844, 860 (1997). The Court did not consider the Internet's status as a forum for free speech, but observed that the Internet "constitutes a vast platform from which to address and hear from a world-wide audience of millions of readers, viewers, researchers, and buyers. Any person or organization with a computer connected to the Internet can 'publish' information." *Id.* at 853.

[676] *American Library Association*, 539 U.S. at 199; *see also id.* at 206 ("A public library does not acquire Internet terminals in order to create a public forum for Web publishers to express themselves, any more than it collects books in order to provide a public forum for the authors of books to speak.").

[677] Packingham v. North Carolina, 582 U.S. ___, No. 15-1194, slip op. at 4–5 (2017) (quoting *Am. Civil Liberties Union*, 521 at 868); *see also id.* at 6 ("This case is one of the first this Court has taken to address the relationship between the First Amendment and the modern Internet. As a result, the Court must exercise extreme caution before suggesting that the First Amendment provides scant protection for access to vast networks in that medium.").

[678] *Id.* at 6, 8; *see id.* at 7 ("[G]iven the broad wording of the North Carolina statute at issue, it might well bar access not only to commonplace social media websites but also to websites as varied as Amazon.com, Washingtonpost.com, and Webmd.com."). The Court was careful to point out, however, that its opinion should not be read as barring states from enacting laws more specific than that of North Carolina, noting that "[s]pecific criminal acts are not protected speech even if speech is the means for their commission." *Id.* (citing Brandenburg v. Ohio, 395 U.S. 444, 447–49 (1969)). Indeed, "it can be assumed that the First Amendment permits a State to enact specific, narrowly tailored laws that prohibit a sex offender from engaging in conduct that often presages a sexual crime, like contacting a minor or using a website to gather information about a minor." *Id.*

Public Issue Picketing and Parading.—

[P. 1336, after first partial paragraph, add new paragraph:]

In *McCullen v. Coakley*, the Court retained a content-neutral analysis similar to that in *Hill*, but nonetheless struck down a statutory thirty-five foot buffer zone at entrances and driveways of abortion facilities.[679] The Court concluded that the buffer zone was not narrowly tailored to serve governmental interests in maintaining public safety and preserving access to reproductive healthcare facilities, the concerns claimed by Massachusetts to underlie the law.[680] The opinion cited several alternatives to the buffer zone that would not curtail the use of public sidewalks as traditional public fora for speech, nor significantly burden the ability of those wishing to provide "sidewalk counseling" to women approaching abortion clinics. Specifically, the Court held that, to preserve First Amendment rights, targeted measures, such as injunctions, enforcement of anti-harassment ordinances, and use of general crowd control authority, as needed, are preferable to broad, prophylactic measures.[681]

---

[679] 573 U.S. ___, No. 12-1168, slip op. at 11–18 (2014).

[680] *Id.* at 19–23.

[681] *Id.* at 23–29.

SECOND AMENDMENT

IN GENERAL

[P. 1353, delete n.12 and substitute with:]

554 U.S. 570 (2008)

[P. 1353, n.13, delete citation at end of footnote and substitute with:]

Id. at 578–80.

[P. 1354, delete n.14 and substitute with:]

Id. at 580–91. In so doing, the *Heller* Court rejected the argument that "only those weapons useful in warfare are protected" by the Second Amendment, as the "traditional militia was formed from a pool of men bringing arms 'in common use at the time' for lawful purposes like self-defense." *Id.* at 624–25 (quoting United States v. Miller, 307 U.S. 174, 179 (1939)) ("We therefore read *Miller* to say only that the Second Amendment does not protect those weapons not typically possessed by law-abiding citizens for lawful purposes, such as short-barreled shotguns."); *see also* Caetano v. Massachusetts, 577 U.S. ___, No. 14-10078, slip op. at 2 (2016) (vacating a ruling by a state court that a ban on stun guns did not violate the Second Amendment because such weapons were "not readily adaptable to use in the military.").

[P. 1354, delete n.15 and substitute with:]

Heller, 554 U.S. at 594–96. Similarly, the phrase "security of a free state" was found to refer not to the defense of a particular state, but to the protection of the national polity. *Id.* at 596–98.

[P. 1354, delete n.16 and substitute with:]

Id. at 628–29. Subsequently, in *Caetano v. Massachusetts,* the Court emphasized that, under *Heller,* the protections of the Second Amendment extend to firearms that were not in existence at the time of the Framers. *See Caetano,* slip op. at 2 (per curiam) (vacating and remanding a Massachusetts state court ruling upholding a state law that prohibited the possession of stun guns, in part, on the grounds that stun guns were not in common use when the Second Amendment was adopted).

[P. 1354, after sentence starting "Similarly, the requirement . . .", add new footnote:]

Heller, 554 U.S. at 630.

[P. 1354, after sentence starting "However, the Court specifically stated . . .", add new footnote:]

Id. at 626.

[P. 1354, after sentence "The Court also noted that there was a historical tradition . . . would not be affected.", add new footnote:]

Id. at 627 (2008). *But see Caetano*, slip op. at 2 (rejecting, as inconsistent with *Heller*, the view that a weapon may be deemed "unusual" if it was not in common use at the time when the Second Amendment was adopted, as well as the view that the Second Amendment only protects weapons that are "useful in warfare").

[P. 1354, delete n.17 and substitute with:]

Heller, 554 U.S. at 629 n.27 (discussing the non-application of rational basis review).

FOURTH AMENDMENT

[P. 1361, in third line of Fourth Amendment text, delete semicolon (;) following word "violated" and substitute with:]

",
"

SEARCH AND SEIZURE

History and Scope of the Amendment

Scope of the Amendment.—

[P. 1366, after n.26, add new sentence:]

> The Court has also recognized that exigent circumstances may justify performing a blood test without a warrant on a motorist to determine his or her blood alcohol concentration (BAC).[682]

[P. 1369, after sentence starting "Permitting all off-the-wall observations, . . .", add new sentence:]

> To some extent, the Court has grounded this concern about expectations of privacy in "Founding-era understandings,"[683] explaining that the Fourth Amendment "seeks to secure 'the privacies of life' against 'arbitrary power,'"[684] and that "a central aim of the Framers was 'to place obstacles in the way of a too permeating police surveillance.'"[685]

[P. 1370, after n.48, add new sentence:]

> On the other hand, the Court has held that "a person has no legitimate expectation of privacy in information he voluntarily turns over to third parties."[686]

---

[682] *See* Missouri v. McNeely, 569 U.S. 141, 156 (2013) (rejecting a *per se* exception to the warrant requirement for BAC blood testing in suspected "drunk-driving" cases and requiring that exigent circumstances be evaluated under a "totality of the circumstances" test). *Cf.* Mitchell v. Wisconsin, 588 U.S. ___, No. 18-6210, slip op. at 8–9 (2019) (plurality opinion) (declining to "revisit" the rule established in *McNeely* but concluding that in circumstances involving unconscious drivers, where a breath test for BAC cannot be performed, exigent circumstances generally exist to take a warrantless blood test).

[683] Carpenter v. United States, 585 U.S. ___, No. 16-402, slip op. at 6 (2018).

[684] *Id.* (quoting Boyd v. United States, 116 U.S. 616, 630 (1886)).

[685] *Id.* (quoting United States v. Di Re, 332 U.S. 581, 595 (1948)).

[686] Smith v. Maryland, 442 U.S. 735, 743–44 (1979). *See also* United States v. Miller, 425 U.S. 435, 442 (1976). Concurring in *United States v. Jones*, 565 U.S. 400 (2012), Justice Sotomayor questioned the continuing viability of this principle in "the digital age, in which people reveal a great deal of information about themselves to third parties in the course of carrying out mundane tasks." *Id.* at 417 (Sotomayor, J., concurring). Relying on this concurrence, the *Carpenter* Court recognized a limit to the third-party doctrine when it "decline[d] to extend *Smith* and *Miller*" to "the qualitatively different category of cell-site

The Interest Protected.—

[P. 1372, delete paragraph starting "In *United States v. Jones . . .*" and substitute with:]

In *United States v. Jones*,[687] the Court seemed to revitalize the significance of governmental trespass in determining whether a Fourth Amendment search has occurred. In *Jones*, the Court considered whether the attachment of a Global-Positioning-System (GPS) device to a car used by a suspected narcotics dealer, and the monitoring of such device for twenty-eight days, constituted a search. Although the Court ruled unanimously that this month-long monitoring violated Jones's rights, it splintered on the reasoning. A majority of the Court relied on the theory of common law trespass to find that the attachment of the device to the car represented a physical intrusion into Jones's constitutionally protected "effect" or private property.[688] While this holding obviated the need to assess the month-long tracking under *Katz*'s reasonable expectation of privacy test, five Justices, who concurred either with the majority opinion or concurred with the judgment, would have held that long-term GPS tracking can implicate an individual's expectation of privacy.[689] Some have read these concurrences as partly premised on the idea that while government access to a small data set—for example, one trip in a vehicle—might not violate one's expectation of privacy, aggregating a month's worth of personal data allows the government to

---

records." *Carpenter*, slip op. at 11. The Court noted that this data provides "an all-encompassing record of the [cell phone] holder's whereabouts," tracking "nearly exactly the movements of [the cell phone's] owner" and operating both prospectively and retroactively. *Id.* at 12–13. Instead, the Court held that "an individual maintains a legitimate expectation of privacy in the record of his physical movements as captured through" cell-site location information. *Id.* at 11.

[687] 565 U.S. 400 (2012).

[688] *Id.* at 403–07. The physical trespass analysis was reprised in subsequent opinions. In its 2013 decision in *Florida v. Jardines*, the Court assessed whether a law enforcement officer had the legal authority to conduct a drug sniff with a trained canine on the front porch of a suspect's home. Reviewing the law of trespass, the Court observed that visitors to a home, including the police, must have either explicit or implicit authority from the homeowner to enter upon and engage in various activities in the curtilage (i.e., the area immediately surrounding the home). Finding that the use of the dog to find incriminating evidence exceeded "background social norms" of what a visitor is normally permitted to do on another's property, the Court held that the drug sniff constituted a search. 569 U.S. 1, 7–10 (2013). Similarly, in its 2015 per curiam opinion in *Grady v. North Carolina*, the Court emphasized the "physical intru[sion]" on a person when it found that attaching a device to a person's body, without consent, for the purpose of tracking the person's movements, constitutes a search within the meaning of the Fourth Amendment. 575 U.S. ___, No. 14-593, slip op. at 4–5 (2015). Neither the majority in *Jardines* nor the Court in *Grady* addressed whether the challenged conduct violates a reasonable expectation of privacy under *Katz v. United States*. *Grady*, slip op. at 5; *Jardines*, 569 U.S. 10–12.

[689] *Jones*, slip op. at 14 (Alito, J., concurring in the judgment, joined by Ginsburg, Breyer, Kagan, JJ.) (concluding that respondent's reasonable expectations of privacy were violated by the long-term monitoring of the movements of the respondent's vehicle); *id.* at 3 (Sotomayor, J., concurring) (disagreeing with Justice Alito's "approach" to the specific case but agreeing "longer term GPS monitoring in investigations of most offenses impinges on expectations of privacy.").

create a "mosaic" about an individual's personal life that violates that individual's reasonable expectation of privacy.[690]

The Court confirmed in *Carpenter v. United States* that the Fourth Amendment is implicated when government action violates individuals' "reasonable expectation of privacy in the whole of their physical movements," regardless of whether the challenged conduct constitutes a physical trespass.[691] The Court held that the government could not, without a warrant, access seven days of a defendant's cell-site location information, which is data that continuously tracks the location of a cell phone.[692] Observing that "historical cell-site records present even greater privacy concerns than the GPS monitoring of a vehicle we considered in *Jones*," the Court highlighted the continuing importance of the expectations-of-privacy test.[693] The Court acknowledged that it had previously declined to extend Fourth Amendment protection to information that a person had voluntarily given to a third party like a wireless carrier, but declined to extend that line of cases to "the qualitatively different category of cell-site records."[694]

Arrests and Other Detentions.—

[P. 1373, after sentence ending " . . . whether a warrant has been obtained," add new sentence:]

To determine whether an officer has probable cause to make a warrantless arrest, courts consider the "totality of the circumstances," examining "the events leading up to the arrest" and deciding "whether these historical facts, viewed from the standpoint of an objectively reasonable police

---

[690] *See, e.g., In re* Application for Telephone Information Needed for a Criminal Investigation, 119 F. Supp. 3d 1011, 1021–22 (N.D. Cal. 2015) (discussing the import of the two concurring opinions from *Jones*); United States v. Brooks, 911 F. Supp. 2d 836, 842 (D. Ariz. 2012) (noting that "[w]hile it does appear that in some future case, a five justice 'majority' is willing to accept the principle that Government surveillance can implicate an individual's reasonable expectation of privacy over time, *Jones* does not dictate the result of the case at hand . . ."); *but see* United States v. Graham, 824 F.3d 421, 435–36 (4th Cir. 2016) (arguing that Justice Alito's *Jones* concurrence should be read more narrowly so as to not implicate government access to information collected by third-party actors, no matter the quantity of information collected); In re Application of FBI, No. BR 14-01, 2014 WL 5463097, at *10 (FISA Ct. Mar. 20, 2014) ("While the concurring opinions in Jones may signal that some or even most of the Justices are ready to revisit certain settled Fourth Amendment principles, the decision in)Jones itself breaks no new ground . . .").

[691] 585 U.S. ___, No. 16-402, slip op. at 12 (2018).

[692] *Id.* at 11.

[693] *Id.* at 13.

[694] *Id.* at 11.

officer, amount to" probable cause.[695] Probable cause is not a "high bar,"[696] requiring only a "probability or substantial chance of criminal activity, not an actual showing of such activity."[697]

[P. 1374, at end of n.66, delete "." and substitute with:]

; Plumhoff v. Rickard, 572 U.S. 765 (2014) (police use of fifteen gunshots to end a police chase).

The Court has also made clear that the Fourth Amendment applies to pre-trial detention. *See* Manuel v. Joliet, 580 U.S. ___, No. 14-9496, slip op. at 1 (2017) (holding that a petitioner who "was held in jail for seven weeks after a judge relied on allegedly fabricated evidence to find probable cause that he had committed a crime" could "challenge his pretrial detention on the ground that it violated the Fourth Amendment").

[P. 1375, n.73, after "Virginia v. Moore, 128 S. Ct. 1598 (2008)", add:]

See also Heien v. North Carolina, 574 U.S. ___, No. 13-604, slip op. at 5 (2014) (holding that a mistake of law can give rise to the reasonable suspicion necessary to uphold the seizure of a vehicle). The law enforcement officer in *Heien* had stopped the vehicle because it had only one working brake light, which the officer understood to be a violation of the North Carolina vehicle code. *Id.* at 2. However, a North Carolina court subsequently held, in a case of first impression, that the vehicle code only requires one working brake light. *Id.* at 3. In holding that reasonable suspicion can rest on a mistaken understanding of a legal prohibition, a majority of the Supreme Court noted prior cases finding that mistakes of fact do not preclude reasonable suspicion and concluded that "reasonable men make mistakes of law, too." *Id.* at 5–6 (citing Illinois v. Rodriguez, 497 U.S. 177, 183–86 (1990), and Hill v. California, 401 U.S. 797, 802–05 (1971), as cases involving mistakes of fact).

Searches and Inspections in Noncriminal Cases.—

[P. 1377, delete first sentence and substitute with:]

In *Donovan v. Dewey,*[698] however, the Court seemingly limited *Barlow*'s reach and articulated a new standard that appeared to permit extensive governmental inspection of commercial property without a warrant.

[P. 1378, delete sentence "*Dewey* suggests, therefore, that warrantless inspections of commercial establishments are permissible so long as the legislature carefully drafts its statute."]

---

[695] Maryland v. Pringle, 540 U.S. 366, 371 (2003) (internal citations and quotations omitted). The totality of circumstances approach requires courts to consider the "whole picture" and to not look at each fact as presented to the reasonable officer in isolation. *See* District of Columbia v. Wesby, 583 U.S. ___, No. 15-1485, slip op. at 11 (2018). Moreover, the existence of an "innocent explanation" for a particular circumstance is insufficient to deny probable cause for an arrest when, in considering all of the circumstances, including any plausible innocent explanations, a reasonable officer can conclude that there is a "substantial chance of criminal activity." *Id.* at 12.

[696] Kaley v. United States, 571 U.S. 320, 338 (2014).

[697] Illinois v. Gates, 462 U.S. 213, 232 (1983).

[698] 452 U.S. 594 (1981).

[P. 1379, after paragraph starting *"Dewey* was applied in *New York v. Burger* . . .", add new paragraph:]

Most recently, however, in *City of Los Angeles v. Patel*, the Court declined to extend the "more relaxed standard" applicable to searches of closely regulated businesses to hotels when invalidating a Los Angeles ordinance that gave police the ability to inspect hotel registration records without advance notice and carried a six-month term of imprisonment and a $1,000 fine for hotel operators who failed to make such records available.[699] The *Patel* Court, characterizing inspections pursuant to this ordinance as "administrative searches,"[700] held "that a hotel owner must be afforded an *opportunity* to have a neutral decision maker review an officer's demand to search the registry before he or she faces penalties for failing to comply" for such a search to be permissible under the Fourth Amendment.[701] In so doing, the Court expressly declined to treat the hotel industry as a "closely regulated" industry subject to the more relaxed standard applied in *Dewey* and *Burger* on the grounds that doing so would "permit what has always been a narrow exception to swallow the rule."[702] The Court emphasized that, over the prior 45 years, it had recognized only four industries as having "such a history of government oversight that no reasonable expectation of privacy . . . could exist for a proprietor over the stock of such an enterprise."[703] These four industries involve liquor sales, firearms dealing, mining, and running an automobile junkyard, and the Court distinguished hotel operations from these industries, in part, because "nothing inherent in the operation of hotels poses a clear and significant risk to the public welfare."[704] However, the Court also suggested that, even if hotels were to be seen as pervasively regulated, the Los Angeles ordinance would still be deemed unreasonable because (1) there was no substantial government interest informing the regulatory scheme; (2) warrantless inspections were not necessary to further the government's purpose; and (3) the inspection program did not provide, in

---

[699] 576 U.S. ___, No. 13-1175, slip op. at 14 (2015). *Patel* involved a facial, rather than an as-applied, challenge to the Los Angeles ordinance. The Court clarified that facial challenges under the Fourth Amendment are "not categorically barred or especially disfavored." *Id.* at 4. Some had apparently taken the Court's earlier statement in *Sibron v. New York*, 392 U.S. 40 (1968), that "[t]he constitutional validity of a warrantless search is pre-eminently the sort of question which can only be decided in the concrete factual context of the individual case," *id.* at 59, to foreclose facial Fourth Amendment challenges. *Patel*, slip op. at 5. However, the *Patel* Court construed *Sibron*'s language to mean only that "claims for facial relief under the Fourth Amendment are unlikely to succeed when there is substantial ambiguity as to what conduct a statute authorizes." *Id.*

[700] *Patel*, slip op. at 10.

[701] *Id.* at 11. The Court further noted that actual pre-compliance review need only occur in those "rare instances" where a hotel owner objects to turning over the registry, and that the Court has never "attempted to prescribe" the exact form of such review. *Id.* at 10–11.

[702] *Id.* at 14.

[703] *Id.* (quoting *Barlow's*, 436 U.S. at 313).

[704] *Id.* The majority further stated that the existence of regulations requiring hotels to maintain licenses, collect taxes, and take other actions did not establish a "comprehensive scheme of regulation" distinguishing hotels from other industries. *Id.* at 15. It also opined that the historical practice of treating hotels as public accommodations does not necessarily mean that hotels are to be treated as comprehensively regulated for purposes of warrantless searches. *Id.* at 14–15.

terms of the certainty and regularity of its application, a constitutionally adequate substitute for a warrant.[705]

[P. 1379, after "In other contexts," add:]

not directly concerned with whether an industry is comprehensively regulated,

Searches and Seizure Pursuant To Warrant

Probable Cause.—

[P. 1386, n.123, after ".", add:]

For an application of the *Gates* "totality of the circumstances" test to the warrantless search of a vehicle by a police officer, see, e.g., Florida v. Harris, 568 U.S. 237 (2013).

Execution of Warrants.—

[P. 1395, after n.186, add new paragraph:]

Limits on detention incident to a search were addressed in *Bailey v. United States*, a case in which an occupant exited his residence and traveled some distance before being stopped and detained.[706] The *Bailey* Court held that the detention was not constitutionally sustainable under the rule announced in *Summers*.[707] According to the Court, application of the categorical exception to probable cause requirements for detention incident to a search is determined by spatial proximity, that is, whether the occupant is found "within the immediate vicinity of the premises to be searched,"[708] and not by temporal proximity, that is, whether the occupant is detained "as soon as reasonably practicable" consistent with safety and security. In so holding, the Court reasoned that limiting the *Summers* rule to the area within which an occupant poses a real threat ensures that the

---

[705] *Id.* at 16. Specifically, the Court noted that the government's alleged interest in ensuring that hotel operators not falsify their records, as they could if given an opportunity for pre-compliance review, applied to every recordkeeping requirement. *Id.* The Court similarly noted that there were other ways to further the city's interest in warrantless inspections (e.g., *ex parte* warrants) and that the ordinance failed to sufficiently constrain a police officer's discretion as to which hotels to search and under what circumstances. *Id.*

[706] 568 U.S. 186 (2013). In *Bailey*, the police obtained a warrant to search Bailey's residence for firearms and drugs. *Id.* at 190. Meanwhile, detectives staked out the residence, saw Bailey leave and drive away, and then called in a search team. *Id.* While the search was proceeding, the detectives tailed Bailey for about a mile before stopping and detaining him. *Id.* at 190–92.

[707] As an alternative ground, the district court had found that stopping Bailey was lawful as an investigatory stop under *Terry v. Ohio*, 392 U.S. 1, 20 (1968), but the Supreme Court offered no opinion on whether, assuming the stop was valid under *Terry*, the resulting interaction between law enforcement and Bailey could independently have justified Bailey's detention. *Bailey*, 568 U.S. at 202.

[708] *Bailey*, slip op. at 202–04.

scope of the rule regarding detention incident to a search is confined to its underlying justification.[709]

Valid Searches and Seizures Without Warrants

Detention Short of Arrest: Stop and Frisk.—

[P. 1399, delete n.209 and substitute with:]

> *See, e.g.*, Prado Navarette v. California, 572 U.S. 393 (2014) (anonymous 911 call reporting an erratic swerve by a particular truck traveling in a particular direction held to be sufficient to justify stop); United States v. Sokolow, 490 U.S. 1, 9 (1989) (airport stop based on drug courier profile may rely on a combination of factors that individually may be "quite consistent with innocent travel"); United States v. Hensley, 469 U.S. 221 (1985) (reasonable suspicion to stop a motorist may be based on a "wanted flyer" as long as issuance of the flyer has been based on reasonable suspicion).

[P. 1402, n.225, after "462 U.S. at 707.", delete and substitute with:]

> However, the search in *Place* was not expeditious, and hence exceeded Fourth Amendment bounds, when agents took ninety minutes to transport luggage to another airport for administration of the canine sniff. The length of a detention short of an arrest has similarly been a factor in other cases. *Compare* Illinois v. Caballes, 543 U.S. 405 (2005) (a canine sniff around the perimeter of a car following a routine traffic stop does not offend the Fourth Amendment if the duration of the stop is justified by the traffic offense), *with* Rodriguez v. United States, 575 U.S. ___, No. 13-9972, slip op. at 3, 5–6 (2015) (finding that the stop in question had been prolonged for 7 to 8 minutes beyond the time needed to resolve the traffic offense in order to conduct a canine sniff).

Search Incident to Arrest.—

[P. 1402, at end of n.230, add:]

> The Court, in *Birchfield v. North Dakota*, explained that the precedent allowing for a warrantless search of an arrestee in order to prevent the destruction of evidence applies to both evidence that could be actively destroyed by a suspect and to evidence that can be destroyed due to a natural process, such as the natural dissipation of the alcohol content in a suspect's blood. 579 U.S. ___, No. 14-1468, slip op. at 30–31 (2016).

[P. 1403, after n.231, add new paragraphs:]

The Court has disavowed a case-by-case evaluation of searches made post-arrest[710] and instead has embraced categorical evaluations as to post-arrest searches. Thus, in *Riley v. California*,[711] the Court declined to extend the holding of *United States v. Robinson* to the search of the digital data contained in a cell phone found on an arrestee. Specifically,

---

[709] *Id.* at 13.

[710] In this vein, the search incident to arrest exception to the warrant requirement differs from other exceptions to the warrant requirement, such as the exigent circumstances exception. *See Birchfield*, slip op. at 15–16 (noting that while "other exceptions to the warrant requirement 'apply categorically'," the exigent circumstances exception to the warrant requirement applies on a case-by-case basis (quoting Missouri v. McNeely, 569 U.S. 141, 150 n.3 (2013)).

[711] 573 U.S. ___, No. 13-132, slip op. (2014).

the Court distinguished a search of cell phones, which contain vast quantities of personal data, from the limited physical search at issue in *Robinson*.[712] Focusing primarily on the rationale that searching cell phones would prevent the destruction of evidence, the government argued that cell phone data could be destroyed remotely or become encrypted by the passage of time. The Court, however, both discounted the prevalence of these events and the efficacy of warrantless searches to defeat them. Rather, the Court noted that other means existed besides a search of a cell phone to secure the data contained therein, including turning the phone off or placing the phone in a bag that isolates it from radio waves.[713] Because of the more substantial privacy interests at stake when digital data is involved in a search incident to an arrest and because of the availability of less intrusive alternatives to a warrantless search, the Court in *Riley* concluded that, as a "simple" categorical rule, before police can search a cell phone incident to an arrest, the police must "get a warrant."[714]

Two years after *Riley*, the Court again crafted a new brightline rule with respect to searches following an arrest in another "situation[] that could not have been envisioned when the Fourth Amendment was adopted."[715] In *Birchfield v. North Dakota*, the Court examined whether compulsory breath and blood tests administered in order to determine the blood alcohol concentration (BAC) of an automobile driver, following the arrest of that driver for suspected "drunk driving," are unreasonable under the search incident to arrest exception to the Fourth Amendment's warrant requirement.[716] In examining laws criminalizing the refusal to submit to either a breath or blood test, similar to *Riley*, the Court relied on a general balancing approach used to assess whether a given category of searches is reasonable, weighing the individual privacy interests implicated by such tests against any legitimate state interests.[717] With respect to *breath* tests, the *Birchfield* Court viewed the privacy intrusions posed by such tests as "almost negligible" in that a breath test is functionally equivalent to the process of using a straw to drink a beverage and yields a limited amount of useful information for law enforcement agents.[718] In contrast, the Court concluded that a mandatory *blood* test raised more serious privacy interests,[719] as blood tests pierce the skin, extract a part of the subject's body, and provide far more information than a breathalyzer test.[720] Turning to the state's interest in obtaining BAC readings for persons arrested for drunk driving, the *Birchfield* Court

---

[712] "Cell phones differ in both a quantitative and a qualitative sense from other objects that might be kept on an arrestee's person." *Id.* at 17.

[713] *Id.* at 14.

[714] *Id.* at 28.

[715] *See Birchfield*, slip op. at 19.

[716] *Id.* at 19.

[717] *Id.*

[718] *Id.* at 20–22. The Court disclaimed a criminal defendant's possessory interest in the air in his lungs, as air in one's lungs is not a part of one's body and is regularly exhaled from the lungs as a natural process. *Id.* at 21.

[719] "Blood tests are a different matter." *Id.* at 22.

[720] *Id.* at 21–23.

acknowledged the government's "paramount interest" in preserving public safety on highways, including the state's need to deter drunk driving from occurring in the first place through the imposition of criminal penalties for failing to cooperate with drunk driving investigations.[721] Weighing these competing interests, the Court ultimately concluded that the Fourth Amendment permits warrantless breath tests incident to arrests for drunk driving because the "impact of breath tests on privacy is slight," whereas the "need for BAC testing is great."[722] In so doing, the Court rejected the alternative of requiring the state to obtain a warrant prior to the administration of a BAC breath test, noting (1) the need for clear, categorical rules to provide police adequate guidance in the context of a search incident to an arrest and (2) the potential administrative burdens that would be incurred if warrants were required prior to every breathalyzer test.[723] Nonetheless, the Court reached a "different conclusion" with respect to *blood* tests, finding that such tests are "significantly more intrusive" and their "reasonability must be judged in light of the availability of the less intrusive alternative of a breath test."[724] As a consequence, the Court held that while a warrantless breath test following a drunk-driving arrest is categorically permissible as a reasonable search under the Fourth Amendment, a warrantless blood test cannot be justified by the search incident to arrest doctrine.[725]

Vehicular Searches.—

[P. 1407, after n.259, add new paragraph:]

The Court has stated, however, that the automobile exception "does not permit an officer without a warrant to enter a home or its curtilage in order to search a vehicle therein."[726] This limit to the exception exists because "the scope of the automobile exception extends no further than the automobile itself."[727] To search a vehicle under the automobile exception, an officer "must have a lawful right of access" to that vehicle,[728] and generally, law enforcement officers have no right to enter a home or its curtilage without express or implied permission or without a warrant.[729]

---

[721] *Id.* at 24–25.

[722] *Id.* at 33.

[723] *Id.* at 25–28. The *Birchfield* Court also rejected "more costly" and previously tried alternatives to penalties for refusing a breath test, such as sobriety checkpoints, ignition interlocks, and the use of treatment programs. *Id.* at 29–30.

[724] *Id.* at 33. In so doing, the Court rejected the argument that warrantless blood tests are needed as an alternative to warrantless breath tests to detect impairing substances other than alcohol or to obtain the BAC of an unconscious or uncooperative driver. *Id.* at 34. In such situations, the Court reasoned that the state could obtain a warrant for the blood test, or in the case of an uncooperative driver, prosecute the defendant for refusing to undergo the breath test. *Id.* at 34–35.

[725] *Id.* at 37–38.

[726] Collins v. Virginia, 584 U.S. ___, No. 16-1027, slip op. at 14 (2018).

[727] *Id.* at 7.

[728] *Id.* at 9.

[729] *See, e.g.*, Florida v. Jardines, 569 U.S. 1, 7–8 (2013).

[P. 1408, n.260, after ".", add:]

Cf. Florida v. Harris, 568 U.S. 237 (2013).

[P. 1408, after n.263, add new sentence:]

A driver with lawful possession and control of a rental car may also be able to challenge the constitutionality of a stop, even if that driver is not listed as an authorized driver on the rental agreement.[730]

[P. 1408, n.262, before first sentence, add:]

For example, an officer who learns, through a license plate search of a vehicle, that the registered owner has a revoked license may have a reasonable suspicion to stop that vehicle if it matches the description of the registered car and if, at the time of the stop, the officer has no countervailing reason to think the driver is not the registered owner. Kansas v. Glover, 140 S. Ct. 1183, 1184, 1191 (2020).

[P. 1409, n.269, after "New York v. Class, 475 U.S. 106 (1986)." delete and substitute with:]

Because there also is no legitimate privacy interest in possessing contraband, and because properly conducted canine sniffs are "generally likely[] to reveal only the presence of contraband," police may conduct a canine sniff around the perimeter of a vehicle stopped for a traffic offense so long as the stop is not prolonged beyond the time needed to process the traffic violation. *Compare* Illinois v. Caballes, 543 U.S. 405 (2005) (a canine sniff around the perimeter of a car following a routine traffic stop does not offend the Fourth Amendment if the duration of the stop is justified by the traffic offense), *with* Rodriguez v. United States, 575 U.S. ___, No. 13-9972, slip op. at 3, 5–6 (2015) (finding that the stop in question had been prolonged for seven to eight minutes beyond the time needed to resolve the traffic offense in order to conduct a canine sniff).

Consent Searches.—

[P. 1412, after n.293, add:]

Moreover, while the Court has appeared to endorse implied consent laws that view individuals who engage in certain regulated activities as having implicitly agreed to certain searches related to that activity and the enforcement of such laws through civil penalties,[731] the implied consent doctrine does not extend so far as to deem individuals to have impliedly consented to a search on "pain of committing a criminal offense."[732]

---

[730] Byrd v. United States, 584 U.S. ___, No. 16-371, slip op. at 2 (2018). *But see id.* at 13 (noting that a "car thief would not have a reasonable expectation of privacy in a stolen car").

[731] *See, e.g.,* Missouri v. McNeely, 569 U.S. 141, 161 (2013) (plurality opinion) (discussing implied consent laws that "require motorists, as a condition of operating a motor vehicle, . . . to consent to [blood alcohol concentration] testing if they are arrested or otherwise detained on suspicion of a drunk-driving offense" or risk losing their license); South Dakota v. Neville, 459 U.S. 553, 554, 563–64 (1983).

[732] *See* Birchfield v. North Dakota, 579 U.S. ___, No. 14-1468, slip op. at 36–37 (2016).

[P. 1413, at end of section, add new sentences:]

Common social expectations inform the analysis. A person at the threshold of a residence could not confidently conclude he was welcome to enter over the express objection of a present co-tenant. Expectations may change, however, if the objecting co-tenant leaves, or is removed from, the premises with no prospect of imminent return.[733]

"Open Fields".—

[P. 1416, at end of n.311, add:]

See also Collins v. Virginia, 584 U.S. ___, No. 16-1027, slip op. at 6 (2018) ("Just like the front porch, side garden, or area 'outside the front window,' . . . the driveway enclosure where Officer Rhodes searched the motorcycle . . . is properly considered curtilage." (quoting Florida v. Jardines, 569 U.S. 1, 6 (2013))).

Prisons and Regulation of Probation and Parole.—

[P. 1420, after n.339, add new paragraph:]

The Court in *Maryland v. King* cited a legitimate interest in having safe and accurate booking procedures to identify persons being taken into custody in order to sustain taking DNA samples from those charged with serious crimes.[734] Tapping the "unmatched potential of DNA identification" facilitates knowing with certainty who the arrestee is, the arrestee's criminal history, the danger the arrestee poses to others, the arrestee's flight risk, and other relevant facts.[735] By comparison, the Court characterized an arrestee's expectation of privacy as diminished and the intrusion posed by a cheek swab as minimal.[736]

Electronic Surveillance and the Fourth Amendment

The Burger and Katz Cases.—

[P. 1429, at end of n.386, add:]

See also Carpenter v. United States, 585 U.S. ___, No. 16-402, slip op. at 22 (2018) (holding government generally must obtain warrant before acquiring cell-site location information, "in light of the deeply revealing nature of [that data], its depth, breadth, and comprehensive reach, and the inescapable and automatic nature of its collection").

---

[733] Fernandez v. California, 571 U.S. 292, 300–02 (2014) (discussing consent by co-occupant sufficient to overcome objection of a second co-occupant who was arrested and removed from the premises, so long as the arrest and removal were objectively reasonable).

[734] 569 U.S. 435, 449 (2013).

[735] *Id.* at 449–56, 460–61.

[736] *Id.* at 460–64.

Warrantless "National Security" Electronic Surveillance.—

[P. 1430, after sentence starting "In *Katz* . . .", add new footnote:]

See also Carpenter v. United States, 585 U.S. ___, No. 16-402, slip op. at 18 (2018) ("[O]ur opinion does not consider other collection techniques involving foreign affairs or national security.").

Enforcing the Fourth Amendment: The Exclusionary Rule

Alternatives to the Exclusionary Rule.—

[P. 1432, n.400, delete "Scott v. Harris" and substitute with:]

Scott v. Harris

[P. 1432, n.400, after ". . . was found reasonable.", add:]

Thus, the Court has noted, "[a]s in other areas of our Fourth Amendment jurisprudence, '[d]etermining whether the force used to effect a particular seizure is reasonable' requires balancing of the individual's Fourth Amendment interests against the relevant government interests." Cty. of Los Angeles v. Mendez, 581 U.S. ___, No. 16-369, slip op. at 6 (2017) (quoting *Graham*, 490 U.S. at 396) (rejecting the Ninth Circuit's "provocation rule" under which law enforcement officers who "make a 'seizure' of a person using force that is judged to be reasonable based on a consideration of the circumstances relevant to that determination" can "nevertheless be held liable for injuries caused by the seizure on the ground that they committed a separate Fourth Amendment violation that contributed to their need to use force"). "The operative question in excessive force cases is 'whether the totality of the circumstances justifie[s] a particular sort of search or seizure.'" *Id.* (quoting Tennessee v. Garner, 471 U.S. 1, 8–9 (1985)).

[P. 1433, n.406, after citation to *Malley v. Briggs,* add:]

But see Mullenix v. Luna, 577 U.S. ___, No. 14-1143, slip op. at 8 (2015) (per curiam) ("The Court has . . . never found the use of deadly force in connection with a dangerous car chase to violate the Fourth Amendment, let alone be the basis for denying qualified immunity.").

Narrowing Application of the Exclusionary Rule.—

[P. 1441, n.449, delete "." at end of first sentence and substitute with:]

; Utah v. Strieff, 579 U.S. ___, No. 14-1373, slip op. (2016).

[P. 1443, delete first sentence of first paragraph and substitute with:]

A significant curtailment of the exclusionary rule came in 1984 with the adoption of a "good faith" exception.

[P. 1445, after second paragraph, add new paragraphs:]

Another significant curtailment of the exclusionary rule involves the attenuation exception, which permits the use of evidence discovered through the government's unconstitutional conduct if the "causal link" between that misconduct and the discovery of the evidence is seen by the reviewing courts as sufficiently remote or has been interrupted by some intervening circumstances.[737] In a series of decisions issued over several decades, the Court has invoked this exception in upholding the admission of challenged evidence. For example, in *Wong Sun v. United States*, the Court upheld the admission of an unsigned statement made by a defendant who initially had been unlawfully arrested because, thereafter, the defendant was lawfully arraigned, released on his own recognizance, and, only then, voluntarily returned several days later to make the unsigned statement.[738] Similarly, in its 1984 decision in *Segura v. United States*, the Court upheld the admission of evidence obtained following an illegal entry into a residence because the evidence was seized the next day pursuant to a valid search warrant that had been issued based on information obtained by law enforcement before the illegal entry.[739]

More recently, in its 2016 decision in *Utah v. Strieff*, the Court rejected a challenge to the admission of certain evidence obtained as the result of an unlawful stop on the grounds that the discovery of an arrest warrant after the stop attenuated the connection between the unlawful stop and the evidence seized incident to the defendant's arrest.[740] As a threshold matter, the Court rejected the state court's view that the attenuation exception applies only in cases involving "an independent act of a defendant's 'free will.'"[741] Instead, the Court relied on three factors it had set forth in a Fifth Amendment case, *Brown v. Illinois*,[742] to determine whether the subsequent lawful acquisition of evidence was sufficiently attenuated from the initial misconduct: (1) the "temporal proximity" between the two acts; (2) the presences of intervening circumstances; and (3) the purpose and flagrancy of the official misconduct.[743] On the whole, the *Strieff* Court, reiterating that "suppression of evidence should be the courts' 'last resort, not our first impulse,'"[744] concluded that the circumstances of the case weighed in favor of the admission of the challenged evidence. While the closeness in time between the initial stop and the search was seen by the Court as favoring suppression,[745] the presence of intervening circumstances in the form of a valid warrant for the defendant's arrest strongly favored the state,[746] and in the Court's

---

[737] Utah v. Strieff, 579 U.S. ___, No. 14-1373, slip op. at 5 (2016).

[738] 371 U.S. 471, 491 (1963).

[739] 468 U.S. 796, 813–16 (1984).

[740] *Strieff*, slip op. at 1. The state in *Strieff* had conceded that law enforcement lacked reasonable suspicion for the stop, *id.* at 2, and the Supreme Court characterized the search of the defendant following his arrest as a lawful search incident to arrest, *id.* at 8.

[741] *Id.* at 5 (quoting State v. Strieff, 457 P.3d 532, 544 (Utah 2015)).

[742] *See* 422 U.S. 590, 603–04 (1970) (holding that the state supreme court in this case had erroneously concluded that *Miranda* warnings always served to purge the taint of an illegal arrest).

[743] *See Strieff*, slip op. at 6–9.

[744] *Id.* at 8 (quoting Hudson v. Michigan, 547 U.S. 586, 591 (2006) (internal quotations omitted)).

[745] *Id.* at 6 (noting that "only minutes" passed between the unlawful stop and the discovery of the challenged evidence).

[746] *Id.* at 6–7. The *Strieff* Court emphasized that it viewed the warrant as "compelling" the officer to arrest the suspect. *Id.* at 9; *see also id.* at 7 (similar).

view, there was no indication that this unlawful stop was part of any "systematic or recurrent police misconduct."[747] In particular, the Court, relying on the second factor, emphasized that the discovery of a warrant "broke the causal chain" between the unlawful stop and the discovery of the challenged evidence.[748] As such, the *Strieff* Court appeared to establish a rule that the existence of a valid warrant, "predat[ing the] investigation" and "entirely unconnected with the stop," generally favors finding sufficient attenuation between the unlawful conduct and the discovery of evidence.[749]

Operation of the Rule: Standing.—

[P. 1446, after first full paragraph, add new sentence:]

The Court has clarified that this "concept of standing in Fourth Amendment cases . . . should not be confused with Article III standing," emphasizing that "Fourth Amendment standing is subsumed under substantive Fourth Amendment doctrine" and is not a preliminary "jurisdictional question."[750]

[P. 1446, delete paragraph starting "The *Katz* reasonable expectation of privacy rationale . . ." and substitute with:]

The *Katz* reasonable-expectation-of-privacy inquiry largely supplanted property-ownership concepts that previously might have supported either standing to suppress or the establishment of an interest that has been invaded—but has not entirely replaced or "repudiate[d]" the Fourth Amendment's "concern for government trespass."[751] In the 1960 case *Jones v. United States*, the Supreme Court held that a person could establish standing to challenge a search or seizure where that person was "legitimately on [the] premises" as a guest or invitee of the owner of the premises.[752] This statement about legitimate presence was later limited by the Court in *Rakas v. Illinois*,[753] which emphasized that to challenge a

---

[747] *Id.* at 8.

[748] *Id.* at 9.

[749] *Id.* at 7.

[750] Byrd v. United States, 584 U.S. ___, No. 16-371, slip op. at 14 (2018).

[751] United States v. Jones, 565 U.S. 400, 406–07 (2012) ("[F]or most of our history the Fourth Amendment was understood to embody a particular concern for government trespass upon the areas . . . it enumerates. *Katz* did not repudiate that understanding."). *See also* Grady v. North Carolina, 575 U.S. ___, No. 14-593, slip op. at 3 (2015) (per curiam); Florida v. Jardines, 569 U.S. 1, 5–6 (2013).

[752] 362 U.S. 257, 266–67 (1960). *See also* United States v. Jeffers, 342 U.S. 48, 51–53 (1951) (allowing defendant with access to a hotel room to challenge the seizure of narcotics that were his property, concluding that the search and the seizure were "incapable of being untied").

[753] 439 U.S. 128, 143 (1978) ("[T]he *Jones* statement that a person need only be 'legitimately on premises' in order to challenge the validity of the search of a dwelling place cannot be taken in its full sweep beyond the facts of that case."). In *Jones*, the Court had also held that a person had standing "where the indictment itself charges possession." 362 U.S. at 264. But in *Simmons v. United States*, 390 U.S. 377, 390 (1968), the Court held "that testimony given by a defendant" to establish possession of things searched or seized and meet

search, a person must assert a *personal* interest protected by the Fourth Amendment.[754] And while prior case law had seemed to suggest that ownership of a seized item would alone suffice to establish standing, the Court clarified in *Rakas* that under *Katz*, "capacity to claim the protection of the Fourth Amendment depends . . . upon whether the person who claims the protection of the Amendment has a legitimate expectation of privacy in the invaded place."[755] Under the reasonable-expectations-of-privacy test, a person may "have a legally sufficient interest" to implicate the protections of the Fourth Amendment even if that interest "might not have been a recognized property interest at common law."[756] Nonetheless, a "property" or "possessory interest" in the premises searched remains relevant to the inquiry.[757]

---

standing requirements is not "admissible against him at trial on the question of guilt or innocence." The Court recognized that *Simmons* (among other legal developments) had undermined the justification for "automatic standing" on the basis of an indictment and overruled this part of *Jones* in *United States v. Salvucci*, 448 U.S. 83, 88–89 (1980).

[754] *See Rakas*, 439 U.S. at 136 ("A person who is aggrieved by an illegal search and seizure only through the introduction of damaging evidence secured by a search of a third person's premises or property has not had any of his Fourth Amendment rights infringed.") (citing Alderman v. United States, 394 U.S. 165, 171–72 (1969)). *See, e.g., id.* at 143 (holding that defendants' "claims must fail" where, even though the defendants were in a car with the permission of the car's owner, "[t]hey asserted neither a property nor a possessory interest in the automobile, nor an interest in the property seized"). In *Rakas*, the Court distinguished *United States v. Jeffers*, 342 U.S. 48 (1951), by holding that "[s]tanding in *Jeffers* was based on Jeffers' possessory interest in both the premises searched and the property seized." 439 U.S. at 136.

[755] *Rakas*, 439 U.S. at 143. *See also* United States v. Salvucci, 448 U.S. 83, 92 (1980) ("We simply decline to use possession of a seized good as a substitute for a factual finding that the owner of the good had a legitimate expectation of privacy in the area searched."); *see, e.g.,* Rawlings v. Kentucky, 448 U.S. 98, 105–06 (1980) (holding defendant could not challenge seizure of his drugs from another's purse, where defendant had no legitimate expectation of privacy in the purse). In *Rakas*, the Court distinguished *Jones v. United States*, 362 U.S. 257 (1960), by stating that in that case, "Jones not only had permission to use the apartment of his friend, but had a key to the apartment . . . . [and] [e]xcept with respect to his friend, Jones had complete dominion and control over the apartment and could exclude others from it," 439 U.S. at 149. *Cf.* Florida v. Jardines, 569 U.S. 1, 5 (2013) ("When 'the Government obtains information by physically intruding' on persons, houses, *papers, or effects*, 'a "search"' within the original meaning of the Fourth Amendment has 'undoubtedly occurred.'" (quoting United States v. Jones, 565 U.S. 400, 406 n.3 (2012)) (emphasis added)).

[756] *Rakas*, 439 U.S. at 143.

[757] *Id.* at 148. *See also, e.g.,* United States v. Padilla, 508 U.S. 77, 82 (1993) (per curiam) ("Expectations of privacy and property interests govern the analysis of Fourth Amendment search and seizure claims.").

FIFTH AMENDMENT

DOUBLE JEOPARDY

Development and Scope

[P. 1460, delete "The 'dual sovereignty' doctrine . . ." through n.57 and substitute with:]

In *Gamble v. United States*, the Court explained that "where there are two sovereigns, there are two laws, and two 'offences.'"[758]

The Supreme Court has been asked to overrule this "dual sovereignty" doctrine in a number of cases, and has repeatedly declined to do so.[759] Although some early cases establishing this doctrine cited the now-overruled principle that the Double Jeopardy Clause did not apply to the states,[760] the Court has since clarified that the dual sovereignty doctrine survived ratification of the Fourteenth Amendment.[761] The Court said in *Gamble*, issued in 2019, that the dual sovereignty doctrine was justified by historical understandings of the Double Jeopardy Clause.[762] Observing that the Clause prohibits dual prosecution for the same "offence," the Court explained that at the time the Constitution was written, an "offence" was defined as a violation of a particular law.[763] In the Court's view, two sovereigns will have two different laws, meaning that violations of those laws will be two different offenses.[764] Further, the Court emphasized that by 2019, the doctrine had been applied in "a chain of precedent linking dozens of cases over 170 years."[765] In prior cases, the Court also recognized the practical considerations justifying the dual sovereignty doctrine, noting that without this principle, states could "hinder[]" federal law enforcement by imposing more lenient sentences on defendants under state law, thereby barring federal prosecution even if the "defendants' acts impinge more seriously on a federal interest than on a state interest."[766] And in *Gamble*, the Court noted the international consequences of the doctrine, stating that if "only one sovereign may prosecute for a single act, no American court—state or federal—could

---

[758] 587 U.S. ___, No. 17-646, slip op. at 4 (2019) (quoting U.S. CONST. amend. V).

[759] *Gamble*, slip op. at 2; Abbate v. United States, 359 U.S. 187, 195 (1959); Bartkus v. Illinois, 359 U.S. 121, 138 (1959). The Court has applied the dual sovereignty doctrine without expressly reconsidering and reaffirming its validity in a number of additional cases, as detailed in *Gamble*, slip op. at 8, and *Bartkus*, 359 U.S. at 129–33.

[760] *See Bartkus*, 359 U.S. at 129; *Lanza*, 260 U.S. at 382. The Court subsequently held in *Benton v. Maryland*, 395 U.S. 784, 794 (1969), that "the double jeopardy prohibition of the Fifth Amendment represents a fundamental ideal in our constitutional heritage, and . . . should apply to the States through the Fourteenth Amendment."

[761] *Gamble*, slip op. at 30.

[762] *Id.* at 3–4.

[763] *Id.* at 4.

[764] *Id.*

[765] *Id.* at 12.

[766] Abbate v. United States, 359 U.S. 187, 195 (1959); *accord, e.g.*, United States v. Wheeler, 435 U.S. 313, 318 (1978).

prosecute conduct already tried in a foreign court."[767] If the Double Jeopardy Clause did bar such U.S. prosecutions, the Court said that this could raise prudential concerns about the U.S. government's ability to vindicate its interests in enforcing its own criminal laws, particularly if the foreign government's legal system is seen as somehow inadequate.[768]

[P. 1460, before sentence starting "The dual sovereignty doctrine has also been applied . . .", add new paragraph break]

[P. 1461, delete n.59 and substitute with:]

E.g., United States v. Lara, 541 U.S. 193, 199 (2004); United States v. Wheeler, 435 U.S. 313, 329–30 (1978).

[P. 1461, delete n.60 and substitute with:]

See, e.g., Waller v. Florida, 397 U.S. 387 (1970) (trial by municipal court precluded trial for same offense by state court); Grafton v. United States, 206 U.S. 333 (1907) (trial by military court-martial precluded subsequent trial in territorial court). More recently, in *Puerto Rico v. Sanchez Valle,* the Court held that the separate prosecution of an individual by the United States and Puerto Rico for the same underlying conduct ran afoul of the Double Jeopardy Clause because the two governments are not "separate sovereigns." *See* 579 U.S. ___, No. 15-108, slip op. at 17–18 (2016). Even though Puerto Rico came to exercise self-rule through a popularly ratified constitution in the mid-twentieth century, the Court concluded that the "original source" for its authority to prosecute crimes ultimately derived from Congress and, specifically, a federal statute which authorized the people of Puerto Rico to draft their own constitution, meaning that the challenged prosecution amounted to a reprosecution by the same sovereign. *See id.* at 14–16 (2016).

Reprosecution Following Acquittal

[P. 1468, after n.96, add new sentence:]

Thus, an acquittal resting on the trial judge's misreading of the elements of an offense precludes further prosecution.[769]

Trial Court Rulings Terminating Trial Before Verdict.—

[P. 1471, after n.114, add new sentence:]

This is so even where the trial court's ruling on the sufficiency of the evidence is based on an erroneous interpretation of the statute defining the elements of the offense.[770]

---

[767] *Gamble,* slip op. at 7.

[768] *Id.*

[769] Evans v. Michigan, 568 U.S. 313 (2013) (acquittal after judge ruled the prosecution failed to prove that a burned building was not a dwelling, but such proof was not legally required for the arson offense charged).

[770] *See* Evans v. Michigan, 568 U.S. ___, No. 11-1327, slip op. (2013).

The "Same Transaction" Problem.—

"For the Same Offence"

The "Same Transaction" Problem.—

[P. 1482, delete entire section and substitute with:]

The Supreme Court has also interpreted the Double Jeopardy Clause to incorporate the doctrine of "collateral estoppel" or "issue preclusion"[771]—that is, the general legal principle that prohibits the relitigation of an issue of fact or law raised and necessarily resolved by a prior judgment.[772] The Court first recognized the Double Jeopardy Clause's issue-preclusion component in *Ashe v. Swenson.*[773] *Ashe* involved a robbery of six poker players.[774] The defendant in *Ashe*, after being acquitted of robbing *one* of the players because of insufficient evidence, was tried and convicted of robbing *another* player.[775] The Court held that because the sole issue in dispute in the first trial was whether Ashe had been one of the robbers, "[o]nce a jury had determined . . . that there was at least a reasonable doubt" as to that issue, the Constitution generally[776] protects a "man who has been acquitted from having to 'run the gantlet' a second time."[777] In so holding, *Ashe* explained that issue preclusion in criminal cases must be applied with "realism and rationality" with a close examination of the underlying record to determine what was "actually decided" by the prior jury's verdict of acquittal.[778] If a criminal judgment does not depend on a jury's determination of a particular factual issue, relitigation of that issue *can* occur.[779]

---

[771] *See* Ashe v. Swenson, 397 U.S. 436, 445 (1970). Collateral estoppel and issue preclusion are synonymous terms. *See* BLACK'S LAW DICTIONARY 318 (10th ed. 2014) (defining "collateral estoppel").

[772] *See* RESTATEMENT (SECOND) OF JUDGMENTS § 27 (Am. Law Inst. 1981).

[773] 397 U.S. at 445. Previously, the Court in *Hoag v. New Jersey*, concluded that successive trials arising out of a tavern hold-up in which five customers were robbed did not violate the Due Process Clause of the Fourteenth Amendment. *See* 356 U.S. 464, 466 (1958).

[774] 397 U.S. at 437.

[775] *Id.* at 439–40.

[776] A defendant who *agrees* to have charges against him arising out of the same event considered in two trials cannot later argue that an acquittal in the first trial means that a second trial offends the Double Jeopardy Clause. *See* Currier v. Virginia, 585 U.S. ___, No. 16-1348, slip op. at 5 (2018) (noting that a defendant's consent to a retrial of the same offense is a "critical difference" from the situation that arose in *Ashe*).

[777] *Ashe*, 397 U.S. at 446 (quoting Green v. United States, 355 U.S. 184, 190 (1957)).

[778] *Id.* at 444.

[779] *See* Bobby v. Bies, 556 U.S. 825, 834 (2009) (citing RESTATEMENT (SECOND) OF JUDGMENTS § 27 cmt. h)).

SELF-INCRIMINATION

Development and Scope

[P. 1485, delete first new paragraph and through paragraph carrying-over from P. 1486 to P. 1487 and substitute with:]

The historical studies cited demonstrate that in England and the colonies the privilege was narrower than the interpretation now prevailing. Of course, constitutional guarantees often expand, or contract, over time as judges adapt underlying rules to new factual patterns and practices. The difficulty is that the Court has generally not articulated the objectives underlying the privilege, usually citing a "complex of values" when it has attempted to state the interests served.[780] Commonly mentioned in numerous cases was the assertion that the privilege was designed to protect the innocent and further the search for the truth.[781]

It appears now, however, that the Court has rejected both of these as inapplicable and has settled upon the principle that the clause serves two interrelated interests: the preservation of an accusatorial system of criminal justice, which goes to the integrity of the judicial system, and the preservation of personal privacy from unwarranted governmental intrusion.[782] To protect these interests and to preserve these values, the

---

[780] Discussing the privilege in one case, the Court stated:

It reflects many of our fundamental values and most noble aspirations: our unwillingness to subject those suspected of crime to the cruel trilemma of self-accusation, perjury or contempt; our preference for an accusatorial rather than an inquisitorial system of criminal justice; our fear that self-incriminating statements will be elicited by inhumane treatment and abuses; our sense of fair play which dictates "a fair state-individual balance by requiring the government to leave the individual alone until good cause is shown for disturbing him and by requiring the government in its contest with the individual to shoulder the entire load"; our respect for the inviolability of the human personality and of the right of each individual "to a private enclave where he may lead a private life"; our distrust of self-deprecatory statements; and our realization that the privilege, while sometimes "a shelter to the guilty," is often "a protection to the innocent." Murphy v. Waterfront Comm'n, 378 U.S. 52, 55 (1964) (internal citations omitted).

[781] *E.g.*, Ullmann v. United States, 350 U.S. 422, 426 (1956); Quinn v. United States, 349 U.S. 155, 162-63 (1955); Twining v. New Jersey, 211 U.S. 78, 91 (1908).

[782] In *Tehan v. United States ex rel. Shott*, the Court noted:

[T]he basic purposes that lie behind the privilege against self-incrimination do not relate to protecting the innocent from conviction, but rather to preserving the integrity of a judicial system in which even the guilty are not to be convicted unless the prosecution "shoulder[s] the entire load.". . . The basic purpose of a trial is the determination of truth, and it is self-evident that to deny a lawyer's help through the technical intricacies of a criminal trial or to deny a full opportunity to appeal a conviction because the accused is poor is to impede that purpose and to infect a criminal proceeding with the clear danger of convicting the innocent. . . . By contrast, the Fifth Amendment's privilege against self-incrimination is not an adjunct to

privilege "is not to be interpreted literally." Rather, the "sole concern [of the privilege] is, as its name indicates, with the danger to a witness forced to give testimony leading to the infliction of penalties affixed to the criminal acts."[783] Furthermore, "[t]he privilege afforded not only extends to answers that would in themselves support a conviction . . . but likewise embraces those which would furnish a link in the chain of evidence needed to prosecute . . ."[784]

The privilege against self-incrimination parries the general obligation to provide testimony under oath when called upon, but it also applies in police interrogations. In all cases, the privilege must be supported by a reasonable fear that a response will be incriminatory. The issue is a matter of law for a court to determine,[785] and therefore, with limited exceptions, one must claim the privilege to benefit from it.[786] Otherwise, silence in the face of questioning may be insufficient to invoke the privilege because it may not afford an adequate opportunity either to test whether information withheld falls within the privilege or to cure a violation through a grant of immunity.[787] A witness who fails to claim the privilege explicitly when an affirmative claim is required is deemed to have waived it, and waiver may be found where the witness has answered some preliminary questions but desires to stop at a certain point.[788]

---

the ascertainment of truth. That privilege, like the guarantees of the Fourth Amendment, stands as a protection of quite different constitutional values—values reflecting the concern of our society for the right of each individual to be let alone.

382 U.S. 406, 415, 416 (1966); *see also* California v. Byers, 402 U.S. 424, 448–58 (1971) (Harlan, J., concurring); Schmerber v. California, 384 U.S. 757, 760–65 (1966); Miranda v. Arizona, 384 U.S. 436, 460 (1966). For a critical view of the privilege, see Henry Friendly, *The Fifth Amendment Tomorrow: The Case for Constitutional Change*, 37 U. Cin. L. Rev. 671 (1968).

[783] *Ullmann*, 350 U.S. at 438–39.

[784] Hoffman v. United States, 341 U.S. 479, 486 (1951); *see also* Emspak v. United States, 349 U.S. 190 (1955); Blau v. United States, 340 U.S. 332 (1951); Blau v. United States, 340 U.S. 159 (1950).

[785] *E.g.*, Mason v. United States, 244 U.S. 362 (1917).

[786] The primary exceptions are for a criminal defendant not taking the stand and a suspect being subject to inherently coercive circumstances (*e.g.*, custodial interrogation). *See* Salinas v. Texas, 570 U.S. 178, 183–86 (2013) (plurality opinion).

[787] In *Salinas v. Texas*, the defendant—Salinas—answered all questions during noncustodial questioning about a double murder, other than one about whether his shotgun would match shells recovered at the murder scene. He fell silent on this inquiry, but did not assert the privilege against self- incrimination. At closing argument at Salinas's murder trial, the prosecutor argued that this silence indicated guilt, and a majority of the Court found the comments constitutionally permissible. The Court affirmed the Texas Supreme Court's ruling that Salinas had failed to invoke his Fifth Amendment rights because he did not do so explicitly. Although no opinion drew a majority of Justices, in an opinion joined by Chief Justice Roberts and Justice Kennedy, Justice Alito observed that a defendant could choose to remain silent for numerous reasons other than avoiding self-incrimination. *Id.* at 188–89 (plurality opinion).

[788] Rogers v. United States, 340 U.S. 367 (1951); United States v. Monia, 317 U.S. 424 (1943). The "waiver" concept here has been pronounced "analytically [un]sound," with the Court preferring to reserve the term "waiver" "for the process by which one affirmatively renounces the protection of the privilege." Garner v. United States, 424 U.S. 648, 654, n.9 (1976). Thus, the Court has settled upon the concept of "compulsion" as applied to "cases where disclosures are required in the face of claim of privilege." *Id.* "[I]n the ordinary case, if

However, an assertion of innocence in conjunction with a claim of the privilege does not obviate the right of witnesses to invoke it, as their responses still may provide the government with evidence it may later seek to use against them.[789]

Although individuals must have reasonable cause to apprehend danger and cannot be the judge of the validity of their claims, a court that would deny a claim of the privilege must be *"perfectly clear*, from a careful consideration of all the circumstances in the case, that the individual is mistaken, and that the answer[s] *cannot possibly* have such tendency to incriminate."[790] To reach a determination, furthermore, a trial judge may not require a witness to disclose so much of the danger as to render the privilege nugatory. As the Court observed:

> [I]f the witness, upon interposing his claim, were required to prove the hazard . . . he would be compelled to surrender the very protection which the privilege is designed to guarantee. To sustain the privilege, it need only be evident from the implications of the question, in the setting in which it is asked, that a responsive answer to the question or an explanation of why it cannot be answered might be dangerous because injurious disclosure could result.[791]

Confessions: Police Interrogation, Due Process, and Self-Incrimination

Miranda v. Arizona.—

[P. 1518, n.355, before period at end of first citation sentence, add:]

; Salinas v. Texas, 570 U.S. 178 (2013) (plurality opinion) (voluntarily accompanying police to station for questioning)

---

a witness under compulsion to testify makes disclosures instead of claiming the privilege, the government has not 'compelled' him to incriminate himself." *Id.* at 654. Similarly, the Court has enunciated the concept of "voluntariness" to be applied in situations where it is claimed that a particular factor denied the individual a "free choice to admit, to deny, or to refuse to answer." *Id.* at 654 n.9, 656–65.

[789] Ohio v. Reiner, 532 U.S. 17 (2001).

[790] Hoffman v. United States, 341 U.S. 479, 488 (1951) (quoting Temple v. Commonwealth, 75 Va. 892, 898 (1881)). For an application of these principles, see Malloy v. Hogan, 378 U.S. 1, 11–14 (1964), and *id.* at 33 (White, Stewart, JJ., dissenting). Where the government is seeking to enforce an essentially noncriminal statutory scheme through compulsory disclosure, some Justices would apparently relax the *Hoffman* principles. *Cf.* California v. Byers, 402 U.S. 424 (1971) (plurality opinion).

[791] *Hoffman*, 341 U.S. at 486–87.

DUE PROCESS

Procedural Due Process

Aliens: Entry and Deportation.—

[P. 1538, delete n.452 and substitute with:]

See Dep't of Homeland Sec. v. Thuraissigiam, 140 S. Ct. 1959, 1982 (2020); *see also* Landon v. Plasencia, 459 U.S. 21, 32 (1982); United States *ex rel.* Knauff v. Shaughnessy, 338 U.S. 537, 544 (1950); Nishimura Ekiu v. United States, 142 U.S. 651, 660 (1892).

[P. 1539, after paragraph ending ". . . a judicial hearing on *habeas corpus*.", add new paragraphs:]

In certain cases, the exclusion of an alien has been seen to implicate the rights of U.S. citizens.[792] These cases have often been decided by the lower courts and often involve U.S. citizens' First Amendment rights, which the Supreme Court appeared to recognize in its 1972 decision in *Kleindienst v. Mandel*.[793] In *Trump v. Hawaii*, the Supreme Court held that a U.S. citizen's "interest in being reunited with his relatives," where those relatives were foreign nationals seeking to enter the U.S., was "sufficiently concrete and particularized to form the basis of an Article III injury in fact."[794]

However, U.S. citizens have also asserted that the exclusion of an alien has impinged upon the citizen's due process rights.[795] In *Kerry v. Din*, five Justices agreed that denying an immigrant visa to the husband of a U.S. citizen on the grounds that he was inadmissible under a provision of federal immigration law (which pertains to "terrorist activities"), without further explanation, did not violate the due process rights of the

---

[792] *See* Kleindienst v. Mandel, 408 U.S. 753, 762 (1972) (apparently recognizing that citizens' First Amendment rights were affected by the denial of a nonimmigrant visa to a Marxist journalist who had been invited to speak in the United States); *see also* Kerry v. Din, 576 U.S. ___, No. 13-1402, slip op. (2015) (plurality and concurring opinions, taken together, suggesting that at least a majority of the Court accepts that *Kleindienst* allows U.S. citizens to challenge visa denials that affect other rights beyond their First Amendment rights); *cf.* Trump v. Int'l Refugee Assistance Project, 582 U.S. ___, No. 16-1436, slip op. at 11 (June 26, 2017) (per curiam) (noting that "foreign nationals abroad who have no connection to the United States at all" can be denied entry as such a denial does not "impose any legally relevant hardship" on the foreign nationals themselves).

[793] *See, e.g.*, Am. Acad. of Religion v. Napolitano, 573 F.3d 115, 117 (2d Cir. 2009) ("The Supreme Court has recognized a First Amendment right to 'hear, speak, and debate with' a visa applicant."); Adams v. Baker, 909 F.2d 643, 647 n.3 (1st Cir. 1990) ("[I]t is important to recognize that the only issue which may be addressed by this court is the possibility of impairment of United States citizens' First Amendment rights through the exclusion of the alien."); Abourezk v. Reagan, 785 F.2d 1043, 1063 n.1 (D.C. Cir. 1986) (noting that the government defendants had "concede[d] that the Supreme Court has already implicitly decided the issue of whether plaintiffs who wish to meet with excluded aliens have standing to raise a constitutional (first amendment) claim") (Bork, J., dissenting).

[794] 585 U.S. ___, No. 17-965, slip op. at 25 (2018).

[795] *See, e.g.*, Bustamante v. Mukasey, 531 F.3d 1059, 1062 (9th Cir. 2008).

U.S. citizen spouse.[796] These Justices differed in their reasoning, though. A three-Justice plurality found that none of the various "interests" asserted by the U.S. citizen wife constituted a protected liberty interest for purposes of the Due Process Clause.[797] For this reason, the plurality rejected the wife's argument that, insofar as enforcement of the law affected her enjoyment of an "implied fundamental liberty," the government must provide her "a full battery of procedural-due-process protections," including stating the specific grounds on which her husband's visa had been denied.[798] A two-Justice concurrence did not reach the question of whether the U.S. citizen wife had asserted a protected liberty interest, but instead concluded that the consular officials' citation of a particular statutory ground for inadmissibility as the basis for denying the visa application satisfied due process under *Kleindienst*, which requires only that the government state a "facially legitimate and *bona fide* reason" for the denial.[799]

[P. 1539, after sentence ending ". . . against aliens already within the country.", add new footnote:]

An alien arriving at a U.S. port of entry, whether at a land border or an international airport, is "'treated' for due process purposes 'as if stopped at the border,'" despite being on U.S. soil. Dep't of Homeland Sec. v. Thuraissigiam, 140 S. Ct. 1959, 1982 (2020) (quoting Shaughnessy v. United States *ex rel.* Mezei, 345 U.S. 206, 215 (1953)). That rule extends to those aliens who arrive at a port of entry and are later paroled in the country pending removal. *Id.*; *see also Shaughnessy*, 345 U.S. at 215. Accordingly, aliens who arrive at a port of entry and enter the country pending a decision concerning their removability are entitled to "only those rights regarding admission that Congress has provided by statute." *Thuraissigiam*, 140 S. Ct. at 1983.

[PP. 1545–46, delete n.494 and substitute with:]

Hampton v. Mow Sun Wong, 426 U.S. 88, 100 (1976). For example, the power to regulate immigration has permitted the federal government to discriminate on the basis of alienage, at least so long as the discrimination satisfies the rational basis standard of review. *See* Mathews v. Diaz, 426 U.S. 67, 79–80, 83 (1976) (holding that federal conditions upon alien eligibility for public assistance were not "wholly irrational," and observing that "In the exercise of its broad power over naturalization and immigration, Congress regularly makes rules that would be unacceptable if applied to citizens . . . The fact that an Act of Congress

---

[796] 576 U.S. ___, No. 13-1402, slip op. (2015).

[797] *Id.* at 5–6. (Scalia, J., joined by Roberts, C.J. & Thomas, J.) (plurality opinion). According to the plurality, the U.S. citizen spouse's alleged interests had been variously formulated as a "liberty interest in her marriage"; a "right of association with one's spouse"; a "liberty interest in being reunited with certain blood relatives"; and the "liberty interest of a U.S. citizen under the Due Process Clause to be free from arbitrary restrictions on his right to live with his spouse." *Id.* at 7. The plurality also expressly noted that no fundamental right to marriage, as such, had been infringed, because "the Federal Government has not attempted to forbid a marriage." *Id.* (contrasting the case at hand with *Loving v. Virginia*, 388 U.S. 1 (1967)).

[798] *Id.* at 6. The plurality took issue with the dissenting Justices' view that procedural due process rights attach to liberty interests that are not created by nonconstitutional law, such as a statute, but are "sufficiently important" so as to "flow 'implicit[ly]' from the design, object, and nature of the Due Process Clause." *Id.* at 11. According to the plurality, this view is a "novel" one that is inconsistent with the Court's established methodology for identifying fundamental rights that are subject to protection under the Due Process Clause. *Id.* at 12.

[799] *Id.* at 3 (Kennedy, J., concurring, joined by Alito, J.).

treats aliens differently from citizens does not in itself imply that such disparate treatment is 'invidious.'"). Nonetheless, with regard to statutes that touch upon immigration-related matters but do not address the entry or exclusion of aliens, the Court has suggested that if such a law discriminates on the basis of suspect factors other than alienage or national origin a more "exacting standard of review" may be required. *See* Sessions v. Morales-Santana, 582 U.S. ___, No. 15-1191, slip op. 14–17 (2017) (distinguishing between immigration and citizenship contexts, and applying heightened scrutiny to hold that a derivative citizenship statute which discriminated by gender violated equal protection principles).

NATIONAL EMINENT DOMAIN POWER

Just Compensation

Rights for Which Compensation Must Be Made.—

[P. 1566, after paragraph ending ". . . as any part of his just compensation.", add new paragraphs:]

The Court has also held that the government has a "categorical duty to pay just compensation" when it physically takes personal property, just as when it takes real property.[800]

In *Horne v. Department of Agriculture*, the Court held that a raisin marketing order issued under a Depression-era statute requiring raisin growers to reserve a percentage of their total crop for the federal government to dispose of in its discretion constituted "a clear physical taking" because, even though the scheme was intended to benefit the growers by maintaining stable markets for raisins, the "[a]ctual raisins are transferred from the growers to the Government."[801] The Court further held the government could not avoid paying just compensation for this physical taking by providing for the return to the raisin growers of any net proceeds from the government's sale of the reserve raisins.[802] The majority also rejected the government's argument that the reserve requirement was not a physical taking because raisin growers voluntarily participated in the raisin market.[803] In so doing, the Court noted that selling produce

---

[800] *See* Horne v. Dep't of Agric., 576 U.S. ___, No. 14-275, slip op. at 5 (2015). In deciding this case, the Court presumably intended to leave intact established exceptions when the government seizes personal property (e.g., confiscation of adulterated drugs). *See, e.g.,* Bennis v. Michigan, 516 U.S. 442, 452 (1996) ("Petitioner also claims that the forfeiture in this case was a taking of private property for public use in violation of the Takings Clause of the Fifth Amendment, made applicable to the States by the Fourteenth Amendment. But if the forfeiture proceeding here in question did not violate the Fourteenth Amendment, the property in the automobile was transferred by virtue of that proceeding from petitioner to the State. The government may not be required to compensate an owner for property which it has already lawfully acquired under the exercise of governmental authority other than the power of eminent domain.").

[801] *Horne*, slip op. at 8.

[802] *Id.* at 9–12.

[803] The government's argument might have carried more weight had the marketing order been viewed as a regulatory taking. Tahoe-Sierra Pres. Council, Inc. v. Tahoe Reg'l Planning Agency, 535 U.S. 302, 321–22 (2002) ("The text of the Fifth Amendment itself provides a basis for drawing a distinction between physical takings and regulatory takings. Its plain language requires the payment of compensation whenever the government acquires private property for a public purpose, whether the acquisition is the result of a condemnation

in interstate commerce is not a "special government benefit that the Government may hold hostage, to be ransomed by the waiver of constitutional protection."[804] In addition, the Court determined that the value of the raisins for takings purposes was their fair market value, with no deduction for the offsetting benefits of the overall statutory scheme, which is intended to maintain stable markets for raisins.[805]

When Property Is Taken

Government Activity Not Directed at Property.—

[P. 1570, delete first sentence at beginning of paragraph and n.667 and substitute with:]

But the Court also decided long ago that land can be "taken" in the constitutional sense by physical invasion or occupation by the government, as occurs when the government floods land permanently or recurrently.[806]

Regulatory Takings.—

[P. 1574, after n.689, delete "Rather, as one commentator remarked, its decisions constitute a 'crazy quilt pattern' of judgments." and n.690, and substitute with:]

More recently the Court has observed that, "[i]n the near century since *Mahon*, the Court for the most part has refrained from elaborating this principle through definitive rules."[807] Indeed, "[t]his area of the law has

---

proceeding or a physical appropriation. But the Constitution contains no comparable reference to regulations that prohibit a property owner from making certain uses of her private property."); Bowles v. Willingham, 321 U.S. 503, 519 (1944) (rent control cannot be a taking of premises if "[t]here is no requirement that the apartments be used for purposes which bring them under the [rent control] Act").

[804] *Horne*, slip op. at 13. Here, the Court expressly rejected the argument that the raisin growers could avoid the physical taking of their property by growing different crops, or making different uses of their grapes, by quoting its earlier decision in *Loretto v. Teleprompter Manhattan CATV Corp.*, 458 U.S. 419, 439 n.17 (1982) ("[A] landlord's ability to rent his property may not be conditioned on his forfeiting the right to compensation for a physical occupation."). The Court also distinguished the raisin reserve provisions from the requirement that companies manufacturing pesticides, fungicides, and rodenticides disclose trade secrets in order to sell those products at issue in *Ruckelshaus v. Monsanto Co.*, 467 U.S. 986 (1984). It did so because the manufacturers in *Ruckelshaus* were seen to have taken part in a "voluntary exchange" of information that included their trade secrets, recognized as property under the Takings Clause, in exchange for a "valuable Government benefit" in the form of a license to sell dangerous chemicals. No such government benefit was seen to be involved with the raisin growers because they were making "basic and familiar uses" of their property.

[805] *Horne*, slip op. at 14–16.

[806] Pumpelly v. Green Bay Co., 80 U.S. (13 Wall.) 166, 177–78 (1872). Recurrent, temporary floodings are not categorically exempt from Takings Clause liability. Ark. Game & Fishing Comm'n v. United States, 568 U.S. 23 (2012) (downstream timber damage caused by changes in seasonal water release rates from government dam).

[807] Murr v. Wisconsin, 582 U.S. ___, No. 15-214, slip op. at 7 (2017) (rejecting the argument of the owners of two adjoining undeveloped lots that a regulatory taking occurred through the enactment of regulations that forbade improvement or separate sale of the lots).

been characterized by 'ad hoc, factual inquiries, designed to allow careful examination and weighing of all the relevant circumstances.'"[808]

[P. 1574, end of first full paragraph after "in the area.", add new footnote:]

While observing that the "central dynamic of the Court's regulatory takings jurisprudence . . . is its flexibility," the Court in *Murr v. Wisconsin* reiterated the "two guidelines . . . for determining when government regulation is so onerous that it constitutes a taking." *Id.* at 7. First, with some qualifications, "'a regulation which denies all economically beneficial or productive use of land will require compensation under the Takings Clause.'" *Id.* (quoting Palazzolo v. Rhode Island, 533 U.S. 606, 617 (2001)). Second, if "a regulation impedes the use of property without depriving the owner of all economically beneficial use, a taking still may be found based on 'a complex of factors,' including (1) the economic impact of the regulation on the claimant; (2) the extent to which the regulation has interfered with distinct investment-backed expectations; and (3) the character of the governmental action." *Id.* at 7–8 (quoting *Palazzolo*, 533 U.S. at 617).

[P. 1577, after sentence ending ". . . that sets the scope of analysis.", add new footnote:]

The "parcel as a whole" analysis refers to the precept that takings law "does not divide a single parcel into discrete segments and attempt to determine whether rights in a particular segment have been entirely abrogated." *Penn Central*, 438 U.S. at 130; *see also* Concrete Pipe & Prods. of Cal., Inc. v. Constr. Laborers Pension Tr., 508 U.S. 602, 644 (1993); Keystone Bituminous Coal Ass'n v. DeBenedictis, 480 U.S. 470, 497 (1987). In *Tahoe-Sierra Preservation Council v. Tahoe Regional Planning Agency*, the Court affirmed the established spatial dimension of the doctrine, under which the court must consider the entire relevant tract, as well as the functional dimension, under which the court must consider plaintiff's full bundle of rights. *See* 535 U.S. 302, 327 (2002). The spatial dimension is perhaps best illustrated by the analysis in *Penn Central*, wherein the Court declined to segment Grand Central Terminal from the air rights above it. 438 U.S. at 130. And the functional dimension of the parcel as a whole is demonstrated by the Court's refusal in *Andrus v. Allard* to segment one "stick" in the plaintiff's "bundle" of property rights in holding that denial of the right to sell Indian artifacts was not a taking in light of rights in the artifacts that were retained. 444 U.S. 51, 65-66 (1979). In *Tahoe-Sierra*, the Court also added a temporal dimension to the "parcel as a whole" analysis, under which a court considers the entire time span of plaintiff's property interest. Invoking this temporal dimension, the Court held that temporary land-use development moratoria do not effect a total elimination of use because use and value return in the period following the moratorium's expiration. *Tahoe-Sierra*, 535 U.S. at 327. Thus, such moratoria are to be analyzed under the ad hoc, multifactor *Penn Central* test, rather than a per se "total takings" approach.

[P. 1577, after sentence ending ". . . that sets the scope of analysis.", delete through "discussed further on" and substitute with:]

In *Murr v. Wisconsin*, the Court stated that, "[l]ike the ultimate question whether a regulation has gone too far, the question of the proper parcel in regulatory takings cases cannot be solved by any simple test. Courts must instead define the parcel in a manner that reflects *reasonable expectations* about the property."[809] In *Murr*, the owners of two small adjoining lots, previously owned separately, wished to sell one of the lots and build on the other. The landowners were prevented from doing so by state and local

---

[808] *Id.* (quoting Tahoe-Sierra Pres. Council, Inc. v. Tahoe Reg'l Planning Agency, 535 U.S. 302, 322 (2002)).

[809] Murr v. Wisconsin, 582 U.S. ___, No. 15-214, slip op. at 20 (2017) (internal citation omitted) (emphasis added).

regulations, enacted to implement a federal act, which effectively merged the lots when they came under common ownership, thereby barring the separate sale or improvement of the lots. The landowners therefore sought just compensation, alleging a regulatory taking of their property.

In ruling against the landowners, the Supreme Court set forth a flexible multi-factor test for defining "the proper unit of property" to analyze whether a regulatory taking has occurred.[810] The Court continued the approach of prior cases whereby the boundaries of the parcel determine the "denominator of the fraction" of value taken from a property by a governmental regulation, which in turn can determine whether the government has "taken" private property.[811] Under this formula, regulators have an interest in a larger denominator—in the *Murr* case, combining the two adjoining lots—to reduce the likelihood of having to provide compensation, while property owners seeking to show that their property has been taken have an interest in the denominator being as small as possible. The *Murr* Court instructed that, in determining the parcel at issue in a regulatory takings case, "no single consideration can supply the exclusive test for determining the denominator. Instead, courts must consider a number of factors," including (1) "the treatment of the land under state and local law"[812]; (2) "the physical characteristics of the land"[813]; and (3) "the prospective value of the regulated land."[814]

[P. 1582, after ". . . be dedicated for public roads)", add new footnote:]

A third type of inverse condemnation, in addition to regulatory and *Nollan*, also applies to exactions imposed as conditions precedent to permit approval. Koontz v. St. Johns River Water Mgmt. Dist., 570 U.S. 595 (2013). To the argument that nothing is "taken" when a permit is denied for failure to agree to a condition precedent, the Court stated that what is at stake is not whether a taking has occurred, but whether the right not to have property taken without just compensation has been burdened impermissibly. *Id.* at 607–08. The Court in *Koontz* did not discuss what remedies might be available to a plaintiff who refuses to accept certain conditions precedent and thereby is refused a permit.

---

[810] *Id.* at 11. In doing so, the Court rejected arguments for the adoption of "a formalistic rule to guide the parcel inquiry," one that would "tie the definition of the parcel to state law." *See id.* at 14.

[811] *Id.* at 9 ("[B]ecause our test for regulatory taking requires us to compare the value that has been taken from the property with the value that remains in the property, one of the critical questions is determining how to define the unit of property 'whose value is to furnish the denominator of the fraction.' As commentators have noted, the answer to this question may be outcome determinative." (quoting *Keystone*, 480 U.S. at 497)).

[812] *Id.* at 11–12 ("[C]ourts should give substantial weight to the treatment of the land, in particular how it is bounded or divided, under state and local law.").

[813] *Id.* ("[C]ourts must look to the physical characteristics of the landowner's property. These include the physical relationship of any distinguishable tracts, the parcel's topography, and the surrounding human and ecological environment. In particular, it may be relevant that the property is located in an area that is subject to, or likely to become subject to, environmental or other regulation.")

[814] *Id.* at 11, 13 ("[C]ourts should assess the value of the property under the challenged regulation, with special attention to the effect of burdened land on the value of other holdings.").

[P. 1582, after n.735, add new sentence:]

The Court clarified this uncertainty in *Koontz v. St. Johns River Water Management District* by holding that monetary exactions imposed under land use permitting were subject to essential nexus/rough proportionality analysis.[815]

[P. 1585, delete sentence starting "In the leading decision . . ." and substitute with:]

In *Williamson County Regional Planning Commission v. Hamilton Bank*,[816] the Court announced a two-part ripeness test for takings actions brought in federal court—although the second part of this test was subsequently overturned by *Knick v. Township of Scott*.[817]

[P. 1585, after sentence starting "First, for an as-applied challenge . . .", add new footnote:]

Williamson Cty., 473 U.S. at 191.

[P. 1585, after sentence starting "Second, when suing . . .", add new footnote:]

Id. at 195.

[P. 1585, after sentence starting "Thus, the claim in *Williamson County* . . .", add new footnote:]

Id. at 194, 196–97.

[PP. 1586–87, delete paragraph starting "The requirement that state remedies be exhausted . . ." and substitute with:]

As noted, *Williamson County* also required litigants to exhaust state remedies before bringing a federal takings claim.[818] This aspect of the Court's decision had significant, and, as the Court came to conclude, "unanticipated" consequences for plaintiffs.[819] In *San Remo Hotel, LP v. City and County of San Francisco*, the plaintiffs had lost an inverse condemnation claim in state court after a federal court dismissed their earlier attempt to file in federal court, citing *Williamson County*'s exhaustion requirement.[820] When the litigants attempted to return to federal court, the court dismissed their claim, holding that the legal doctrine of issue preclusion prevented the court from relitigating those

---

[815] 570 U.S. 595 (2013).

[816] 473 U.S. 172 (1985).

[817] 588 U.S. ___, No. 17-647, slip op. at 23 (2019).

[818] Williamson Cty. Reg'l Planning Comm'n v. Hamilton Bank of Johnson City, 473 U.S. 172, 195 (1985).

[819] Knick v. Twp. of Scott, 588 U.S. ___, No. 17-647, slip op. at 5 (2019).

[820] 545 U.S. 323, 331–32 (2005).

claims.[821] Under common-law preclusion doctrines, which are "implemented by" the federal full faith and credit statute,[822] federal courts are in some circumstances required to abide by state court decisions that have already resolved the issues presently before the federal court.[823] In *San Remo*, the Supreme Court held that these preclusion doctrines barred the plaintiffs' takings claim, declining to create any special exceptions in the context of the Takings Clause.[824] Thus, as the Court later described this outcome, "[t]he adverse state court decision that . . . gave rise to a ripe federal takings claim simultaneously barred that claim."[825] In a concurring opinion in *San Remo*, four Justices said that while they agreed that the plaintiffs were precluded from relitigating their takings claim in federal court, they believed that *Williamson County* "may have been mistaken" in creating an exhaustion requirement.[826] The concurring Justices believed it was "not obvious" that this exhaustion requirement was required by "constitutional or prudential principles,"[827] and they further contended that "*Williamson County*'s state-litigation rule . . . . all but guarantees that claimants will be unable to utilize the federal courts to enforce the Fifth Amendment's just compensation guarantee."[828]

The Supreme Court overruled *Williamson County*'s exhaustion requirement in *Knick v. Township of Scott*.[829] Instead, the Court held that property owners have a "Fifth Amendment right to full compensation" and a concomitant right to bring a federal suit at the time the government takes their property, "regardless of post-taking remedies that may be available to the property owner."[830] The Court said its cases had long established that a right to compensation "arises at the time of the taking," and that *Williamson County*'s conclusion otherwise had rested on a misunderstanding of precedent.[831] The Supreme Court concluded that *Williamson County* was wrongly decided and that *stare decisis* considerations did not preclude it from overruling the exhaustion aspects of that decision.[832]

---

[821] *Id.* at 334–35.

[822] 28 U.S.C. § 1738 ("[J]udicial proceedings . . . shall have the same full faith and credit in every court within the United States and its Territories and Possessions as they have by law or usage in the courts of such State, Territory or Possession from which they are taken.").

[823] *San Remo*, 545 U.S. at 336.

[824] *Id.* at 338.

[825] Knick v. Twp. of Scott, 588 U.S. ___, No. 17-647, slip op. at 6 (2019).

[826] *San Remo*, 545 U.S. at 348 (Rehnquist, C.J., concurring).

[827] *Id.* at 349.

[828] *Id.* at 351.

[829] 588 U.S. ___, No. 17-647, slip op. at 23 (2019).

[830] *Id.* at 7, 11.

[831] *Id.* at 7, 12–15.

[832] *Id.* at 20.

SIXTH AMENDMENT

RIGHT TO A SPEEDY AND PUBLIC TRIAL

Speedy Trial

Application and Scope.—

[P. 1593, delete sentence after n.18 and substitute with:]

> But beyond its widespread applicability in state and federal prosecutions
> are questions of when the right attaches and detaches, when it is violated,
> and how violations may be remedied.

[P. 1595, after n.23, add new paragraph:]

The Court has, however, distinguished the concluding phase of a criminal prosecution—or the period between conviction and sentencing—from earlier phases involving (1) the investigation to determine whether to arrest a suspect and bring charges and (2) the period between when charges are brought and when the defendant is convicted upon trial or a guilty plea.[833] In *Betterman v. Montana,* the Court held that the constitutional guarantee of a speedy trial "detaches" once the defendant is convicted and, thus, does not protect against delays in sentencing.[834] The Court reached this conclusion, in part, by analogizing the speedy trial right to other protections that cease to apply upon conviction.[835] The *Betterman* Court's conclusion was also based on originalist reasoning, noting that when the Sixth Amendment was adopted, the term "accused" implied a status preceding conviction, while the term "trial" connoted a discrete event that would be followed by sentencing.[836] Practical considerations also informed the Court's conclusion. In particular, the *Betterman* Court raised concerns about the potential "windfall" that defendants would enjoy if the standard remedy for speedy trial violations—namely, dismissal of the charges—were to be applied after conviction.[837] Finally, the Court, relying on the federal government's and states' practices in implementing the speedy trial guarantee, observed that the federal Speedy Trial Act and "numerous state analogs" impose precise time limits for charging and trial, but are silent with respect to sentencing, suggesting that historical practice was consistent with the Court's interpretation of the scope of the Speedy Trial Clause.[838] At the same time, the Court did not view the reliance on plea agreements, instead of trials, in the contemporary criminal justice system as requiring a

---

[833] Betterman v. Montana, 578 U.S. ___, No. 14-1457, slip op. at 3 (2016).

[834] *Id.* at 1, 3.

[835] *Id.* at 4 (noting, for example, that proof beyond a reasonable doubt is required for conviction, but sentencing factors need only be proved by a preponderance of the evidence).

[836] *Id.* at 4–5.

[837] *Id.* at 6–7.

[838] *Id.* at 7–8.

different outcome, noting that there are other protections against excessive delays in sentencing available to defendants, including the Due Process Clause and Federal Rule of Criminal Procure 32(b)(1).[839]

RIGHT TO TRIAL BY IMPARTIAL JURY

Jury Trial

Attributes and Function of the Jury.—

[P. 1601, delete "and in subsequent cases it has done so." and change comma before n.60 to period]

[P. 1602, delete sentence starting "Applying the same type of analysis . . ." and substitute with:]

> In *Apodaca v. Oregon*, a four-Justice plurality applied the same type of analysis used in *Williams* to conclude that, while unanimity was the rule at common law, the framers of the Sixth Amendment likely had not intended to preserve that requirement within the term "jury."[840]

[P. 1603, after n.68, add new paragraph:]

> The Supreme Court departed from *Apodaca*'s "badly fractured" opinions in *Ramos v. Louisiana*, holding that "the Sixth Amendment's unanimity requirement applies to state and federal criminal trials equally."[841] The Court confirmed that, at the time of the Founding, the Sixth Amendment's guarantee of a jury trial included the requirement of unanimity.[842] And since then, the majority opinion observed, the Supreme Court "commented on the Sixth Amendment's unanimity requirement" in a number of opinions over the years.[843] The Court described the *Apocada* plurality's analysis as "a breezy cost-benefit analysis"[844] and said that "the ancient guarantee of a unanimous jury verdict" should not have been subjected to such a "functionalist assessment."[845] With respect to Justice Powell's "dual-track theory of incorporation," the Justices disagreed as to

---

[839] *Id.* at 8–10 (noting, among other things that the Due Process Clause serves as a "backstop against exorbitant delay"). The majority in *Betterman* did not address how a due process claim for an allegedly excessive delay in sentencing should be analyzed.

[840] 406 U.S. at 407–09 (1972).

[841] 140 S. Ct. 1390, 1397 (2020) .

[842] *Id.* at 1395 ("Wherever we might look to determine what the term 'trial by an impartial jury trial' meant at the time of the Sixth Amendment's adoption—whether it's the common law, state practices in the founding era, or opinions and treatises written soon afterward—the answer is unmistakable. A jury must reach a unanimous verdict in order to convict.").

[843] *Id.* at 1395–96.

[844] *Id.* at 1401.

[845] *Id.* at 1402.

whether this aspect of the *Apodaca* ruling was "a governing precedent,"[846] but ultimately, a majority of the Court overruled the decision.[847]

[P. 1603, delete sentence starting "Certain functions of the jury. . ." and substitute with:]

Accordingly, after *Ramos*, the unanimity requirement joins other aspects of the Sixth Amendment right to a jury trial that must exist in both the federal and state court systems.

When the Jury Trial Guarantee Applies.—

[P. 1606, after n.93, add new sentence:]

In *Alleyne v. United States*, the Court extended *Apprendi* to require "that any fact that increases the mandatory minimum [sentence] . . . must be submitted to the jury."[848]

[P. 1607, delete first paragraph and substitute with:]

Apprendi's importance soon became evident as the Court applied its reasoning in other situations to strike down state or federal laws on Sixth Amendment grounds.[849] In *Ring v. Arizona*, the Court applied *Apprendi* to invalidate an Arizona law that authorized imposition of the death penalty only if the judge made a factual determination as to the existence of any of several aggravating factors.[850] Although Arizona had required that the judge's findings as to aggravating factors be made beyond a reasonable doubt, and not merely by a preponderance of the evidence, the Court held that a jury must make those findings if the

---

[846] *Compare id.* at 1402 (plurality opinion) (Gorsuch, J., joined by Ginsburg and Breyer, JJ.) (arguing that *Apodaca* did not supply "a governing precedent" and that "a single Justice writing only for himself" should not have "the authority to bind this Court to propositions it has already rejected"), *and id.* at 1424–25 (Thomas, J., concurring in judgment) ("I would simply hold that, because all of the opinions in *Apodaca* addressed the Due Process Clause, its Fourteenth Amendment ruling does not bind us because the proper question here is the scope of the Privileges or Immunities Clause."), *with id.* at 1428 (Alito, J., dissenting, joined by Roberts, C.J., and Kagan, J.) (arguing that *Apodaca* is a binding precedent).

[847] *Id.* at 1404–06 (majority opinion).

[848] 570 U.S. 99, 102 (2013) (overruling Harris v. United States, 536 U.S. 545 (2002)).

[849] *Apprendi* has also influenced the Court's ruling on matters of statutory interpretation. For example, in *Mathis v. United States*, 579 U.S. ___, No. 15-6092, slip op. (2016), a plurality of the Court concluded that the "elements based approach" to interpreting the Armed Career Criminal Act (ACCA)—wherein a judge is prohibited from inquiring into the specific conduct of a particular offender's previous acts in determining whether a sentence enhancement applies—is necessitated by *Apprendi*'s holding that generally only a jury, and not a judge, may find facts that increase a maximum penalty. *Id.* at 10; *see also id.* at 1 (Kennedy, J., concurring) (joining the five-Justice majority opinion, but expressing a "reservation" about the majority's reliance on *Apprendi* because that case "was incorrect, and . . . does not compel the elements based approach."); Descamps v. United States, 570 U.S. ___, No. 11-9540, slip op. at 14 (2013) (noting the "serious Sixth Amendment concerns" that would arise if the element-centric, categorical approach was not adopted with regard to interpreting the ACCA).

[850] 536 U.S. 584 (2002).

existence of particular facts is a precondition for imposing a judgment within a particular range.[851] Similarly, in *Hurst v. Florida*, the Court applied *Apprendi* and *Ring* to invalidate a Florida statute authorizing a "hybrid" proceeding in which the "jury renders an advisory verdict, but the judge makes the ultimate sentencing determination."[852] According to the Court, such proceedings run afoul of the Sixth Amendment because the judge, not the jury, makes the findings of fact that are necessary before imposing the death penalty.[853]

[P. 1609, delete second paragraph and substitute with:]

The Court, however, has refused to extend *Apprendi* to a judge's decision to impose sentences for discrete crimes consecutively rather than concurrently.[854] The Court explained that, when a defendant has been convicted of multiple offenses, each involving discrete sentencing prescriptions, the states apply various rules regarding whether a judge may impose the sentences consecutively or concurrently.[855] The Court held that "twin considerations—historical practice and respect for state sovereignty—counsel against extending *Apprendi*'s rule" to preclude judicial fact-finding in this situation, as well.[856]

---

[851] "Because Arizona's enumerated aggravating factors operate as 'the functional equivalent of an element of a greater offense,' . . . the Sixth Amendment requires that they be found by a jury." *Id.* at 509 (quoting *Apprendi*, 530 U.S. at 494 n.19). The Court rejected Arizona's request that it recognize an exception for capital sentencing so as not to interfere with elaborate sentencing procedures designed to comply with the Eighth Amendment. *Id.* at 605–07.

[852] 577 U.S. ___, No. 14-7505, slip op. at 1–2 (2016) (quoting *Ring*, 536 U.S. at 584 n.6) (quotation marks omitted). In so doing, the Court expressly overruled its earlier decisions in *Spaziano v. Florida*, 468 U.S. 447 (1984), and *Hildwin v. Florida*, 490 U.S. 638 (1989) (per curiam), which approved of Florida's "hybrid" proceedings on the grounds that "the Sixth Amendment does not require that the specific findings authorizing the imposition of the sentence of death be made by a jury." *Id.* at 9 (quoting *Hildwin*, 490 U.S. at 640–41). Both decisions were issued prior to *Ring*. Nonetheless, as the Court held in *McKinney v. Arizona*, neither *Ring* nor *Hurst* held that a jury is constitutionally required to weigh the aggravating and mitigating circumstances or make the ultimate sentencing decision within the relevant range. *See* 140 S. Ct. 702, 707–08 (2020). Instead, building on *Apprendi*, those cases concluded that the Sixth Amendment merely requires a jury to find the existence of aggravating facts necessary to qualify for the death penalty. *Id.* at 708. As a result, the *McKinney* Court concluded that *Ring* and *Hurst* did not cast doubt on the Court's ruling in *Clemons v. Mississippi*, 494 U.S. 738 (1990). *McKinney*, 140 S. Ct. at 708. *Clemons* allowed an appellate court, following a determination that the jury relied on an impermissible aggravating circumstance in sentencing a defendant to death, to reweigh the aggravating and mitigating circumstances. 494 U.S. at 741. The *Clemons* Court reasoned that such review was akin to harmless-error review because the appellate court was simply determining whether the remaining factual findings that the jury already considered still warranted the death penalty. *Id.*

[853] *Hurst*, slip op. at 6.

[854] Oregon v. Ice, 555 U.S. 160 (2009).

[855] Most states follow the common law tradition of giving judges unfettered discretion over the matter, while some states presume that sentences will run consecutively but allow judges to order concurrent sentences upon finding cause to do so. "It is undisputed," the Court noted, "that States may proceed on [either of these] two tracks without transgressing the Sixth Amendment." *Id.* at 163.

[856] *Id.* at 168. The Court also noted other decisions judges make that are likely to evade

[P. 1612, after paragraph ending " . . . sentences under it.", add new paragraph:]

A splintered Court extended *Apprendi* and its progeny to the setting of a supervised release revocation in *United States v. Haymond.*[857] *Haymond* centered on the constitutionality of 18 U.S.C. § 3583(k), which provided (among other things) that if a judge finds by the preponderance of the evidence that a sex-offender defendant on supervised release has committed one of several enumerated offenses, including the possession of child pornography, the judge must impose an additional term of imprisonment of at least five years and up to life, regardless of the nature of the initial crime of conviction.[858] A felon who was found with child pornography while on supervised release and was sentenced under § 3583(k) challenged the constitutionality of that law.[859] A four-Justice plurality concluded in an opinion by Justice Gorsuch that the statute was unconstitutional, at least as applied to the defendant's case.[860] Citing *Apprendi* and *Alleyne,* the plurality reasoned that because the statute compelled a judge to sentence the defendant to a minimum of five years in prison without empaneling a jury or requiring the government to prove his guilt beyond a reasonable doubt, the application of the statute to the defendant violated the Fifth and Sixth Amendments.[861]

Providing a fifth vote on the constitutional question, Justice Breyer concurred only in the judgment of the Court.[862] His opinion limited the scope of the plurality opinion, which he argued could potentially reach other, more commonplace provisions governing supervised release proceedings.[863] Specifically, Justice Breyer distinguished ordinary supervised release proceedings, which typically result in fairly limited terms of imprisonment based on the severity of the original crime, from § 3583(k) because the latter (1) mandated that the judge impose a minimum term of imprisonment that (2) applied only when a defendant committed a discrete set of criminal offenses.[864] Consequently, rather than constituting an "ordinary revocation" of supervised release, in Justice Breyer's view the statute "more closely resemble[d] the punishment of new

---

the strictures of *Apprendi*, including determining the length of supervised release, attendance at drug rehabilitation programs, terms of community service, and imposition of fines and orders of restitution. *Id.* at 171–72.

[857] *See* 588 U.S. ___, No. 17-1672, slip op. (2019).

[858] *Id.* at 3 (plurality opinion).

[859] *Id.* at 2.

[860] *Id.* at 1.

[861] *Id.* at 10. The plurality declined to resolve the question of how to remedy the constitutional violation, concluding that the "wiser course" was to return the case to the appellate court for "it to have the opportunity to address" whether the constitutional infirmity can be cured by requiring a jury acting under the reasonable doubt standard decide whether the defendant violated § 3583(k). *Id.* at 22–23.

[862] *Id.* at 1 (Breyer, J., concurring).

[863] *Id.*

[864] *Id.* at 2.

criminal offenses" without the protection of Fifth and Sixth Amendment rights.[865]

Impartial Jury

[P. 1615, after paragraph ending ". . . against a co-defendant which it implicates.", add new paragraphs:]

Nonetheless, there are limits on the extent to which an inquiry can be made into whether a criminal defendant's right to a jury trial has been denied by a biased jury. With origins dating from the English common law, a rule of evidence has been adopted by the federal rules of evidence[866] and by the vast majority of the states[867] that forbids the "impeachment" or questioning of a verdict by inquiring into the internal deliberations of the jury.[868] The "no impeachment" rule, which aims to promote "full and vigorous discussion" by jurors and to preserve the "stability" of jury verdicts, has limited the ability of criminal defendants to argue that a jury's internal deliberations demonstrated bias amounting to a deprivation of the right to a jury trial.[869] Indeed, the Court has held that the Sixth Amendment justifies an exception to the no impeachment rule in only the "gravest and most important cases."[870] As a result, the Court has rejected a Sixth Amendment exception to the rule when evidence existed that jurors were under the influence of alcohol and drugs during the trial.[871] Likewise, the Court concluded that the no-impeachment rule prevented evidence from being introduced indicating that a jury forewoman had failed to disclose a prodefendant bias during jury selection (*voir dire*) and allegedly influenced the jury with such bias.[872] In the Court's view, three safeguards—(1) the *voir dire* process, (2) the ability for the court and counsel to observe the jury during trial, and (3) the potential for jurors to report untoward behavior to the court before rendering a verdict—adequately protect Sixth Amendment interests while preserving the values underlying the no impeachment rule.[873]

---

[865] *Id.*

[866] *See* FED. R. EVID. 606(b)(1) ("During an inquiry into the validity of a verdict or indictment, a juror may not testify about any statement made or incident that occurred during the jury's deliberations; the effect of anything on that juror's or another juror's vote; or any juror's mental processes concerning the verdict or indictment.").

[867] *See* Pena-Rodriguez v. Colorado, 580 U.S. ___, No. 15-606, slip op. at 9 (2017) (noting that 42 jurisdictions follow the federal rule).

[868] The no-impeachment rule does have three central exceptions, allowing a juror to testify about (1) extraneous prejudicial information improperly brought to the jury's attention; (2) outside influences brought to bear on any juror; and (3) a mistake made in entering the verdict on the verdict form. *See* FED. R. EVID. 606(b)(2). As a result, the rule prohibits all juror testimony excepting for when the jury considers prejudicial extraneous evidence or is subject to other outside influence. *See Pena-Rodriguez*, slip op. at 8.

[869] *See Pena-Rodriguez*, slip op. at 11.

[870] *See* McDonald v. Pless, 238 U.S. 264, 269 (1915).

[871] *See* Tanner v. United States, 483 U.S. 107, 127 (1987).

[872] *See* Warger v. Shauers, 574 U.S. ___, No. 13-517, slip op. at 3–4 (2014).

[873] *See Tanner*, 483 U.S. at 127. In addition, while the no-impeachment rule, by its very nature, prohibits testimony by jurors, evidence of misconduct *other than juror testimony* can

However, in *Pena-Rodriguez v. Colorado,* the Court for the first time recognized a Sixth Amendment exception to the no-impeachment rule.[874] In that case, a criminal defendant contended that his conviction by a Colorado jury for harassment and unlawful sexual contact should be overturned on constitutional grounds because evidence from two jurors revealed that a fellow juror had expressed anti-Hispanic bias toward the petitioner and his alibi witness during deliberations.[875] The Court agreed, concluding that where a juror makes a "clear statement" indicating that he relied on "racial stereotypes or animus to convict a criminal defendant, the Constitution requires that the no-impeachment rule give way . . . ."[876] In so holding, *Pena-Rodriguez* emphasized the "imperative to purge racial prejudice from the administration of justice" that underlies the Fourteenth Amendment, which, in turn, makes the Sixth Amendment applicable to the states.[877] Contrasting the instant case from earlier rulings that involved "anomalous behavior from a single jury—or juror—gone off course," the Court noted that racial bias in the judicial system was a "familiar and recurring evil" that required the judiciary to prevent "systematic injury to the administration of justice."[878] Moreover, the Court emphasized "pragmatic" rationales for its holding, noting that other checks on jury bias, such as questioning during *voir dire* or jurors reporting inappropriate statements during the course of deliberations, unlikely would disclose racial bias.[879]

[P. 1615, at the beginning of paragraph starting "In *Witherspoon v. Illinois* . . . ", add new sentence:]

Inquiries into jury bias have arisen in the context of the imposition of the death penalty.

---

be used to impeach the verdict. *Id.*

[874] *See Pena-Rodriguez,* slip op. at 17.

[875] *Id.* at 3–4.

[876] *Id.* at 17. The Court noted that "[n]ot every offhand comment indicating racial bias or hostility will justify setting aside the no-impeachment bar to allow further judicial inquiry," but that instead the no-impeachment rule does not govern when a juror makes a statement exhibiting "overt racial bias" that was a "significant motivating factor in the juror's vote to convict." *Id.* If the *Pena-Rodriguez* exception to the no-impeachment rule applies, the trial court must examine the underlying evidence and determine whether a retrial is necessary in "light of all the circumstances, including the content and timing of the alleged statements and the reliability of the proffered evidence." *Id.*

[877] *Id.* at 13.

[878] *Id.* at 15–16.

[879] *Id.* ("[T]his Court has noted the dilemma faced by trial court judges and counsel in deciding whether to explore potential racial bias at *voir dire* . . . The stigma that attends racial bias may make it difficult for a juror to report inappropriate statements during the court of juror deliberations.").

[P. 1616, after n.145, add new sentence:]

Instead, a juror may be excused for cause "where the trial judge is left with the definite impression that a prospective juror would be unable to faithfully and impartially apply the law."[880]

[P. 1617, delete n.151 and substitute with:]

551 U.S. at 9 (citations omitted). In *Uttecht*, the Court reasoned that deference was owed to trial courts because the lower court is in a "superior position to determine the demeanor and qualifications of a potential juror." *See id.* at 22. In *White v. Wheeler*, the Court recognized that a trial judge's decision to excuse a prospective juror in a death penalty case was entitled to deference even when the judge does not make the decision to excuse the juror contemporaneously with jury selection (*voir dire*). *See* 577 U.S. ___, No. 14-1372, slip op. at 7–8 (2015) (per curiam). The Court explained that the deference due under *Uttecht* to a trial judge's decision was not limited to the judge's evaluation of a juror's demeanor, but extended to a trial judge's consideration of "the substance of a juror's response." *See id.* at 8. When a trial judge "chooses to reflect and deliberate" over the record regarding whether to excuse a juror for a day following the questioning of the prospective juror, that judge's decision should be "commended" and is entitled to substantial deference. *See id.* at 8.

[P. 1617, after sentence ending ". . . by reviewing courts.", add new sentence:]

If there is ambiguity in a prospective juror's statement, a court is "entitled to resolve it in favor of the State."[881]

CONFRONTATION

[P. 1631, before first full paragraph, add new paragraph:]

The Court continued its shift away from a broader reading of *Crawford* in *Ohio v. Clark*,[882] a case that held that the Confrontation Clause did not bar the introduction of statements that a child made to his preschool teacher regarding abuse committed by the defendant.[883] To reach its holding, the Court, relying on a multi-factor approach to the primary purpose test similar to *Bryant*, noted that the statements in question (1) occurred in the context of an ongoing emergency involving suspected child abuse; (2) were made by a very young child, who did not intend his statements to be a substitute for trial testimony; (3) historically were admissible at common law; and (4) were not made to law enforcement officers.[884] In so holding, the Court appeared to lessen the importance of the primary purpose test, concluding that the primary purpose test is a "necessary, but not always sufficient, condition" for the exclusion of out-of-court statements under the Sixth Amendment, as evidence that

---

[880] *See Witt*, 469 U.S. at 425–26.
[881] *See Uttecht*, 551 U.S. at 7 (internal citations omitted).
[882] *See* 576 U.S. ___, No. 13-1352, slip op. (2015).
[883] *Id.* at 1.
[884] *Id.* at 7–10.

satisfies the primary purpose test may still be presented at trial if the evidence would have been admissible at the time of the founding.[885]

ASSISTANCE OF COUNSEL

Absolute Right to Counsel at Trial

Development of Right.—

[P. 1639, delete n.287 and substitute with:]

> Loper v. Beto, 405 U.S. 473 (1972) (error to have permitted counseled defendant in 1947 trial to have his credibility impeached by introduction of prior uncounseled convictions in the 1930s; Chief Justice Burger and Justices Blackmun, Powell, and Rehnquist dissented); United States v. Tucker, 404 U.S. 443 (1972) (error for sentencing judge in 1953 to have relied on two previous convictions at which defendant was without counsel); Burgett v. Texas, 389 U.S. 109 (1967) (admission of record of prior conviction without the assistance of counsel at trial, with instruction to jury to regard it only for purposes of determining sentence if it found defendant guilty, but not to use it in considering guilt, was inherently prejudicial); *but see* United States v. Bryant, 579 U.S. ___, No. 15-420, slip op. at 13 (2016) (holding that the use of prior, uncounseled tribal-court domestic abuse convictions as the predicates for a sentence enhancement in a subsequent conviction does not violate the Sixth Amendment right to counsel, as repeat offender laws penalize only the last offense committed by the defendant); Nichols v. United States, 511 U.S. 738 (1994) (as Scott v. Illinois, 440 U.S. 367 (1979) recognized that an uncounseled misdemeanor conviction is valid if defendant is not incarcerated, such a conviction may be used as the basis for penalty enhancement upon a subsequent conviction).

Limits on the Right to Retained Counsel.—

[P. 1641, in first full paragraph, delete first sentence and substitute with:]

> The right to retain counsel of choice generally does not bar operation of forfeiture provisions, even if the forfeiture serves to deny to a defendant the wherewithal to employ counsel.

[P. 1641, at end of first full paragraph, add:]

> Moreover, on the same day *Caplin & Drysdale* was decided, the Court, in *United States v. Monsanto,* held that the government may, prior to trial, freeze assets that a defendant needs to hire an attorney if probable cause exists to "believe that the property will ultimately be proved forfeitable."[886] Nonetheless, the holdings from *Caplin & Drysdale* and *Monsanto* are limited in that the Court, in *Luis v. United States,* has held

---

[885] *Id.* at 7.

[886] *Monsanto*, 491 U.S. at 615 ("Indeed, it would be odd to conclude that the Government may not restrain property, such as the home and apartment in respondent's possession, based on a finding of probable cause, when we have held that . . . the Government may restrain persons where there is a finding of probable cause to believe that the accused has committed a serious offense."). A subsequent case held that where a grand jury had returned an indictment based on probable cause, that conclusion was binding on a court during forfeiture proceedings and the defendants do not have a right to have such a conclusion re-examined in a separate judicial hearing in order to unfreeze the assets to pay for their counsel. Kaley v. United States, 571 U.S. 320 (2014).

that the Sixth Amendment provides criminal defendants the right to preserve *legitimate, untainted* assets unrelated to the underlying crime in order to retain counsel of their choice.[887]

Effective Assistance of Counsel.—

[P. 1645, delete last sentence of n.320 and substitute with:]

See also Burt v. Titlow, 571 U.S. 12 (2013); Cullen v. Pinholster, 563 U.S. 170 (2011).

[P. 1645, at end of n.321, add:]

See also Maryland v. Kulbicki, 577 U.S. ___, No. 14-848, slip op. at 3 (2015) (per curiam) (reversing an opinion by Maryland's highest state court, which found that counsel was ineffective because the defendant's attorneys did not question the methodology used by the state in analyzing bullet fragments, on the grounds that this methodology "was widely accepted" at the time of trial, and courts "regularly admitted [such] evidence").

[P. 1645, at end of n.325, delete "." and substitute with:]

; *Burt*, 571 U.S. at 23–24 (where a reasonable interpretation of the record indicated that a criminal defendant claimed actual innocence, the defendant's attorney was justified in withdrawing a guilty plea).

[P. 1646, delete n.329 and substitute with:]

See Andrus v. Texas, 140 S. Ct. 1875, 1882 (2020) (per curiam) (concluding the defendant's counsel provided constitutionally ineffective assistance by inadequately investigating mitigating evidence, providing evidence that bolstered the state's case, and failing to scrutinize the state's aggravating evidence); Buck v. Davis, 580 U.S. ___, No. 15-8049, slip op. at 17 (2017) (concluding that "[n]o competent defense attorney would introduce" evidence that his client was a future danger because of his race); *see also* Hinton v. Alabama, 571 U.S. 263, 274 (2014) (per curiam) (holding an attorney's hiring of a questionably competent expert witness because of a mistaken belief in the legal limit on the amount of funds payable on behalf of an indigent defendant constitutes ineffective assistance); Sears v. Upton, 561 U.S. 945, 952 (2010) (concluding that the "cursory nature" of a defense counsel's investigation into mitigation evidence was constitutionally ineffective); Porter v. McCollum, 558 U.S. 30, 40 (2009) (holding an attorney's failure to interview witnesses or search records in preparation for penalty phase of capital murder trial constituted ineffective assistance of counsel); Rompilla v. Beard, 545 U.S. 374, 385 (2005) (concluding that a defendant's attorneys' failure to consult trial transcripts from a prior conviction that the attorneys knew the prosecution would rely on in arguing for the death penalty was inadequate); Wiggins v. Smith, 539 U.S. 510, 526–28 (2003) (holding an attorney's failure to investigate defendant's personal history

---

[887] 578 U.S. ___, No. 14-419, slip op. at 1 (2016) (announcing the judgment of the Court). The Court in *Luis* split as to the reasoning for holding that a pretrial freeze of untainted assets violates a criminal defendant's Sixth Amendment right to counsel of choice. Four Justices employed a balancing test, weighing the government's contingent future interest in the untainted assets against the interests in preserving the right to counsel — a right at the "heart of a fair, effective criminal justice system" — in concluding that the defendant had the right to use innocent property to pay a reasonable fee for assistance of counsel. *See id.* at 11–16 (Breyer, J., joined by Roberts, C.J., Ginsburg & Sotomayor, JJ.). Justice Thomas, in providing the fifth and deciding vote, concurred in judgment only, contending that "textual understanding and history" alone suffice to "establish that the Sixth Amendment prevents the Government from freezing untainted assets in order to secure potential forfeiture." *See id.* at 1 (Thomas, J., concurring); *see also id.* at 9 ("I cannot go further and endorse the plurality's atextual balancing analysis.").

and present important mitigating evidence at capital sentencing was objectively unreasonable).

[P. 1647, at end of first partial paragraph, add new footnote:]

In *Chaidez v. United States*, 568 U.S. 342 (2013), the Court held that *Padilla* announced a "new rule" of criminal procedure that did not apply "retroactively" during collateral review of convictions then already final. For a discussion of retroactive application of the Court's criminal procedure decisions, *see supra* Article III: Section 2. Judicial Power and Jurisdiction: Clause 1. Cases and Controversies; Grants of Jurisdiction: Judicial Power and Jurisdiction-Cases and Controversies: The Requirements of a Real Interest: Retroactivity Versus Prospectivity.

[P. 1647, delete n.336 and substitute with:]

See Strickland, 466 U.S. at 694. This standard does not require that a "defendant show that counsel's deficient conduct more likely than not altered the outcome in the case." *Id.* at 693. At the same time, the Court has concluded that the "prejudice inquiry under *Strickland*" applies to cases beyond those in which there was only "little or no mitigation evidence" presented. *See* Sears v. Upton, 561 U.S. 945, 955 (2010); Porter v. McCollum, 558 U.S. 30, 40 (2009) (evaluating the "totality of mitigating evidence" to conclude that there was "a reasonable probability that the advisory jury—and the sentencing judge—'would have struck a different balance'" but for the counsel's deficiencies). For a recent example of a criminal defendant who succeeded on the prejudice prong of the *Strickland* test, *see* Buck v. Davis, 580 U.S. ___, No. 15-8049, slip op. at 18–19 (2017) (holding that, in a case where the focus of a capital sentencing proceeding was on the defendant's likelihood of recidivism, defense counsel had been ineffective by introducing racially charged testimony about the defendant's future dangerousness, and "[r]easonable jurors might well have valued [the testimony] concerning the central question before them.").

[P. 1648, delete n.337 and substitute with:]

See, e.g., Smith v. Spisak, 558 U.S. 139, 154–56 (2010). In *Hill v. Lockhart,* the Court applied the *Strickland* test to attorney decisions to accept a plea bargain, holding that a defendant must show a reasonable probability that, but for counsel's errors, the defendant would not have pleaded guilty and would have insisted on going to trial. *See* 474 U.S. 52, 59 (1985). As a result, the prejudice question with respect to when a counsel's deficient performance leads the defendant to accept a guilty plea rather than go to trial is not whether the trial would have resulted in a not guilty verdict. *See* Roe v. Flores-Ortega, 528 U.S. 470, 482–83 (2000). Instead, the issue is whether the defendant was prejudiced by the "denial of the entire judicial proceeding . . . to which he had a right." *Id.* at 483. As a result, prejudice may be very difficult to prove if the defendant's decision about going to trial turns on his prospects of success and those chances are affected by an attorney's error. *See* Premo v. Moore, 562 U.S. 115, 118 (2011). However, when a defendant's choice to accept a plea bargain has nothing to do with his chances of success at trial, such as if the defendant is primarily concerned with the respective consequences of a conviction after trial or by plea, a defendant can show prejudice by providing evidence contemporaneous with the acceptance of the plea that he would have rejected the plea if not for the erroneous advice of counsel. *See* Lee v. United States, 582 U.S. ___, No. 16-327, slip op. at 7–9 (2017) (holding that a defendant whose fear of deportation was the determinative factor in whether to accept a plea agreement could show prejudice resulting from his attorney's erroneous advice that a felony charge would not lead to deportation even when a different result at trial was remote).

[P. 1649, delete sentences starting "In *Lafler v. Cooper,* four dissenters . . ." through ". . . did not prevail, however."]

[P. 1649, after sentence ending ". . . to meaningful adversarial testing." add new sentence:]

Moreover, prejudice is presumed "when counsel's constitutionally deficient performance deprives a defendant of an appeal that he otherwise would have taken."[888]

[P. 1649, delete n.343 and substitute with:]

466 U.S. at 657-59.

[P. 1649, delete n.344 and substitute with:]

Cronic, 466 U.S. at 659 n.26.

[P. 1649, delete n.345 and substitute with:]

See, e.g., Weaver v. Massachusetts, 582 U.S. ___, No. 16-240, slip op. at 12 (2017) (holding that "when a defendant raises a public-trial violation via an ineffective-assistance-of-counsel claim, *Strickland* prejudice is not shown automatically"); Florida v. Nixon, 543 U.S. 175, 189-90 (2004) (holding that a concession-of-guilt strategy in a capital trial does not automatically rank as prejudicial ineffective assistance of counsel); Bell v. Cone, 535 U.S. 685, 697 (2002) (concluding that *Cronic*'s rule that prejudice can be presumed when counsel "entirely fails" to subject the prosecution's case to meaningful adversarial testing does not extend to situations where counsel's failings were limited to specific points in the trial); Mickens v. Taylor, 535 U.S. 162, 173-74 (2002) (holding that, to demonstrate a Sixth Amendment violation where the trial court fails to inquire into a potential conflict of interest, the defendant must establish that the conflict adversely affected his counsel's performance).

[P. 1649, after paragraph ending " . . . by the *Strickland* standard.", add new section:]

Limits on the Role of the Attorney.—While the Sixth Amendment guarantees the right of assistance of counsel, that right does not require the defendant to surrender control entirely to his representative.[889] Defense counsel's central province is in trial management, providing assistance in deciding what arguments to make, what evidentiary objections to raise, and what evidence should be submitted.[890] At the same time, the accused has the "ultimate authority to make certain fundamental decisions regarding the case," including "whether to plead guilty, waive a jury, testify in his or her own behalf, or take an appeal."[891] Such decisions are for the criminal defendant to make notwithstanding

---

[888] *See* Roe v. Flores-Ortega, 528 U.S. 470, 484 (2000). In *Garza v. Idaho*, the Court clarified that the presumption of prejudice that applies when counsel's deficient performance forfeits an appeal that a defendant otherwise would have taken remains even when the defendant has signed an appeal waiver, because issues may remain as to the scope or validity of the waiver and the presumption-of-prejudice rule does not depend upon the prospects of the defendant's appeal. *See* 586 U.S. ___, No. 17-1026, slip op. at 4–6, 10 (2019).

[889] *See* Faretta v. California, 422 U.S. 806, 819–20 (1975) (noting that counsel, by providing "assistance," no matter how expert, is "still an assistant").

[890] *See* Gonzalez v. United States, 553 U.S. 242, 248 (2008).

[891] *See* Jones v. Barnes, 463 U.S. 745, 751 (1983).

the defendant's own inexperience or lack of professional qualifications.[892] Allowing counsel to usurp such decisions from the accused violates the Sixth Amendment's right to counsel, amounting to a structural error that obviates any need to inquire into whether the criminal defendant was prejudiced in any way.[893]

In this vein, the Court held in *McCoy v. Louisiana* that a criminal defendant's choice to maintain his innocence at the guilt phase of a capital trial was not a strategic choice for a counsel to make, notwithstanding the counsel's view that confessing guilt offered the best chance to avoid the death penalty.[894] Instead, Justice Ginsburg, writing on behalf of the Court, viewed such a decision as a fundamental choice about the client's objectives for the criminal proceeding.[895] More specifically, while acknowledging that counsel "may reasonably assess a concession of guilt as best suited to avoiding the death penalty," the Court noted that a criminal defendant may not share the objective of avoiding such a punishment and instead may wish, above all else, to avoid admitting guilt or living the rest of his life in prison.[896] Because the Sixth Amendment requires the assistance of counsel, the *McCoy* Court concluded that a lawyer cannot concede his client's guilt and must instead assist in achieving his client's express objective to maintain his innocence of the charged criminal acts.[897]

---

[892] *See* McCoy v. Louisiana, 584 U.S. ___, No. 16-8255, slip op. at 6 (2018).

[893] *See id.* at 11 ("Because a client's autonomy, not counsel's competence, is in issue, we do not apply our ineffective-assistance-of-counsel jurisprudence.").

[894] *Id.* at 6–7.

[895] *Id.* at 7.

[896] *Id.*

[897] *Id.* Because the criminal defendant in *McCoy* expressly stated his desire to maintain his innocence, the Court found the case distinguishable from *Florida v. Nixon*, 543 U.S. 175 (2004), wherein the defendant did not protest the counsel's proposed approach to concede guilt during sentencing and only objected after trial. *See McCoy,* slip op. at 9. The *McCoy* Court also distinguished *Nix v. Whiteside*, 475 U.S. 157 (1986), as, unlike in McCoy's case, in *Nix* the defendant told his lawyer that he intended to commit perjury, raising an "ethical conundrum" between the client's rights under Sixth Amendment and the attorney's professional obligations to not suborn perjury. *See McCoy,* slip op. at 9.

SEVENTH AMENDMENT

TRIAL BY JURY IN CIVIL CASES

Application of the Amendment

Cases "at Common Law".—

[P. 1669, at end of n.39, add:]

> *See also* Oil States Energy Servs., LLC v. Greene's Energy Grp., LLC, 584 U.S. ___, No. 16-712, slip op. at 17 (2018) ("This Court's precedents establish that, when Congress properly assigns a matter to adjudication in a non-Article III tribunal, 'the Seventh Amendment poses no independent bar to the adjudication of that action by a nonjury factfinder.'" (quoting Granfinanciera, 492 U.S. at 53–54)).

EIGHTH AMENDMENT

CRUEL AND UNUSUAL PUNISHMENTS

Application and Scope

[PP. 1688–89, delete three paragraphs starting "'Difficulty would attend the effort to define . . ." and substitute with:]

Well over a century ago, the Court began defining limits on the scope of criminal punishments allowed under the Eighth Amendment, noting that while "[d]ifficulty would attend the effort to define with exactness the extent of the constitutional provision which provides that cruel and unusual punishments shall not be inflicted," "it is safe to affirm that punishments of torture," such as drawing and quartering, disemboweling alive, beheading, public dissection, and burning alive, are "forbidden by . . . [the] Constitution."[898] Nonetheless, in the context of capital punishment, the Court has upheld the use of a firing squad[899] and electrocution,[900] generally viewing the Eighth Amendment to prohibit punishments that "involve the unnecessary and wanton infliction of pain."[901] In three more recent cases, the Supreme Court held that the various lethal injection protocols withstood scrutiny under the Eighth Amendment, finding that none of the challenged protocols presented a "substantial risk of serious harm" or an "objectively intolerable risk of harm."[902]

Capital Punishment

[P. 1691, delete last paragraph and substitute with:]

Changed membership on the Court has had an effect. Gone from the Court are several Justices who believed that all capital punishment

---

[898] *See* Wilkerson v. Utah, 99 U.S. 130, 135–36 (1879).

[899] *Id.* at 137–38.

[900] *See In re* Kemmler, 136 U.S. 436, 447 (1890) ("Punishments are cruel when they involve torture or a lingering death; but the punishment of death is not cruel, within the meaning of that word as used in the Constitution. It implies there something inhuman and barbarous, something more than the mere extinguishment of life."); *see also* Louisiana *ex rel.* Francis v. Resweber, 329 U.S. 459 (1947).

[901] *See* Gregg v. Georgia, 428 U.S. 153, 173 (1976) (joint opinion); *see also* Bucklew v. Precythe, 139 S. Ct. 1112, 1124 (2019) (declaring that "the Eighth Amendment was understood to forbid . . . forms of punishment that intensified the sentence of death" by superadding "terror, pain, or disgrace") (internal citations and quotations omitted).

[902] *See* Baze v. Rees, 553 U.S. 35, 50 (2008) (plurality opinion) (upholding Kentucky's use of a three-drug cocktail consisting of an anesthetic (sodium thiopental), a muscle relaxant, and an agent that induced cardiac arrest); *see also Bucklew*, 139 S. Ct. at 1130 (in an as-applied challenged, concluding that the petitioner's claims that the State of Missouri's execution protocol would result in severe pain rested on "speculation unsupported, if not affirmatively contradicted, by the evidence" before the lower court); Glossip v. Gross, 576 U.S. ___, No. 14-7955, slip op. at 29 (2015) (upholding Oklahoma's use of a three-drug cocktail that utilized a sedative called midazolam in lieu of sodium thiopental).

constitutes cruel and unusual punishment, often resulting in consistent votes to issue stays against any challenged death sentence.[903] While two current members of the Court have recently concluded that the "death penalty, in and of itself, now likely constitutes a legally prohibited 'cruel and unusual punishment,'"[904] a majority of the Court has held that it is "settled that capital punishment is constitutional," resulting in most challenges focusing on how the death penalty is applied, such as the consideration of aggravating and mitigating circumstances and the appropriate scope of federal review.[905]

General Validity and Guiding Principles.—

[P. 1697, delete n.86 and substitute with:]

The Stewart plurality noted its belief that jury sentencing in capital cases performs an important social function in maintaining the link between contemporary community values and the penal system, but agreed that sentencing may constitutionally be vested in the trial judge. Gregg v. Georgia, 428 U.S. 153, 190 (1976). Subsequently, however, the Court issued several opinions holding that the Sixth Amendment right to a jury trial is violated if a judge makes factual findings (e.g., as to the existence of aggravating circumstances) upon which a death sentence is based. Hurst v. Florida, 577 U.S. ___, No. 14-7505, slip op. at 1–2 (2016); Ring v. Arizona, 536 U.S. 584 (2002). Notably, one Justice in both cases would have found that the Eighth Amendment—not the Sixth Amendment—requires that "a jury, not a judge, make the decision to sentence a defendant to death." *Ring*, 536 U.S. at 614 (Breyer, J., concurring in the judgment). *See also Hurst*, slip op. at 1 (Breyer, J., concurring in the judgment).

[P. 1698, at end of n.92, add:]

See also Hurst v. Florida, 577 U.S. ___, No. 14-7505, slip op. at 1–2 (2016).

---

[903] For example, the position of Justices Brennan and Marshall that the "death penalty is unconstitutional in all circumstances" resulted in two automatic votes against any challenged death sentence during their time on the Court. *See, e.g.*, Lenhard v. Wolff, 444 U.S. 807, 808 (1979) (Brennan & Marshall, JJ., dissenting). Justice Blackmun, who retired in 1994, concluded late in his career that the Court's effort to reconcile the twin goals of fairness to the individual defendant and consistency and rationality of sentencing had failed and that the death penalty, "as currently administered, is unconstitutional." *See* Callins v. Collins, 510 U.S. 1141, 1159 (1994) (Blackmun, J., dissenting). Justice Stevens, who retired from the Court in 2010, concluded in a 2008 case that the death penalty is "patently excessive and cruel and unusual punishment violative of the Eighth Amendment" because of what he perceived as its "negligible returns." *See* Baze v. Rees, 553 U.S. 35, 86 (2008) (Stevens, J., concurring) (internal citations and quotations omitted). Nonetheless, because the "Court has held the death penalty constitutional" and out of "respect" for the Court's precedents, Justice Stevens' remaining years on the Court did not yield automatic votes against the death penalty akin to those of Justices Brennan, Marshall, and Blackmun.

[904] *See* Glossip v. Gross, 576 U.S. ___, No. 14-7955, slip op. at 2 (2015) (Breyer & Ginsburg, JJ., dissenting).

[905] *See id.* at 4 (Alito, J., joined by Roberts, C.J., and Scalia, Kennedy, and Thomas, JJ.); *see also* Bucklew v. Precythe, 139 S. Ct. at 1122 (2019) ("The Constitution allows capital punishment. . . . While the Eighth Amendment doesn't forbid capital punishment, it does speak to how States may carry out that punishment, prohibiting methods that are 'cruel and unusual.'").

Implementation of Procedural Requirements.—

[P. 1699, delete n.98 and sentence starting "If, however, actual sentencing authority is conferred on the trial judge, . . . specified crimes.")]

[P. 1702, after sentence ending ". . . rulings on substantive Eighth Amendment law.", add new footnote:]

As such, the Court has opined that it is not the role of the Eighth Amendment to establish a special "federal code of evidence" governing "the admissibility of evidence at capital sentencing proceedings." *See* Romano v. Oklahoma, 512 U.S. 1, 11–12 (1994). Instead, the test for a constitutional violation attributable to evidence improperly admitted at a capital sentencing proceeding is whether the evidence "so infected the sentencing proceeding with unfairness as to render the jury's imposition of the death penalty a denial of due process." *Id.* at 12. As a consequence, the Court found nothing constitutionally impermissible with a state having joint sentencing proceedings for two defendants whose underlying conviction arose from the same single chain of events. *See* Kansas v. Carr, 577 U.S. ___, No. 14-449, slip op. at 15–16 (2016) (rejecting the argument that joinder of two defendants was fundamentally unfair because evidence that one defendant unduly influenced another defendant's conduct may have "infected" the jury's decision making). Indeed, the Court approvingly noted that joint proceedings before a single jury for defendants that commit the same crimes are "not only permissible but are often preferable" in order to avoid the "wanto[n] and freakis[h]" imposition of the death sentence. *See id.* at 17 (citing Gregg v. Georgia, 428 U.S. 153, 206–07 (1976) (joint opinion of Stewart, Powell, & Stevens, JJ.)).

[P. 1703, n. 118, after citation to *Buchanan v. Angelone*, add:]

In this vein, the Court has held that capital sentencing courts are not obliged to inform the jury affirmatively that mitigating circumstances lack the need for proof beyond a reasonable doubt. *See* Kansas v. Carr, 577 U.S. ___, No. 14-449, slip op. at 11 (2016) (noting that ambiguity in capital sentencing instructions gives rise to constitutional error only if there is a reasonable likelihood that the jury has applied the challenged instruction in a way that prevents consideration of constitutionally relevant evidence).

[P. 1704, delete first string cite following citation to *Simmons* and substitute with:]

See also Lynch v. Arizona, 578 U.S. ___, No. 15-8366, slip op. at 3–4 (2016) (holding that the possibility of clemency and the potential for future "legislative reform" does not justify a departure from the rule of *Simmons*); Kelly v. South Carolina, 534 U.S. 246, 252 (2002) (concluding that a prosecutor need not express an intent to rely on future dangerousness; logical inferences may be drawn); Shafer v. South Carolina, 532 U.S. 36, 40 (2001) (holding that an amended South Carolina law still runs afoul of *Simmons*).

[P. 1705, delete n.126 and substitute with:]

See Clemons v. Mississippi, 494 U.S. 738, 741 (1990) (authorizing appellate reassessment of a death sentence on an improper aggravating circumstance); *see also* McKinney v. Arizona, 140 S. Ct. 702, 706–07 (2020) (extending *Clemons* review so that a reassessment could occur when a trial court improperly ignored a mitigating circumstance).

[P. 1705, delete paragraph starting "Focus on the character . . ." and substitute with:]

Focus on the character and culpability of the defendant led the Court, initially, to hold that the Eighth Amendment "prohibits a capital sentencing jury from considering victim impact evidence" that does not "relate directly to the circumstances of the crime."[906] Four years later, the Court largely overruled[907] these decisions, however, holding that the Eighth Amendment does allow "'victim impact' evidence relating to the personal characteristics of the victim and the emotional impact of the crimes on the victim's family."[908] The Court reasoned that the admissibility of victim impact evidence was necessary to restore balance to capital sentencing. In the Court's view, exclusion of such evidence "unfairly weighted the scales in a capital trial" because there are no corresponding limits on "relevant mitigating evidence a capital defendant may introduce concerning his own circumstances."[909]

[P. 1706, before section "Limitations on Capital Punishment: Proportionality" add new section:]

Limitations on Capital Punishment: Methods of Execution.— Throughout the history of the United States, various methods of execution have been deployed by the states in carrying out the death penalty. In the early history of the nation, hanging was the "nearly universal form of execution."[910] In the late 19th century and continuing into the 20th century, the states began adopting electrocution as a substitute for hanging based on the "well-grounded belief that electrocution is less painful and more humane than hanging."[911] And by the late 1970s, following *Gregg*, states began adopting statutes allowing for execution by lethal injection, perceiving lethal injection to be a more humane alternative to electrocution or other popular pre-*Gregg* means of carrying out the death penalty, such as firing squads or gas chambers.[912] Today the overwhelming majority of the states that allow for the death penalty use lethal injection as the "exclusive or primary method of execution."[913]

Despite a national evolution over the past two hundred years with respect to the methods deployed in carrying out the death penalty, the choice to adopt arguably more humane means of capital punishment has not been the direct result of a decision from the Supreme Court. Citing public understandings from the time of the Framing, the Court has articulated some limits to the methods that can be employed in carrying

---

[906] *See* Booth v. Maryland, 482 U.S. 496, 501–02 (1987); *see also* South Carolina v. Gathers, 490 U.S. 805, 811 (1989) (concluding that *Booth* extended to a prosecutor's statements about a victim's personal qualities).

[907] The Court has refrained from overturning *Booth*'s holding that the admission of a victim's family members' characterizations and opinions about the "underlying crime, the defendant, and the appropriate sentence" violate the Eighth Amendment. *See* Bosse v. Oklahoma, 580 U.S. ___, No. 15-9173, slip op. at 1 (2016). Instead, the Court has overruled *Booth*'s central holding that "evidence and argument relating to the victim and the impact of the victim's death on the victim's family are inadmissible at a capital sentencing hearing." *See* Payne v. Tennessee, 501 U.S. 808, 830 n.2 (1991).

[908] *See Payne*, 501 U.S. at 817.

[909] *Id.* at 822.

[910] *See* State v. Frampton, 627 P. 2d 922, 934 (Wash. 1981).

[911] *See* Malloy v. South Carolina, 237 U.S. 180, 185 (1915).

[912] *See* Baze v. Rees, 553 U.S. 35, 42 (2008) (plurality opinion).

[913] *Id.*

out death sentences, such as those that "superadd" terror, pain, or disgrace to the penalty of death[914] by, for example, torturing someone to death.[915] Nonetheless, the Supreme Court has "never invalidated a State's chosen procedure" for carrying out the death penalty as a violation of the Eighth Amendment.[916] In 1878, the Court, relying on a long history of using firing squads in carrying out executions in military tribunals, held that the "punishment of shooting as a mode of executing the death penalty" did not constitute a cruel and unusual punishment.[917] Twelve years later, the Court upheld the use of the newly created electric chair, deferring to the judgment of the New York state legislature and finding that it was "plainly right" that electrocution was not "inhuman and barbarous."[918] Fifty-seven years later, a plurality of the Court concluded that it would not be "cruel and unusual" to execute a prisoner whose first execution failed due to a mechanical malfunction, as an "unforeseeable accident" did not amount to the "wanton infliction of pain" barred by the Eighth Amendment.[919]

The declaration in *Trop* that the Eighth Amendment "must draw its meaning from the evolving standards of decency that mark the progress of a maturing society"[920] and the continued reliance on that declaration by a majority of the Court in several key Eighth Amendment cases[921] set the stage for potential "method of execution" challenges to the newest mode for the death penalty: lethal injection. Following several decisions clarifying the proper procedural mechanism to raise challenges to methods of execution,[922] the Court, in *Baze v. Rees*, rejected a method of execution challenge to Kentucky's lethal injection protocol, a three-drug protocol consisting of (1) an anesthetic that would render a prisoner unconscious; (2) a muscle relaxant; and (3) an agent that would induce cardiac arrest.[923] A plurality opinion, written by Chief Justice Roberts and joined by Justices Kennedy and Alito, concluded that to constitute cruel

---

[914] *See* Bucklew v. Precythe, 139 S. Ct. at 1123 (2019) (citing 4 W. BLACKSTONE, COMMENTARIES ON THE LAWS OF ENGLAND 370 (1769)).

[915] *See* Wilkerson v. Utah, 99 U.S. 130, 135–36 (1879) (noting in dicta that certain forms of torture, such as drawing and quartering, disemboweling alive, beheading, public dissection, and burning alive, are "forbidden by . . . [the] Constitution"); *see also Bucklew*, 139 S. Ct. at 1122–23 (similar).

[916] *See Baze*, 553 U.S. at 48 (plurality opinion).

[917] *See Wilkerson*, 99 U.S. at 134–35.

[918] *See In re* Kemmler, 136 U.S. 436, 447 (1890).

[919] *See* Louisiana *ex rel.* Francis v. Resweber, 329 U.S. 459, 464 (1947) (plurality opinion). Justice Frankfurter concurred in judgment, providing the fifth vote for the Court's judgment. *Id.* at 466 (Frankfurter, J., concurring). He grounded his decision on whether the Eighth Amendment had been incorporated against the states through the Fourteenth Amendment, ultimately concluding that Louisiana's choice of execution cannot be said to be "repugnant to the conscience of mankind." *Id.* at 471.

[920] *See* Trop v. Dulles, 356 U.S. 86, 101 (1958) (plurality opinion).

[921] *See, e.g.*, Kennedy v. Louisiana, 554 U.S. 407, 419 (2008); Hudson v. McMillian, 503 U.S. 1, 8 (1992); Rhodes v. Chapman, 452 U.S. 337, 346 (1981); Gregg v. Georgia, 428 U.S. 153, 173 (1976) (joint opinion).

[922] *See, e.g.*, Hill v. McDonough, 547 U.S. 573 (2006) (ruling that a challenge to the constitutionality of an execution method could be brought as a civil rights claim under 28 U.S.C. § 1983); Nelson v. Campbell, 541 U.S. 637 (2004) (same).

[923] 553 U.S. 35, 44 (2008).

and unusual punishment, a particular method for carrying out the death penalty must present a "substantial" or "objectively intolerable" risk of harm.[924] In so concluding, the plurality opinion rejected the view that a prisoner could succeed on an Eighth Amendment method of execution challenge by merely demonstrating that a "marginally" safer alternative existed, because such a standard would "embroil" the courts in ongoing scientific inquiries and force courts to second guess the informed choices of state legislatures respecting capital punishment.[925] As a result, the plurality reasoned that to address a "substantial risk of serious harm" effectively, the prisoner must propose an alternative method of execution that is feasible, can be readily implemented, and can significantly reduce a substantial risk of severe pain.[926] Given the "heavy burden" that the plurality placed on those pursuing an Eighth Amendment method of execution claim, the plurality upheld Kentucky's protocol in light of (1) the consensus of state lethal injection procedures; (2) the safeguards Kentucky put in place to protect against any risks of harm; and (3) the lack of any feasible, safer alternative to the three-drug protocol.[927] Four other Justices, for varying reasons, concurred in the judgment of the Court.[928]

Seven years later, in a seeming reprise of the *Baze* litigation, a majority of the Court in *Glossip v. Gross* formally adopted the *Baze* plurality's reasoning with respect to Eighth Amendment claims involving methods of execution, resulting in the rejection of a challenge to Oklahoma's three-drug lethal injection protocol.[929] Following *Baze,* anti-death penalty advocates successfully persuaded pharmaceutical companies to stop providing states with the anesthetic that constituted the first of the three drugs used in the protocol challenged in the 2008 case, resulting in several states, including Oklahoma, substituting a sedative called midazolam in the protocol.[930] In *Glossip*, the Court held that Oklahoma's use of midazolam in its execution protocol did not violate the Eighth Amendment, because the challengers had failed to present a known and available alternative to midazolam and did not adequately demonstrate that the drug was ineffective in rendering a prisoner insensate to pain.[931]

---

[924] *Id.* at 50.

[925] *Id.* at 51.

[926] *Id.* at 52.

[927] *Id.* at 53–61.

[928] Justice Stevens, while announcing his skepticism regarding the constitutionality of the death penalty as a whole, concluded that, based on existing precedent, the petitioners' evidence failed to prove a violation of the Eighth Amendment. *Id.* at 71–87 (Stevens, J., concurring). Justice Thomas, on behalf of himself and Justice Scalia, rejected the idea that the Court had the capacity to adjudicate claims involving methods of execution properly and instead argued that an execution method violates the Eighth Amendment only if it is deliberately designed to inflict pain. *Id.* at 94–107 (Thomas, J., concurring). Justice Breyer concluded that insufficient evidence in either the record or in available medical literature demonstrated that Kentucky's lethal injection method created significant risk of unnecessary suffering. *Id.* at 107–13 (Breyer, J., concurring).

[929] *See* 576 U.S. ___, No. 14-7955, slip op. (2015).

[930] *Id.* at 5–7.

[931] *Id.* at 16–29.

Four years after *Glossip*, the Court further clarified its method-of-execution jurisprudence in *Bucklew v. Precythe*.[932] In that case, a death row inmate challenged the State of Missouri's use of the drug pentobarbital in executions because, regardless of its effect on *other inmates*, the drug would result in *him* experiencing "severe pain" due to his "unusual medical condition."[933] The Court, in an opinion by Justice Gorsuch, began by framing the *Baze-Glossip* test as fundamentally asking whether a state's chosen method of execution is one that "cruelly superadds pain to the death sentence" relative to an alternative method of execution.[934] With this framework in mind, the Court first rejected the petitioner's argument that *Baze* and *Glossip*, which involved facial challenges, did not govern his *as-applied* challenge.[935] Justice Gorsuch reasoned that determining whether the state is cruelly "superadding" pain to a punishment necessarily requires comparing that method with a viable alternative, an inquiry that simply does not hinge on whether a death row inmate's challenge rests on facts unique to his particular medical condition. [936] In so concluding, the Court clarified that an inmate seeking to identify an alternative method of execution is not limited to choosing a method that the state *currently* authorizes and can instead point, for example, to a well-established protocol in another state.[937] Applying the *Baze-Glossip* framework, the Court then rejected the petitioner's proposed alternative of using the drug nitrogen hypoxia because (1) the proposal was insufficiently detailed to permit a finding that the state could carry out the execution easily and quickly;[938] (2) the proposed drug was an

---

[932] *See* Bucklew v. Precythe, 139 S. Ct. 1112, 1118–19 (2019).

[933] *Id.* at 1118–21. Specifically, the petitioner argued that the state's protocol would cause him severe pain because he suffered from a disease that causes vascular tumors, which could rupture upon being injected with the drug that Missouri used in its death penalty protocol. *Id.* at 1120–21.

[934] *Id.* at 1125 (observing that *Baze* and *Glossip* "teach[]" that a prisoner must show a "feasible and readily implemented alternative method of execution that would significantly reduce a substantial risk of severe pain and that the State has refused to adopt without a legitimate penological reason.").

[935] *Id.* at 1126.

[936] *Id.* at 1126–27 (concluding that the argument that the Constitution categorically forbids some particular methods of execution was foreclosed by *Baze* and *Glossip*, as well as the "original and historical understanding" of the Eighth Amendment, which rejected ancient and barbaric methods of execution only because, in comparison to alternatives available at the Founding, they went far beyond what was necessary to carry out a death sentence). In so concluding, the Court rejected the argument that the comparator in an as-applied challenge should be a typical execution. *Id.* at 1127. For the Court, this argument rested on the assumption that executions must be carried out painlessly, a standard the Court "has rejected time and time again." *Id.* Instead, to determine whether the state is cruelly "superadding" pain, *Bucklew* concluded that a death row inmate must show that the state had some other "feasible and readily available method" to carry out the execution that would have "significantly reduced a substantial risk of pain." *Id.* Justice Gorsuch also saw other problems with the petitioner's distinction between an as-applied challenge and a facial challenge. Viewing this distinction as simply a question of the breadth of the remedy afforded the plaintiff, the Court concluded that the meaning of the Constitution should not hinge on the particular remedy being sought. *Id.* at 1127–28. Moreover, the Court raised the concern that creating a distinction based on the nature of the plaintiff's preferred remedy would result in "pleading games" over the labels a plaintiff assigned to his complaint. *Id.* at 1128.

[937] *Id.* at 1128.

[938] *Id.* at 1129–30.

"untried and untested" method of execution;[939] and (3) the underlying record showed that any risks created by pentobarbital and mitigated by nitrogen hypoxia were speculative in nature.[940]

As a result of *Baze, Glossip,* and *Bucklew,* it appears that only those modes of the death penalty that demonstrably result in substantial risks of harm for the prisoner relative to viable alternatives can be challenged as unconstitutional.[941] This standard appears to result in the political process (as opposed to the judicial process) being the primary means of making wholesale changes to a particular method of execution.[942]

Limitations on Capital Punishment: Diminished Capacity.—

[PP. 1709–10, delete paragraph starting "In *Panetti v. Quarterman,* . . ." and substitute with:]

The Court in *Panetti v. Quarterman* clarified when a prisoner's current mental state can bar his execution under the rule of *Ford.*[943] Relying on the understanding that the execution of a prisoner who cannot comprehend the reasons for his punishment offends both moral values and serves "no retributive purpose," the Court concluded that the operative test was whether a prisoner can "reach a rational understanding for the reason for his execution."[944] Under *Panetti,* if a prisoner's mental state is so distorted by mental illness that he cannot grasp the execution's "meaning and purpose" or the "link between [his] crime and its punishment," he cannot be executed.[945]

Twelve years after *Panetti,* the Court further clarified two aspects of the *Ford-Panetti* inquiry in *Madison v. Alabama.*[946] First, on behalf of the Court, Justice Kagan concluded that a prisoner challenging his execution on the ground of a mental disorder cannot prevail "merely because he cannot remember committing his crime."[947] Recognizing that a

---

[939] *Id.*

[940] *Id.* at 1130–33 (noting (1) evidence in the record that the state was making accommodations to further reduce any risks to the petitioner and (2) insufficient evidence indicating that pentobarbital would create risks of severe pain and that nitrogen hypoxia would not carry the same risks).

[941] Bucklew v. Precythe, 139 S. Ct. 1112, 1125 (2019).

[942] *Id.* at 1133–34 ("Under our Constitution, the question of capital punishment belongs to the people and their representatives, not the courts, to resolve. The proper role of courts is to ensure that method-of-execution challenges to lawfully issued sentences are resolved fairly and expeditiously."); *see also* Barr v. Lee, 140 S. Ct. 2590, 2590–94 (2020) (per curiam) (relying on *Bucklew*'s views on the proper role of the judiciary with respect to method-of-execution challenges to reject a challenge raised "hours before" execution concerning the safety of using pentobarbital to carry out the death penalty).

[943] 551 U.S. 930 (2007).

[944] *Id.* at 958.

[945] *Id.* at 958–60. In a separate part of the opinion, the Court held that the Due Process Clause of the Fourteenth Amendment required the state to provide the petitioner with an "adequate opportunity to submit expert evidence in response to the report filed by the court-appointed experts" on the petitioner's sanity. *Id.* at 951.

[946] *See* 586 U.S. ___, No. 17-7505, slip op. (2019).

[947] *Id.* at 8–9.

prisoner who can no longer remember a crime "may yet recognize the retributive message society intends to convey with a death sentence," the Court declined to impose a categorical rule prohibiting the execution of such a prisoner.[948] Instead, Justice Kagan viewed a prisoner's memory loss as a factor that a court may consider in determining whether he has a "rational understanding" of the reason for his execution.[949] Second, the *Madison* Court concluded that while *Ford* and *Panetti* pertained to prisoners suffering from psychotic delusions, the logic of those opinions extended to a prisoner who suffered from dementia.[950] For the Court, the *Ford-Panetti* inquiry is not so much concerned with the precise *cause* for whether a prisoner can rationally understand why the state is seeking an execution and is instead focused on whether the prisoner's mental condition has the *effect* of preventing such an understanding.[951]

[P. 1711, after n.160, add new paragraphs:]

In *Hall v. Florida,*[952] however, the Court limited the states' ability to define intellectual disability by invalidating Florida's "bright line" cutoff based on Intelligence Quotient (IQ) test scores. A Florida statute stated that anyone with an IQ above 70 was prohibited from offering additional evidence of mental disability and was thus subject to capital punishment.[953] The Court invalidated this rigid standard, observing that "[i]ntellectual disability is a condition, not a number."[954] The majority found that, although IQ scores are helpful in determining mental capabilities, they are imprecise in nature and may only be used as a factor of analysis in death penalty cases.[955] This reasoning was buttressed by a consensus of mental health professionals who concluded that an IQ test score should be read not as a single fixed number, but as a range.[956]

Building on *Hall,* in *Moore v. Texas* the Supreme Court rejected the standards used by Texas state courts to evaluate whether a death row inmate was intellectually disabled, concluding that the standards created an "unacceptable risk that persons with intellectual disability will be executed."[957] First, Justice Ginsburg, on behalf of the Court, held that a

---

[948] *Id.* at 11.

[949] *Id.* In so holding, the Court noted that evidence that a prisoner has difficulty preserving *any* memories may contribute to a finding that the prisoner may not rationally understand the reasons for his death sentence. *Id.*

[950] *Id.* at 12.

[951] *Id.* at 12–13 ("[I]f and when that failure of understanding is present, the rationales kick in—irrespective of whether one disease or another . . . is to blame.").

[952] 572 U.S. ___, No. 12-10882, slip op. (2014).

[953] FLA. STAT. § 921.137.

[954] *Hall,* slip op. at 21.

[955] *Id.* Of those states that allow for the death penalty, a number of them do not have strict cut-offs for IQ scores. *See, e. g.,* CAL. PENAL CODE § 1376 (West 2016); LA. CODE CRIM. PROC. ANN. art. 905.5.1 (2016); NEV. REV. STAT. § 174.098.7; UTAH CODE ANN. § 77–15a–102 (Lexis-Nexis 2016). Similarly, the U.S. Code does not set a strict IQ cutoff. *See* 18 U.S.C. § 3596(c) (2012).

[956] This range, referred to as a "standard error or measurement" or "SEM," is used by many states in evaluating the existence of intellectual disability. *Hall,* slip op. at 12.

[957] *See* 581 U.S. ___, No. 15-797, slip op. at 2 (2017) [hereinafter *Moore I*].

Texas court's conclusion that a prisoner with an IQ score of 74 could be executed was "irreconcilable with *Hall*" because the state court had failed to consider standard errors that are inherent in assessing intellectual disability.[958] Second, the *Moore* Court determined that Texas deviated from prevailing clinical standards respecting the assessment of a death row inmate's intellectual capabilities by (1) emphasizing the petitioner's perceived adaptive strengths and his behavior in prison;[959] (2) dismissing several traumatic experiences from the petitioner's past;[960] and (3) requiring the petitioner to show that his adaptive deficits were not due to a personality disorder or a mental health issue.[961] Third, the Court criticized the prevailing standard used in Texas courts for assessing intellectual disability in death penalty cases, which had favored the "'consensus of *Texas citizens'* on who 'should be exempted from the death penalty,'" with regard to those with "mild" intellectual disabilities in the state's capital system, concluding that those with even "mild" levels of intellectual disability could not be executed under *Atkins*.[962] Finally, *Moore* rejected the Texas courts' skepticism of professional standards for assessing intellectual disability, standards that the state courts had viewed as being "exceedingly subjective."[963] The Supreme Court instead held that "lay stereotypes" (and not established professional standards) on an individual's intellectual capabilities should "spark skepticism."[964] As a result, following *Hall* and *Moore,* while the states retain "some flexibility" in enforcing *Atkins,* the medical community's prevailing standards appear to "supply" a key constraint on the states in capital cases.[965]

---

[958] *Id.* at 10.

[959] *Id.* at 12 ("[T]he medical community focuses the adaptive-functioning inquiry on adaptive *deficits*."); *see also id.* at 13 ("Clinicians, however, caution against reliance on adaptive strengths developed in a controlled setting, as prison surely is.") (internal citations and quotations omitted).

[960] *Id.* at 13–14 ("Clinicians rely on such factors as cause to explore the prospect of intellectual disability further, not to counter the case for a disability determination.").

[961] *Id.* at 14 ("The existence of a personality disorder or mental-health issue, in short, is not evidence that a person does not also have intellectual disability.") (internal citations and quotations omitted).

[962] *Id.* at 15. In so concluding, the Court noted that "[m]ild levels of intellectual disability . . . nevertheless remain intellectual disabilities," and "States may not execute anyone in the *entire* category of intellectually disabled offenders." *Id.* (internal citations and quotations omitted).

[963] *See Ex parte* Briseno, 135 S.W.3d 1, 8 (Tex. Crim. App. 2004).

[964] *See Moore I*, slip op. at 15.

[965] *Id.* at 17. Two years after *Moore I*, the case returned to the High Court, where, in a per curiam opinion, the Court again reversed the Court of Criminal Appeals of Texas. *See* Moore v. Texas, 586 U.S. ___, No. 18-443, slip op. at 1 (2019) (per curiam) (hereinafter *Moore II*). That court had concluded that the prisoner did not have an intellectual disability and was, therefore, eligible for the death penalty. *Id.* Finding that the lower court's opinion "repeat[ed] the analysis" the Supreme Court "previously found wanting" in its 2017 opinion, *Moore II* criticized the Texas court's (1) reliance on the petitioner's adaptive strengths in lieu of his adaptive deficits; (2) emphasis on the petitioner's adaptive improvements made in prison; (3) tendency to consider the petitioner's social behavior to be caused by "emotional problems," instead of his general mental abilities; and (4) continued reliance on the *Briseno* case the Court had previously criticized in *Moore I. Id.* at 6–9. Ultimately, the Court concluded that the record from the trial court demonstrated that the petitioner was "a person with intellectual disability," reversing the lower court's judgment and remanding the case.

Proportionality

Limitations on Capital Punishment: Proportionality.—

[P. 1725, after sentence ending "greater prospects for reform.", add new footnote:]

> *Id.* at 8.

[P. 1725, after sentence ending ". . . in homicide cases categorically.", add new footnote:]

> *Id.* at 20.

[P. 1726, after sentence ending ". . . immaturity, vulnerability, suggestibility, and the like.", add new footnote:]

> *Id.* at 15.

[P. 1726, after sentence ending ". . . meting out society's severest penalties.", add new footnote:]

> *Id.* at 8. In *Montgomery v. Louisiana*, the Court cautioned, however, that *Miller* should not be read as merely imposing additional procedural hurdles before a juvenile offender could be sentenced to life without parole. *See* 577 U.S. ___, No. 14-280, slip op. at 16 (2016). Instead, according to the *Montgomery* Court, *Miller* barred a sentence of life without parole for "all but the rarest of juvenile offenders, those whose crimes reflect permanent incorrigibility." *Id.* at 17.

[P. 1726, delete sentences starting "In leading four Justices in dissent . . ." to ". . . barring a type of sentence altogether."]

> *Id.* at 10.

TENTH AMENDMENT

RESERVED POWERS

Effect of Provision on Federal Powers

Federal Regulations Affecting State Activities and Instrumentalities.—

[P. 1747, after sentence ending ". . . as well as states.", add new paragraph:]

The Court's most recent consideration of the anti-commandeering principle occurred in 2018 in *Murphy v. NCAA*.[966] In *Murphy*, Justice Alito, writing on behalf of the Court, invalidated on anti-commandeering grounds a provision in the Professional and Amateur Sports Protection Act (PASPA) that prohibited states from authorizing sports gambling schemes.[967] Noting the rule from *New York* and *Printz* that Congress lacks "the power to issue orders directly to the States,"[968] the Court concluded that PASPA's prohibition of state authorization of sports gambling violated the anti-commandeering rule by putting state legislatures under the "direct control of Congress."[969] In so concluding, Justice Alito rejected the argument that the anti-commandeering doctrine only applies to "affirmative" congressional commands, as opposed to when Congress prohibits certain state action.[970] Finding the distinction between affirmative requirements and prohibitions "empty," the Court held that both types of commands equally intrude on state sovereign interests.[971]

In holding that Congress cannot command a state legislature to refrain from enacting a law, the *Murphy* Court reconciled its holding with two related doctrines.[972] First, the Court noted that while cases like *Garcia, Baker* establish that the anti-commandeering doctrine "does not apply when Congress evenhandedly regulates activity in which both States and private actors engage,"[973] PASPA's anti-authorization provision was, in contrast, solely directed at the activities of state legislatures.[974] Second, the Court rejected the argument that PASPA

---

[966] 584 U.S. ___, No. 16-476, slip op. at 14–24 (2018).

[967] *See* Pub. L. No. 102-559, § 2(a), 106 Stat. 4227, 4228 (1992) (codified at 28 U.S.C. § 3702).

[968] *See Murphy*, slip op. at 14. *Murphy* offered three justifications for the anti-commandeering rule: (1) to protect liberty by ensuring a "healthy balance of power" between the states and the federal government; (2) to promote political accountability by avoiding the blurring of which government is to credit or blame for a particular policy; (3) to prevent Congress from shifting the costs of regulation to the states. *Id.* at 17–18.

[969] *Id.* at 18.

[970] *Id.* at 18–19.

[971] *Id.* at 19.

[972] *Id.* at 19–24.

[973] *Id.* at 20.

[974] *Id.* at 21. The Court also distinguished two other cases in which the Court rejected anti-commandeering challenges to federal statutes. First, the *Murphy* Court found PASPA to be distinct from the "cooperative federalism" of the law at issue in *Hodel v. Virginia*

constituted a "valid preemption provision" under the Supremacy Clause.[975] While acknowledging that the "language used by Congress and this Court" with respect to preemption is sometimes imprecise,[976] Justice Alito viewed "every form of preemption" to be based on a federal law that regulates the conduct of private actors—either by directly regulating private entities or by conferring a federal right to be free from state regulation.[977] In contrast, PASPA's anti-authorization provision did not "confer any federal rights on private actors interested in conducting sports gambling operations" or "impose any federal restrictions on private actors."[978] As a result, the *Murphy* Court viewed the challenged provision to be a direct command to the states in violation of the anti-commandeering rule.[979]

Surface Mining & Reclamation Assn., Inc., 452 U.S. 264 (1981), in which, unlike PASPA, Congress provided the states with the *choice* of either implementing a federal program or allowing the federal program to preempt contrary state laws. *See Murphy*, slip op. at 20. Likewise, the *Murphy* Court found *FERC v. Mississippi*, 456 U.S. 742 (1982) inapplicable, as the law at issue in *FERC* did not, like PASPA, issue a command to a state legislature. *See Murphy*, slip op. at 20. Instead, the *Murphy* Court viewed the law in *FERC* as imposing the "modest requirement" that states "consider, but not necessarily" adopt federal regulations pertaining to the consumption of oil and natural gas. *Id.*

[975] *See Murphy*, slip op. at 21. *Murphy* identified two requirements for a preemption provision to be deemed valid: (1) the provision must represent an exercise of power conferred on Congress by the Constitution; (2) the provision must regulate private actors and not the states. *Id.* In so concluding, the Court noted that the Supremacy Clause was not an independent grant of legislative power and that "pointing to the Supremacy Clause" as the basis for Congress's authority "will not do." *Id.* (citing Armstrong v. Exceptional Child Ctr., Inc., 575 U.S. ___, No. 14-15, slip op. at 3 (2015)).

[976] *Id.* at 22–23. In particular, the Court noted that while express preemption clauses in federal statutes often appear to operate directly on the states, it would be a "mistake to be confused by the way in which a preemption provision is phrased" because Congress is not required to "employ a particular linguistic formulation when preempting state law." *Id.* at 22 (quoting Coventry Health Care of Missouri, Inc. v. Nevils, 581 U.S. ___, No. 16-149, slip op. at 10–11 (2017)).

[977] *Id.* at 23–24.

[978] *Id.* at 24 (noting that if a private actor started a sports gambling operation, either with or without state authorization, PASPA's anti-authorization provision would not be violated).

[979] *Id.* The Court ultimately invalidated PASPA in its entirety, holding that other provisions of the law that *did* regulate private conduct were not severable from the anti-authorization provision and therefore could exist independently from the unconstitutional provision. *See id.* at 24–30.

ELEVENTH AMENDMENT

STATE SOVEREIGN IMMUNITY

The Nature of the States' Immunity

[P. 1759, delete sentence starting "A great deal of the difficulty . . . ."]

[P. 1759, delete "One view of the Amendment" and substitute with:]

One view of the Eleventh Amendment

[P. 1759, delete sentence "That view finds present day expression." and n.43.]

[P. 1761, delete paragraph starting "Outside the area of federal court jurisdiction . . ."]

[P. 1762, after n.63, add new paragraphs:]

Questions regarding the constitutional dimensions of sovereign immunity have also arisen in the context of *interstate* sovereign immunity when a private party institutes an action against a state in another state's court. In the now-overturned 1979 decision of *Nevada v. Hall*, the Court held that while states are free as a matter of comity "to accord each other immunity or to respect any established limits on liability," the Constitution does not compel a state to grant another state immunity in its courts.[980] In *Hall*, California residents who were severely injured in a car crash with a Nevada state university employee on official business sued the university and the State of Nevada in California court.[981] After considering the scope of sovereign immunity as it existed prior to and "in the early days of independence," the doctrine's effect on "the framing of the Constitution," and specific "aspects of the Constitution that qualify the sovereignty of the several States," such as the Full Faith and Credit Clause,[982] the Court concluded that "[n]othing in the Federal Constitution authorizes or obligates this Court to frustrate" California's policy of "full compensation in its courts for injuries on its highways resulting from the negligence" of state or non-state actors "out of enforced respect for the sovereignty of Nevada."[983]

---

[980] 440 U.S. 410, 426 (1979), *overruled by* Franchise Tax Bd. v. Hyatt, 587 U.S. ___, No. 17-1299, slip op. at 4 (2019) [hereinafter *Franchise Tax Bd. III*].

[981] *Id.* at 411–12.

[982] *Id.* at 414–18.

[983] *Id.* at 426. In the Court's view, for a federal court to infer "from the structure of our Constitution and nothing else, that California is not free in this case to enforce its policy of full compensation, that holding would constitute the real intrusion on the sovereignty of the States—and the power of the people—in our Union." *Id.* at 426–27.

Forty years later, the Court overruled *Hall* in *Franchise Tax Board of California v. Hyatt (Franchise Tax Board III)*, holding that "States retain their sovereign immunity from private suits brought in the courts of other States."[984] The case involved a tort action by a private party against a California state agency in Nevada's courts.[985] The "sole question" before the Court was whether to overrule *Nevada v. Hall*, a question over which the Court divided in 2016.[986] As the majority in *Franchise Tax Board III* read the historical record, although interstate sovereign immunity may have existed as a voluntary practice of comity at the time of the founding, the Constitution "fundamentally adjust[ed] the States' relationship with each other and curtail[ed] their ability, as sovereigns, to decline to recognize each other's immunity."[987] The Court reiterated the view embraced in several of its decisions since *Hall* that in proposing the Eleventh Amendment in response to *Chisholm v. Georgia*, "Congress acted not to change but to restore the original constitutional design."[988] Accordingly, the Court explained, the "sovereign immunity of the States . . . neither derives from, nor is limited by, the terms of the Eleventh Amendment."[989] Moreover, the Court reasoned, "[n]umerous provisions" in the Constitution support the view that interstate sovereign immunity is "embe[dded] . . . within the constitutional design."[990] Among other provisions, the Court cited Article I insofar as it "divests the States of the traditional diplomatic and military tools that foreign sovereigns possess" and Article IV's Full Faith and Credit Clause, which requires that "state-court judgments be accorded full effect in other States and preclude[s] States from 'adopt[ing] any policy of hostility to the public Acts' of other States."[991] Accordingly, because sovereign immunity was inherent in the constitutional design, the Court concluded that the State of California could not be sued in Nevada absent the former state's consent.[992]

---

[984] *Franchise Tax Bd. III*, slip op. at 4.

[985] *Id.* at 1–3.

[986] *Id.* at 3; *see also* Franchise Tax Bd. of Cal. v. Hyatt, 136 S. Ct. 1277, 1279 (2016) ("The Court is equally divided on this question, and we consequently affirm the Nevada courts' exercise of jurisdiction over California."); *Franchise Tax Bd. III*, slip op. at 2–3 (explaining that the two prior *Franchise Tax Board* decisions centered on interpretations of the Full Faith and Credit Clause of Article IV of the Constitution).

[987] *Franchise Tax Bd. III*, slip op. at 5, 13.

[988] *Id.* at 12 (quoting Alden v. Maine, 527 U.S. 706, 722 (1999)).

[989] *Id.* (quoting *Alden*, 527 U.S. at 713).

[990] *Id.* at 13.

[991] *Id.* at 13–14 (citation omitted).

[992] *Id.* at 16, 17–18. The Court reasoned that *stare decisis* did not compel it to follow *Hall* even though "some plaintiffs, such as Hyatt," relied on that decision in litigation against states. *Id.* at 17. In the Court's view, *Hall* "failed to account for the historical understanding of state sovereign immunity" and stood "as an outlier in [the Court's] sovereign immunity jurisprudence." *Id.*

Suits Against States

[P. 1762, n.65, after citation to "*Central Virginia Community College v. Katz*", add:]

The Court has cautioned, however, that *Katz*'s analysis is limited to the context of the Bankruptcy Clause. Specifically, the Court has described the Clause as "sui generis" or "unique" among Article I's grants of authority, and, unlike other such grants, the Bankruptcy Clause itself abrogated state sovereign immunity in bankruptcy proceedings. *See* Allen v. Cooper, 140 S. Ct. 994, 1002–03 (2020) (observing that *Katz* "points to a good-for-one-clause-only holding" and does not cast further doubt on *Seminole Tribe*'s "general rule that Article I cannot justify haling a State into federal court").

Congressional Withdrawal of Immunity.—

[P. 1768, at end of n.99, delete "." and add:]

; Allen v. Cooper, 140 S. Ct. 994 (2020) (the Copyright Remedy Clarification Act of 1990 did not validly abrogate state sovereign immunity).

Suits Against State Officials

[P. 1770, delete n.113 and substitute with:]

See, e.g. Larson v. Domestic & Foreign Corp., 337 U.S. 682 (1949). It should be noted, however, that as a threshold issue in lawsuits against state employees or entities, courts must look to whether the sovereign is the real party in interest to determine whether state sovereign immunity bars the suit. *See* Hafer v. Melo, 502 U.S. 21, 25 (1991). Court must determine "whether the remedy sought is truly against the sovereign," and if an "action is in essence against a State even if the State is not a named party, then the State is the real party in interest and is entitled to invoke the Eleventh Amendment's protections." *See* Lewis v. Clarke, 581 U.S. ___, No. 15-1500, slip op. 5–6 (2017). As a result, arms of the state, such as a state university, enjoy sovereign immunity. *Id.* at 6. Likewise, lawsuits brought against employees in their official capacity "may also be barred by sovereign immunity." *Id.*

TWELFTH AMENDMENT

ELECTION OF PRESIDENT

[P. 1782, after n.3, add:]

The Supreme Court has said that the Twelfth Amendment "both acknowledg[ed] and facilitat[ed] the Electoral College's emergence as a mechanism not for deliberation but for party-line voting."[993] Accordingly, the Court has concluded that the Twelfth Amendment generally does not prevent states from enacting laws intended to ensure that electors vote for the parties' nominees.[994]

---

[993] Chiafalo v. Washington, 140 S. Ct. 2316, 2327 (2020).

[994] *See id.* at 2327–28; *see also* discussion *supra* Article II: Section 1: Clauses 2–4. Election: Electoral College: Electors as Free Agents.

FOURTEENTH AMENDMENT

Section 1. Rights Guaranteed

DUE PROCESS OF LAW

Jurisdiction to Tax

Generally.—

[P. 1871, delete sentences starting "Taxation of an interstate business . . ." and ending ". . . may prove useful." and substitute with:]

> In 2018, the Court, however, reversed course in *South Dakota v. Wayfair,* overturning *Quill*'s Commerce Clause holding and upholding a South Dakota law that required certain large retailers that lacked a physical presence in the state to collect and remit sales taxes from retail sales to South Dakota residents.[995] In so holding, the *Wayfair* Court concluded that while the Due Process and Commerce Clause standards "may not be identical or coterminous," they are "closely related," and there are "significant parallels" between the two standards.[996]

Intangible Personalty.—

[P. 1876, after sentence ending ". . . under its control.", add:].

> Likewise, the more recent case of *North Carolina Department of Revenue v. Kimberly Rice Kaestner 1992 Family Trust,* which saw the Court invalidating a state tax imposed on trust income of an in-state beneficiary, appears to be limited to its facts, where the beneficiaries (1) had not received any trust income, (2) had no right to demand that income, and (3) were uncertain to ever receive that income.[997]

Fundamental Rights (Noneconomic Substantive Due Process)

[P. 1892, delete n.536 and substitute with:]

> *See supra* Bill of Rights, The Fourteenth Amendment and Incorporation.

[P. 1892, delete heading "Development of the Right of Privacy" and substitute with:]

> *Determining Noneconomic Substantive Due Process Rights.—*

---

[995] 585 U.S. ___, No. 17-494, slip op.at 22 (2018).

[996] *Id.* at 11.

[997] *See* N.C. Dept. of Revenue v. Kimberly Rice Kaestner 1992 Family Trust, 588 U.S. ___, No. 18-457, slip op. at 7 (2019).

Development of the Right of Privacy.—

[P. 1897, after sentence ending ". . . conduct violates the Due Process Clause.", add new paragraph:]

More broadly, in *Washington v. Glucksberg,* the Court, in an effort to guide and "restrain" a court's determination of the scope of substantive due process rights, held that the concept of "liberty" protected under the Due Process Clause should first be understood to protect only those rights that are "deeply rooted in this Nation's history and tradition."[998] Moreover, the Court in *Glucksberg* required a "careful description" of fundamental rights that would be grounded in specific historical practices and traditions that serve as "crucial guideposts for responsible decision making."[999] However, the Court in *Obergefell v. Hodges* largely departed from *Glucksberg's* formulation for assessing fundamental rights in holding that the Due Process Clause required states to license and recognize marriages between two people of the same sex.[1000] Instead, the *Obergefell* Court recognized that fundamental rights do not "come from ancient sources alone" and instead must be viewed in light of evolving social norms and in a "comprehensive" manner.[1001] For the *Obergefell* Court, the two-part test relied on in *Glucksberg*—relying on history as a central guide for constitutional liberty protections and requiring a "careful description" of the right in question—was "inconsistent" with the approach taken in cases discussing certain fundamental rights, including the rights to marriage and intimacy, and would result in rights becoming stale, as "received practices could serve as their own continued justification and new groups could not invoke rights once denied."[1002]

Abortion.—

[P. 1909, after n.621 and before heading "Privacy After Roe: Informational Privacy, Privacy of the Home or Personal Autonomy?", add new paragraphs:]

The Court revisited the question of whether particular restrictions place a "substantial obstacle" in the path of women seeking a pre-viability abortion and constitute an "undue burden" on abortion access in its 2016 decision in *Whole Woman's Health v. Hellerstedt.*[1003] At issue in *Whole Woman's Health* was a Texas law that required (1) physicians performing or inducing abortions to have active admitting privileges at a hospital located not more than thirty miles from the facility; and (2) the facility itself to meet the minimum standards for ambulatory surgical centers under Texas law.[1004] Texas asserted that these requirements served

---

[998] *See* 521 U.S. 702, 720–21 (1997).

[999] *See id.* at 721 (internal citations and quotations omitted).

[1000] *See* 576 U.S. ___, No. 14-556, slip op. at 18 (2015).

[1001] *See id.* at 18–19.

[1002] *See id.* at 18.

[1003] 579 U.S. ___, No. 15-274, slip op. (2016).

[1004] *Id.* at 1–2.

various purposes related to women's health and the safety of abortion procedures, including ensuring that women have easy access to a hospital should complications arise during an abortion procedure and that abortion facilities meet heightened health and safety standards.[1005]

In reviewing Texas's law, the *Whole Woman's Health* Court began by clarifying the underlying "undue burden" standard established in *Casey*. First, the Court noted that the relevant standard from *Casey* requires that courts engage in a balancing test to determine whether a law amounts to an unconstitutional restriction on abortion access by considering the "burdens a law imposes on abortion access together with the benefits those laws confer."[1006] As a consequence, the *Whole Woman's Health* articulation of the undue burden standard necessarily requires that courts "consider the existence or nonexistence of medical benefits" when considering whether a regulation constitutes an undue burden.[1007] In such a consideration, a reviewing court, when evaluating an abortion regulation purporting to protect woman's health, may need to closely scrutinize (1) the relative value of the protections afforded under the new law when compared to those prior to enactment[1008] and (2) health regulations with respect to comparable medical procedures.[1009] Second, the *Whole Woman's Health* decision rejected the argument that judicial scrutiny of abortion regulations was akin to rational basis review,[1010] concluding that courts should not defer to legislatures when resolving questions of medical uncertainty that arise with respect to abortion regulations.[1011] Instead, the Court found that reviewing courts are permitted to place "considerable weight upon evidence and argument presented in judicial proceedings" when evaluating legislation under the undue burden standard, notwithstanding contrary conclusions by the legislature.[1012]

Applying these standards, the *Whole Woman's Health* Court viewed the alleged benefits of the Texas requirements as inadequate to justify the challenged provisions under the precedent of *Casey*, given both

---

[1005] *Id.* at 22.

[1006] *Id.* at 19.

[1007] *Id.*

[1008] *Id.* at 22, 28–30 (reviewing the state of the law prior to the enactment of the abortion regulation to determine whether there was a "significant health-related problem that the new law helped to cure.").

[1009] *Id.* at 30 (comparing the health risks associated with abortion relative to other medical procedures).

[1010] *But cf.* Box v. Planned Parenthood of Ind. & Ky., Inc., 587 U.S. ___, No. 18-483, slip op. at 1–3 (2019) (per curiam) (applying rational basis review and ultimately upholding a state law "alter[ing] the manner in which abortion providers may dispose of fetal remains" after noting that the law's challengers "never argued that [the] law creates an undue burden on a woman's right to obtain an abortion" and "instead litigated [the] case on the assumption that the law does not implicate a fundamental right and is therefore subject only to ordinary rational basis review").

[1011] *Whole Woman's Health*, slip op. at 20.

[1012] *See id.* (noting that in *Gonzales v. Carhart*, 550 U.S. 124, 165 (2007), the Court maintained that courts have an "independent constitutional duty" to review factual findings when reviewing legislation as inconsistent with abortion rights).

the burdens they imposed upon women's access to abortion and the benefits provided.[1013] Specifically as to the admitting privileges requirement, the Court determined that nothing in the underlying record showed that this requirement "advanced Texas's legitimate interest in protecting women's health" in any significant way as compared to Texas's previous requirement that abortion clinics have a "working arrangement" with a doctor with admitting privileges.[1014] In particular, the Court rejected the argument that the admitting privileges requirements were justified to provide an "extra layer" of protection against abusive and unsafe abortion facilities, as the Court concluded that "[d]etermined wrongdoers, already ignoring existing statutes and safety measures, are unlikely to be convinced to adopt safe practices by a new overlay of regulations."[1015] On the contrary, in the Court's view, the evidentiary record suggested that the admitting-privileges requirement placed a substantial obstacle in the path of women's access to abortion because (1) of the temporal proximity between the imposition of the requirement and the closing of a number of clinics once the requirement was enforced; [1016] and (2) the necessary consequence of the requirement of foreclosing abortion providers from obtaining such privileges for reasons having "nothing to do with ability to perform medical procedures."[1017] In the view of the Court, the resulting facility closures that the Court attributed to the first challenged requirement meant fewer doctors, longer wait times, and increased crowding for women at the remaining facilities, and the closures also increased driving distances to an abortion clinic for some women, amounting to an undue burden.[1018]

Similarly as to the surgical-center requirement, the *Whole Woman's Health* Court viewed the record as evidencing that the requirement "provides no benefits" in the context of abortions produced through medication and was "inappropriate" as to surgical abortions.[1019] In so doing, the Court also noted disparities between the treatment of abortion facilities and facilities providing other medical procedures, such as colonoscopies, which the evidence suggested had greater risks than abortions.[1020] The Court viewed the underlying record as demonstrating that the surgical-center requirement would also have further reduced the

---

[1013] *Id.* at 19 (quoting and citing Planned Parenthood v. Casey, 505 U.S. 833, 877–78 (1992) (plurality opinion)).

[1014] *Id.* at 23. The Court further noted that Texas had admitted it did not know of a "single instance" where the requirement would have helped "even one woman" obtain "better treatment." *Id.*

[1015] *Id.* at 27.

[1016] *Id.* at 24.

[1017] Specifically, the Court noted that hospitals typically condition admitting privileges based on the number admissions a doctor has to a hospital—policies that, because of the safety of abortion procedures, meant that providers likely would be unable to obtain and maintain such privileges. *Id.* at 25.

[1018] *Id.* at 26. The Court noted that increased driving distances are not necessarily an undue burden, but in this case viewed them as "one additional burden" which, when taken together with the other burdens—and the "virtual absence of any health benefit"—lead to the conclusion that the admitting-privileges requirement constitutes an undue burden. *Id.*

[1019] *Id.* at 30.

[1020] *Id.* at 30–31.

number of abortion facilities in Texas to seven or eight and, in so doing, would have burdened women's access to abortion in the same way as the admitting-privileges requirement (e.g., creating crowding, increasing driving distances).[1021] Ultimately, the Court struck down the two provisions in the Texas law, concluding that the regulations in question imposed an undue burden on a "large fraction" of women for whom the provisions are an "actual" restriction.[1022]

Four years after *Whole Woman's Health*, the Court examined a Louisiana statute that was "almost word-for-word identical to Texas'[s] admitting privileges law."[1023] Following the approach enunciated in *Whole Woman's Health*, four Justices balanced the law's "'asserted benefits'" against the "'burdens' it impose[d] on abortion access" to determine whether the law ran afoul of the undue burden standard.[1024] After examining the district court's findings and the legislative record in detail, the plurality concluded that, like Texas's law, Louisiana's admitting-privileges requirement imposed an undue, and thus unconstitutional, burden on women seeking an abortion.[1025] Chief Justice Roberts provided the fifth vote in support of the Court's judgment that the law was unconstitutional.[1026] Although the Chief Justice viewed *Whole Woman's Health* as "wrongly decided" and disagreed with the plurality's interpretation of *Casey's* undue burden standard as a balancing test, he concluded that the Court was bound by stare decisis to follow that decision and "treat like cases alike."[1027]

Privacy After Roe: Informational Privacy, Privacy of the Home or Personal Autonomy?.—

[P. 1912, after n.636, delete paragraph and substitute with:]

More than two decades after *Whalen,* the Court remains ambivalent about whether such a privacy right exists. In its 2011 decision in *NASA v. Nelson,* the Supreme Court unanimously ruled against 28 NASA workers who argued that the extensive background checks required

---

[1021] *Id.* at 32, 35–36.

[1022] *Id.* at 39. In so concluding, the *Whole Woman's Health* Court appears to have clarified that the burden for a plaintiff to establish that an abortion restriction is unconstitutional on its face (as opposed to unconstitutional as applied in a particular circumstance) is to show that the law would be unconstitutional with respect to a "large fraction" of women for whom the provisions are relevant. *Id.* (rejecting Texas's argument that the regulations in question would not affect most women of reproductive age in Texas); *cf.* United States v. Salerno, 481 U.S. 739, 745 (1987) ("A facial challenge to a legislative Act is, of course, the most difficult challenge to mount successfully, since the challenger must establish that no set of circumstances exists under which the Act would be valid."). A plurality of the Court again applied the "large fraction" standard in *June Medical Services LLC v. Russo,* discussed *infra.* 140 S. Ct. 2103, 2131–33 (2020) (plurality opinion).

[1023] *June Med. Servs. LLC,* 140 S. Ct. at 2112.

[1024] *Id.* (quoting *Whole Woman's Health,* 136 S. Ct. at 2310).

[1025] *Id.* at 2133.

[1026] *Id.* at 2141 (Roberts, C.J., concurring in the judgment).

[1027] *Id.* at 2133, 2135–40, 2141.

to work at NASA facilities violated their constitutional privacy rights.[1028] In so doing, the Court assumed without deciding that a right to informational privacy could be protected by the Constitution, but held that any such right would not prevent the government from asking reasonable questions in light of the government's interest as an employer and in light of the statutory protections that provide meaningful checks against unwarranted disclosures.[1029] As a result, the questions about the scope of the right to informational privacy suggested by *Whalen* remain.

Family Relationships.—

[P. 1919, delete sentence "Unlike the shifting definitions of the 'privacy' line of case, the Court's treatment of the 'liberty' of familial relationships has a relatively principled doctrinal basis."]

[P. 1919, after sentence ending ". . . to rigorous scrutiny.", add new paragraph:]

In 2015, in *Obergefell v. Hodges*, the Supreme Court clarified that the "right to marry" applies with "equal force" to same-sex couples, as it does to opposite-sex couples, holding that the Fourteenth Amendment requires a state to license a marriage between two people of the same sex and to recognize a marriage between two people of the same sex when their marriage was lawfully licensed and performed out of state.[1030] In so holding, the Court recognized marriage as being an institution of "both continuity and change," and, as a consequence, recent shifts in public attitudes respecting gay individuals and more specifically same-sex marriage necessarily informed the Court's conceptualization of the right to marry.[1031] More broadly, the *Obergefell* Court recognized that the right to marry is grounded in four "principles and traditions." These involve the concepts that (1) marriage (and choosing whom to marry) is inherent to individual autonomy protected by the Constitution; (2) marriage is fundamental to supporting a union of committed individuals; (3) marriage safeguards children and families;[1032] and (4) marriage is essential to the nation's social order, because it is at the heart of many legal benefits.[1033] With this conceptualization of the right to marry in mind, the Court found no difference between same- and opposite-sex couples with respect to any of the right's four central principles, concluding that a denial of marital

---

[1028] *See* 562 U.S. 134 (2011).

[1029] *Id.* at 148–56.

[1030] *See* 576 U.S. ___, No. 14-556, slip op. at 12 (2015).

[1031] *See id.* at 6–10.

[1032] In *Pavan v. Smith*, the Court reviewed an Arkansas law providing that when a married woman gives birth, her husband must be listed as the second parent on the child's birth certificate, including when he is not the child's genetic parent. 582 U.S. ___, No. 16-992, slip op. at 1 (2017). The lower court had interpreted the law to not require the state to extend the rule to similarly situated same-sex couples. *Id.* Relying on *Obergefell*, the Court struck down the law, noting that the "differential treatment" of the Arkansas rules "infringes *Obergefell*'s commitment to provide same-sex couples 'the constellation of benefits that the States have linked to marriage.'" *Id.* (quoting *Obergefell*, slip op. at 17).

[1033] *See Obergefell*, slip op. at 12–16.

recognition to same-sex couples ultimately "demean[ed]" and "stigma[tized]" those couples and any children resulting from such partnerships.[1034] Given this conclusion, the Court held that, while limiting marriage to opposite-sex couples may have once seemed "natural," such a limitation was inconsistent with the right to marriage inherent in the "liberty" of the person as protected by the Fourteenth Amendment.[1035]

PROCEDURAL DUE PROCESS: CIVIL

Generally

[P. 1926, delete sentence starting "One of the basic criteria . . ." and substitute with:]

A basic threshold issue respecting whether due process is satisfied is whether the government conduct being examined is a part of a criminal or civil proceeding.[1036] The "appropriate framework" for assessing procedural rules in the field of criminal law is determining whether the procedure is offensive to the concept of fundamental fairness.[1037] In civil contexts, however, a balancing test is used that evaluates the government's chosen procedure with respect to the private interest affected, the risk of erroneous deprivation of that interest under the chosen procedure, and the government interest at stake.[1038]

The Requirements of Due Process.—

[P. 1931, after n.742 and before paragraph starting "(4) Confrontation and Cross-Examination, . . .", add new paragraph:]

Subsequently, in *Williams v. Pennsylvania*, the Court found that the right of due process was violated when a judge on the Pennsylvania Supreme Court—who participated in case denying post-conviction relief to a prisoner convicted of first-degree murder and sentenced to death—had, in his former role as a district attorney, given approval to seek the death penalty in the prisoner's case.[1039] Relying on *Caperton*, which the Court viewed as having set forth an "objective standard" that requires

---

[1034] *See id.* at 17.

[1035] *See id.* at 17–18. The Court also grounded its *Obergefell* decision in the Equal Protection Clause of the Fourteenth Amendment. *Id.* at 19 ("The right of same-sex couples to marry that is part of the liberty promised by the Fourteenth Amendment is derived, too, from that Amendment's guarantee of the equal protection of the laws."). For a discussion of *Obergefell*'s Equal Protection holding, *see infra* Fourteenth Amendment: Equal Protection of the Laws: The New Equal Protection: Sexual Orientation.

[1036] *See* Medina v. California, 505 U.S. 437, 443 (1992).

[1037] *Id.*

[1038] *See* Mathews v. Eldridge, 424 U.S. 319, 335 (1976). In *Nelson v. Colorado*, the Supreme Court held that the *Mathews* test controls when evaluating state procedures governing the continuing deprivation of property *after* a criminal conviction has been reversed or vacated, with no prospect of reprosecution. *See* 581 U.S. ___, No. 15-1256, slip op. at 6 (2017).

[1039] 579 U.S. ___, No. 15-5040, slip op. at 1 (2016).

recusal when the likelihood of bias on the part of the judge is "too high to be constitutionally tolerable,"[1040] the *Williams* Court specifically held that there is an impermissible risk of actual bias when a judge had previously had a "significant, personal involvement as a prosecutor in a critical decision regarding the defendant's case."[1041] The Court based its holding, in part, on earlier cases which had found impermissible bias occurs when the same person serves as both "accuser" and "adjudicator" in a case, which the Court viewed as having happened in *Williams*.[1042] It also reasoned that authorizing another person to seek the death penalty represents "significant personal involvement" in a case,[1043] and took the view that the involvement of multiple actors in a case over many years "only heightens"—rather than mitigates—the "need for objective rules preventing the operation of bias that otherwise might be obscured."[1044] As a remedy, the case was remanded for reevaluation by the reconstituted Pennsylvania Supreme Court, notwithstanding the fact that the judge in question did not cast the deciding vote, as the *Williams* Court viewed the judge's participation in the multi-member panel's deliberations as sufficient to taint the public legitimacy of the underlying proceedings and constitute reversible error.[1045]

The Procedure That is Due Process

Proceedings in Which Procedural Due Process Need Not Be Observed.—

[P. 1945, after n.818, delete heading "When Process is Due" and substitute with "What Process is Due"]

What Process is Due.—

[P. 1949, after sentence ending ". . . burdensome for the city.", add new paragraph:]

In another context, the Supreme Court applied the *Mathews* test to strike down a provision in Colorado's Exoneration Act.[1046] That statute required individuals whose criminal convictions had been invalidated to prove their innocence by clear and convincing evidence in order to recoup any fines, penalties, court costs, or restitution paid to the state as a result

---

[1040] *Id.* (internal quotations omitted).

[1041] *Id.* at 5–6.

[1042] *Id.* at 6 (citing *In re* Murchison, 349 U.S. 133, 136–37 (1955)). The Court also noted that "[n]o attorney is more integral to the accusatory process than a prosecutor who participates in a major adversary decision." *Id.* at 7.

[1043] *Id.* at 9. *See also id.* at 10 (noting that the judge in this case had highlighted the number of capital cases in which he participated when campaigning for judicial office).

[1044] *Id.* at 8.

[1045] *Id.* at 12–13. Likewise, the Court rejected the argument that remanding the case would not cure the underlying due process violation because the disqualified judge's views might still influence his former colleagues, as an "inability to guarantee complete relief for a constitutional violation . . . does not justify withholding a remedy altogether." *Id.* at 14.

[1046] *See* Nelson v. Colorado, 581 U.S. ___, No. 15-1256, slip op. at 1 (2017).

of the conviction.[1047] The Court, noting that "[a]bsent conviction of crime, one is presumed innocent,"[1048] concluded that all three considerations under *Mathews* "weigh[ed] decisively against Colorado's scheme."[1049] Specifically, the Court reasoned that (1) those affected by the Colorado statute have an "obvious interest" in regaining their funds;[1050] (2) the burden of proving one's innocence by "clear and convincing" evidence unacceptably risked erroneous deprivation of those funds;[1051] and (3) the state had "no countervailing interests" in withholding money to which it had "zero claim of right."[1052] As a result, the Court held that the state could not impose "anything more than minimal procedures" for the return of funds that occurred as a result of a conviction that was subsequently invalidated.[1053]

Jurisdiction

In Personam Proceedings Against Individuals.—

[P. 1955, at end of section, add new paragraph:]

> *Walden v. Fiore* further articulated what "minimum contacts" are necessary to create jurisdiction as a result of the relationship between the defendant, the forum, and the litigation.[1054] In *Walden*, the plaintiffs, who were residents of Nevada, sued a law enforcement officer in federal court in Nevada as a result of an incident that occurred in an airport in Atlanta as the plaintiffs were attempting to board a connecting flight from Puerto Rico to Las Vegas. The Court held that the court in Nevada lacked jurisdiction because of insufficient contacts between the officer and the state relative to the alleged harm, as no part of the officer's conduct

---

[1047] *See id.* at 4–5 (describing Colorado's Exoneration Act). Initially, the Court concluded that because the case concerned the "continuing deprivation of property after a [criminal] conviction" was reversed or vacated and "no further criminal process" was implicated by the case, the appropriate lens to examine the Exoneration Act was through the *Mathews* balancing test that generally applies in civil contexts. *Id.* at 5–6. The Court noted, however, that even under the test used to examine criminal due process rights—the fundamental fairness approach—Colorado's Exoneration Act would still fail to provide adequate due process because the state's procedures offend a fundamental principle of justice—the presumption of innocence. *Id.* at 7 n.9.

[1048] *Id.* at 1.

[1049] *Id.* at 6.

[1050] *Id.* In so concluding, the Court rejected Colorado's argument that the money in question belonged to the state because the criminal convictions were in place at the time the funds were taken. *Id.* The Court reasoned that after a conviction has been reversed, the criminal defendant is presumed innocent and any funds provided to the state as a result of the conviction rightfully belong to the person that was formerly subject to the prosecution. *Id.* at 7 ("Colorado may not presume a person, adjudged guilty of no crime, nonetheless guilty *enough* for monetary exactions.").

[1051] *Id.* at 8–9. In particular, the Court noted that when a defendant seeks to recoup small amounts of money under the Exoneration Act, the costs of mounting a claim and retaining a lawyer "would be prohibitive," amounting to "no remedy at all" for any minor assessments under the Act. *Id.* at 9.

[1052] *Id.* at 10.

[1053] *Id.*

[1054] 571 U.S. ___, No. 12-574, slip op. (2014). This type of "jurisdiction" is often referred to as "specific jurisdiction."

occurred in Nevada. In so holding, the Court emphasized that the minimum contacts inquiry should not focus on the resulting injury to the plaintiffs; instead, the proper question is whether the defendant's conduct connects him to the forum in a meaningful way.[1055]

Suing Out-of-State (Foreign) Corporations.—

[P. 1956, delete paragraphs and substitute with:]

Presence alone, however, does not expose a corporation to all manner of suits through the exercise of general jurisdiction. Only corporations, whose "continuous and systematic" affiliations with a forum make them "essentially at home" there, are broadly amenable to suit.[1056] While the paradigmatic examples of where a corporate defendant is "at home" are the corporation's place of incorporation and principal place of business,[1057] the Court has recognized that in "exceptional cases" general jurisdiction can be exercised by a court located where the corporate defendant's operations are "so substantial" as to "render the corporation at home in that State."[1058] Nonetheless, insubstantial in-state business, in and of itself, does not suffice to permit an assertion of jurisdiction over claims that are unrelated to any activity occurring in a state.[1059] Without the protection of such a rule, foreign corporations would be exposed to the manifest hardship and inconvenience of defending, in any state in which they happened to be carrying on business, suits for torts wherever committed and claims on contracts wherever made.[1060] And if the

---

[1055] *Id.* at 6–8.

[1056] Daimler AG v. Bauman, 571 U.S ___, No. 11-965, slip op. at 8 (2014) (quoting Goodyear Dunlop Tires Operations, S.A. v. Brown, 564 U.S. 915, 920 (2011)) (holding Daimler Chrysler, a German public stock company, could not be subject to suit in California with respect to acts taken in Argentina by Argentinian subsidiary of Daimler, notwithstanding the fact that Daimler Chrysler had a U.S. subsidiary that did business in California).

[1057] *Id.* at 18–19.

[1058] *Id.* at 20 n.19. For example, the Court held that an Ohio court could exercise general jurisdiction over a defendant corporation who was forced to relocate temporarily from the Philippines to Ohio, making Ohio the "center" of the corporation's activities. *See* Perkins v. Benguet Consol. Mining Co., 342 U.S. 437, 447–48 (1952).

[1059] *See* BNSF R.R. Co. v. Tyrrell, 581 U.S. ___, No. 16-405, slip op. at 11–12 (2017) (holding that Montana courts could not exercise general jurisdiction over a railroad company that had over 2,000 miles of track and more than 2,000 employees in the state because the company was not incorporated or headquartered in Montana and the overall activity of the company in Montana was not "so substantial" as to render the corporation "at home" in the state).

[1060] *E.g.*, Helicopteros Nacionales de Colombia v. Hall, 466 U.S. 408 (1984); Davis v. Farmers Co-operative Co., 262 U.S. 312 (1923); Rosenberg Bros. & Co., Inc. v. Curtis Brown Co., 260 U.S. 516 (1923); Simon v. S. Ry., 236 U.S. 115, 129–30 (1915); Green v. Chicago, B. & Q. Ry., 205 U.S. 530 (1907); Old Wayne Life Ass'n v. McDonough, 204 U.S. 8 (1907). Continuous operations were sometimes sufficiently substantial and of a nature to warrant assertions of jurisdiction. St. Louis S.W. Ry. Co. v. Alexander, 227 U.S. 218 (1913); *see also* Goodyear Dunlop Tires Operations, S.A. v. Brown, 564 U.S. 915, 922 (2011) (distinguishing application of stream-of-commerce analysis in specific cases of in-state injury from the degree of presence a corporation must maintain in a state to be amenable to general jurisdiction there).

corporation stopped doing business in the forum state before suit against it was commenced, it might well escape jurisdiction altogether.[1061]

In early cases, the issue of the degree of activity and, in particular, the degree of solicitation that was necessary to constitute doing business by a foreign corporation, was much disputed and led to very particularistic holdings.[1062] In the absence of enough activity to constitute doing business, the mere presence of an agent, officer, or stockholder, who could be served, within a state's territorial limits was not sufficient to enable the state to exercise jurisdiction over the foreign corporation.[1063] The touchstone in jurisdiction cases was recast by *International Shoe Co. v. Washington* and its "minimum contacts" analysis.[1064] International Shoe, an out-of-state corporation, had not been issued a license to do business in the State of Washington, but it systematically and continuously employed a sales force of Washington residents to solicit therein and thus was held amenable to suit in Washington for unpaid unemployment compensation contributions for such salesmen. The Court deemed a notice of assessment served personally upon one of the local sales solicitors, and a copy of the assessment sent by registered mail to the corporation's principal office in Missouri, sufficient to apprise the corporation of the proceeding.

[P. 1963, after n.904, delete sentences starting "Writing in dissent for herself . . ." until n.905.]

[P. 1963, after n.906, add new paragraph:]

Nonetheless, in order for a state court to exercise specific jurisdiction, the suit must arise out of or relate to the defendant's contacts with the forum,[1065] and when there is "no such connection, specific jurisdiction is lacking regardless of the extent of a defendant's unconnected activities in the State."[1066] As a result, the Court, in *Bristol-Myers Squibb Co. v. Superior Court of California,* concluded that the California Supreme Court erred in employing a "relaxed" approach to personal jurisdiction by holding that a state court could exercise *specific* jurisdiction over a corporate defendant who was being sued by non-state residents for out-of-state activities solely because the defendant had

---

[1061] Robert Mitchell Furniture Co. v. Selden Breck Constr. Co., 257 U.S. 213 (1921); Chipman, Ltd. v. Thomas B. Jeffery Co., 251 U.S. 373, 379 (1920). Jurisdiction would continue, however, if a state had conditioned doing business on a firm's agreeing to accept service through state officers should it and its agent withdraw. Washington *ex rel.* Bond & Goodwin & Tucker v. Superior Court, 289 U.S. 361, 364 (1933).

[1062] Solicitation of business alone was inadequate to constitute "doing business," *Green,* 205 U.S. at 534, but when connected with other activities could suffice to confer jurisdiction. Int'l Harvester Co. v. Kentucky, 234 U.S. 579 (1914). Hutchinson v. Chase & Gilbert, 45 F.2d 139, 141–42 (2d Cir. 1930) (Hand, J.) (providing survey of cases).

[1063] *E.g.,* Riverside Mills v. Menefee, 237 U.S. 189, 195 (1915); Conley v. Mathieson Alkali Works, 190 U.S. 406 (1903); Goldey v. Morning News, 156 U.S. 518 (1895); *but see* Conn. Mut. Life Ins. Co. v. Spratley, 172 U.S. 602 (1899).

[1064] 326 U.S. 310 (1945).

[1065] Daimler AG v. Bauman, 571 U.S ___, No. 11-965, slip op. at 8 (2014).

[1066] Bristol-Myers Squibb Co. v. Superior Court of Cal., San Francisco Cty., 582 U.S. ___, No. 16-466, slip op. at 7 (2017).

"extensive forum contacts" unrelated to the claims in question.[1067] Concluding that California's approach was a "loose and spurious form of general jurisdiction,"[1068] the Court held that without a "connection between the forum and the specific claims at issue," California courts lacked jurisdiction over the corporate defendant.[1069]

PROCEDURAL DUE PROCESS—CRIMINAL

Generally: The Principles of Fundamental Fairness

[P. 1981, n.1020, after sentence ending ". . . required by due process.", delete and substitute with:]

> For other recurrences to general due process reasoning, as distinct from reliance on more specific Bill of Rights provisions, see, e.g., United States v. Bryant, 579 U.S. ___, No. 15-420, slip op. at 15–16 (2016) (holding that principles of due process did not prevent a defendant's prior uncounseled convictions in tribal court from being used as the basis for a sentence enhancement, as those convictions complied with the Indian Civil Rights Act, which itself contained requirements that "ensure the reliability of tribal-court convictions"). *See also* Hicks v. Oklahoma, 447 U.S. 343 (1980) (where sentencing enhancement scheme for habitual offenders found unconstitutional, defendant's sentence cannot be sustained, even if sentence falls within range of unenhanced sentences); Sandstrom v. Montana, 442 U.S. 510 (1979) (conclusive presumptions in jury instruction may not be used to shift burden of proof of an element of crime to defendant); Kentucky v. Whorton, 441 U.S. 786 (1979) (fairness of failure to give jury instruction on presumption of innocence evaluated under totality of circumstances); Taylor v. Kentucky, 436 U.S. 478 (1978) (requiring, upon defense request, jury instruction on presumption of innocence); Patterson v. New York, 432 U.S. 197 (1977) (defendant may be required to bear burden of affirmative defense); Henderson v. Kibbe, 431 U.S. 145 (1977) (sufficiency of jury instructions); Estelle v. Williams, 425 U.S. 501 (1976) (a state cannot compel an accused to stand trial before a jury while dressed in identifiable prison clothes); Mullaney v. Wilbur, 421 U.S. 684 (1975) (defendant may not be required to carry the burden of disproving an element of a crime for which he is charged); Wardius v. Oregon, 412 U.S. 470 (1973) (defendant may not be held to rule requiring disclosure to prosecution of an alibi defense unless defendant is given reciprocal discovery rights against the state); Chambers v. Mississippi, 410 U.S. 284 (1973) (defendant may not be denied opportunity to explore confession of third party to crime for which defendant is charged).

The Elements of Due Process

Clarity in Criminal Statutes: The Void-for-Vagueness Doctrine.—

[P. 1983, after first full paragraph ending "'. . . meaning of [an] enactment.'", add new sentences:]

> In other situations, a statute may be unconstitutionally vague because the statute is worded in a standardless way that invites arbitrary enforcement. In this vein, the Court has invalidated two kinds of criminal

---

[1067] *Id.* at 7.

[1068] *Id.* A court may exercise "general" jurisdiction for any claim—even if all the incidents underlying the claim occurred in a different state—against an individual in that person's domicile or against a corporation where the corporation is fairly regarded as "at home," such as the company's place of incorporation or headquarters. *See* Goodyear Dunlop Tires Operations, S.A. v. Brown, 564 U.S. 915, 919–24 (2011).

[1069] *See Bristol-Myers Squibb Co.*, slip op. at 8.

laws as "void for vagueness": (1) laws that define criminal offenses; and (2) laws that fix the permissible sentences for criminal offenses.[1070] With respect to laws that define criminal offenses, the Court has required that a penal statute provide a definition of the offense with "sufficient definiteness that ordinary people can understand what conduct is prohibited and in a manner that does not encourage arbitrary and discriminatory enforcement."[1071]

[P. 1983, at end of first full paragraph, add new sentence:]

The Court may also apply the void-for-vagueness doctrine to analyze statutes governing civil "removal cases,"[1072] "in view of the grave nature of deportation."[1073]

[P. 1985, in first sentence, delete "*FCC v. Fox*, 567 U.S. ___, No. 10–1293, slip op. (2012)" and substitute with:]

FCC v. Fox Television Stations, Inc.,[1074]

[P. 1986, after first sentence in first full paragraph, add new footnote:]

See, e.g., McDonnell v. United States, 579 U.S. ___, No. 15-474, slip op. at 23 (2016) (narrowly interpreting the term "official act" to avoid a construction of the Hobbs Act and federal honest-services fraud statute that would allow public officials to be subject to prosecution without fair notice "for the most prosaic interactions" between officials and their constituents).

[P. 1987, after first full paragraph ending ". . . abrogation of the common law rule.", add new paragraphs:]

With regard to statutes that fix criminal sentences,[1075] the Court has explained that the law must specify the range of available sentences with "sufficient clarity."[1076] For example, in *Johnson v. United States*, after

---

[1070] *See* United States v. Beckles, 580 U.S. ___, No. 15-8544, slip op. at 5 (2017).

[1071] *See* Kolender v. Lawson, 461 U.S. 352, 357 (1983).

[1072] Sessions v. Dimaya, 584 U.S. ___, No. 15-1498, slip op. at 5 (2018) (plurality opinion).

[1073] Jordan v. De George, 341 U.S. 223, 231 (1951).

[1074] 567 U.S. 239, 258 (2012).

[1075] In *United States v. Beckles*, the Supreme Court concluded that the federal sentencing guidelines "do not fix the permissible range of sentences" and, therefore, are not subject to a vagueness challenge under the Due Process Clause. *See* 580 U.S. ___, No. 15-8544, slip op. at 5 (2017). Rather, the sentencing guidelines "merely guide the district courts' discretion." *Id.* at 8. In so concluding, the Court noted that the sentencing system that predated the use of the guidelines gave nearly unfettered discretion to judges in sentencing, and that discretion was never viewed as raising vagueness concerns. *Id.* Thus, the Court reasoned that it was "difficult to see how the present system of guided discretion" could raise vagueness concerns. *Id.* Moreover, the *Beckles* Court explained that "the advisory Guidelines . . . do not implicate the twin concerns underlying [the] vagueness doctrine—providing notice and preventing arbitrary enforcement." *Id.* According to the Court, the only notice that is required regarding criminal sentences is provided to the defendant by the applicable statutory range, and the guidelines. Further, the guidelines, which serve to advise courts how to exercise their discretion within the bounds set by Congress, simply do not regulate any conduct that can be arbitrarily enforced against a criminal defendant. *Id.* at 9.

[1076] *See* United States v. Batchelder, 442 U.S. 114, 123 (1979).

years of litigation on the meaning and scope of the "residual clause" of the Armed Career Criminal Act of 1984 (ACCA),[1077] the Court concluded that the clause in question was void for vagueness.[1078] In relevant part, the ACCA imposes an increased prison term upon a felon who is in possession of a firearm, if that felon has previously been convicted for a "violent felony," a term defined by the statute to include "burglary, arson, or extortion, [a crime that] involves use of explosives, or" crimes that fall within the residual clause—that is, crimes that "otherwise involve[] conduct that presents a serious potential risk of physical injury to another."[1079] In *Johnson,* prosecutors sought an enhanced sentence for a felon found in possession of a firearm, arguing that one of the defendant's previous crimes—unlawful possession of a short-barreled shotgun— qualified as a violent felony because the crime amounted to one that "involve[d] conduct that presents a serious potential risk of physical injury to another."[1080] To determine whether a crime falls within the residual clause, the Court had previously endorsed a "categorical approach"—that is, instead of looking to whether the facts of a specific offense presented a serious risk of physical injury to another, the Supreme Court had interpreted the ACCA to require courts to look to whether the underlying crime falls within a category such that the "ordinary case" of the crime would present a serious risk of physical injury.[1081]

The Court in *Johnson* concluded that the residual clause was unconstitutionally vague because the clause's requirement that courts determine what an "ordinary case" of a crime entails led to "grave uncertainty" about (1) how to estimate the risk posed by the crime and (2) how much risk was sufficient to qualify as a violent felony.[1082] For example, in determining whether attempted burglary ordinarily posed serious risks of physical injury, the Court suggested that reasonable minds could differ as to whether an attempted burglary would typically end in a violent encounter, resulting in the conclusion that the residual clause provided "no reliable way" to determine what crimes fell within its scope.[1083] In so holding, the Court relied heavily on the difficulties that federal courts (including the Supreme Court) have had in establishing consistent standards to adjudge the scope of the residual clause, noting that the failure of "persistent efforts" to establish a standard can provide evidence of vagueness.[1084]

In *Sessions v. Dimaya,* the Court extended *Johnson* to conclude that a statute allowing the deportation of any alien who committed a

---

[1077] *See, e.g.,* Sykes v. United States, 564 U.S. 1 (2011); Chambers v. United States, 555 U.S. 122 (2009); Begay v. United States, 553 U.S. 137 (2008); James v. United States, 550 U.S. 192 (2007).

[1078] *See* Johnson v. United States, 576 U.S. ___, No. 13-7120, slip op. (2015).

[1079] *See* 18 U.S.C. § 924(e)(2)(B) (2012).

[1080] *Johnson,* slip op. at 2–3.

[1081] *See James,* 550 U.S. at 208.

[1082] *Johnson,* slip op. at 5–6.

[1083] *Id.*

[1084] *See id.* at 6–10 ("Nine years' experience trying to derive meaning from the residual clause convinces us that we have embarked upon a failed enterprise.").

"crime of violence" was unconstitutionally vague.[1085] Similar to the statute at issue in *Johnson*, the statute at issue in *Dimaya* defined the phrase "crime of violence" by reference to a statutory "residual clause" covering felonious conduct that "involve[d] a substantial risk that physical force . . . may be used in the course of committing the offense," and lower courts had again adopted the categorical approach to determine whether any particular offense fell within the ambit of the residual clause.[1086] The Court concluded that *Johnson* had "straightforward application" to the case before it,[1087] because in both cases, the statutes required courts to impermissibly speculate about the "ordinary version" of an offense, and about whether that offense involved sufficient risk of violence to fall within the ambit of the provision. In so doing, the Court rejected purported distinctions between the two residual clauses.[1088] The government raised a number of textual differences between the two statutes—the *Dimaya* statute used the phrase "in the course of," while the *Johnson* statute did not; the *Dimaya* statute referenced the risk of "physical force," while the *Johnson* statute referred to "physical injury"; and the *Dimaya* statute, unlike the *Johnson* statute, did not include an exemplary list of covered crimes.[1089] In the eyes of the Court, these were "the proverbial distinction[s] without a difference," because none related "to the pair of features—the ordinary-case inquiry and a hazy risk threshold—that *Johnson* found to produce impermissible vagueness."[1090]

The Court subsequently considered the constitutionality of another residual clause in *United States v. Davis*, and as in *Johnson* and *Dimaya*, held that the clause was unconstitutionally vague.[1091] The challenged federal statute created a sentence enhancement for offenders "using or carrying a firearm 'during and in relation to,' or possessing a firearm 'in furtherance of,' any federal 'crime of violence or drug trafficking crime.'"[1092] The statutory definition of "crime of violence" included a residual clause stating that a felony offense would be included in the definition if, "by its nature," the offense "involve[d] a substantial risk that physical force . . . may be used in the course of committing the

---

[1085] 584 U.S. ___, No. 15-1498, slip op. at 7 (2018). Justice Gorsuch did not join that portion of the Court's opinion detailing how the void-for-vagueness doctrine applies in the context of non-criminal removal cases. *See id.* at 4–6. Justice Gorsuch suggested that he believed the Due Process Clause required the same standard in both criminal and civil cases, *id.* at 10–12 (Gorsuch, J., concurring), but he ultimately resolved the issue by citing to the relevant statute, noting that Congress had *chosen* to "extend existing forms of liberty" to certain individuals—and once it had done so, the government could take away that "liberty . . . only after affording due process." *Id.* at 13.

[1086] *Id.* at 2 (majority opinion).

[1087] *Id.* at 11.

[1088] *Id.* at 16.

[1089] *Id.* at 16–21.

[1090] *Id.* at 16. Nor did it matter to the Court that there were fewer lower court and Supreme Court cases wrestling with the proper meaning of the statute than had divided on the proper interpretation of the *Johnson* statute; the cases interpreting the *Dimaya* statute still demonstrated divisive problems of application. *Id.* at 21–24.

[1091] 588 U.S. ___, No. 18-431, slip op. at 1–2 (2019).

[1092] *Id.* at 2 (quoting 18 U.S.C. § 924(c)(1)(A)).

offense."[1093] In light of *Johnson* and *Dimaya*, the government acknowledged that if this statute also used the categorical approach to determine whether a crime was a "crime of violence," the provision would be unconstitutional.[1094] Instead, the government defended the provision by arguing that courts should adopt a "case-specific approach" to interpreting this statute, asking whether a defendant, through his or her "actual conduct," posed a "substantial risk of physical violence."[1095] Although the Court acknowledged that this case-specific method would "avoid the vagueness problem" by focusing on the specific defendant's actual conduct, it nonetheless concluded that the statute could not be read to embrace this approach.[1096] The Court emphasized that it had already interpreted very similar statutory provisions to require the categorical approach,[1097] concluding that the word "offense" is "most naturally" read to "refer to a generic crime"[1098] and expressing concerns about an approach that would give different meanings to the phrase "crime of violence" in different parts of the criminal code.[1099] Consequently, because the statute employed a categorical approach, the Court held that the provision in *Davis*, like the ones at issue in *Johnson* and *Dimaya*, was "unconstitutionally vague."[1100]

Fair Trial.—

[P. 1991, n.1067, before sentence starting "Bias or prejudice of . . .", add:]

Similarly, in *Rippo v. Baker*, the Supreme Court vacated the Nevada Supreme Court's denial of a convicted petitioner's application for post-conviction relief based on the trial judge's failure to recuse himself. 580 U.S. ___, No. 16-6316, slip op. (2017). During Rippo's trial, the trial judge was the target of a federal bribery probe by the same district attorney's office that was prosecuting Rippo. Rippo moved for the judge's disqualification under the Fourteenth Amendment's Due Process Clause, arguing the "judge could not impartially adjudicate a case in which one of the parties was criminally investigating him." *Id.* at 1. After the judge was indicted on federal charges, a different judge subsequently assigned to the case denied Rippo's motion for a new trial. In vacating the Nevada Supreme Court's decision, the Supreme Court noted that "[u]nder our precedents, the Due Process Clause may sometimes demand recusal even when a judge 'ha[s] no actual bias.' Recusal is required when, objectively speaking, 'the probability of actual bias on the part of the judge or decisionmaker is too high to be constitutionally tolerable.'" *Id.* at 2 (quoting Aetna Life Ins. Co. v. Lavoie, 475 U.S. 813, 825 (1986); Withrow v. Larkin, 421 U.S. 35, 47 (1975)).

[1093] *Id.* at 3 (quoting 18 U.S.C. § 924(c)(3)). This provision was almost identical to the residual clause considered in *Sessions v. Dimaya*, 584 U.S. ___, No. 15-1498, slip op. at 2 (2018).

[1094] *Davis*, slip op. at 7.

[1095] *Id.*

[1096] *Id.* at 8–9.

[1097] *Id.* at 9–10.

[1098] *Id.* at 10 (quoting Nijhawan v. Holder, 557 U.S. 29, 33–34 (2009)) (internal quotation mark omitted).

[1099] *Id.* at 12.

[1100] *Id.* at 24.

Prosecutorial Misconduct.—

[P. 1998, at end of n.1100, add:]

See also Wearry v. Cain, 577 U.S. ___, No. 14-10008, slip op. at 9 (2016) (per curiam) (finding that a state post-conviction court had improperly (1) evaluated the materiality of each piece of evidence in isolation, rather than cumulatively; (2) emphasized reasons jurors might disregard the new evidence, while ignoring reasons why they might not; and (3) failed to consider the statements of two impeaching witnesses).

[P. 1998, delete n.1101 and substitute with:]

Strickler v. Greene, 527 U.S. 263, 296 (1999); *see also* Turner v. United States, 582 U.S. ___, No. 15-1503, slip op. at 12 (2017) (holding that, when considering the withheld evidence in the context of the entire record, the evidence was "too little, too weak, or too distant" from the central evidentiary issues in the case to meet *Brady*'s standards for materiality).

Proof, Burden of Proof, and Presumptions.—

[P. 2000, delete n.1110 and substitute with:]

Id. at 316, 18–19. *See also* Musacchio v. United States, 577 U.S. ___, No. 14-1095, slip op. (2016) ("When a jury finds guilt after being instructed on all elements of the charged crime plus one more element," the fact that the government did not introduce evidence of the additional element—which was not required to prove the offense, but was included in the erroneous jury instruction—"does not implicate the principles that sufficiency review protects."); Griffin v. United States, 502 U.S. 46 (1991) (general guilty verdict on a multiple-object conspiracy need not be set aside if the evidence is inadequate to support conviction as to one of the objects of the conviction, but is adequate to support conviction as to another object).

The Problem of the Incompetent or Insane Defendant.—

[P. 2005, delete n.1134 and substitute with:]

Pate v. Robinson, 383 U.S. 375, 378 (1966); *see also* Drope v. Missouri, 420 U.S. 162, 180 (1975) (noting the relevant circumstances that may require a trial court to inquire into the mental competency of the defendant). In *Ake v. Oklahoma,* the Court established that, when an indigent defendant's mental condition is both relevant to the punishment and seriously in question, the state must provide the defendant with access to a mental health expert who is sufficiently available to the defense and independent from the prosecution to effectively "assist in evaluation, preparation, and presentation of the defense." 470 U.S. 68, 83 (1985). While the Court not decided whether *Ake* requires that the state provide a qualified mental health expert that is available exclusively to the defense team, *see McWilliams v. Dunn,* 582 U.S. ___, No. 16-5294, slip op.at 13 (2017), a state nevertheless deprives an indigent defendant of due process when it provides a competent psychiatrist only to *examine* the defendant without also requiring that an expert provide the defense with help in evaluating, preparing, and presenting its case. *Id.* at 15.

[P. 2006, after n.1141, add new sentences:]

For example, in *Kahler v. Kansas,* the Court held that the Due Process Clause does not require a state to adopt *M'Naghten*'s moral-incapacity test as a complete insanity defense resulting in an acquittal.[1101] The Court

---

[1101] 140 S. Ct. 1021, 1027, 1037 (2020).

stated that "[d]efining the precise relationship between criminal culpability and mental illness," because it involves "hard choices" among competing values and evolving understandings of mental health, "is a project for state governance, not constitutional law."[1102]

[P. 2007, delete sentences starting "The Court held in *Ford* . . ." through n.1149.]

Guilty Pleas.—

[P. 2008, at end of n.1154, add:]

Release-dismissal agreements, pursuant to which the prosecution agrees to dismiss criminal charges in exchange for the defendant's agreement to release his right to file a civil action for alleged police or prosecutorial misconduct, are not *per se* invalid. Town of Newton v. Rumery, 480 U.S. 386, 394 (1987).

[P. 2008, delete n.1155 and substitute with:]

See Tollett v. Henderson, 411 U.S. 258, 265–66 (1973); North Carolina v. Alford, 400 U.S. 25, 38 (1970); Parker v. North Carolina, 397 U.S. 790, 795 (1970); McMann v. Richardson, 397 U.S. 759, 771 (1970); Brady v. United States, 397 U.S. 742, 758 (1970).

[P. 2008, after n.1155, add new sentence:]

However, some constitutional challenges may survive a plea if they go to "'the very power of the State' to prosecute the defendant."[1103]

Sentencing.—

[P. 2012, in second sentence, delete "in*Simmons*" and substitute with:]

in *Simmons*

[P. 2012, delete last sentence of n.1172 and substitute with:]

See also Lynch v. Arizona, 578 U.S. ___, No. 15-8366, slip op. at 3–4 (2016) (holding that the possibility of clemency and the potential for future "legislative reform" does not justify a departure from the rule of *Simmons*); Kelly v. South Carolina, 534 U.S. 246, 252 (2002) (concluding that a prosecutor need not express intent to rely on future dangerousness; logical

---

[1102] *Id.* at 1037.

[1103] Class v. United States, 583 U.S. ___, No. 16-424, slip op. at 4 (2018) (quoting Blackledge v. Perry, 417 U.S. 21, 30 (1974)) (holding guilty plea did not bar defendant "from challenging the constitutionality of the statute of conviction on direct appeal"). *See also* Menna v. New York, 423 U.S. 61, 62 n.2 (1975) (per curiam) (holding guilty plea did not waive defendant's claim on direct appeal that double jeopardy prohibited his prosecution); *Blackledge*, 417 U.S. at 31 (holding guilty plea did not foreclose defendant in *habeas* challenge from arguing that due process prohibited his prosecution). The state can permit pleas of guilty in which the defendant reserves the right to raise constitutional questions on appeal, and federal *habeas* courts will honor that arrangement. Lefkowitz v. Newsome, 420 U.S. 283, 293 (1975).

inferences may be drawn); Shafer v. South Carolina, 532 U.S. 36 (2001) (amended South Carolina law still runs afoul of *Simmons*).

Rights of Prisoners.—

[P. 2016, delete n.1198 and substitute with:]

See Bell v. Wolfish, 441 U.S. 520, 535–40 (1979). Persons not yet convicted of a crime may be detained by the government upon the appropriate determination of probable cause, and the government is entitled to "employ devices that are calculated to effectuate [a] detention." *Id.* at 537. Nonetheless, the Court has held that the Due Process Clause protects a pretrial detainee from being subject to conditions that amount to punishment, which can be demonstrated through (1) actions taken with the "express intent to punish" or (2) the use of restrictions or conditions on confinement that are not reasonably related to a legitimate goal. *See Wolfish,* 441 U.S. at 538, 561. More recently, the Court clarified the standard by which the due process rights of pretrial detainees are adjudged with respect to excessive force claims. Specifically, in *Kingsley v. Hendrickson,* the Court held that, in order for a pretrial detainee to prove an excessive force claim in violation of his due process rights, a plaintiff must show that an officer's use of force was objectively unreasonable, depending on the facts and circumstances from the perspective of a reasonable officer on the scene, *see* 576 U.S. ___, No. 14-6368, slip op. at 6–7 (2015), aligning the due process excessive force analysis with the standard for excessive force claims brought under the Fourth Amendment. *Cf.* Graham v. Connor, 490 U.S. 386, 388 (1989) (holding that a "free citizen's claim that law enforcement officials used excessive force . . . [is] properly analyzed under the Fourth Amendment's 'objective reasonableness' standard"). Liability for actions taken by the government in the context of a pretrial detainee due process lawsuit does not, therefore, turn on whether a particular officer subjectively knew that the conduct being taken was unreasonable. *See Kingsley,* slip op. at 1.

EQUAL PROTECTION OF THE LAWS

Equal Protection: Judging Classifications by Law

The New Standards: Active Review.—

[P. 2059, delete last paragraph starting "Thus, the nature of active review . . ." and substitute with:]

An open question after *Obergefell v. Hodges,* the 2015 case finding the right to same-sex marriage is protected by the Constitution, is the extent to which the Court is re-conceptualizing equal protection analysis.[1104] In *Obergefell,* the Court concluded that state laws that distinguished between marriages between same- and opposite-sex married couples violated the Equal Protection Clause.[1105] However, in lieu of more traditional equal protection analysis, the *Obergefell* Court did not identify whether the base classification made by the challenged state marriage laws was "suspect." Nor did the *Obergefell* Court engage in a balancing test to determine whether the purpose of the state classification was tailored to or fit the contours of the classification. Instead, the Court merely declared that state laws prohibiting same-sex marriage "abridge[d] central precepts of equality."[1106] It remains to be seen whether *Obergefell*

[1104] *See* 576 U.S. ___, No. 14-556, slip op. (2015).

[1105] *Id.* at 22.

[1106] *Id.*

signals a new direction for the Court's equal protection jurisprudence or is merely an anomaly that indicates the fluctuating nature of active review, as the doctrine has been subject to shifting majorities and varying degrees of concern about judicial activism and judicial restraint. Nonetheless, as will be more fully reviewed below, the sliding scale of review underlies many of the Court's most recent equal protection cases, even if the jurisprudence and its doctrinal basis have not been fully elucidated or consistently endorsed by the Court.

Testing Facially Neutral Classifications Which Impact on Minorities

[P. 2065, before heading "Traditional Equal Protection: Economic Regulation and Related Exercises of the Police Power," add new paragraph:]

In *Department of Homeland Security v. Regents of the University of California*, a four-Justice plurality rejected an equal protection challenge to the Department of Homeland Security's decision to rescind the Deferred Action for Childhood Arrivals (DACA) program.[1107] The DACA program offered "immigration relief" in the form of "favorable treatment" for certain people who arrived in the United States as children.[1108] The plaintiffs argued that the rescission decision violated equal protection guarantees because it was motivated by impermissible animus, "evidenced by (1) the disparate impact of the rescission on Latinos from Mexico, who represent 78% of DACA recipients; (2) the unusual history behind the rescission," which included shifting positions about whether to continue the program; "and (3) pre- and post-election statements by President Trump" that were critical of Latinos.[1109] With respect to the first factor, the plurality found that this disparate impact was "expected" based on the fact that "Latinos make up a large share of the unauthorized alien population."[1110] On the second factor, the plurality said the Administration's "decision to reevaluate DACA . . . was a natural response" to new concerns about the program's legality.[1111] And finally, the plurality concluded that the President's statements, "remote in time and made in unrelated contexts," were not probative of other executive officials' decision to rescind the program.[1112]

[1107] 140 S. Ct. 1891, 1915 (2020) (plurality opinion). A majority of the Court held that the Department's decision to rescind DACA was "arbitrary and capricious" under the Administrative Procedure Act and remanded the case so the Department could "consider the problem anew." *Id.* at 1914, 1916 (majority opinion). Four Justices who dissented from this aspect of the Court's decision concurred in the judgment rejecting the equal protection claim. *Id.* at 1919 (Thomas, J., concurring in the judgment in part and dissenting in part); *id.* at 1935–36) (Kavanaugh, J., concurring in the judgment in part and dissenting in part).

[1108] *Id.* at 1901 (majority opinion).

[1109] *Id.* at 1915 (plurality opinion).

[1110] *Id.* at 1915–16.

[1111] *Id.* at 1916.

[1112] *Id.*

EQUAL PROTECTION AND RACE

Education

Efforts to Curb Busing and Other Desegregation Remedies.—

[P. 2098, after n.1655, add new paragraph:]

The Court subsequently declined to extend the reasoning of these cases to remedies for exclusively *de facto* racial segregation. In *Schuette v. Coalition to Defend Affirmative Action*,[1113] the Court considered the constitutionality of an amendment to the Michigan Constitution, approved by that state's voters, to prohibit the use of race-based preferences as part of the admissions process for state universities. A plurality of the *Schuette* Court restricted its prior holdings as applying only to those situations where state action had the serious risk, if not purpose, of causing specific injuries on account of race.[1114] Finding no similar risks of injury with regard to the Michigan Amendment and no similar allegations of past discrimination in the Michigan university system, the Court declined to "restrict the right of Michigan voters to determine that race-based preferences granted by state entities should be ended."[1115] The plurality opinion and a majority of the Court, however, explicitly rejected a broader "political process theory" with respect to the constitutionality of race-based remedies. Specifically, the Court held that state action that places effective decision making over a policy that "inures primarily to the benefit of the minority" at a different level of government is not subject to heightened constitutional scrutiny.[1116]

Juries

[P. 2103, delete n.1679 and substitute with:]

See, e.g., Flowers v. Mississippi, 588 U.S. ___, No. 17-9572, slip op. at 2–3 (2019) (reasoning that "[f]our critical facts" when "taken together" established the trial court's "clear error" in concluding that the state's exercise of a peremptory strike was not "motivated in substantial part by discriminatory intent": (1) the state's use of "peremptory challenges to strike 41 of the 42 black prospective jurors" over the course of the defendant's six trials; (2) the state's

---

[1113] 572 U.S. ___, No. 12-682, slip op. (2014).

[1114] The plurality opinion was written by Justice Kennedy, joined by Chief Justice Roberts and Justice Alito. Justice Scalia authored an opinion concurring in judgment, joined by Justice Thomas, arguing that *Seattle School District* and the case on which it was based should be overturned in their entirety. *Schuette*, slip op. at 7–8 (Scalia, J., concurring in judgment). Justice Breyer also wrote an opinion concurring in judgment that the Michigan amendment did not violate the Equal Protection Clause. Specifically, Justice Breyer relied on the facts that (1) the amendment forbid racial preferences aimed at achieving diversity in education (as opposed to remedying past discrimination); (2) the amendment was aimed at ensuring that the democratic process (as opposed to the university administration) controlled with respect to affirmative action policy; and (3) the underlying racial preference policy had been adopted by individual school administrations, not by elected officials. *Id.* at 5 (Breyer, J., concurring in judgment). Justice Sotomayor, joined by Justice Ginsburg, dissented. *Id.* at 5, 22 (Sotomayor, J., dissenting). Justice Kagan recused herself.

[1115] *Id.* at 3–4.

[1116] *Id.* at 11.

exercise of "peremptory strikes against five of the six black prospective jurors" at the sixth trial; (3) the "dramatically disparate questioning of black and white prospective jurors"; and (4) the state's use of a peremptory strike against one black prospective juror who was "similarly situated to white prospective jurors who were not struck" (internal quotation marks omitted)); Foster v. Chatman, 578 U.S. ___, No. 14-8349, slip op. at 10–23 (2016) (applying the three-step process set forth in *Batson* to allow a death row inmate to pursue an appeal on the grounds that the state court's conclusion that the defendant had not shown purposeful discrimination during voir dire was clearly erroneous given that the prosecution's justifications for striking African-American jurors, while seeming "reasonable enough," had "no grounding in fact," were contradicted by the record, and had shifted over time); Snyder v. Louisiana, 552 U.S. 472, 483 (2008) (finding the prosecution's race-neutral explanation for its peremptory challenge of an African-American juror to be implausible, and that this "implausibility" was "reinforced by the prosecutor's acceptance of white jurors" whom the prosecution could have challenged for the same reasons that it claimed to have challenged the African-American juror); Miller-El v. Dretke, 545 U.S. 231, 240–41 (2005) (finding discrimination in the use of peremptory strikes based on various factors, including the high ratio of African-Americans struck from the venire panel, some of whom were struck on grounds that "appeared equally on point as to some white jurors who served").

"Affirmative Action": Remedial Use of Racial Classifications

[P. 2109, at end of first full paragraph after ". . . opinion.", add new footnote:]

For a detailed discussion of the use of racial considerations in apportionment and districting by the States, see *infra* Amendment 14: Section 1: Rights Guaranteed: Fundamental Interests: The Political Process: Apportionment and Districting.

[P. 2116, at end of first full paragraph, add new footnote:]

Grutter, 539 U.S. at 315. While an educational institution will receive deference in its judgment as to whether diversity is essential to its educational mission, the courts must closely scrutinize the means by which this goal is achieved. Thus, the institution will receive no deference regarding the question of the necessity of the means chosen and will bear the burden of demonstrating that "each applicant is evaluated as an individual and not in a way that an applicant's race or ethnicity is the defining feature of his or her application." Fisher v. Univ. of Tex. at Austin (*Fisher I*), 570 U.S. 297, 312 (2013) (citation omitted). In its 2013 decision in *Fisher*, the Court did not rule on the substance of the challenged affirmative action program and instead remanded the case so that the reviewing appellate court could apply the correct standard of review. However, the Court issued a subsequent decision in *Fisher* addressing the Texas program directly. *See* Fisher v. Univ. of Tex. at Austin (*Fisher II*), 579 U.S. ___, No. 14-981, slip op. (2016).

[P. 2117, after first full paragraph, add new paragraph:]

The Court subsequently revisited the question of affirmative action in undergraduate education in its 2016 decision in *Fisher v. University of Texas at Austin*, upholding the University of Texas at Austin's (UT's) use of "scores" based, in part, on race in filling approximately 25% of the slots in its incoming class that were not required by statute to be awarded to Texas high school students who finished in the top 10% of their graduating class (Top Ten Percent Plan or TTPP).[1117] The Court itself suggested that the "sui generis" nature of the UT program,[1118]

[1117] *Fisher II*, slip op. at 3–4.
[1118] *Id.* at 8.

coupled with the "fact that this case has been litigated on a somewhat artificial basis" because the record lacked information about the impact of Texas's TTPP,[1119] may limit the decision's value for "prospective guidance."[1120] Nonetheless, certain language in the Court's decision, along with its application of the three "controlling factors" set forth in the Court's 2013 decision in *Fisher*,[1121] seem likely to have some influence, as they represent the Court's most recent jurisprudence on whether and when institutions of higher education may take race into consideration in their admission decisions. Specifically, the 2016 *Fisher* decision began and ended with broad language recognizing constraints on the implementation of affirmative action programs in undergraduate education, including language that highlights the university's "continuing obligation to satisfy the burden of strict scrutiny in light of changing circumstances"[1122] and emphasized that "[t]he Court's affirmance of the University's admissions policy today does not necessarily mean the University may rely on that same policy without refinement."[1123] Nonetheless, while citing these constraints, the 2016 *Fisher* decision held that the challenged UT program did not run afoul of the Fourteenth Amendment. In particular, the Court concluded that the state's compelling interest in the case was not in enrolling a certain number of minority students, but in obtaining the educational benefits that flow from student body diversity, noting that the state cannot be faulted for not specifying a particular level of minority enrollment.[1124] The Court further concurred with UT's view that the alleged "critical mass" of minority students achieved under the 10% plan was not dispositive, as the university had found that it was insufficient,[1125] and that UT had found other means of promoting student-body diversity were unworkable.[1126] In so concluding, the Court held that the university had met its burden in surviving strict scrutiny by providing sworn

---

[1119] *Id.* at 10.

[1120] *Id.*

[1121] Fisher v. Univ. of Tex. at Austin (*Fisher I*), 570 U.S. 297, 312 (2013). The first of these principles is that strict scrutiny requires the university to demonstrate with clarity that its "purpose or interest is both constitutionally permissible and substantial, and that its use of the classification is necessary . . . to the accomplishment of its purpose." *Id.* at 309. The second principle is that the decision to pursue the educational benefits that flow from student body diversity is, in substantial measure, an "academic judgment" to which "some, but not complete, judicial deference is proper." *Id.* at 311. The third is that no deference is owed in determining whether the use of race is narrowly tailored; rather, the university bears burden of proving a non-racial approach would not promote its interests "about as well" and "at tolerable administrative expense." *Id.* at 312.

[1122] *Fisher II*, slip op. at 10.

[1123] *Id.*

[1124] *Id.* at 11–13. On the other hand, the Court emphasized that the university cannot claim educational benefits in "diversity writ large." *Id.* at 12. "A university's goals cannot be elusory or amorphous—they must be sufficiently measurable to permit judicial scrutiny of the policies adopted to reach them." *Id.* The Court also noted that the asserted goals of UT's affirmative action program "mirror" those approved in earlier cases (e.g., ending stereotypes and promoting cross-racial understanding). *Id.* at 13.

[1125] *Id.* at 13–15. The Court further emphasized that the fact that race allegedly plays a minor role in UT admissions, given that approximately 75% of the incoming class is admitted under the 10% plan, shows that the challenged use of race in determining the composition of the rest of the incoming class is narrowly tailored, not that it is unconstitutional. *Id.* at 15.

[1126] *Id.* at 15–19.

affidavits from UT officials and internal assessments based on months of studies, retreats, interviews, and reviews of data that amounted, in the view of the Court, to a "reasoned, principled explanation" of the university's interests and its efforts to achieve those interests in a manner that was no broader than necessary.[1127] The Court refused to question the motives of university administrators and did not further scrutinize the underlying evidence relied on by the respondents, which may indicate that there are some limits to the degree in which the Court will evaluate a race-conscious admissions policy once the university has provided sufficient support for its approach.[1128]

THE NEW EQUAL PROTECTION

Classifications Meriting Close Scrutiny

Alienage and Nationality.—

[P. 2118, delete n.1762 and substitute with:]

> Graham v. Richardson, 403 U.S. 365, 371 (1971); *see also* Takahashi v. Fish & Game Comm'n, 334 U.S. 410, 420 (1948); Truax v. Raich, 239 U.S. 33, 39 (1915); Yick Wo v. Hopkins, 118 U.S. 356, 369 (1886). Aliens in the United States, including whose presence is not authorized by the federal government, are "persons" to whom the Fifth and Fourteenth Amendments apply. *See, e.g.,* Zadvydas v. Davis, 533 U.S. 678, 693 (2001) ("[O]nce an alien enters the country, the legal circumstance changes, for the Due Process Clause applies to all 'persons' within the United States, including aliens, whether their presence here is lawful, unlawful, temporary, or permanent."); Plyler v. Doe, 457 U.S. 202, 210–16 (1982).However, the power to regulate immigration has permitted the federal government to discriminate on the basis of alienage, at least so long as the discrimination satisfies the rational basis standard of review. *See* Mathews v. Diaz, 426 U.S. 67,79–80, 83 (1976) (holding that federal conditions upon alien eligibility for public assistance were not "wholly irrational," and observing that "In the exercise of its broad power over naturalization and immigration, Congress regularly makes rules that would be unacceptable if applied to citizens . . . The fact that an Act of Congress treats aliens differently from citizens does not in itself imply that such disparate treatment is 'invidious.'"). Nonetheless, with regard to statutes that touch upon immigration-related matters but do not address the entry or exclusion of aliens, the Court has suggested that if such a law discriminates on the basis of suspect factors other than alienage or national origin a more "exacting standard of review" may be required. *See* Sessions v. Morales-Santana, 582 U.S. ___, No. 15-1191, slip op. 14–17 (2017) (distinguishing between immigration and citizenship contexts and applying heightened scrutiny to hold that a derivative citizenship statute which discriminated by gender violated equal protection principles).

Sex.—

[P. 2131, n.1820, delete sentence starting "*See also* Miller v. Albright . . ." and substitute with:]

> *See also* Miller v. Albright, 523 U.S. 420, 424 (1998) (opinion of Stevens, J.) (concluding that a requirement in a citizenship statute that children born abroad and out of wedlock to citizen fathers, but not to citizen mothers, obtain formal proof of paternity by age 18 does not violate

---

[1127] *Id.* at 13 ("Petitioner's contention that the University's goal was insufficiently concrete is rebutted by the record").

[1128] *Id.* at 13–14.

the equal protection component of the Fifth Amendment's Due Process Clause). Importantly, however, the Court in *Sessions v. Morales-Santana* distinguished *Nguyen* and *Miller* in ruling that a derivative citizenship statute for children born abroad and out of wedlock to a U.S. citizen and foreign national violated equal protection principles because the statute imposed lengthier physical presence requirements on citizen fathers than citizen mothers. *See* 582 U.S. ___, No. 15-1191, slip op. 15–16 (2017). Specifically, the *Morales-Santana* Court held that unlike the statute at issue in *Nguyen* and *Miller*, the physical presence requirement being challenged in *Morales-Santana* did nothing to demonstrate the parent's tie to the child and was not a "minimal" burden on the citizen parent. *Id.* at 16. The *Morales-Santana* Court also concluded that, while the Court in *Fiallo v. Bell*, 430 U.S. 787 (1977), had applied a very deferential standard when reviewing gender-based distinctions in the context of alien admission preferences, a more "exacting standard of review" was appropriate when assessing the permissibility of such distinctions in the application of derivative citizenship statutes. *Id.* at 14–17 (describing the *Fiallo* Court's ruling as being supported by the "extremely broad power to admit or exclude aliens" and concluding that heightened scrutiny was appropriate in the review of gender-based distinctions made by a derivative citizenship statute, which did not touch upon the "entry preference for aliens" governed by *Fiallo*).

[P. 2136, after sentence ending ". . . facilities, prestige or alumni network.", add new paragraph:]

The Court in *Sessions v. Morales-Santana* applied the "exceedingly persuasive justification" test to strike down a gender-based classification found in a statute that allowed for the acquisition of U.S. citizenship by a child born abroad to an unwed couple if one of the parents was a U.S. citizen.[1129] The law at issue in *Morales-Santana,* which had been enacted many decades earlier, conditioned the grant of citizenship on the U.S. citizen parent's physical presence in the United States prior to the child's birth, providing a shorter presence requirement for an unwed U.S. citizen mother relative to the unwed U.S. citizen father.[1130] According to the majority, such a classification "must substantially serve an important government interest *today*,"[1131] and the law in question was based on "two once habitual, but now untenable, assumptions": (1) that marriage presupposes that the husband is dominant and the wife is subordinate; (2) an unwed mother is the natural and sole guardian of a non-marital child.[1132] Having found that the law was an "overbroad generalization[]" about males and females and was based on the "obsolescing view" about unwed fathers,[1133] the Court concluded that the citizenship provision's "discrete duration-of-residency requirements for unwed mothers and fathers who have accepted parental responsibility [was] stunningly anachronistic."[1134]

[1129] *See* Sessions v. Morales-Santana, 582 U.S. ___, No. 15-1191, slip op. at 2 (2017) (holding that "the gender line Congress drew is incompatible with the requirement that the Government accord to all persons 'the equal protection of the laws.'").

[1130] *Id.* at 2–3 (describing 8 U.S.C. §§ 1401 & 1409 (1958 ed.)).

[1131] *Id.* at 9 (citing Obergefell v. Hodges, 576 U.S. ___, No. 14-556, slip op. at 20 (2015)).

[1132] *Id.* at 10.

[1133] *Id.* at 13.

[1134] *Id.* at 14. In so holding, the *Morales-Santana* Court rejected the government's argument that the challenged law's gender distinction helped ensure that the child born abroad and out of wedlock to a U.S. citizen and foreign nationalwould have a strong connection with the United States. *Id.* at 17. The government's argued that an unwed alien mother, on account of being the only legally recognized parent, would have a "competing

In response to what the lower court had described as the "most vexing problem" in the case,[1135] the *Morales-Santana* Court, in crafting a remedy for the equal protection violation, deviated from the presumption that "extension, rather than nullification" of the denied benefit is generally the "proper course."[1136] The Court observed that Congress had established derivative citizenship rules that varied depending upon whether one or both parents were U.S. citizens and whether the child was born in or outside marriage.[1137] Justice Ginsburg writing for the majority concluded that extending the much-shorter physical presence requirement applicable to unwed U.S. citizen mothers to unwed U.S. citizen fathers would run significantly counter to Congress's intentions when it established this statutory scheme, because such a remedy would result in a longer physical presence requirement for a *married* U.S. citizen who had a child abroad than for a similarly situated *unmarried* U.S. citizen.[1138] As a result, the Court held that the longer physical presence requirement for unwed U.S. citizen fathers governed, as that is the remedy that "Congress likely would have chosen had it been apprised of the constitutional infirmity."[1139]

Fundamental Interests: The Political Process

Apportionment and Districting.—

[P. 2156, delete n.1921 and substitute with:]

In *Evenwel v. Abbott*, a case involving representation in the state legislature, the Court rejected the argument that the Equal Protection Clause prohibits states from using total population in determining voting districts and instead requires the use of the voting population. 578 U.S. ___, No. 14-940, slip op. (2016). The Court based its conclusion here, in part, on the debates over representation in the U.S. House and Senate at the time of the Constitution's framing, as well as subsequent debates over the Fourteenth Amendment at

---

national influence" upon the child that warranted the requirement that the U.S. father have a longer physical connection with the United States. *Id.* The Court concluded that the argument was based on the assumption that an alien father of a nonmarital child would not accept parental responsibility, a "[l]ump characterization" about gender roles that did not pass equal protection inspection. *Id.* at 18. Moreover, even assuming that an interest in ensuring a connection to the United States could support the law, the Court held that the law's gender-based means could not serve the desired end because the law allowed for an individual with no ties whatsoever to the United States to become a citizen if his U.S. citizen mother lived in the country for a year prior to his birth. *Id.* at 18–19.

The Court also rejected the government's argument that Congress wished to reduce the risk of "statelessness" for the foreign-born child of a U.S. citizen mother; an argument premised on the belief that countries are more likely to grant citizenship to the child of a citizen mother than to the child of a citizen father. *Id.* at 19. The Court noted there was little evidence that a statelessness concern prompted the physical presence requirements, *id.* at 19–20, and the Court also was skeptical that the risk of statelessness in actuality disproportionately endangered the children of unwed U.S. citizen mothers. *Id.* at 21–23.

[1135] *See* Morales-Santana v. Lynch, 804 F.3d 521, 535 (2d Cir. 2015).

[1136] *See Morales-Santana*, slip op. at 25 (quoting Califano v. Westcott, 443 U.S. 76, 89 (1979)).

[1137] *Id.* at 2–4, 26.

[1138] *Id.* at 26 ("For if [the] one-year dispensation were extended to unwed citizen fathers, would it not be irrational to retain the longer term when the U.S.-citizen parent is married?").

[1139] *Id.* at 27 (internal citations and quotations omitted).

the time of its ratification. *Id.* at 8–12. The Court also noted prior decisions focusing on "equality of representation," and not "voter equality," *id.* at 16, and the settled practices of all fifty states and "countless local jurisdictions" in apportioning representation based on total population. *Id.* at 18. It is important to note, however, that the *Evenwel* Court declined to find that apportionment based on total population is constitutionally required, and the Court has, in other cases, upheld the use of districts based on voting population. *See* Burns v. Richardson, 384 U.S. 73, 93–94 (1966) (rejecting a challenge to Hawaii's use of the registered-voter population).

[P. 2157, after n.1927, add new paragraph:]

Subsequently, in its 2016 decision in *Harris v. Arizona Independent Redistricting Commission*, the Court reiterated the significance of the 10% threshold in challenges to state legislative voting districts, observing that "attacks on deviations under 10% will succeed only rarely, in unusual cases."[1140] Instead, challengers must show that it is "more probable than not" that the deviation "reflects the predominance of illegitimate reapportionment factors rather than . . . legitimate considerations."[1141] The Court unanimously agreed that the challengers in *Harris* had failed to meet this burden, as the record supported the district court's conclusion that the deviation here—which was 8.8%—reflected the redistricting commission's efforts to achieve compliance with the Voting Rights Act, and not to secure political advantage for the Democratic party.[1142] In particular, the Court noted that the difference in population between Democratic- and Republican-leaning districts may simply reflect the residential and voting patterns of minorities, and the redistricting commission's efforts to maintain "ability-to-elect districts" (i.e., districts favorable to the election of minority candidates).[1143] In the Court's view, there was no showing of "illegitimate factors" here, unlike in certain earlier cases (e.g., the creation of districts that seem to have no relation to keeping counties whole or preserving the cores of prior districts).[1144] The Court further noted that its decision in *Shelby County v. Holder*,[1145] which held unconstitutional a section of the Voting Rights Act relevant to this case, did not mean that Arizona's attempt to comply with the Act could not have been a legitimate state interest, as Arizona created the plan at issue in 2010, and *Shelby County* was not decided until 2013.[1146]

[P. 2158, delete sentence after n.1928 and substitute with:]

Even if racial gerrymandering is intended to benefit minority voting populations, it is subject to strict scrutiny under the Equal Protection Clause[1147] if "race was the predominant factor motivating the legislature's

---

[1140] 578 U.S. ___, No. 14-232, slip op. at 5 (2016). *See also id.* (noting the "inherent difficulties" of measuring and comparing factors that may legitimately account for small deviations from strict mathematical equality).

[1141] *Id.* at 1.

[1142] *See id.* at 5–9.

[1143] *Id.* at 9–10.

[1144] *Id.* at 10.

[1145] 570 U.S. 529 (2013).

[1146] *See* 578 U.S. ___, No. 14-232, slip op. at 10 (2016).

[1147] *See* Abbott v. Perez, 138 S. Ct. 2305, 2314 (2018) ("The Equal Protection Clause

decision to place a significant number of voters within or without a particular district."[1148] A challenger can show racial predominance by "demonstrating that the legislature 'subordinated' other factors—compactness, respect for political subdivisions, partisan advantage, what have you—to 'racial considerations.'"[1149]

[P. 2158, n.1930, after sentence ending ". . . compelling government interest.", add:]

Moreover, in discussing a challenger's reliance on the "bizarreness" of a district's shape, the Court has cautioned that "[t]he Equal Protection Clause does not prohibit misshapen districts. It prohibits unjustified racial classifications." Bethune-Hill v. Va. State Bd. of Elections, 580 U.S. ___, No. 15-680, slip op. at 9 (2017) (holding that racial considerations predominated in the redrawing of twelve Virginia state legislative districts, but left it to the district court to determine whether the state succeeded in "demonstrat[ing] that its districting legislation is narrowly tailored to achieve a compelling interest").

[P. 2158, n.1931, after sentence ending ". . . (also involving congressional districts).", add:]

When a state relies on compliance with the Voting Rights Act "to justify race-based districting," however, the state "must show (to meet the 'narrow tailoring' requirement) that it had 'a strong basis in evidence' for concluding that the statute required its action." Cooper, 581 U.S. at ___, slip op. at 3 (quoting Ala. Legislative Black Caucus, 575 U.S. at 278). In other words, "the State must establish that it had 'good reasons' to think that it would transgress the Act if it did not draw race-based district lines." Id. at 3 (quoting Ala. Legislative Black Caucus, 575 U.S. at 278). See Perez, 138 S. Ct. at 2334 (rejecting Texas's claim that "it had good reasons to believe" that its use of race as a predominant factor in the design of a Texas House District "was necessary to satisfy § 2 of the Voting Rights Act," and noting "where we have accepted a State's 'good reasons' for using race in drawing district lines, the State made a strong showing of a pre-enactment analysis with justifiable conclusions" (internal quotation marks and citation omitted)). In Bethune-Hill v. Virginia State Board of Elections, the Court found that the State had established that the primary mapdrawer "discussed the district with incumbents from other majority-minority districts[,] . . . considered turnout rates, the results of the recent contested primary and general elections . . . , and the district's large population of disenfranchised black prisoners," which the Court characterized as a "functional analysis" that "achieved an informed bipartisan consensus," meeting the narrow tailoring requirement. No. 15-680, 580 U.S. ___, slip op. at 15, 14 (2017)).

[P. 2158, after n.1931, delete sentence starting "On the other hand, . . ." and substitute with:]

While the Court appeared to have weakened a challenger's ability to establish equal protection claims in the early 2000s by deferring to a legislature's articulation of legitimate political explanations for districting

---

forbids 'racial gerrymandering,' that is, intentionally assigning citizens to a district on the basis of race without sufficient justification." (quoting Shaw v. Reno, 509 U.S. 630, 641 (1993))).

[1148] Miller v. Johnson, 515 U.S. 900, 916 (1995); see also Shaw v. Hunt, 517 U.S. 899, 904–05 (1996). Furthermore, in determining whether racial criteria predominate in the drawing of a district, the Court has noted that the determination must be made with respect to a specific electoral district, as opposed to a state as an undifferentiated whole. See Ala. Legislative Black Caucus v. Alabama, 575 U.S. 254, 255 (2015)

[1149] Cooper v. Harris, 581 U.S. ___, No. 15-1262, slip op. at 2 (2017) (quoting Miller, 515 U.S. at 916).

decisions, and by allowing for a correlation between race and political affiliation,[1150] more recent cases have shown such challenges are not entirely foreclosed.[1151]

[P. 2159, delete "however, in a decision of potentially major import reminiscent of _Baker v. Carr_,"]

[PP. 2160–62, delete four paragraphs starting "Justice White's plurality opinion . . ." and substitute with:]

Following _Bandemer_'s holding that claims of partisan gerrymandering were justiciable, the Court could not reach a consensus on the proper test for adjudicating these claims, and eventually concluded that claims of unconstitutional partisan gerrymandering were nonjusticiable.[1152] First, in 2004's _Vieth v. Jubelirer_, a four-Justice plurality would have overturned _Bandemer_ and held that "political gerrymandering claims are nonjusticiable."[1153] Justice Kennedy, concurring in the Court's judgment, agreed that the challengers before the Court had not yet articulated "comprehensive and neutral principles for drawing electoral boundaries" or any rules that would properly "limit and confine judicial intervention."[1154] But he held out hope that in the future the Court could find "some limited and precise rationale" to adjudicate other partisan gerrymandering claims, leaving _Bandemer_ intact.[1155] Two years later, in _League of United Latin American Citizens v. Perry_, a splintered Court again neither adopted a standard for adjudicating political gerrymandering claims, nor overruled _Bandemer_ by deciding such claims were nonjusticiable.[1156] Ultimately, in _Rucho v. Common Cause_, issued in 2019, the Supreme Court held that there were no judicially manageable standards by which courts could adjudicate claims of unconstitutional partisan gerrymandering, implicitly overruling

---

[1150] _See_ Easley v. Cromartie, 532 U.S. 234 (2001). 532 U.S. 234, 242 (2001) ("Caution is especially appropriate in this case, where the State has articulated a legitimate political explanation for its districting decision, and the voting population is one in which race and political affiliation are highly correlated."). Nonetheless, in considering a state's legitimate reasons for a particular redistricting decision, the Court has held that legislative efforts to create districts of approximately equal population should not be weighed against the use of race to determine whether race predominates, as the "equal population" goal is a "background rule" that animates all redistricting decisions. _See Ala. Legislative Black Caucus_, slip op. at 17.

[1151] _See Cooper_, slip op. at 34 (holding that racial considerations predominated in the redrawing of two congressional districts in North Carolina and "that §2 of the [Voting Rights Act] gave North Carolina no good reason to reshuffle voters because of their race").

[1152] Rucho v. Common Cause, 588 U.S. ___, Nos. 18-422, 18-726, slip op. at 30 (2019).

[1153] 541 U.S. 267, 281 (2004).

[1154] _Id._ at 306–07.

[1155] _Id._ at 306.

[1156] 548 U.S. 399, 414 (2006) (declining to "revisit [_Bandemer's_] justiciability holding"); _see also id._ at 417 (Kennedy, J.) (rejecting proposed test for adjudicating partisan gerrymandering claims); _id._ at 492 (Roberts, J., concurring in part) (agreeing that proposed test was not a reliable standard for adjudicating partisan gerrymandering claims); _id._ at 512 (Scalia, J., dissenting) (arguing that claims of unconstitutional partisan gerrymandering are nonjusticiable).

Bandemer's conclusion that such claims were justiciable under the Equal Protection Clause.[1157]

[P. 2162, delete "It had been thought that the use of multimember districts to submerge racial, ethnic, and political minorities might be treated differently" and substitute with:]

In another line of cases, courts suggested that challenges to multimember districts that allegedly minimize or cancel out the votes of racial and political minorities might be justiciable under the Equal Protection Clause,[1158]

[P. 2164, after sentence ending ". . . defeats preferred candidates of the minority.", add new footnote:]

With regard to the interplay between the demands of the Equal Protection Clause and the Voting Rights Act (VRA), the Court recently explained:

> Since the Equal Protection Clause restricts consideration of race and the VRA demands consideration of race, a legislature attempting to produce a lawful districting plan is vulnerable to "competing hazards of liability." In an effort to harmonize these conflicting demands, we have assumed that compliance with the VRA may justify the consideration of race in a way that would not otherwise be allowed. In technical terms, we have assumed that complying with the VRA is a compelling state interest, and that a State's consideration of race in making a districting decision is narrowly tailored and thus satisfies strict scrutiny if the State has 'good reasons' for believing that its decision is necessary in order to comply with the VRA.

Abbott v. Perez, 138 S. Ct. 2305, 2315 (2018) (quoting Bush v. Vera, 517 U.S. 952, 977 (1996) (plurality opinion); Cooper v. Harris, , 581 U.S. ___, No. 15-1262, slip op. at 3 (2017)) (citing Bethune-Hill v. Va. State Bd. of Elections, 580 U.S. ___, No. 15-680, slip op. at 13 (2017); Shaw v. Hunt, 517 U.S. 899, 915 (1996)). The Court further clarified that, under *Thornburg v. Gingles*, "[t]o make out a § 2 'effects' claim [under the VRA], a plaintiff must establish the three so-called 'Gingles factors.' These are (1) a geographically compact minority population sufficient to constitute a majority in a single-member district, (2) political cohesion among the members of the minority group, and (3) bloc voting by the majority to defeat the minority's preferred candidate." *Id.* at 2330–31 (citing *Gingles*, 478 U.S. at 48–51).

[P. 2164, n.1965, after "*E.g.*," add:]

North Carolina v. Covington, 585 U.S. ___, No. 17-1364, slip op. at 9–10 (2018) (per curiam) ("The District Court's decision to override the legislature's remedial map on that basis was clear error. '[S]tate legislatures have primary jurisdiction over legislative reapportionment,' and a legislature's 'freedom of choice to devise substitutes for an apportionment plan found unconstitutional, either as a whole or in part, should not be restricted beyond the clear commands' of federal law. A district court is 'not free . . . to disregard the political program of' a state legislature on other bases." (quoting White v. Weiser, 412 U.S. 783, 795 (1973); Burns v. Richardson, 384 U.S. 73, 85 (1966); Upham v. Seamon, 456 U.S. 37, 43 (1982) (per curiam)));

[1157] 588 U.S. ___, Nos. 18-422, 18-726, slip op. at 30 (2019).

[1158] *See* Kilgarlin v. Hill, 386 U.S. 120, 125 n.3 (1967); Burns v. Richardson, 384 U.S. 73, 88–89 (1966); Fortson v. Dorsey, 379 U.S. 433, 439 (1965).

Sexual Orientation

[P. 2172, at end of section, add new paragraphs:]

In *United States v. Windsor*,[1159] the Court struck down Section 3 of the Defense of Marriage Act (DOMA), which provided that for purposes of any federal act, ruling, regulation, or interpretation by an administrative agency, the word "spouse" would mean a person of the opposite sex who is a husband or a wife.[1160] In *Windsor*, the petitioner had been married to her same-sex partner in Canada and she lived in New York, where the marriage was recognized. After her partner died, the petitioner sought to claim a federal estate tax exemption for surviving spouses.[1161] In examining the federal statute, the Court initially noted that, while "[b]y history and tradition the definition and regulation of marriage . . . has been treated as being within the authority and realm of the separate States,"[1162] Section 3 of DOMA took the "unusual" step of departing from the "history and tradition of reliance on state law to define marriage" in order to alter the reach of over 1,000 federal laws and limit the scope of federal benefits.[1163] Citing to *Romer*, the Court noted that discrimination of "unusual character" warranted more careful scrutiny.[1164] In approving of same-sex marriages, the State of New York was conferring a "dignity and status of immense import,"[1165] and the federal government, with Section 3 of DOMA, was aiming to impose "restrictions and disabilities" on and "injure the very class" New York sought to protect.[1166] In so doing, the Court concluded that Section 3 of DOMA was motivated by improper animus or purpose because the law's avowed "purpose and practical" effect was to "impose a . . . stigma upon all who enter into same- sex marriages made lawful" by the states.[1167] Holding that "no legitimate purpose overcomes the purpose and effect to disparage and injure those whom the State, by its marriage laws, sought to protect in personhood and dignity,"[1168] the Court held that Section 3 of DOMA violates "basic due process and equal protection principles applicable to the Federal Government."[1169] In striking down Section 3, the Court did not expressly set out what test the government must meet to

---

[1159] 570 U.S. 744 (2013).

[1160] Defense of Marriage Act, Pub. L. No. 104-199, § 3, 110 Stat. 2419 (2006) (codified at 1 U.S.C. §7.)

[1161] Section 3 also provided that "marriage" would mean only a legal union between one man and one woman.

[1162] *Windsor*, 570 U.S. at 763–66.

[1163] *Id.* at 767–69.

[1164] *Id.* at 768 (citing Romer v. Evans, 517 U.S. 620, 633 (1996)).

[1165] *Id.* at 768.

[1166] *Id.* at 769–70.

[1167] *Id.* at 770–71.

[1168] *Id.* at 774–75.

[1169] *Id.* at 769. Because the case was decided under the Due Process Clause of the Fifth Amendment, which comprehends both substantive due process and equal protection principles (as incorporated through the Fourteenth Amendment), this statement leaves unclear precisely how each of these doctrines bears on the presented issue.

justify laws calling for differentiated treatment based on sexual orientation.

Two years after *Windsor,* the Court, in *Obergefell v. Hodges,* invalidated several state laws limiting the licensing and recognition of marriage to two people of the opposite sex.[1170] While the decision primarily rested on substantive due process grounds,[1171] the Court noted that the "right of same sex couples to marry" is "derived, too," from the Fourteenth Amendment's Equal Protection Clause.[1172] In so holding, the Court recognized a general "synergy" between the Due Process Clause and the Equal Protection Clause, noting that just as evolving societal norms inform the liberty rights of same-sex couples, so too do "new insights and societal understandings" about homosexuality reveal "unjustified inequality" with respect to traditional concepts about the institution of marriage.[1173] In this sense, the Court viewed marriage laws prohibiting the licensing and recognition of same-sex marriages as working a grave and continuing harm to same-sex couples, serving to "disrespect and subordinate them."[1174] As a result, the Court ruled that the Equal Protection Clause prevents states from excluding same-sex couples from civil marriage on the same terms and conditions as opposite-sex couples.[1175]

Section 5. Enforcement

ENFORCEMENT

Congressional Definition of Fourteenth Amendment Rights

[PP. 2195–96, delete n.2127 and substitute with:]

527 U.S. at 639–46; *see also* Allen v. Cooper, 140 S. Ct. 994, 1005–07 (2020) (holding that evidence of unconstitutional state-copyright infringement was not materially different than the record for state-patent infringement at issue in *Florida Prepaid*); *cf.* Coll. Sav. Bank v. Fla. Prepaid Postsecondary Educ. Expense Bd., 527 U.S. 666, 673–75 (1999) (concluding that Congress, by subjecting states to suits for false advertisement, exceeded its powers under the Fourteenth Amendment because the statute did not implicate property interests protected by the Due Process Clause).

[1170] *See* 576 U.S. ___, No. 14-556, slip op. at 2, 28 (2015).

[1171] *Id.* at 10–19.

[1172] *Id.* at 19.

[1173] *Id.* at 19–21.

[1174] *Id.* at 22.

[1175] *Id.* at 23. Interestingly, however, the *Obergefell* Court did not engage in any traditional equal protection analysis in which a government's classification is adjudged based on the nature of the classification and the relationship between the classification and the underlying justifications for the government policy. Instead the *Obergefell* Court concluded that state classifications distinguishing between opposite- and same-sex couples violated equal protection principles on their face and therefore were unconstitutional. *Id.* at 21–22; *see also supra* Equal Protection of the Laws: Equal Protection: Judging Classifications by Law: The New Standards: Active Review.

[P. 2199, delete "However, as Justice Rehnquist . . ." through n.2148.]

FIFTEENTH AMENDMENT

Sections 1 and 2. Right of Citizens to Vote

ABOLITION OF SUFFRAGE QUALIFICATIONS ON BASIS OF RACE

Adoption and Judicial Enforcement

Racial Gerrymandering.—

[PP. 2207–08, delete sentence starting "Congressional amendment of § 2 . . ."]

Congressional Enforcement

Federal Remedial Legislation.—

[P. 2212, after first paragraph, delete remaining paragraphs in section and substitute with:]

But, it was in upholding the constitutionality of the 1965 Act in *South Carolina v. Katzenbach* that the Court sketched the outlines of a broad power in Congress to enforce the Fifteenth Amendment.[1176] Although Section 1 authorized the courts to strike down state statutes and procedures that denied the vote on the basis of race, the Court held Section 2 authorized Congress to go beyond proscribing certain discriminatory statutes and practices to "enforce" the guarantee by any rational means at its disposal.[1177] Congress was therefore justified in deciding that certain areas of the nation were the primary locations of voting discrimination and in directing its remedial legislation to those areas.[1178] The Court concluded that Congress chose a rational formula based on the existence of voting tests that could be used to discriminate and on low registration or voting rates, which demonstrated the likelihood that the tests had been so used; that Congress could properly suspend for a period all literacy tests in the affected areas upon findings that they had been administered discriminatorily and that illiterate whites had been registered while both literate and illiterate African-Americans had not been; and that Congress could require the states to seek federal permission to reinstitute old tests or institute new ones; and it could provide for federal examiners to register qualified voters.[1179] The *Katzenbach* decision appeared to afford Congress discretion to enact measures designed to enforce the Amendment through broad affirmative prescriptions rather than through proscriptions of specific practices.[1180] Subsequent decisions of the Burger Court confirmed

---

[1176] 383 U.S. 301 (1966).

[1177] *Id.* at 325–26.

[1178] *Id.* at 331.

[1179] *Id.* at 333–37.

[1180] Justice Black dissented from the portion of the decision that upheld the requirement that before a state could change its voting laws it must seek approval of the Attorney General

the reach of this power. In one case, the Court held that evidence of past discrimination in the educational opportunities available to African-American children precluded a North Carolina county from reinstituting a literacy test.[1181] And, in 1970, when Congress suspended for a five-year period literacy tests throughout the nation,[1182] the Court unanimously sustained the action as a valid measure to enforce the Fifteenth Amendment.[1183] Moreover, in *City of Rome v. United States*,[1184] the Court read the scope of Congress's remedial powers under Section 2 of the Fifteenth Amendment to parallel similar reasoning under Section 5 of the Fourteenth Amendment. In *City of Rome*, the City had sought to escape from coverage of the Voting Rights Act by showing that it had not utilized any discriminatory practices within the prescribed period.[1185] The lower court found that the City had engaged in practices without any discriminatory motive, but that its practices had had a discriminatory impact.[1186] The City thus argued that, because the Fifteenth Amendment reached only purposeful discrimination, the Act's proscription of effect, as well as of purpose, went beyond Congress's power.[1187] The Court held, however, that, even if discriminatory intent was a prerequisite to finding a violation of Section 1 of the Fifteenth Amendment,[1188] Congress still had authority to proscribe electoral devices that had the effect of discriminating.[1189] The Court held that Section 2, like Section 5 of the Fourteenth Amendment, was in effect a "Necessary and Proper Clause," which enabled Congress to enact enforcement legislation that was rationally related to the end sought, and that section 2 of the Fifteenth Amendment did not prohibit such legislation since the legislation was consistent with the letter and spirit of the Constitution, even though the actual practice, which the legislation outlawed or restricted, would not, in itself, violate the Fifteenth Amendment.[1190] In so acting, Congress could prohibit state action that perpetuated the effect of past discrimination, or that, because of the existence of past purposeful discrimination, raised a risk of purposeful discrimination that might not lend itself to judicial invalidation.[1191]

The Court stated:

> It is clear, then, that under § 2 of the Fifteenth Amendment Congress may prohibit practices that in and of themselves do not violate § 1 of the Amendment, so long as the prohibitions attacking racial discrimination in voting are "appropriate," as

---

or a federal court. *Id.* at 355 (Black, J., dissenting).

[1181] Gaston Cty. v. United States, 395 U.S. 285 (1969).

[1182] 84 Stat. 315, 42 U.S.C. § 1973aa (transferred to 52 U.S.C. § 10501 (2012)).

[1183] Oregon v. Mitchell, 400 U.S. 112, 131–34, 144–47, 216–17, 231–36, 282–84 (1970).

[1184] 446 U.S. 156 (1980).

[1185] *Id.* at 172.

[1186] *Id.*

[1187] *Id.* at 173.

[1188] *Cf.* City of Mobile v. Bolden, 446 U.S. 55, 60–61 (1980).

[1189] *See City of Rome*, 446 U.S. at 173.

[1190] *Id.* at 174–77.

[1191] *Id.* at 175–76.

that term is defined in *McCulloch v. Maryland* and *Ex parte Virginia* . . . . Congress could rationally have concluded that, because electoral changes by jurisdictions with a demonstrable history of intentional racial discrimination in voting create the risk of purposeful discrimination, it was proper to prohibit changes that have a discriminatory impact.[1192]

In 1975 and 1982, Congress extended and revised the Voting Rights Act.[1193] Congress used the 1982 Amendments to revitalize Section 2 of the Act, which, unlike Section 5, applies nationwide.[1194] As enacted in 1965, Section 2 largely tracked the language of the Fifteenth Amendment. In *City of Mobile v. Bolden*,[1195] a majority of the Court agreed that the Fifteenth Amendment and Section 2 of the Act were coextensive, but the Justices did not agree on the meaning to be ascribed to the statute. A plurality believed that, because the constitutional provision reached only purposeful discrimination, Section 2 was similarly limited. A major purpose of Congress in 1982 had been to set aside this possible interpretation and to provide that any electoral practice "which results in a denial or abridgement" of the right to vote on account of race or color will

---

[1192] City of Rome v. United States, 446 U.S. 156, 177 (1980). In *Lopez v. Monterey Cty.*, 525 U.S. 266 (1999), the Court reiterated its prior holdings that Congress may exercise its enforcement power based on discriminatory effects, and without any finding of discriminatory intent.

[1193] The 1975 amendments, Pub. L. No. 94-73, 89 Stat. 400, extended the Act for seven years; expanded it to include those areas having minorities distinguished by their language, i.e., "persons who are American Indian, Asian American, Alaskan Natives or of Spanish heritage," *id.* at § 207, in which certain statistical tests are met; and required election materials to be provided in an alternative language if more than five percent of the voting age citizens of a political subdivision are members of a single language minority group whose illiteracy rate is higher than the national rate. *Id.* at § 301. The 1982 amendments, Pub. L. No. 97-205, 96 Stat. 131, in addition to the Section 2 revision, provided that a covered jurisdiction may remove itself from the Act's coverage by proving to the special court in the District of Columbia that the jurisdiction has complied with the Act for the previous ten years and that it has taken positive steps both to encourage minority political participation and to remove structural barriers to minority electoral influence. *Id.* at § 2. Moreover, the 1982 amendments changed the result in *Beer v. United States*, 425 U.S. 130 (1976), in which the Court had held that a covered jurisdiction was precluded from altering a voting practice covered by the Act only if the change would lead to a retrogression in the position of racial minorities; if a change in voting practice merely perpetuated a practice that was not covered by the Voting Rights Act because it was enacted prior to November 1964, the jurisdiction could implement it. The 1982 amendments provide that the change may not be approved if it would "perpetuate voting discrimination," in effect applying the new Section 2 results test to preclearance procedures. S. REP. NO. 97-417, at 12 (1982); H.R. REP. NO. 97-227, at 28 (1981).

[1194] Private parties may bring suit to challenge electoral practices under Section 2.

[1195] 446 U.S. 55 (1980). *See id.* at 60–61 (Burger, C.J., Stewart, Powell, Rehnquist, JJ.), and *id.* at 105 n.2 (Marshall, J. dissenting).

violate the Act.[1196] The Court in *Shelby County v. Holder*,[1197] however, emphasized the limits to the enforcement power of the Fifteenth Amendment in striking down Section 4 of the Act, which provided the formula that determined which states or electoral districts are required to submit electoral changes to the Department of Justice or a federal court for preclearance under Section 5 of the Act. In 2006, Congress had reauthorized the Act for twenty-five years and provided that the preclearance requirement extended to jurisdictions that had a voting test and less than fifty percent voter registration or turnout as of 1972.[1198] In *Shelby County*, the Court described the Section 5 preclearance process as an "extraordinary departure from the traditional course of relations between the States and the Federal Government"[1199] and as "extraordinary legislation otherwise unfamiliar to our federal system."[1200] This led the Court to find the formula in Section 4 violated the "fundamental principle of equal sovereignty" among states because the section, by definition, applied to only some states and not others.[1201] While the Court acknowledged that the disparate treatment of states under Section 4 could be justified by "unique circumstances," such as those before Congress at the time of enactment of the Voting Rights Act,[1202] the Court held that Congress could no longer "distinguish between States in such a fundamental way based on fourty-year-old-data, when today's statistics tell an entirely different story" with respect to racial discrimination in covered jurisdictions.[1203] The Court added, however, that Congress could "draft another formula [for pre-clearance] based on current conditions"

[1196] Before the 1982 amendments, Section 2 provided that "[n]o voting qualification or prerequisite to voting, or standard, practice, or procedure shall be imposed or applied by any State or political subdivision to deny or abridge the right of any citizen of the United States to vote on account of race or color." Pub. L. No. 89-110, § 2, 79 Stat. 437. Section 3 of the 1982 amendments amended Section 2 of the Act by inserting the language quoted and by setting out a nonexclusive list of factors making up a "totality of circumstances test" by which a violation of Section 2 would be determined. 96 Stat. 131, 134, amending 42 U.S. § 1973. Without any discussion of the Fifteenth Amendment, the Court in *Thornburg v. Gingles*, 478 U.S. 30 (1986), interpreted and applied the "totality of the circumstances" test in the context of multimember districting. *Id.* at 80.

[1197] 570 U.S. 529 (2013).

[1198] Fannie Lou Hamer, Rosa Parks, and Coretta Scott King Voting Rights Act Reauthorization and Amendments Act, Pub. L. No. 109-246, 120 Stat. 577 (2006).

[1199] *Shelby County*, 570 U.S. at 545–46.

[1200] *Id.* (citation omitted).

[1201] *Id.* at 542 (quoting Nw. Austin Mun. Util. Dist. No. One v. Holder, 557 U.S. 193, 203 (2009)).The significance of the principle of equal sovereignty as enunciated in *Coyle v. Smith* had been considered by the Court in a previous challenge to the Act. *See* South Carolina v. Katzenbach, 383 U.S. 301, 328–29 (1966) . Considering the disparate treatment of states under the Section 5 preclearance requirement, the *Katzenbach* Court had referenced the case of *Coyle v. Smith*, 221 U.S. 559 (1911), which upheld the authority of Oklahoma to move its state capitol despite language to the contrary in the enabling act providing for its admission as a state. This case, while based on the theory that the United States "was and is a union of States, equal in power, dignity and authority," 221 U.S. at 580, was distinguished by the Court in *Katzenbach* as concerning only the admission of new states and not remedies for actions occurring subsequent to that event. The Court in *Shelby County* held, however, that a broader principle regarding equal sovereignty "remains highly pertinent in assessing subsequent disparate treatment of States." *Shelby County*, 570 U.S. at 544 (citing *Nw. Austin*, 557 U.S. at 203).

[1202] *Id.* at 545–46 (quoting *Katzenbach*, 383 U.S. at 334, 335).

[1203] *Id.* at 546–47, 556.

that demonstrate "that exceptional conditions still exist justifying such an 'exceptional departure from the traditional course of relations between the States and the Federal Government.'"[1204]

[1204] *Id.* at 545 (quoting Presley v. Etowah Cty. Comm'n, 502 U.S. 491, 500–01 (1992)).

TWENTY-FIRST AMENDMENT

REPEAL OF THE EIGHTEENTH AMENDMENT

Scope of Regulatory Power Conferred upon the States

Discrimination Between Domestic and Imported Products.—

[P. 2245, delete subheading "Discrimination Between Domestic and Imported Products.—" and substitute with:]

Discrimination Against Interstate Commerce.—

[P. 2245, before n.1, delete period and substitute with comma and after n.1, add:]

also known as the dormant Commerce Clause.[1205]

[P. 2247, delete n.13 and substitute with:]

Bacchus Imports, Ltd. v. Dias, 468 U.S. 263, 276 (1984). *See also, e.g.,* Capital Cities Cable, Inc. v. Crisp, 467 U.S. 691, 713 (1984) ("In rejecting the claim that the Twenty-first Amendment ousted the Federal Government of all jurisdiction over interstate traffic in liquor, we have held that when a State has not attempted directly to regulate the sale or use of liquor within its borders—the core § 2 power—a conflicting exercise of federal authority may prevail.").

[P. 2247, after sentence ending ". . . the Court stated in 2005.", add new footnote:]

Granholm v. Heald, 544 U.S. 460, 487 (2005). *See also* Bacchus Imports, Ltd. v. Dias, 468 U.S. 263, 276 (1984) (invalidating tax that discriminated in favor of specific locally produced products); Healy v. The Beer Institute, 491 U.S. 324, 343 (1989) (invalidating "price affirmation" statute requiring out-of-state brewers and beer importers to affirm that their prices are not higher than prices charged in border states); Brown-Forman Distillers Corp. v. N.Y. State Liquor Auth., 476 U.S. 573, 585 (1986) (invalidating "price affirmation" statute requiring distillers or agents who sell to in-state wholesalers to affirm that their prices would not be higher than prices elsewhere in the United States).

[P. 2248, at end of n.15, add:]

Accord Tenn. Wine and Spirits Retailers Ass'n v. Thomas, 588 U.S. ___, No. 18-96, slip op. at 21 (2019). However, in *Tennessee Wine,* the Court rejected the suggestion that a law should be deemed constitutional under the Twenty-first Amendment merely because it—or a similar law—predated Prohibition. *Id.* at 30. The Court clarified that pre-Prohibition laws that were "never tested" in the Supreme Court could have been held invalid then and, consequently, might remain invalid in modern times. *Id.*

[1205] *See, e.g.,* Tenn. Wine and Spirits Retailers Ass'n. v. Thomas, 588 U.S. ___, No. 18-96, slip op. at 15 (2019).

[P. 2248, after n.15, add new paragraphs:]

Consequently, in *Granholm v. Heald*, the Supreme Court struck down regulatory schemes employed by Michigan and New York that discriminated against out-of-state wineries.[1206] Both states employed a "three-tier system," in which producers, wholesalers, and retailers had to be separately licensed by the state.[1207] The Court first affirmed its prior cases holding that as a general matter, "States can mandate a three-tier distribution scheme in the exercise of their authority under the Twenty-first Amendment."[1208] But within their three-tier systems, Michigan and New York gave certain advantages to in-state wineries by creating special licensing systems allowing them to directly ship wine to in-state consumers.[1209] While recognizing that both states did have significant authority to regulate the importation and sale of liquor, the Court said that the challenged systems "involve[d] straightforward attempts to discriminate in favor of local producers . . . contrary to the Commerce Clause," and that these schemes could not be "saved by the Twenty-first Amendment."[1210]

The states argued in *Granholm* that their restrictions on direct shipments by out-of-state wineries passed muster under dormant Commerce Clause principles because they advanced two legitimate local purposes: "keeping alcohol out of the hands of minors and facilitating tax collection."[1211] The Supreme Court rejected these claims, concluding that there was insufficient evidence to show that prohibiting direct shipments would solve either of these problems.[1212] The Court also suggested that the states could achieve "their regulatory objectives . . . without discriminating against interstate commerce."[1213]

The Court struck down another discriminatory regulation in *Tennessee Wine and Spirits Retailers Association v. Thomas*.[1214] In that case, the Court considered specific aspects of Tennessee's three-tier system.[1215] In particular, Tennessee would only issue new retail licenses to individuals who had been residents of the state for the previous two years.[1216] In defense of the law, a trade association representing Tennessee liquor stores argued that the case was not governed by

---

[1206] 544 U.S. 460, 493 (2005).

[1207] *Id.* at 466–67.

[1208] *Id.* at 466 (discussing North Dakota v. United States, 495 U.S. 423, 444 (1990) (plurality opinion); *id.* at 444 (Scalia, J., concurring)).

[1209] *Id.* at 469–70.

[1210] *Id.* at 489.

[1211] *Id.*

[1212] *Id.* at 490–91.

[1213] *Id.* at 491.

[1214] 588 U.S. ___, No. 18-96, slip op. at 36 (2019).

[1215] *Id.* at 2.

[1216] *Id.* at 3. Some additional aspects of Tennessee's regulatory scheme had been invalidated by the lower courts, and the state did not defend those provisions on appeal to the Supreme Court. *Id.* at 1.

Granholm.[1217] In its view, *Granholm*'s analysis was limited to laws that discriminate against out-of-state products and producers, whereas Tennessee's provision concerned "the licensing of domestic retail alcohol stores."[1218] The Court disagreed, explaining that instead, *Granholm* established that the Constitution "prohibits state discrimination against all 'out-of-state economic *interests.*'"[1219]

Ultimately, the Court concluded in *Tennessee Wine* that the challenged law was unconstitutional because its predominant effect was protectionism, saying that the law had "at best a highly attenuated relationship to public health or safety."[1220] The trade association argued that the provision was justified because it made retailers "amenable to the direct process of state courts," allowed the state "to determine an applicant's fitness to sell alcohol," and "promote[d] responsible alcohol consumption."[1221] But in the Court's view, there was no "'concrete evidence' showing that the 2-year residency requirement actually promotes public health or safety; nor [was] there evidence that nondiscriminatory alternatives would be insufficient to further those interests."[1222]

Regulation of Transportation and "Through" Shipments.—

[P. 2248, delete subheading "Regulation of Transportation and 'Through' Shipments.—"]

Foreign Imports, Exports; Taxation, Regulation.—

[P. 2249, delete subheading "Foreign Imports, Exports; Taxation, Regulation.—" and substitute with:]

[1217] *Id.* at 26.

[1218] *Id.*

[1219] *Id.* at 27 (quoting Granholm v. Heald, 544 U.S. 460, 472 (2005)). The Court also characterized the association's reading of the Twenty-first Amendment as "implausible." *Id.* While the association conceded that § 2 of the Twenty-first Amendment could not shield discriminatory laws that address the importation of alcohol, it argued that § 2 authorized its discriminatory law regarding licensing domestic stores. *Id.* The Court noted that the Twenty-first Amendment specifically prohibits the "importation" of alcohol into a state in violation of that state's laws, but does not literally address states' ability to license domestic retailers. *Id.* The majority argued that "if § 2 granted States the power to discriminate in the field of alcohol regulation, that power would be at its apex when it comes to regulating the activity to which the provision expressly refers." *Id.* at 26–27. But because § 2 did *not* shield importation laws from analysis under the dormant Commerce Clause, the Court reasoned that it would be odd for the provision to nonetheless protect other types of discriminatory regulations. *Id.*

[1220] *Id.* at 33.

[1221] *Id.* at 33–35.

[1222] *Id.* at 33.

AMENDMENT 21—REPEAL OF EIGHTEENTH AMENDMENT

Imports, Exports, and Foreign Commerce.—

[P. 2250, delete sentence starting, "Similarly, a state 'affirmation law' . . .":]

ACTS OF CONGRESS HELD UNCONSTITUTIONAL IN WHOLE OR IN PART BY THE SUPREME COURT OF THE UNITED STATES

[This entry should follow #75 in the main volume:]

___ Act of October 14, 1940 (Pub. L. No. 76-853, § 205, 54 Stat. 1169–70), later recodified by Act of June 27, 1952 (Pub. L. No. 82-414, § 309, 66 Stat. 238–39) at 8 U.S.C. § 1409(c)

Section 1409(c) of the Immigration and National Act, which required children born abroad to an unwed citizen father and a non-citizen mother to demonstrate that the citizen father was physically present in the United States for longer time period than if the child was born to a citizen mother and non-citizen father, is incompatible with the equal protection component of the Fifth Amendment's Due Process Clause.

Sessions v. Morales-Santana, 582 U.S. ___, No. 15-1191, slip op. (2017).
Justices concurring: Roberts, C.J., Kennedy, Ginsburg, Breyer, Sotomayor, Kagan
Justices concurring in judgment in part: Thomas, Alito

[This entry should follow #77 in the main volume:]

___ Act of July 5, 1946 (Pub. L. No. 79-489, § 2(a), 60 Stat. 428)

A provision of the Lanham Act prohibiting the registration of trademarks that may "disparage . . . or bring . . . into contemp[t] or disrepute" any "persons, living or dead" is facially unconstitutional under the First Amendment's Free Speech Clause.

Matal v. Tam, 582 U.S. ___, No. 15-1293, slip op. (2017).
Justices concurring in the judgment: Roberts, C.J., Kennedy, Thomas, Ginsburg, Breyer, Alito, Sotomayor, Kagan

___ Act of July 5, 1946 (Pub. L. No. 79-489, § 2(a), 60 Stat. 428)

A provision of the Lanham Act prohibiting the registration of trademarks that "consist[] of or comprise[] immoral . . . or scandalous matter" is facially unconstitutional under the First Amendment's Free Speech Clause.

Iancu v. Brunetti, 588 U.S. ___, No. 18-302, slip op. (2019).
Justices concurring: Kagan, Thomas, Ginsburg, Alito, Gorsuch, Kavanaugh
Justices concurring in part and dissenting in part: Roberts, C.J., Breyer, Sotomayor

[This entry should follow #109 in the main volume:]

___ Act of August 6, 1965 (Pub. L. No. 89-110, § 4(b), 79 Stat. 438, 42 U.S.C. § 1973(b))

Section 4 of the Voting Rights Act of 1965, which provides the formula for determining the states or electoral districts that are required to submit electoral changes to the Department of Justice or a federal court for preclearance approval under Section 5 of the Act, exceeds Congress's enforcement power under the Fifteenth Amendment by violating the "fundamental principle of equal sovereignty" among states without sufficient justification.

> *Shelby Cty. v. Holder*, 570 U.S. 529 (2013).
> Justices concurring: Roberts, C.J., Scalia, Kennedy, Thomas, Alito
> Justices dissenting: Ginsburg, Breyer, Sotomayor, Kagan

[This entry should follow #135 in the main volume:]

___ Act of October 12, 1984 (Pub. L. No. 98-473, § 1001(a), 98 Stat. 2136, 18 U.S.C. § 16(b))

The residual clause of the provision of the federal criminal code that defines the term "crime of violence" violates the Due Process Clause of the Fifth Amendment as being void for vagueness.

> *Sessions v. Dimaya*, 584 U.S. ___, No. 15-1498, slip op. at 5 (2018).
> Justices concurring: Kagan, Ginsburg, Breyer, Sotomayor, Gorsuch

[This entry should follow #138 in the main volume:]

___ Act of May 19, 1986 (Pub. L. No. 99-308, § 104(a)(1), 100 Stat. 457, 18 U.S.C. § 924(c)(3))

A residual clause in the "Firearms Owners' Protection Act" that defines the term "crime of violence" violates the Due Process Clause of the Fifth Amendment as being void for vagueness.

> *United States v. Davis*, 588 U.S. ___, No. 18-431, slip op. at 24 (2019).
> Justices concurring: Gorsuch, Ginsburg, Breyer, Sotomayor, Kagan
> Justices dissenting: Kavanaugh, Roberts, C.J., Thomas, Alito

[This entry should follow #139 in the main volume:]

___ Act of October 27, 1986 (Pub. L. No. 99-570, § 1401, 100 Stat. 3207, 3207–40, 18 U.S.C. § 924(e)(2)(B)(ii))

Imposing an increased sentence under the residual clause of the Armed Career Criminal Act violates the Due Process Clause of the Fifth Amendment as being void for vagueness.

> *Johnson v. United States*, 576 U.S. ___, No. 13-7120, slip op. (2015).
> Justices concurring: Roberts, C.J., Scalia, Ginsburg, Breyer, Sotomayor, Kagan
> Justices concurring in judgment only: Kennedy, Thomas
> Justice dissenting: Alito

[This entry should follow #147 in the main volume:]

___ Act of November 15, 1990 (Pub. L. No. 101-553, § 2, 104 Stat. 2749–50, 17 U.S.C. § 511(a))

The Copyright Remedy Clarification Act of 1990, which purported to abrogate state sovereign immunity in copyright infringement cases, exceeds Congress's powers under either the Intellectual Property Clause of Article I, Section 8 or Section 5 of the Fourteenth Amendment.

> *Allen v. Cooper*, 140 S. Ct. 994 (2020).
> Justices concurring: Roberts, C.J., Alito, Sotomayor, Kagan, Gorsuch, Kavanaugh
> Justices concurring in the judgment: Thomas, Ginsburg, Breyer

[This entry should follow #149 in the main volume:]

___ Act of November 29, 1990 (Pub. L. No. 101-647, § 2521, 104 Stat. 4844, 18 U.S.C. § 1345(a)(2))

Allowing a pretrial freeze of legitimate, untainted assets violates a criminal defendant's Sixth Amendment right to counsel of choice.

> *Luis v. United States,* 578 U.S. ___, No. 14-419, slip op. (2016).
> Justices concurring: Roberts, C.J., Ginsburg, Breyer, Sotomayor
> Justice concurring in judgment only: Thomas
> Justices dissenting: Kennedy, Alito, Kagan

[This entry should follow #153 in the main volume:]

___ Act of October 28, 1992 (Pub. L. No. 101-559, § 3792, 106 Stat. 4227, 28 U.S.C.S. § 3702(1))

Federal law prohibiting states from authorizing sports gambling schemes violates the anticommandeering rule, which prohibits Congress from issuing orders directly to the states.

> *Murphy v. NCAA,* 584 U.S. ___, No. 16-476, slip op. (2018).
> Justices concurring: Roberts, C.J., Kennedy, Thomas, Alito, Kagan, Gorsuch
> Justices dissenting: Ginsburg, Breyer, Sotomayor

[This entry should follow #162 in the main volume:]

___ Act of September 21, 1996 (Pub. L. No. 104-199, § 2(a), 110 Stat. 2419, 1 U.S.C. § 7)

Section 3 of the Defense of Marriage Act (DOMA), which provides that—for purposes of any federal act, ruling, regulation, or interpretation by an administrative agency—the word "spouse" is defined as a person of the opposite sex who is a husband or a wife, was "motivated by improper animus or purpose" to disparage and injure those whom a state, by its marriage laws, "sought to protect in personhood and dignity," amounting to a deprivation of the equal liberty of persons that is protected by the Fifth Amendment.

> *United States v. Windsor*, 570 U.S. 744 (2013).
> Justices concurring: Kennedy, Ginsburg, Breyer, Sotomayor, Kagan
> Justices dissenting: Roberts, C.J., Scalia, Thomas, Alito

[This entry should follow #168 in the main volume:]

___ Act of March 27, 2002 (Pub. L. 107-155, § 307(b), 116 Stat. 102, 2 U.S.C. § 441a(a)(3))

Aggregate limits on the amount of money individuals are allowed to contribute to candidates, political action committees, national party committees, and state or local party committees violate the First Amendment by restricting participation in the political process without furthering the government's interest in preventing quid pro quo corruption or the appearance thereof.

> *McCutcheon v. FEC*, 572 U.S. 185 (2014).
> Justices concurring: Roberts, C.J., Scalia, Kennedy, Alito
> Justice concurring in judgment only: Thomas
> Justices dissenting: Ginsburg, Breyer, Sotomayor, Kagan

[This entry should follow #169 in the main volume:]

___ Act of September 30, 2002 (Pub. L. No. 107-228, § 214(d), 116 Stat. 1350)

Section 214(d) of the Foreign Relations Authorization Act, FY2003—which states that, "[f]or purposes of the registration of birth, certification of nationality, or issuance of a passport of a United States citizen born in the city of Jerusalem, the Secretary [of State] shall, upon the request of the citizen or the citizen's legal guardian, record the place of birth as Israel"— is unconstitutional because it forces the Executive to contradict a prior recognition decision made pursuant to the President's exclusive power under Article II, Section 3, to recognize foreign sovereigns.

> *Zivotofsky v. Kerry*, 576 U.S. ___, No. 13-628, slip op. (2014).
> Justices concurring: Kennedy, Ginsburg, Breyer, Sotomayor, Kagan
> Justice concurring in part, and dissenting in part: Thomas
> Justices dissenting: Roberts, C.J., Scalia, Alito

[This entry should follow #171 in the main volume:]

___ Act of May 27, 2003 (Pub. L. No. 108-25, Title III, § 301(f), 117 Stat. 711, 734, 22 U.S.C. § 7631(f))

A condition on the provision of federal funds intended to combat HIV/AIDS requiring a recipient to have a policy "explicitly opposing prostitution and sex trafficking" violates First Amendment free speech rights by improperly interfering with the recipient's protected conduct outside of the federal program.

Agency for Int'l Dev. v. All. for Open Soc'y Int'l, 570 U.S. 205 (2013).
Justices concurring: Roberts, C.J., Kennedy, Ginsburg, Breyer, Alito, Sotomayor
Justices dissenting: Scalia, Thomas

[This entry should follow #173 in the main volume:]

___ Act of July 21, 2010 (Pub. L. No. 111-203, § 1011, 124 Stat. 1376, 1964, 12 U.S.C. § 5491(c)(3))

Provision of the Dodd-Frank Wall Street Reform and Consumer Protection Act restricting the President's power to remove the Director of the Consumer Financial Protection Bureau, providing that the Director may be removed only "for inefficiency, neglect of duty, or malfeasance in office," violates the Constitution's separation of powers.

Seila Law LLC v. Consumer Fin. Prot. Bureau, 140 S. Ct. 2183 (2020).
Justices concurring: Roberts, C.J., Alito, Kavanaugh
Justices concurring in part: Thomas, Gorsuch
Justices concurring in judgment in part and dissenting in part: Kagan, Ginsburg, Breyer, Sotomayor

[Add:]

___ Act of November 2, 2015 (Pub. L. No. 114-74, § 301(a)(1)(A), 129 Stat. 584, 588, 47 U.S.C. § 227(b)(1)(A)(iii))

Government-debt exception added to a robocall restriction in the Telephone Consumer Protection Act of 1991 (TCPA) makes the law an unconstitutional content-based regulation of speech in violation of the First Amendment, but could be severed from the TCPA.

Barr v. Am. Ass'n of Political Consultants, 140 S. Ct. 2335 (2020).
Justices concurring: Kavanaugh, Roberts, C.J., Alito
Justices concurring in part and dissenting in part: Thomas
Justices concurring in judgment: Sotomayor
Justices concurring in judgment in part and dissenting in part: Breyer, Ginsburg, Kagan, Gorsuch

STATE CONSTITUTIONAL AND STATUTORY PROVISIONS AND MUNICIPAL ORDINANCES HELD UNCONSTITUTIONAL OR HELD TO BE PREEMPTED BY FEDERAL LAW

I. STATE LAWS HELD UNCONSTITUTIONAL

[Add:]

___ Hall v. Florida, 572 U.S. ___, No. 12-10882, slip op. (2014).

Florida state law that provides a "bright line" cutoff based on IQ test scores to determine if a defendant is ineligible for capital punishment because of intellectual disability violates the Eighth Amendment because IQ scores are imprecise in nature and may only be used as a factor of analysis in death penalty cases.

> Justices concurring: Kennedy, Ginsburg, Breyer, Sotomayor, Kagan
> Justices dissenting: Roberts, C.J., Scalia, Thomas, Alito

___ McCullen v. Coakley, 573 U.S. ___, No. 12-1168, slip op. (2014).

Massachusetts statute requiring a thirty-five-foot buffer zone at entrances and driveways of abortion facilities violates the First Amendment, as the zone created is not narrowly tailored to serve governmental interests in maintaining public safety and preserving access to reproductive healthcare facilities because less intrusive alternatives were available to the state.

> Justices concurring: Roberts, C.J., Ginsburg, Breyer, Sotomayor, Kagan
> Justices concurring in judgment: Scalia, Kennedy, Thomas, Alito

___ Harris v. Quinn, 573 U.S. ___, No. 11-681, slip op. (2014).

An Illinois law requiring a Medicaid recipient's "personal assistant" (who is part of a bargaining unit but not a member of the bargaining union) to pay an "agency" fee to the union violates the First Amendment's prohibitions against compelled speech and could not be justified under the rationale of *Abood v. Detroit Board of Education*, 431 U.S. 209 (1977).

> Justices concurring: Roberts, C.J., Scalia, Kennedy, Thomas, Alito
> Justices dissenting: Ginsburg, Breyer, Sotomayor, Kagan

___ Comptroller of the Treasury of Md. v. Wynne, 575 U.S. ___, No. 13-485, slip op. (2015).

Maryland's personal income tax scheme—which taxed Maryland residents on their worldwide income and nonresidents on income earned in the state and did not offer Maryland residents a full credit for income taxes they paid to other states—violates the "Dormant Commerce Clause" because it "fails the internal consistency test" and it "inherently discriminates" against interstate commerce.

Justices concurring: Roberts, C.J., Kennedy, Breyer, Alito, Sotomayor
Justices dissenting: Scalia, Thomas, Ginsburg, Kagan

___ Obergefell v. Hodges, 576 U.S. ___, No. 14-556, slip op. (2015).

The laws of Michigan, Kentucky, Ohio, and Tennessee defining marriage as a union between one man and one woman violate the Due Process and Equal Protection Clauses of the Fourteenth Amendment because the fundamental right to marry protected by Due Process Clause and the central precepts of equality undergirding the Equal Protection Clause prohibit states from excluding same-sex couples from civil marriage on the same terms and conditions as opposite-sex couples.

Justices concurring: Kennedy, Ginsburg, Breyer, Sotomayor, Kagan
Justices dissenting: Roberts, C.J., Scalia, Thomas, Alito

___ Hurst v. Florida, 577 U.S. ___, No. 14-7505, slip op. (2016).

Florida's capital sentencing scheme, by allowing a criminal defendant to be sentenced to death upon findings by a court, violates the Sixth Amendment's right to trial by jury.

Justices concurring: Roberts, C.J.; Scalia, Kennedy, Thomas, Ginsburg, Sotomayor, Kagan
Justices concurring in judgment: Breyer
Justices dissenting: Alito

___ Franchise Tax Bd. of Cal. v. Hyatt, 578 U.S. ___, No. 14-1175, slip op. (2016).

Nevada's sovereign immunity statute, as interpreted by the Nevada Supreme Court, by not affording a California state agency the same limited immunity that is provided to Nevada state agencies, embodies a policy of hostility toward its sister state in violation of the Full Faith and Credit Clause and cannot be reconciled with the principle of constitutional equality among the states.

Justices concurring: Kennedy, Ginsburg, Breyer, Sotomayor, Kagan
Justices concurring in judgment: Alito
Justices dissenting: Roberts, C.J., Thomas

___ Birchfield v. North Dakota, 579 U.S. ___, No. 14-1468, slip op. (2016).

A North Dakota law providing criminal sanctions against an arrestee who refuses to submit to a warrantless blood alcohol concentration test administered by taking a blood sample from the arrestee cannot be justified as a search incident to an arrest or on the basis of implied consent and, therefore, violates the Fourth Amendment.

Justices concurring: Roberts, C.J., Kennedy, Breyer, Alito, Kagan
Justices concurring in judgment: Ginsburg, Sotomayor
Justices dissenting: Thomas

___ Whole Woman's Health v. Hellerstedt, 579 U.S. ___, No. 15-274, slip op. (2016).

A Texas law, which requires that (1) physicians performing or inducing an abortion have admitting privileges at a local hospital and (2) abortion facilities meet the minimum standards for ambulatory surgical centers under Texas law, imposes a substantial obstacle to a woman seeking an abortion, imposing an undue burden on a liberty interest protected by the Fourteenth Amendment's Due Process Clause.

Justices concurring: Kennedy, Ginsburg, Breyer, Sotomayor, Kagan
Justices dissenting: Roberts, C.J., Thomas, Alito

___ Pena-Rodriguez v. Colorado, 580 U.S. ___, No. 15-606, slip op. (2017).

A Colorado evidentiary rule prohibiting jurors from testifying about any matter or statement occurring during the course of the jury's deliberations in a proceeding inquiring into the validity of the verdict must yield in the face of a challenge that a juror relied on racial stereotypes or animus to convict a criminal defendant in violation of the Sixth Amendment's right to a jury trial.

Justices concurring: Kennedy, Ginsburg, Breyer, Sotomayor, Kagan
Justices dissenting: Roberts, C.J., Thomas, Alito

___ Nelson v. Colorado, 581 U.S. ___, No. 15-1256, slip op. (2017).

A Colorado statute permitting the state to retain the costs, fees, and restitution paid by an exonerated criminal defendant unless the defendant prevails in a separate civil proceeding by proving her innocence by clear and convincing evidence violates the Fourteenth Amendment's Due Process Clause.

Justices concurring: Roberts, C.J., Kennedy, Ginsburg, Breyer, Sotomayor, Kagan
Justices concurring in judgment: Alito
Justices dissenting: Thomas

___ Cooper v. Harris, 581 U.S. ___, No. 15-1262, slip op. (2017).

North Carolina, in redrawing two legislative districts, impermissibly relied on race as its predominant rationale without sufficient justification in violation of the Fourteenth Amendment's Equal Protection Clause.

Justices concurring in full: Thomas, Ginsburg, Breyer, Sotomayor, Kagan
Justices concurring in judgment: Roberts, C.J., Kennedy, Alito

___ Packingham v. North Carolina, 582 U.S. ___, No. 15-1194, slip op. (2017).

A North Carolina law making it a felony for a registered sex offender "to access a commercial social networking Web site where the sex offender knows that the site permits minor children to become members or to create or maintain personal Web pages," impermissibly restricts lawful speech in violation of the First Amendment.

> Justices concurring in full: Kennedy, Ginsburg, Breyer, Sotomayor, Kagan
> Justices concurring in judgment: Roberts, C.J., Thomas, Alito

___ Trinity Lutheran Church of Columbia, Inc. v. Comer, 582 U.S. ___, No. 15-577, slip op. (2017).

A policy of the Missouri Department of Natural Resources to exclude an otherwise qualified entity from a public grant program because of the entity's religious status violates the First Amendment's Free Exercise Clause.

> Justices concurring in full: Roberts, C.J., Kennedy, Alito, Kagan
> Justices concurring in part: Thomas, Gorsuch
> Justices concurring in judgment: Breyer
> Justices dissenting: Ginsburg, Sotomayor

___ Pavan v. Smith, 582 U.S. ___, No. 16-992, slip op. (2017).

An Arkansas law providing that when a married woman gives birth, her husband must be listed as the second parent on the child's birth certificate, including when he is not the child's genetic parent, violates the Fourteenth Amendment's substantive guarantee of the "constellation of benefits that the States have linked to marriage" to same-sex couples, as announced in *Obergefell v. Hodges,* 576 U.S. ___, No. 14-556, slip op. (2015).

> Justices concurring: Per Curiam (Unannounced by the Court)
> Justices dissenting: Thomas, Alito, Gorsuch

___ National Institute of Family and Life Advocates v. Becerra, 585 U.S. ___, No. 16-1140, slip op. (2018).

California law requiring certain (1) medically licensed pro-life centers that offer pregnancy-related services to notify women that the state provides free or low-cost services, including abortion; and (2) unlicensed pro-life centers that offer-pregnancy-related services to notify women that the state has not licensed the clinics to provide medical services likely violates the First Amendment.

> Justices concurring: Roberts, C.J., Kennedy, Thomas, Alito, Gorsuch
> Justices dissenting: Ginsburg, Breyer, Sotomayor, Kagan

___ Minnesota Voters Alliance v. Mansky, 585 U.S. ___, No. 16-1435 (2018).

Minnesota statute stating that political insignia may not be worn at polling places violates the First Amendment's Free Speech Clause because it is not capable of reasoned application.

> Justices concurring: Roberts, C.J., Kennedy, Thomas, Ginsburg, Alito, Kagan, Gorsuch
> Justices dissenting: Sotomayor, Breyer

___ Janus v. American Federation of State, County, and Municipal Employees, Council 31, 585 U.S. ___, No. 16-1466, slip op. (2018).

Illinois statute that allows exclusive representatives of public employees to enter into collective bargaining agreements that require nonconsenting employees to pay certain fees to the representative unlawfully compels speech in violation of the First Amendment.

> Justices concurring: Alito, Roberts, C.J., Kennedy, Thomas, Gorsuch
> Justices dissenting: Kagan, Ginsburg, Breyer, Sotomayor

___ Dawson v. Steager, 586 U.S. ___, No. 17-419, slip op. (2019).

A West Virginia statute, by providing a tax exemption for the retirement benefits of certain state law enforcement employees but not for federal retirees who had comparable job duties, discriminates against federal employees in violation of 4 U.S.C. § 111 and in violation of the constitutional doctrine of intergovernmental tax immunity.

___ Tennessee Wine and Spirits Retailers Association v. Thomas, 588 U.S. ___, No. 18-96, slip op. (2019).

Tennessee law creating 2-year residency requirement for alcohol retailers to obtain a license violates the dormant Commerce Clause and exceeds the state's authority under Section 2 of the Twenty-first Amendment.

> Justices concurring: Alito, Roberts, C.J., Ginsburg, Breyer, Sotomayor, Kagan, Kavanaugh
> Justices dissenting: Gorsuch, Thomas

___ June Med. Servs. L.L.C. v. Russo, 140 S. Ct. 2103 (2020).

Louisiana state statute requiring abortion providers to have admitting privileges at hospitals within thirty miles of where an abortion is performed or induced violates the Fourteenth Amendment's Due Process Clause.

> Justices concurring: Breyer, Ginsburg, Sotomayor, Kagan
> Justices concurring in judgment: Roberts, C.J.
> Justices dissenting: Thomas, Alito, Gorsuch, Kavanaugh

___ Ramos v. Louisiana, 140 S. Ct. 1390 (2020).

Louisiana state constitutional provision allowing criminal conviction by a nonunanimous jury violates the Sixth Amendment's right to trial by jury.

> Justices concurring: Gorsuch, Ginsburg, Breyer
> Justices concurring in part: Sotomayor, Kavanaugh
> Justices concurring in judgment: Thomas
> Justices dissenting: Alito, Roberts, C.J., Kagan

II.   ORDINANCES HELD UNCONSTITUTIONAL

[Add:]

___ City of Los Angeles v. Patel, 576 U.S. ___, No. 13-1175, slip op. (2015).

A Los Angeles ordinance that gives police the ability to inspect hotel registration records without advance notice and arrest hotel employees for noncompliance is facially unconstitutional. Inspections under the ordinance constitute administrative searches for purposes of the Fourth Amendment and, as such, may only proceed if the subject of the search has been afforded an opportunity to obtain pre-compliance review before a neutral decision-maker.

> Justices concurring: Kennedy, Ginsburg, Breyer, Sotomayor, Kagan
> Justices dissenting: Roberts, C.J., Scalia, Thomas, Alito

___ Reed v. Town of Gilbert, 576 U.S. ___, No. 13-502, slip op. (2015).

A municipality's sign code imposing more stringent restrictions on signs directing the public to a public event than on signs conveying political or ideological messages is a content-based regulation that is not narrowly tailored to serve compelling interests in preserving the aesthetics of a town and promoting traffic safety.

> Justices concurring: Roberts, C.J., Scalia, Kennedy, Thomas, Alito, Sotomayor
> Justices concurring in judgment only: Ginsburg, Breyer, Kagan

III.   STATE AND LOCAL LAWS HELD PREEMPTED BY FEDERAL LAW

[At beginning of list, add:]

The CONSTITUTION OF THE UNITED STATES OF AMERICA: ANALYSIS AND INTERPRETATION is currently undergoing significant revisions as part of a regular review of the document. As part of the revision process, the list of state and local laws held preempted by federal law is being eliminated.

SUPREME COURT DECISIONS OVERRULED BY SUBSEQUENT DECISION

[At beginning of list, add:]

Following the celebration of its one-hundredth anniversary, the *Constitution of the United States of America: Analysis and Interpretation* is currently undergoing significant revisions as part of an ongoing review of the document. In order to provide an objective list of cases in which the Court has overturned a prior ruling, the following list will encompass only those cases in which the Court has explicitly stated that it is overruling a prior case or issues a decision that is the functional equivalent of an express overruling. In instances where a majority of the Court distinguishes (but does not overrule) an earlier holding, that case is not included in this listing. This approach provides consistent and objective treatment, adhering to the Court's repeated statements that only the High Court has the prerogative of overruling its own decisions. *See Agostini v. Felton*, 521 U.S. 203, 237 (1997); *Rodriguez de Quijas v. Shearson/Am. Express, Inc.*, 490 U.S. 477, 484 (1989). As the review of this list continues, other decisions may be added to or deleted from this list based on this criterion.

[Delete 217. and substitute with:]

Overruling Case	*Overruled Case*
Minnesota v. Mille Lacs Band of Chippewa Indians, 526 U.S. 172 (1999) (in part)	Ward v. Race Horse, 163 U.S. 504 (1896)
Herrera v. Wyoming, 587 U.S. ___, No. 17-532 (2019) (in part)	

[Delete 228. Parents Involved in Community Schs. v. Seattle Sch. Dist. No. 1, 551 U.S. 124 (2007); Sch. Comm. of Boston v. Bd. of Educ., 389 U.S. 572 (1968)]

[Delete 229. Gonzales v. Carhart, 550 U.S. 124 (2007); Stenberg v. Carhart, 530 U.S. 914 (2000)]

SUPREME COURT DECISIONS OVERRULED

[Add:]

Overruling Case	*Overruled Case*
Alleyne v. United States, 570 U.S. 99 (2013)	Harris v. United States, 536 U.S. 545 (2002)
Obergefell v. Hodges, 576 U.S. ___, No. 14-556, slip op. (2015)	Baker v. Nelson, 409 U.S. 810 (1972)
Johnson v. United States, 576 U.S. ___, No. 13-7120, slip op. (2015)	Sykes v. United States, 564 U.S. 1 (2011); James v. United States, 550 U.S. 192 (2007)
Hurst v. Florida, 577 U.S. ___ , No. 14-7505, slip op. (2016)	Hildwin v. Florida, 490 U.S. 638 (1989) (per curiam); Spaziano v. Florida, 468 U.S. 447 (1984)
South Dakota v. Wayfair, 585 U.S. ___, No. 17-494, slip op.(2018)	National Bellas Hess v. Department of Revenue of Illinois, 386 U.S. 753 (1967);Quill Corp. v. North Dakota, 504 U.S. 298 (1992)
Trump v. Hawaii, 585 U.S. ___, No. 17-965, slip op. (2018)	Korematsu v. United States, 323 U.S. 214 (1944)
Janus v. American Federation of State, County, and Municipal Employees, Council 31, 585 U.S. ___, No. 16-1466, slip op. (2018)	Abood v. Detroit Bd. of Educ., 431 U.S. 209 (1977)
Knick v. Twp. of Scott, 588 U.S. ___, No. 17-647, slip op. (2019)	Williamson Cty. Reg'l Planning Comm'n v. Hamilton Bank, 473 U.S. 172 (1985) (in part)
Franchise Tax Bd. of Cal. v. Hyatt, 587 U.S. ___, No. 17-1299, slip op. (2019)	Nevada v. Hall, 440 U.S. 410 (1979)
Rucho v. Common Cause, 588 U.S. ___, Nos. 18-422, 18-726, slip op. (2019)	Davis v. Bandemer, 478 U.S. 109 (1986)
Ramos v. Louisiana, 140 S. Ct. 1390 (2020)	Apodaca v. Oregon, 406 U.S. 404 (1972) (plurality opinion); Johnson v. Louisiana, 406 U.S. 366 (1972) (Powell, J., concurring)

TABLE OF CASES

TABLE OF CASES

TABLE OF CASES

TABLE OF CASES

TABLE OF CASES

TABLE OF CASES

TABLE OF CASES

TABLE OF CASES